A Woman's Journey to Freedom

Breaking Free of Harmful Behaviors and Memories to Find Healthy, Joyful Living

TWO BESTSELLING WORKS
COMPLETE IN ONE VOLUME

THE COMPULSIVE WOMAN
THE NOT-SO-COMPULSIVE WOMAN

SANDRA
SIMPSON LeSOURD

Inspirational Press • New York

Inspirational Press
A division of BBS Publishing Corporation
386 Park Avenue South
New York, NY 10016
Inspirational Press is a registered trademark of BBS Publishing Corporation.

Published by arrangement with Baker Book House Company.

Library of Congress Catalog Card Number: 97-77408
ISBN: 0-88486-198-8

Printed in the United States of America

CONTENTS

The Compulsive Woman

To
Brad
Brent
Lisa

CONTENTS

Foreword

This book offers some good news and some bad news. The *bad* news is that you will recognize someone when you read it. You know a compulsive woman. She is your co-worker, your wife, your sister, your mother, or she might be you. She is leading a driven, pain-filled life, acting as if she freely chooses to live this way.

Sandy LeSourd was such a woman. Many people will assume that her story is extreme or unusual. It is not. She did not live on the streets, sleeping in parks or alleys. She had a house, a car, nice clothes, and friends. She looked like a lot of people you know. She appeared to be leading "the good life." The inside, however, did not match the outside. Inside she was far from leading a good life. Her day was full of compulsive behaviors. When her supply of one thing ran out, she turned to something else to numb her pain.

The costs of compulsive behaviors in terms of dollars and human suffering are staggering. Medical science has been successful at eliminating many of the diseases that were dread killers only a few decades ago. But we have made little progress until recently on helping people with illnesses of lifestyle. Many of the things that kill us now are things we do to ourselves. In spite of overwhelming evidence that smoking causes fetal injury, cancer, and heart disease, a third of the population smokes daily. In a world where millions go to sleep hungry and starvation is all too common, we live in a society preoccupied with diets and weight loss and where nearly half of our citizens are obese. Over eighteen million adults drink in a way that causes them serious problems. Cirrhosis of the liver is still the ninth leading cause of death in America. Alcohol abuse alone costs the U.S. economy annually over $49 billion.

Compulsive behaviors are nothing new. They have been with us as long as recorded history. We have called them by various names—sin, weak moral character, possession, insanity—and we have tried to treat them with threats, fines, medications, jail terms, even executions. We haven't been very successful. It is becoming clear, however, that there are important similarities between addictions. We are headed toward the day when professionals will study *addiction,* rather than *addictions.* When the Compulsivity Clinic was founded, we were told that it would not work, that each addiction needed separate treatment and that people with a particular addiction could not relate to someone with a different addiction. We found out different. We found that there are more similarities than differences when it comes to working with compulsive people. This book will show you that as well.

I said that this book offers both good and bad news. The *good* news is that there is hope. Even as you read this, there are thousands of compulsive women (and men) all over the world who are active in recovery programs. They are leading joyful lives free from the restraints of compulsive behavior. Each time a person tells her story of recovery it makes it a little bit easier for the next person to begin the journey. There is hope for the compulsive woman in your life. There is hope for you.

—*Mic Hunter*
Co-Director, Health Activation Services, and
author of The First Step: For People in Relationships
with Sex Addicts

Introduction

Who is the compulsive woman?

The woman who volunteers for everything, who can't say no.

The woman whose TV is on all day long or who lives her life around soap operas.

The woman whose life revolves around food. She eats too much—or too little. Sweets are often her downfall.

The compulsive woman is an exercise nut, jogging miles every day, rain or shine. She is the one who shops when she needs a high while debts pile up. She may be a chain-smoker or a closet alcoholic; hooked on prescription drugs or sex or dependent on male approval for her sense of worth.

The compulsive woman is easy prey for psychics, spiritists, cults of every kind. She's a perfectionist who never lives up to her own expectations. Her natural drive and energy have become distorted; her motor is running wild. She has an irrational need to do something over and over to the point where she has lost control.

In other words, the compulsive woman has a complicated problem, and the solution to her problem has to address more than her primary addiction or symptom. According to a study done by *Ms.* magazine published in February 1987, "The patterns of dependence [for women] have been obscured by the tendency to look at individual addictions rather than the forces that create dependency. . . ."

One of the significant features of the *Ms.* survey was a precedent-setting demonstration that the compulsive personality expresses itself in more than one addiction. "Cross-addictions," that is, multiple or reinforcing addictions, are a tremendous problem for the compulsive woman; a cure is difficult so long as one tries to treat only the symptoms without getting at the root causes: fear, anger, and—in particular—shame.

Another significant feature in compulsion revealed in the *Ms.* study is the gender factor. The survey revealed that women are more likely to have certain kinds of addictions than men (shopping, watching television, compulsive eating and dieting, taking tranquilizers, etc.). More importantly, it revealed that there is a particular pattern in compulsion that most compulsive women demonstrate. "We are trained from early childhood to form at least part of our identity in terms of dependency," observes *Ms.*, "generally upon fathers, boyfriends, male bosses, or husbands who are older. . . ."

The compulsive woman is often addicted to love. Wrong love. Or she is dependent on men as the primary token of her value. And this pattern of dependency leads to lack of self-direction, self-control, and self-esteem.

"Addicted people are willing to endure anything in order to reexperience that physical and psychological state of being," writes Drs. Connell Cowan and Melvyn Kinder in *Smart Women/Foolish Choices*, "that compelling satisfaction they feel whenever they take in that substance, whatever it is—alcohol, drugs, nicotine, food, or a man's love. This hunger for love becomes obsession when it reaches such a proportion that the woman feels she needs it just to feel that life is worth living, just to maintain her everyday emotional balance."

I was led to a study of compulsive behavior not out of any abstract interest, but through the desperate need to understand my own life and behavior. I had not one but all of the compulsions mentioned above. I was cross-addicted to almost *everything* at one time or another. The despair it caused led me at one point to try to kill myself. If some women can identify with my symptoms and my misery, I hope that my pathway to recovery will also inspire and encourage these women in their battle to gain mastery of themselves and their lives gone out of control.

I have built this book around my own life struggles. And as a result of my studies into compulsivity, I have also included at the back of the book self-assessment lists, information about compulsive behavior, and guides on where you can get help.

It is possible for the compulsive woman to break the patterns that control her, to recover her self-worth, and to lead a constructive and joyous life. That is the promise of this book.

—*Sandra Simpson LeSourd*

PART ONE

ILLNESS
AND
RECOVERY

Facing Off

Many people operate in their daily lives as automatons, almost completely unaware that their nearly every action is dictated by compulsion, with little or no freedom of choice and with virtually no spontaneity. Many people don't know the difference between compulsion and choice. . . . {They} are so overwhelmed and tyrannized by their compulsions that they must act out (do things) immediately, impulsively, without thought or consideration in order to overcome complete and utter paralysis.

Theodore Isaac Rubin, M.D.
The Winner's Notebook

A S I WALKED UP TO THE WOODEN GATE OF THE CAMP SPONSORED BY THE Compulsivity Clinics of America, after having been dropped off in the parking lot by a friend, I felt my stomach knot in fear. *Don't be silly,* I told myself. *You're here to learn more about yourself— why you've been a compulsive person all your life. There is nothing to be afraid of.*

I'd felt this way before—the first day of school . . . being dropped off at a Girl Scout camp. But to have these feelings now was ridiculous. I was forty-eight years old!

Anxiously I looked about the crowded parking lot—doors

slamming, men and women tugging suitcases and duffle bags from yawning car trunks. Were all these people as apprehensive as I?

A ruddy-faced young man standing in the center of the parking lot pointed up a blacktop path toward a gray wooden lodge half-hidden in the Minnesota woods. Falling oak leaves swirled about his head as he spoke. "You'll be staying up there at the end of the path. Down here"—he gestured at a brown log building closer by—"is where you get fed."

A comforting thought, being fed. Was I going to be preoccupied with food this week?

Only a month ago my interest had been perked by a telephone conversation with a vivacious young woman who had just "graduated" from this Compulsivity Clinic course. She had enrolled with serious food disorders only to discover she was alcoholic as well.

I knew I had been an alcoholic—correction, was a recovering alcoholic—and that I had other compulsive behavior problems as well. It was time to subdue the rest of these monsters.

The advance information had fascinated me:

The Compulsivity Clinic program offers you the opportunity to uncover the causes of your compulsive behaviors. It provides support to make lifestyle changes. You will learn about:

Addictive relationships
Managing change
Dealing with shame and guilt
Chemical dependencies
Sexual abuse and addiction

Self-defeating lifestyle problems can include:

Workaholism
Relationship dependency
Eating disorders
Smoking
Gambling

As I struggled up the walkway with my suitcase, I was filled with fresh resolve to uncover those hidden areas buried deep within myself. Dread and exhilaration coursed through my veins, unlikely companions.

At the door of the lodge a staff member issued a green plastic three-ring notebook containing the week's schedule and other information, then with a warm smile assigned me to a bed. All the staff people looked energetic, lean, disciplined, bright. I wondered how they viewed us.

What are these people going to find out about me?

More terrifyingly: *What am I going to find out about myself?*

The women's sleeping areas were separated by carpeted room dividers. I found my cubicle at the far end on the right side. Good. I'd have some privacy here. Suddenly I wanted to protect myself from getting too close to these others.

Across the aisle I glimpsed a thin young woman solemnly unpacking an orange nylon duffle bag, methodically and mechanically sorting her personal belongings. A pile of paperback books slid onto the floor with a thud. As she dove to retrieve them, the words *child abuse* on one of the covers caught my eye.

I could only speculate that my silent roommate across the way bore some invisible scars.

After tidying up my tiny cubicle, I looked it over with satisfaction. To counter harsh ceiling lights, I had brought my small gooseneck reading lamp. It now threw a comforting beam of light on my "security blanket"—a new blue down bathrobe, a recent purchase so I would not be cold in the Minnesota night air.

At five o'clock we all streamed back to the brown log dining hall for an early dinner. I fought down nervousness as I filled my plate and selected a seat. *You've been in groups before,* I told myself. *Relax.*

It was a futile command. The thick hero sandwich I began to stuff into my mouth suddenly exploded into a shower of ham, lettuce, tomato, and onions. As I tried to catch the falling food, my paper plate tumbled to the floor. My feet were awash in debris.

As every eye in the room turned to survey the mess, I let out a self-conscious giggle. Immediately the entire room broke into gales of laughter.

"Looks like you'd better start all over again," cracked a large blonde woman seated next to me. As she turned toward me, I noticed a steel brace supporting her back.

Looking around the room at the now-smiling faces, I felt cheered somehow that my blunder had been a welcome icebreaker. Everyone had been as tense as I was.

After dinner the leadership team was introduced, including Terry Kellogg, founder of the Compulsivity Clinics, and we got down to basics. First some important definitions were explained to us.

Obsession: recurring, persistent thoughts, images, or impulses that occur in your mind. They seem to come from nowhere; they are not voluntary. You do not seem to be able to control or suppress them, though you try.

Compulsion: an insistent, repetitive, intrusive, and unwanted urge to perform an act that is contrary to one's ordinary wishes or standards. Since it serves as a defensive substitute for even more unacceptable unconscious ideas or wishes, failure to perform the compulsive act leads to anxiety. Performing it relieves anxiety. Yet performing it is also linked with the desire to resist doing it and often a sense of shame. The compulsive link to a particular act, event, experience (like gambling or shopping), or thing (like alcohol) often leads to addiction.

Addiction: a pathological link or relationship with a mood-altering act, event, experience, or thing that causes major life problems. An addiction is more serious than a compulsion and can be life-threatening if it involves substance abuse (alcohol, drugs, or even food and tobacco). It is behavior that continues despite adverse emotional, medical, financial, or social consequences.

After the introductory staff comments, the twenty-five of us who had enrolled in the Clinic introduced ourselves and spoke briefly about the problems that had brought us there. We were alcoholics, drug addicts, chain-smokers, gamblers, compulsive TV-watchers. Many had come with sexual compulsions or severe relationship dependencies. Most of us had one form of eating disorder or another. Some were given to excessive shopping, spending, or other types of binge behaviors. It was heartening, somehow, to know that my secrets, my problems, were also the secrets and problems of others. Several faces now became brightened by a new sense of hope.

Mic Hunter (who is now the coordinator of the Clinic) assured us that what seemed impossible to resist was indeed resistible, that our problems were treatable and curable. He was later to offer this checklist to help identify compulsive behaviors:

- Is the behavior ritualized? If interrupted, does the person get upset?

- Is there time distortion when the person is involved in this behavior? (Does it go on for much longer than he thinks it does or than he expects?)

- Does the person set rigid rules for himself in this behavior, and then tend to violate them? (He says he'll drink only between the hours of ten and twelve, and then doesn't; etc.)

- Does the person go to extremes, from overdoing to underdoing, in this behavior?

- If there are negative consequences, does the person continue the behavior anyway?

- Is there any "situation stressor" causing this behavior? (A man insulted sexually by a woman who has spurned him, for instance, may launch a succession of promiscuous relationships, but only to prove his masculinity and not as a compulsive behavior. When he understands the reason for what she said, or that it isn't true, he will stop his promiscuity.)

• Is there preoccupation ("obsessing") about this behavior, in which the person thinks more about it than anything else, so that it interferes with his life? (Copyright © 1986 by Mic Hunter; taken from the forthcoming *Excessive Appetites*.)

After the introductory comments, our first group session came in a small room with mahogany-paneled walls and one large window. We all sat on floor pillows. It felt strangely cozy inside these walls, almost womblike. There we met our six group members: two men and four women, including myself.

Our counselor, Maureen, welcomed us: "You are to become a family—to eat together, spend time together when we are not in this room, and 'be there' for each other. I want you to experience trust and love for one another, something you may never have really known in your own families."

She paused a moment. "For the rest of the week please do not contact anyone on the outside. This is especially important for those of you with relationship dependencies. We suggest you don't call out and 'get a fix.' You're here to focus on yourselves, to feel your true feelings and confront your fears. I urge you to stay within the framework of our program so as not to become fragmented."

I liked Maureen, a lovely Irish wisp of a woman with a cloud of short auburn hair and a mellow, soothing voice that was competent and reassuring. Maureen described herself as a recovering alcoholic from a strongly "dysfunctional" family.

"Over ninety percent of American families are dysfunctional to some degree," she added. She defined the dysfunctional family as one in which either father or mother or child has a problem that causes an imbalance in family relationships. A father may be addicted to alcohol; a mother may have a nervous breakdown; a son or daughter may have a serious illness. Whatever the specific issue, the family begins to revolve around the problem, ceasing to function in a healthy, mutually supportive way.

Soon a cover-up of feelings begins. Hurt, angry, confused emotions are stuffed down inside of us, kept concealed even from ourselves. Out-of-touch with our own deepest truth, we feel driven to do things without knowing why. Compulsive behavior is born.

Fred, a heavy-set man in his thirties, sat in the corner frowning. He was a stockbroker in the Gamblers Anonymous program. Wall Street, he confided, was spawning a new breed of gambler, the compulsive investor. Fred spoke slowly, as though physically exhausted.

Maureen bore in on him. "I suspect you are so full of sugar and starch—they act as a medication, you know—that your real feelings can't get through. For the rest of your time here, Fred, I want you to totally abstain from all sugar and white flour. You need to cleanse your body of these substances before you can start to *feel* what you need to feel."

The stories that poured out from this group triggered memories and pain of my own:

"I've always had problems with money and men."

"I'm a chain-smoker and addicted to soap operas."

"My wife said if I didn't get some help for my pornography addiction she would divorce me."

"My father raped me when I was eight; then my uncle and my two brothers took advantage of me. I hate them all."

My contribution: "I've had five years of sobriety, but I know I've only struck the tip of the iceberg in working out my compulsive behavior."

Each person spoke with deep emotion, some with anger, some with tears. An ever-present box of tissues was scooted about the room. Complete strangers a few hours earlier, we began to see ourselves by the end of the session as being bound by a common thread of inner pain.

I was too keyed up after this encounter to go to bed, so I took a short walk under the trees. Geese honked on nearby Lake Minnetonka; the smell of burning leaves recalled fall nights in Vermont where I grew up.

I wondered about how I had come across. Had I sounded too "put together"? Hollow? Superficial? Defensive? Had I used too many humorous quips to keep people from getting too close—because I was too selfish or scared to communicate more meaningfully?

After breakfast the next morning I stopped to talk with the woman in the steel back brace who had sat next to me the night before at dinner. Perched uncomfortably on a straight naugahyde chair, she was wheezing and struggling for breath.

"Can I help you?" I offered weakly.

She pointed to her pack of cigarettes. "You could take these things and throw them in the lake. But I'd probably be fool enough to dive in after them."

"I used to be hooked on them, too," I said, then wondered if my "used to" sounded lofty or self-righteous.

The morning small group session was heavy going. We again sat on pillows in a circle, while Steve, the other male in our group, sobbed uncontrollably and rocked back and forth on his pillow. He told the group about his problem.

"I hate myself!" he kept saying, pounding at the oversized pillow beneath him. "I told myself when I came here I wouldn't read that stuff again, but I did last night before I went to bed. Then I took a fantasy trip and. . . ." He didn't go on.

"Steve, who are you *really* angry at?" Maureen asked.

He was silent for a moment. "I guess it's my parents. It goes 'way back. As kids, we couldn't be normal. You know, no smoking, no drinking, no dancing, no movies."

"So reading sex magazines was a way to get back at them," ventured Maureen.

Steve nodded. "The only thing my parents ever said to me about sex was, 'Don't do it. It's wrong.' Since they wouldn't answer my questions about masturbation, I felt like a freak." He started to pound his thighs with his fists.

"Steve, stop beating yourself up," Maureen ordered. "I want you to get in touch with how lonely you have been, how isolated you've felt."

Steve's realization moments later: "When I started rebelling, voices inside me began saying, 'You're *bad*!' That really scared me. I guess I was scared because I wondered if those voices in my head were from my parents or from God or from the pit of hell."

He talked for a half hour. We all went through his torment with him. Finally spent from this wrenching session, Steve leaned back against the wall. The toes of his stained white tennis shoes were tilted slightly inward, reminding me of a little boy abandoned in his playpen. I had a glimpse then of a little Steve, desperate and lonely, wanting to be picked up and held.

Then the little boy opened his eyes, reached for his horn-rimmed glasses, cleared his throat, and was transformed before our compassionate eyes into the Steve of today, the forty-year-old accountant.

Each day there was some kind of breakthrough in a member of our group. Some of the things I heard resembled my own nightmares. Others represented the secrets and fears of other lives.

Peggy, thirtyish, with green eyes and a sprinkle of freckles, was office manager for a small insurance company. Despite her responsible position, she had come to the Clinic desperately needy and scared. The oldest girl in a family of four, she'd been responsible for the care of her younger brothers and sisters. Her mother, obese and deeply disturbed emotionally, had spent most of her time in bed, getting up only for trips to the bathroom or refrigerator. Her father, a violent and abusive man, had beaten his children unmercifully.

"I became sexually active with boys in my class at age thirteen," Peggy related. "By the time I was seventeen, I'd tried it all except marriage. That was a disaster. All four of my marriages have been failures. I've lost track of the times I've tried to kill myself—six, eight."

"Why suicide?" asked Maureen.

"Maybe suicide was an attempt to kill that part of me I didn't like. The guiltiest I feel is about my abortion twelve years ago. Since my marriage was breaking up, I thought it would be a mistake to bring a child into the world. I never told my husband."

"Would you like to let go of that guilt, Peggy?" Maureen asked.

Peggy wiped her nose with the back of her hand. "Oh, God, *yes!* Is there any way I can?"

Maureen moved across the room to where Peggy was sitting and put her arm around her. "We're going to have a memorial service for your child, right here. Would you like to invite the group to be part of it?"

Peggy blinked, her stricken eyes meeting the gaze of each of us seated around the room. "Would you all like to come?" she asked.

Profoundly affected, we nodded.

What Maureen didn't tell us then is that ritual acts often help to break the pattern of guilt that underlies compulsive behavior. That is why cleansing rituals as an expression of real faith—rituals like baptism and communion—play such an important role in many addicts' recovery.

"Does your daughter have a name, Peggy?" Maureen asked.

"Yes. Her name is Kim."

"Please invite Kim to come into the room and be with us now."

Peggy moved her lips self-consciously, her eyes filling with tears.

"Would you describe Kim to all of us, Peggy?"

"She is twelve years old. Her hair is blonde and she has blue eyes. She looks so sad. There are tears in her eyes. . . ."

"Do you know why she looks so sad, Peggy? It's because she doesn't want you to go on mourning for her. She is happy and at peace in heaven. Is there anything you'd like to say to Kim?"

Breaking a long pause, Peggy blurted in a shaking voice, *"Please* forgive me, Kim. I was so confused when I found out I was pregnant with you. I was so frightened and unhappy. I didn't dare to have you . . . please forgive me!

"I love you, Kim. I miss you and I miss not having you with me now when I could be a mom to you. But I wasn't ready. I hope you can understand that." Peggy broke down, her tears and mascara running together down her cheeks. Most of the women in the group were also weeping.

"Is there anything else you want to say to her, Peggy?"

"Just I love you . . . I love you . . . I know we will be together someday. . . ."

"It's time to say good-bye to her, to let her go."

"Good-bye, Kim . . . good-bye . . . I love you. . . ."

The six days with the Clinic felt like forever, yet when it was over they seemed to have sped by. We had exercise sessions, lectures on the dysfunctional family, sexual disorders, nutrition, and so forth. Information helps us to get a handle on our problems, I learned, because fear plays a major role in compulsive behavior.

The last morning I took an early morning walk alone, past Lake Minnetonka into the forest. The woods were pungent with the smell of moist earth. I found a sunny spot on a gently sloping hill where leaves protected me from the damp ground. Easing my body to the ground, I looked skyward in self-examination. I felt strangely vulnerable, so I began a deep breathing exercise we had been taught in one of our sessions. In . . . out . . . in . . . out. We had been taught that getting proper oxygen to the brain is often enough to help reduce or eliminate the fear response. Agoraphobics and other people afflicted with fear are often able to reduce their anxiety simply by improved breathing. Hyperventilation occurs frequently during anxiety attacks and makes you feel dizzy, that you are losing control.

The breathing exercise helps compulsives as well. We used it in combination with focusing mentally on our grief, pain, or sadness. After a while a surge of emotion welled up from deep inside me. I sobbed wrenching sobs, thinking of my new friends. The intimate details of our lives we had shared, and the mutual support we had given one another, had brought us close together.

The Compulsivity Clinic had provided insights into the nature of the problem millions of women face, but left me with unanswered questions: How can compulsive people change? Were we wounded ones permanently damaged or was there a clearly marked path to wholeness? How far along was I? Were there any positive elements in compulsive behavior?

The root cause of all compulsions, we had been told, was fear and shame. I needed to ponder that deeply, to look for the origins of shame in my own background.

The search would take me not only into my own history, but into the experiences of many others. It would take me to hospitals and clinics, halfway houses and self-help groups, into libraries and research centers. It would set me interviewing health professionals and people struggling with current addictions.

I offer my own story following as an illustration of the genesis and growth of compulsive behavior. It is typical of the inhibiting and self-defeating patterns many women live and suffer under. It also illustrates the process by which you and I can be released from the bondage in which compulsions keep us.

2

The Violated Childhood

*More than other emotions, shame involves a quality of the
unexpected; if in any way we feel it coming we are powerless
to avert it. This is in part because of the difficulty we have
in admitting to ourselves either shame or the circumstances
that give rise to shame. Whatever part voluntary action may
have in the experience of shame is swallowed up in the sense
of something that overwhelms us from without and 'takes us'
unawares. We are taken by surprise, caught off guard, or
off base, caught unawares, made a fool of. It is as if we were
suddenly invaded from the rear where we cannot see, are
unprotected, and can be overpowered.*

Helen Merrell Lynd
On Shame and the Search for Identity

I LEARNED SOMETHING ABOUT MYSELF FROM EVERY PERSON AT THE CLINIC.
Some of their experiences helped me open long-closed doors in
my past. Peggy's story was much sadder and more traumatic than
mine but, her green eyes clouded, she pried open a door I had sealed
shut in my childhood. Peggy traced her low self-worth to unremit-
ting abusive treatment by her father, and the unsupporting, passive
behavior of her obese mother, who became a negative role model
for her.

Because her mother was so disturbed, Peggy had to fill the role of mother to the other children. Before she reached puberty, Peggy found a way to prevent her father from beating his children: sex. If she gave in to her father's demands, he would not abuse the younger children.

"My father wanted to have sex with me all the time. I just didn't have the strength to resist, so I let him," Peggy had told us dispassionately. "I felt it was my fault somehow that my mother acted so strangely."

My heart had ached for her. Basically a talented, responsible person—she'd held her office job for seven years—Peggy's emotional life was a mess. A compulsive eater and drinker, obsessed by fears, she had been looking desperately for help. The memorial service for her aborted child, Kim, had been a good start. A lot more healing had to take place inside Peggy before she could acquire positive feelings about herself.

What was the connection, I wondered, between sexual abuse in childhood and compulsive behavior problems in adulthood?

Reading *Silent Scream* by Martha Janssen on her incestuous relationship with her father helped me understand Peggy's agony of spirit. Martha Janssen's book is written in blank verse:

> *Daughters love to sit*
> *on daddies' laps.*
> *Me too.*
> *I would scramble up*
> *at the end of the day.*
> *We'd talk until Mother left the room.*
> *Then we'd "play."*
>
> *Now I know*
> *why I watch so carefully*
> *little girls sitting*
> *on their daddies' laps.*

Then this indictment addressed to her abusive father:

> *You!*
> *You walk calmly*
> *among people, relatives.*
> *They don't know you*
> *as I do.*
> *You smile*
> *and feel no guilt*
>   *no shame.*
> *You walk away from my pain.*
>
> *This is crazy.*
> *I carry the weight of the sentence*
> *But you are the killer.*[1]

My mind went back to a clinic lecture. If children are sexually molested, then the "boundaries" of their bodies have been violated. It's as though their right to say no has been stolen from them. Thus they grow up confused, with certain protective limits erased, prone to erratic and compulsive behavior. Such people have a lifelong struggle with shame.

Shame, I learned, has to do with how we feel about ourselves, whereas guilt has to do with our behavior. We incur guilt when we violate some value we hold, but it has a constructive purpose in that it motivates us to make amends. Shame has no such constructive purpose, in that it turns us away from others and strikes a blow at our very worth as persons. Shame isolates, alienates. It makes us feel we're no good, that we're unworthy of respect.

Because shame is almost impossible to communicate, and because a person suffering from shame tends not to talk about his problem—or even perhaps be aware of it—he looks for temporary relief through some outlet like food, drugs, or alcohol, any "mood-alterer" to ease his pain.

An estimated seventy percent of all women who come to treatment centers are victims of sexual abuse as children. Estimates of sexual abuse of girls under fourteen range from 45,000 to 500,000 incidents per year. Some estimate that one in every four girls and one in six boys in the U.S. will be sexually molested before they are eighteen. Government statistics, moreover, indicate that nearly fifty percent are victimized by a member of their own family. The *Ms.* study (see page 11) compiled striking anecdotal evidence that "women who have been victims of incest or rape are vastly overrepresented among the addicted population."

Only in recent years have women been able to acknowledge their rejected memories and describe their experiences. The emotional progression of a victim goes something like this:[2]

1. Deep inner hurt and dismay over the sexual violation; a feeling of being damaged goods.

2. Fearful resolve not to tell anyone.

3. An attempt to bury the episode(s) in one's subconscious, where the memory festers and creates an inner disorder.

4. Adult relationships with men are damaged.

5. Trust and intimacy problems with both sexes develop.

6. Suicide can seem the answer—as it had to Peggy.

The road back to health for the victim takes this course:

1. Facing up to the fact of abuse, dredging it up from the subconscious.

2. In a therapeutic setting, admitting to others that it happened, as Peggy did in our small group. Once this exposure gets the abuse into the light, much of the destructive power goes out of it.

3. Seeing it as the abuser's problem and fault, not the victim's.

4. Forgiving him/her for it.

Peggy's experience, outwardly so different from my own, nevertheless had triggered childhood memories. The change from the emotionally charged atmosphere of the six-day Compulsivity Clinic to the more relaxed pace in my small rural community was what I needed to begin to sort them out. I developed a whole new perspective on this period of my life, including one traumatic episode that had burst out of my subconscious. One day with notepad and pen I began to dig into my early years.

At first glance my childhood seemed utterly normal. An only child, I was reared in the small community of St. Johnsbury Center, Vermont. My father, Richard Simpson, was a handsome and gregarious man, and served as a salesman, first for an appliance store, later for an automobile dealer. His wife, Elizabeth, my mother, was a fragile, pretty woman who centered her life on homemaking with few outside interests.

For me going to the old Congregational village church was a high point. On Sunday mornings I'd arrive starched and curled, eager for the Sunday school lesson to begin. The smells linger to this day; men's minty aftershave, the musky, damp odor of the church bell rope (how I longed to give it a hearty tug), coffee, cinnamon, and ham from the church kitchen.

I can still see the ladies dressed in dotted swiss and print voile dresses, their "finger-waved" hair-dos precise as metal washboards. The men in their three-piece suits seemed oddly stiff, as though their legs wouldn't bend in pants with such razor-sharp creases. Their hair slicked down with Brilliantine, noses and cheeks aglow from vigorous scrubbing, their hearty "how-do-you-do's" rang through the building.

My classroom was a clutter of small oak chairs presided over by our teacher, my Aunt Ethel. Next to the large blackboard was an oak-framed picture of Jesus. I recall his strong, sensitive face, long, beautiful, flowing hair—and those eyes. Warm, loving eyes. Jesus was holding the lost sheep in one arm, a staff in the other hand, a red cape over his long white garment.

"Jesus loves you," Aunt Ethel would intone. "He wants you to come to him with whatever is bothering you." What was bothering me in those early years was the fact that my father and mother didn't seem to love each other as other daddies and mommies did, but I couldn't even tell Jesus this.

Then my aunt would teach us from the Bible. A verse she often chose was, "He was wounded for our transgressions, he was bruised for our iniquities . . . and with his stripes we are healed."[3] I couldn't understand these words at all. Aunt Ethel explained that the stripes were the wounds of Christ, but the only wounds I saw in the picture books were in his hands and feet. They looked more like holes in his flesh than stripes. Yet the verse was strangely comforting.

The hour of Bible stories always passed too quickly for me. Soon it was time to join the grown-ups in the auditorium, where the organist extracted loud and wondrous sounds from the quaking mahogany organ with her favorite selection: "Yes, Jesus loves me. . . ."

How I loved these Sunday afternoons when we'd motor around the Vermont countryside in our slate-gray 1938 Plymouth! Occasionally we'd take the hour's journey to where my Uncle Ralph and Aunt Agnes lived. Aunt Agnes always had freshly fried doughnuts and orange Kool-Aid for us, and her house smelled of lavender and polished wood.

One of these visits, however, was not so pleasant. For many years what happened that Sunday at Uncle Ralph's had lain buried deep inside me. Peggy helped me recall it. The rest I discovered in a therapy session. As I began to put the episode down on paper, I trembled so violently I had to get out of my chair and walk around the room.

It happened when I was five. On this particular Sunday we had driven there in time for lunch. Afterward we gathered around the old player piano in the living room for a songfest. Uncle Ralph let me select the music roll from the glass-front cabinet where the player rolls were stored, then sit beside him on the piano bench.

Mother and Aunt Agnes didn't sing, just sat nearby smiling encouragingly as Dad, Uncle Ralph, and I warbled away. Dad sang tenor to Uncle Ralph's bass, with my squeaky child's voice feebly carrying the melody.

Every time a polka was played, I'd slip off the bench and skip about the house, through the dark hall with its ticking clocks, past Uncle Ralph's gun case with the stuffed animals on top, then out through the kitchen past the black wrought-iron stove with its gleaming chrome trim, on into the dining room. Breathless, I'd bound back onto the piano bench, bumping affectionately into Uncle Ralph as he manipulated the brass levers beside the keyboard.

When the music ended, Aunt Agnes, a gardener of great skill, invited us to help pick vegetables for dinner. Usually when she suggested this I'd be the first one out the door, but on this occasion I decided to stay behind while Uncle Ralph rolled his handmade cigarettes, a ritual I found fascinating. All the ingredients were in place to start production when Uncle Ralph sank down into his oak rocking chair. I noticed that his face was flushed and his breathing wheezy.

"Is something wrong, Uncle Ralph?" I asked.

"No, dear, not really, but I would feel better if you'd come over here and sit on my lap."

Eager to please, I approached the seated figure, turning my back to him expecting to be lifted into his lap. Instead his strong hands pressed my small body next to him. He gripped so tightly I could hardly breathe; then one hand groped for my pubic area. I heard his rasping, measured breath, felt the brass fittings on his suspenders digging into my shoulders.

What was going on? Why was he breathing so fast? Now he was pressing and poking and hurting me through my cotton dress.

Terror filled me. Shame . . . horror. What if Dad and Mom and Aunt Agnes were to walk in now? I could hear their voices chatting nonchalantly outside. "Let's dig some more beets," I heard my father say.

What is this man whom I love and trust doing to me? Uncle Ralph wouldn't touch me *there.* . . . But he is, and he's acting crazy and frantic and his false teeth are clicking in my ears. Oh, somebody help me!

Little short gasps and moans, then his hands dropped limply beside me. He slumped back in the squeaking rocker like an exhausted rag doll, his eyes shut, the spittle running down the corners of his mouth. The only sound now was the *tick-tock* of the hall clocks.

Breaking loose from his locked legs, I streaked upstairs to the bathroom, past the stuffed animals, my heart pounding, my stomach heaving, my eyes burning with tears of guilt and fright. There was the beautiful ceramic jar with the blue forget-me-nots where Aunt Agnes saved the long strands of her jet-black hair. This saintly and pristine lady, what would she think of me? I let Uncle Ralph touch those private parts that Mother told me no one was to see or touch. Mother and Dad would be furious if they knew! They must never find out. Deep within me something was dying—a joyfulness and a trust. A passage had been made from innocence to something I wasn't quite sure of, something frightening and unclean.

I pressed my body so hard against the washbasin that my chest ached. Gallons of water must have passed through my desperately scrubbing hands. My nightmare was interrupted by a familiar tap at the door. My dad always knocked that way. *Dum-dum-da-dum-dum—da-dum.*

Poking his head around the door, he teased, "Snookie, are you

36

going to use up all the water in the reservoir? We're waiting on you to come help with dinner."

"I'll be right down, Daddy."

Shyly I entered the kitchen, the skipping child of an hour ago now silent, ashamed, wounded by an encounter she neither understood nor could share. Irrevocably I gave myself an order: *I will never ever tell anyone what happened today.*

The beets stained my small fingers as I scrubbed off the dirt in the old stainless steel sink. My hands were almost raw. Would I ever feel clean again?

Years later at the Compulsivity Clinic, I asked Mic Hunter if this single instance of sexual abuse could be one of the underlying causes of my compulsive behavior.

Compulsivity, he admitted, usually has a complicated genesis. The shame/guilt reaction of the victim in cases of abuse can be a major contributing factor. The key is the way in which the family responds to the person who has been victimized. In my case, he said, there was no one I felt I could talk to. Nor did anyone notice my trauma symptoms. The implication to me as a child was: *Your pain doesn't matter.* So I forced the pain inward and blamed myself.

It was significant, I think, that I tried ritual obsessive handwashing to cleanse myself.

According to psychologists Pamela Vredevelt and Kathryn Rodriguez in their book *Surviving the Secret,* there are five common identity and interpersonal problems suffered by sexual abuse victims:

1. Minimizing their own abilities and maximizing others' strengths.

2. Tending to take responsibility for others' behavior.

3. Having difficulty achieving intimacy with others.

4. Tending to think if they please others they will be considered "perfect."

5. Worrying obsessively about problems and sabotaging their own efforts to change.

In retrospect, I can see that my experience of being abused shattered not only the trust I had in myself, but also in others close to me—and even of the boundaries of the world as I knew it.

3

The Dysfunctional Home

Passive dependent people are so busy seeking to be loved that they have no energy left to love. They are like starving people, scrounging wherever they can for food, and with no food of their own to give to others. It is as if within them they have an inner emptiness, a bottomless pit crying out to be filled but which can never be completely filled.

M. Scott Peck, M.D.
The Road Less Traveled

THOUGH I WAS FORTUNATE THAT NEITHER OF MY PARENTS DRANK—I became an alcoholic in spite of this—it was apparent to me at an early age that my father and mother did not enjoy being with one another. Dad's absence for three years during World War II didn't help. Our home, off-balance because of the problem relationship between my two parents, was dysfunctional.

As the alienation between my mother and father grew, a spirit of sadness took over our home. A dome of silence seemed to settle over us. Yet for years, probably because of me, their only child, my parents struggled to hold their marriage together.

I remember a recurring dream in which I was a lifeguard trying to pull my parents to the ocean's shore. I'd swim frantically to rescue one as the other went under. I could never get them both to safety; one or the other would drown before I could reach him. Choices! Which one to save? Why couldn't I save them both? I'd awaken tangled in my bedclothes, heart pounding, my nightgown soaked in perspiration.

Tensely I'd lie awake until my dad's short, dry cough from the adjoining bedroom, and the sound of Mother's steady breathing, assured me that all was well.

But all was not well. They were playing a charade called marriage. Sometimes my mind would form a strange fantasy. I'd imagine that our rambling three-story house was actually made of cardboard. If you cut on the dotted line you could fold it up and return it to the carton it had come in. One day I'd return home from school and there would be nothing there—just a grassy plot with a few lilac bushes standing sentinel over an empty hole.

Often my heart would race with fear as I hurried up the broken asphalt sidewalk of Elm Street after school. Maybe today was the day the house had vanished. All the other neat clapboard homes were in place, their prim, Priscilla-curtained windows following my anxious odyssey toward home. Eagerly my eyes would sweep up the street to our house on the hill. It was still there!

My steps would quicken. I hoped there would be a simmering pot of chowder on the stove. First I stamped my muddy feet on the square raffia mat, then burst into the kitchen. I was always trying to bring light and sunshine into the house, into my parents' cold marriage.

There was Mother, neatly groomed in her modest cotton house dress, her sad hazel eyes lighting up as her only child came through the door. She seemed so fragile, so vulnerable. I felt responsible for her. How I wanted to throw my arms around her and tell her not to worry, that I would protect her.

After chowder and cookies I would slip out the kitchen door and head for my very own sanctuary. There it was! The golden glow of the afternoon burst through the pink-and-white blossoms of my apple tree, warming my long braids and sprinkling me with diamonds. My skin was dusted with golden flecks of light. The red clover and buttercups in my hand were celestial blooms.

Vermont disappeared in a misty vapor, our house and garage spinning away into space. Here I was away from sad people, unhappy people. My apple tree was a magic place. There was no pain here. No confusion. No one spoke cross or accusing words.

My tree always welcomed me. It never said, "Come back later; I have branches to straighten now." Just, "Come rest in my arms. You're safe here."

My tree had a heartbeat. I could feel the rhythm pulsating as I sat in the branches. I didn't mind sharing my tree with the robins and the fat honeybees.

My earliest "addiction" was for love and approval. There were happy times with my father. He taught me while I was still small to use carpentry tools and do other boyish things. I was only four when I started "helping" him work on our gray Plymouth. He'd take the motor apart, placing nuts and bolts and gaskets in murky baths of lubricating oil. I'd swirl them around with my hands and squeal in delight as the oil ran down my arms. How much I depended on Daddy's approval!

Knowing deep down that my parents' marriage was failing, I tried harder to please. It was at this point that I slipped into what I now know as the "co-dependent role." I so wanted our family life to be happy that I was ready to play any part that could bring this about. Very early, perhaps as a contrast to the joylessness in our home, I determined to be a "fun person." I was always playing jokes on others, mimicking my teachers and friends. I laughed a lot, developed a reputation as a class clown. I was not yet a true compulsive, but already my gaiety had something excessive about it, as though I were telling myself, "I *will* be happy!" Hurting inside, my defense was a perpetual smile.

Years later I was to read my own youthful situation reflected in the words of social philosopher Helen Lynd: "The discovery that our parents are not all-wise and all-good and that we must face the uncertainties of our own judgment . . . is a lonely experience. It becomes still more lonely and poignant, and in a real sense shameful, when it is followed by a realization that, instead of our elders being our interpreters of the world, our protectors, we must, instead, protect them from their own fallibilities and shortcomings, and from the shameful knowledge that we are aware of them" (*On Shame and the Search for Identity*).

I was also to learn that an addiction-prone personality like mine typically manifests an exaggerated degree of compliance, and is overly concerned with pleasing people and winning approval.

But not even my desperately cheerful facade, as it turned out, could stop the breakup of our home. I was fifteen when Mother and Dad separated and filed for divorce. I retreated to my apple tree on the hill. By now my teenage legs were too long for the "stirrup" limbs and it seemed pretty dumb to sit in a tree at my age. So I'd lean up against the warm bark, feeling the heartbeat of the moving sap. Was my parents' separation something I had caused? Was there something I could still do?

All year my heart throbbed like a toothache. Typical of young people in dysfunctional families, I felt increasingly responsible to take care of my mother. To fix everything in her life, to "make it all better"—the phrase she'd often used when she kissed a bump or scratch.

My tree had no answers. So I retreated behind an air of bravado, masking my hurt with a casual veneer. Life was a charade . . . smile . . . pretend. I practiced my act before my dressing table mirror—"so-what" expressions, "I-couldn't-care-less" gestures. Cultivate the quick, merry laugh, Sandra Jean. Crinkle your eyes in merriment.

After the divorce both my parents entered second marriages that proved to be solid and lasting. Not aware of the happiness ahead for them, however, I remained the confused child in-between. Feeling disconnected with family life, I sought love like candy, and tried intensely to be more acceptable to my friends.

One of these friends was Linette. She was a sunny blonde with a dazzling smile and a Bo Derek figure that drove the guys at Spaulding High School wild. We were sophomores when Linette invited me to spend the weekend with her while her parents were away in Montreal.

She set out popcorn and potato chips, then poured Cokes from a frosty twelve-ounce bottle. "Should we put some bourbon in these?" she asked.

"That would be fine with me!" I replied in my best Rita Hayworth imitation. I had never seen a bottle of bourbon.

Linette went to a dining room cabinet and flung open the double doors. Before us stood a dazzling array of liquor—vodka, gin, Scotch, bourbon, brandy, wine, creme de menthe, rum, champagne. What an education!

How worldly I suddenly felt, as she measured a crystal shot glass of bourbon into each glass of Coke. After stirring the swirling mixture with a pink flamingo swizzle stick, she triumphantly handed me my glass.

"Here's to Spaulding High!" she toasted.

The mossy smell of the liquor sifted through the sweet Coke aroma. Now I was in the big leagues—a rite of passage—a woman at last!

Yuk. The first rush of bubbly liquid hit my tongue. "This tastes awful, Linette."

"It gets better as you go along," she assured me.

Sure enough, the second and third swallows were less pungent. A warm, tingly feeling was taking hold. "I see what you mean. This is okay!" I burbled, gulping the contents of the glass.

"Hey, take it easy," Linette warned. "You shouldn't drink it so fast!"

Before long my body felt as though it were floating in warm butterscotch sauce. I felt cozy and cared for. Cared about.

"Do you suppose I could have another?" I don't remember how many times I asked this question that evening.

Sometime later Linette telephoned our boyfriends. When it came my turn to talk, I gushed something wonderfully witty into the phone.

"You all right, Sandy?" the boy on the line asked. "You sound funny."

That's the last thing I remember.

I awakened fully clothed, flat on my back in Linette's guest room bed. By flinging my leg over the side, I stopped the room from spinning. Then waves of nausea came and I rushed for the bathroom. Kneeling on the tile floor I gripped the toilet in a death lock.

I didn't feel at all like Rita Hayworth now.

It would be two years before I had another drink . . . but I had the exact chemistry to become an alcoholic. I see myself in this statement: "The dulling of sensibility, the soothing feeling that all is well, is a powerful experience for some people. . . . Those who depend totally on such an experience do so because it gives their lives a structure and secures them, at least subjectively, against the press of what is novel and demanding. This is what they are addicted to" (Dr. Stanton Peele in *Love and Addiction*).

After graduating from high school, I enrolled at the Rhode Island School of Design in Providence. Weekends several of us would go to nearby Brown University for fraternity house weekend parties. Feeling like a small-town bumpkin in my homemade clothes, unsure of myself in the company of sophisticated Ivy League girls, I began to depend on alcohol for my security.

During exam week in May 1956, at the end of my second year in Rhode Island, I got a telephone call from my father who was now living in Barre, Vermont, with his new wife, Nora. "The Chamber of Commerce wants Barre to have a contestant in the Miss Vermont Pageant this year," he told me, "so I volunteered you. Your picture ran in last night's paper."

I was too stunned to speak. Dad had always been a practical joker, but this time he'd gone too far.

"The pageant is next weekend at the Burlington High School Auditorium," he continued. "You'll need to be there on Friday with a talent presentation."

Panic set in even before I hung up. What would I wear? What in the world could I do for a talent presentation? Could I lose twenty pounds before next weekend? Fretful hazel eyes stared back at me from the bathroom mirror. Dark circles. Jowls. Why did I stuff myself with all those sugar doughnuts at the Bluebird Cafe?

Somehow I completed my exams, got some clothes together, and made the trip to Burlington, Vermont, all in three days' time. The pageant weekend activities were a blur of teas, lunches, interviews, and rehearsals. The night of the finals was brutally hot; the makeshift fans that wheezed asthmatically from the gymnasium balcony raised barely a tickle of breeze. As I went onstage to do my talent, I was sure I would faint.

I'd decided to repeat a skit I'd done at the School of Design, a pantomime about the precocious little six-year-old Eloise who lived in New York's Plaza Hotel. To my amazement the audience in Vermont seemed to like it: riotous laughter and applause.

Still, as the contestants circled the stifling auditorium in formal gowns for the final time, I knew I had no chance of winning in the face of the far more beautiful and talented competition. I was already undressing in the basement as the announcer began to call up to the stage the runners-up for the title of Miss Vermont.

I had just gotten out of my soggy copper-colored velvet gown and was struggling with a jammed hook and eye on my voluminous crinoline hoopskirt when the final announcement came: *"And now, Miss Vermont of 1956, Sandra Jean Simpson of Barre!"*

I couldn't be hearing right.

Struggling back into my clothes, I stumbled up the stairs and burst onto the brilliantly lit stage. Blinking in disbelief, I heard applause pouring from the packed auditorium. People were standing on their chairs. Even the judges were giving me a standing ovation. I was in shock.

A crown of daisies, roses, and ferns was placed ceremoniously on my head. It was too big and slipped down over my ears. A brass trophy was thrust into my hands, while a white satin banner affirmed that I was indeed being named Miss Vermont of 1956.

My eyes scanned the audience for my parents' faces. Mother was weeping copiously on the left side of the auditorium. Dad and Nora were clapping wildly on the right. For one addicted to pleasing others, it was a heady experience.

Suddenly I felt somehow terribly alone, vulnerable. The thorns in a mountainous bouquet of red roses pricked painfully at my arm. In all that noisy, spotlit room, only the pain seemed real.

Though I didn't know it, the pain had just begun.

4

Into the Fast Lane

Suppose a bottle should materialize before him full and unopened. Once assured of its reality, how calmly then, all excitement gone, he would open it and pour, almost not needing it in the security the sight of it gave him. But he would drink it, of course. He wouldn't care how bad it tasted—un-iced, without water or soda, lukewarm, stinking, throttling. He would drink a good half-glass at once— and at once the pricking nerves would die down, the thumping heart quiet, the fatigue and ease come warmly over him at last. That's what liquor and only liquor could do for him. . . .

—Charles Jackson
The Lost Weekend

THE MORNING AFTER THE VERMONT PAGEANT I AWOKE IN MY FATHER'S home to the scent of roses. I rolled over in bed and touched the gleaming trophy on the nightstand. So it wasn't a dream; it had really happened.

"Here's the morning paper, Miss Vermont," my stepmother chirped, bringing coffee. "Your picture's on the front page."

Indeed it was. There above an expanse of bare shoulders, a mass of greenery and flowers obscured my eyes. Only the tip of my nose

47

protruded out from under the foliage like a shiny cautious mouse.

"Oh, no," I groaned. "I look like a tossed salad."

Weeks later the same horrid picture glared at me from the slick pages of *Confidential* magazine. The magazine staff had amassed the most unflattering photos of state pageant winners they could dig up and concocted what they felt was a real pageant exposé. The caption under my picture: *Is This Vermont's Best?*

Shortly thereafter each contestant received an unsettling flood of letters from members of a fundamentalist group as we prepared to go to Atlantic City for the Miss America Pageant. We were informed through elaborate maps and diagrams that we had chosen the road to death and destruction.

My oversized crown was not the only unflattering aspect of the newspaper picture. At 146 pounds I was twenty pounds overweight. A stint as tennis instructor at a summer camp turned out to be a good way to prepare for the Miss America Pageant looming ahead in September in Atlantic City. The campers monitored every mouthful of food I ate and by late August the twenty pounds were gone.

Meanwhile, filling the duties of Miss Vermont had its perilous aspects. Who, for example, would have anticipated horse shows? At these appearances it was my duty to tromp to the center of the field, present trophies to the victorious riders, and pin the ribbons to the bridles of their snorting, gasping mounts. Since horses have terrified me since early childhood, these ribbon ceremonies represented pure torture.

The Stowe Horse Show was almost canceled by heavy rains. But "the show must go on." At the judge's nod I picked my way gingerly through mucky clods of earth toward the biggest, blackest stallion ever born.

As I approached, this black monster reared up on his hind legs. When his right front hoof came down, it pummeled my left foot into the slime, driving my periwinkle pump several inches into the mud. Only my stocking foot emerged, undamaged—but how does one walk off the field with one shoe? My fear of the beast turning to indignation, I began to dig furiously for the submerged pump. Some unseen force was pulling it in the opposite direction. By now my white gloves were two clunky paws. At last I struggled upright, clutching the oozing shoe, while a nervous judge helped me off the field past the tittering onlookers.

Unaware that my insecurity had turned me into an all-out people-pleaser—especially with men to whom I automatically looked for approval—I accepted blindly all suggestions put forward by the Vermont Development Commission, the Chamber of Commerce, and the Vermont Ski Association. In spite of the fact that September was breaking all heat records, I agreed to travel to Atlantic City dressed in ski garb. The outfit they chose made me look like a raspberry-colored walrus. (Raspberry was the newest and most daring shade in ski wear in 1956.) But I lived to please.

Departure day at Burlington's airport was the initial test. Approaching the plane I had my first tussle with my cumbersome skis and poles. Even though laced together, they clearly had a mind of their own and poked out of my frantic grasp in all directions. Trying to be terribly nonchalant, despite the trickles of perspiration running down my face in the 80° heat, I stumbled up the narrow stairs of the DC-7, my ski boots massive lead weights. Somehow the stewardess and my traveling companion, a charming woman named Barbara who was director of the Vermont Pageant, got me sandwiched into the narrow seat.

Getting off the aircraft at LaGuardia Airport for a change of planes was difficult, but a breeze compared to my encounter with the revolving doors inside the terminal. Barbara sensed impending disaster. "Clasp your skis and poles close to your body," she urged. "Take teensie steps until you get around, then step out slowly."

Holding my breath, I clattered into the swirling cubicle. What happened next I can hardly describe. Skis, poles, and I flew from the spinning contraption like an exploding pinwheel. Barbara darted to safety as a pole zipped by her head. Stunned onlookers peered in disbelief at the tangled mass of steel and bamboo that lay sprawled on the marble airport floor.

We did eventually arrive at the Atlantic City airport where we were whisked into a pageant limousine. When we emerged at the Claridge Hotel, Barbara collared the photographer who had been assigned to record my arrival. Where was that promised brisk breeze from the ocean? I was about to faint from the heat.

"Let's set up the shot on the beach," the photographer suggested, leading us across the boardwalk and onto the scalding sand. There I strapped the skis to my boots and crouched in my best downhill position while he took shot after shot.

The blowing sand caked my perspiring face and stuck in my teeth. My knees felt as though they'd never unbend.

Afterward I clomped off dutifully to Registration. Assembled contestants floated about the palatial ballroom perfectly coiffed and groomed—immaculately pressed, buttoned, and zippered. Over in the corner, by contrast, was propped a wretched raspberry robot, fumbling with skis and poles.

The net result of the ski publicity attempt:

1. No picture in any paper—local or otherwise.
2. Two huge blisters on both heels.

Pageant week continued to provide one glitch after another. I spilled food and broke my zipper at a crucial moment. At the end of my talent presentation I forgot the presence of stage hands and bustled about cleaning up my equipment, causing, to my mortification, a burst of laughter from the audience.

Yet this very laughter served as my escape. As I'd learned, first as a child, then as a teenager, I covered my confusion with pranks and pratfalls. It won me acceptance from the other contestants, who voted me Miss Congeniality.

Once again the press handling did little for my ego. One reporter noted that my listed weight of 146 pounds (recorded before I had dropped the twenty pounds) was the highest of any contestant, and wrote this caption under my picture: *Fattest At Pageant Is Friendliest.*

Nevertheless, my future seemed full of promise. The day after the Miss America Pageant (beautiful Marian McKnight of South Carolina won that year), I was flown to New York and introduced to the Broadway columnist Walter Winchell. Winchell delighted in discovering young talent and creating opportunities for them. Thus began an unusual friendship. Probably because my naïveté intrigued him, he took a fatherly interest in my career.

One night I was escorted by Winchell and Joe DiMaggio to a party for Judy Garland at the Plaza Hotel. The small-town girl from Vermont gazed around the room awestruck at the celebrities from sports and show business. In the glow of the flickering candles and flowing champagne, the world seemed a warm and wonderful place. I became hooked on the celebrity lifestyle.

Hoping to launch me in an entertainment career, Winchell got me breaks on television variety shows. But even his clout could not compensate for the fact that I was a lousy actress.

By now I was going to classes at the Parsons School of Design in New York City, and working part-time at the Vermont Development Commission office in the Radio City Music Hall building. There I met the Operations Manager of Disneyland who offered me a job as an artist doing caricature sketches of tourists. Soon I moved into a Newport Beach, California, beach house with three other girls.

After a two-week apprenticeship under a Disneyland instructor, I was assigned a location at Sleeping Beauty's Castle. My first assignment might have served as a warning of trouble to come. A young mother with three sons signed up to have each child sketched. The first two likenesses flew easily from my pad. Not so the third. The little boy wiggled, slid down from his chair, made faces, stuck out his tongue. The first three tries were disastrous, the fourth barely acceptable.

I was close to tears. What was wrong? Why was my hand shaking? Could it have been because of the beach party that had gone on until two that morning? My roommates seemed to feel fine after these late nights. Why couldn't I stop after one or two drinks the way they did?

In any case, the Disneyland job lasted only for a season. Pepsi Cola, one of the Miss America Pageant sponsors, offered me a position in their public relations department with a good salary and an expense account. I moved back to New York City.

One of my first assignments was to go to Providence, Rhode Island, to help with a fashion show promotion put on by the local Pepsi bottler. While strolling down the familiar streets—it was hard to believe three years had passed since my father's phone call ended my stint at the Rhode Island School of Design—an episode occurred that, once again, should have alerted me to the excessive side of my personality.

Ahead I saw a familiar storefront logo: *Kays of Newport.* As a student, I'd drooled over their gorgeous shoe windows, but could never afford a single pair, even on sale. Today the store windows were swathed in wide paper banners. *Relocation Sale! 50–75% off!!*

Seated inside the store on a plush velvet chair, I smiled nervously at the salesman. "I was thinking of a little evening sandal in silver," I said, trying to sound sophisticated.

Soon he returned balancing six shoeboxes.

"Ooooh," I squealed amid a flurry of fuschia tissue paper, as he slipped a gleaming sandal with rhinestone trim onto my foot.

"I'll take them," I gasped enthusiastically, not wanting to appear gauche and ask the price.

"Would you care for something similar in gold?" he asked.

More boxes, more mountains of tissue. "These lucite sling pumps with rhinestone heels are very new. . . ."

If they were very new, I wanted them. After all, I was expected to be a trend-setter, wasn't I?

Back and forth from the treasure trove behind blue velvet curtains he bounced, arms laden with boxes—black patent pumps, red espadrilles, blue-and-white candy-striped "slings," purple iridescent slippers, navy suede sandals, charcoal gray dinner shoes, yellow flats with flower trim.

"Yes . . . yes . . . yes," I kept saying.

By now the tower of boxes around my chair was obscuring me from the rest of the store. The sales staff were clearly impressed. So were other customers. Who was this extravagant mystery woman? I loved the attention.

An hour later my shopping binge was complete: twenty-two pairs of shoes, five matching handbags. One entire month's salary gone. The purchases would be delivered to my hotel that afternoon.

How was I going to pay my rent? Somehow that didn't matter. I floated back to the hotel in a euphoric trance. From then on, shopping would give me what almost amounted to a chemical high.

Dr. David J. Juroe, writing in his book *Money,* comments on just this kind of reaction: "For those inclined toward buying, compulsive spending sprees keep them on excitable highs, away from being bored or listless about life. What really happens is that the compulsive striving, in this case spending, sustains the constant activity that is needed to distract them from the real inner disturbances."

I was to become very much like the Liza Moran described as follows in "Compulsive Shopping" (April 1986 *Glamour*):

It is 7:00 p.m. and twenty-eight-year-old Liza Moran is in tears because her boyfriend has just called to cancel their dinner date. This has happened four times in the past month; Liza is afraid the relationship is falling apart. She looks at the clock, realizes the stores are open until 9:00 tonight, and heads out the door.

Several hours later, Liza returns home with a $200 cashmere sweater and a $150 pair of suede boots. She would have bought even more but she had already used up most of her available credit on an earlier $1000 shopping binge that began after her boyfriend canceled a weekend in the country.

The article went on to describe Liza Moran (not her real name) as a compulsive shopper. When anything goes wrong in her life, she spends money. Liza even uses the language of drug addicts to describe her shopping sprees and their guilty aftermath. "I get high when I catch the first whiff of perfume from the cosmetics counters," she says. "I'm flying the whole time I'm in the stores. The crash comes the next day, when I look at the pricetags on everything I've bought. I tell myself I'll never do it again, but I know I will. The high is worth the letdown."

The pace of my own life speeded up. Early morning plane departures. Cabs, terminals, hotel lobbies. Hands to shake, speeches to make, an endless blur of faces and places. Lonely room service dinners. A drink to blunt the loneliness. Better still, two drinks. . . .

The glamour soon began to wear off as I battled the pinchers and strokers who grabbed at me. At times I felt like a plastic wind-up Barbie doll, at other times like a trained seal: "Throw me a fish and I'll balance a ball on my nose!"

"How many other gals are raking in the dough you're making, doll?" one Pepsi bottler asked.

True. I would be silly to quit such a rewarding job. Yet if people only knew how grim it was to live out of a matched set of turquoise Samsonite. Finally I placed a call to my boss in New York: "Mitch, I can't go another mile. I've been on the road now for five weeks straight. May I take a rest?"

"Sure. Why don't you take a few days in Palm Springs and soak up the sun."

Sitting by the pool of a fancy resort hotel, I let the warm California sun melt away my battle fatigue. I knew I was drinking too much.

Often I'd made promises to myself—one more drink and I'd toddle off to bed. Too often there'd been a rising sun on those words. Time only for a shower, a change of clothes, then it was back to the cola wars.

Reaching for the suntan oil I realized hours had passed. The pool waiter was certainly efficient. I wondered if he'd counted all the drinks he'd served me. It didn't matter if he had. I was an important public relations woman. In the big leagues now.

Weaving slightly toward the thatched snack hut, my toe caught in a chaise lounge leg and down I went onto the pool tarmac. Four waiters in safari uniforms leaped to my rescue. Gently they seated me at a glass table under a tilting purple canvas umbrella. "May I bring you something to eat, miss?" one asked.

My skinned knees burned. "Yes, bring me one of those pineapple things with shrimp . . . and perhaps a vodka martini on the rocks."

After all, it was lunchtime and the guys back in New York would be at the Cub Room starting on their Bloody Marys. It was a ritual I missed. The camaraderie. The comfort of that coterie of bodies pressed together at our end of the bar. The Bloody Marys and the inevitable London broil accompanied by soggy sliced tomatoes and mushy green beans. Nirvana!

Another martini arrived. The whiff of juniper pricked my nostrils as the first bracing jolt of the velvety liquid exploded my taste buds.

Wow, Simpson, you're a fireworks gal! You glitter. You flash. You dance in the sky.

Although for me—at least at first—alcohol acted as a stimulant, it is known to depress the activity of the central nervous system.

Drs. Ray Hodgson and Peter Miller, in *Self-Watching: Addictions, Habits, Compulsions,* describe the effects of alcohol as follows: "In small doses [it] results in a lessening of tension and a feeling of relaxation and lack of inhibition. Increased dosage, however, leads to a progressive loss of control over judgement, skills and emotions, often accompanied by violence and aggression. In large doses alcohol poisons the whole system and may result in coma followed by death. Alcohol also has a long history of inducing a dependence which is notoriously difficult to break."

Traveling with the current Miss America became one of my greatest challenges at Pepsi (I was now the Coordinator of the Miss America/Pepsi Cola Scholarship Foundation). It was my responsibility to see that her public appearance schedule was kept within limits. Not an easy task when the host bottler was paying a thousand dollars a day and wanted her to visit his favorite Aunt Minnie for "just a couple of minutes."

Then there were those harrowing evenings when the new queen was to appear at the same function where Mrs. Alfred Steele (Joan Crawford, wife of the Pepsi Board Chairman) was also to be. As Walter Winchell warned: "Don't invite Miss America (any Miss America) and La Belle Crawford to the same party." When it happened, as it had to, we staffers went into maneuvers not unlike a beachhead invasion, complete with walkie-talkies, to make sure those two stellar females didn't cross paths. Mrs. Steele didn't like to share the spotlight with beautiful younger women.

I used to have the cold sweats hearing in Mrs. Steele's icy voice the words I most feared: "Miss Simmmmmmmmsunnnnn!"

Joan Steele was a diminutive dynamo in matching couture creations. Her hat, gloves, handbag, and dress were frequently stitched from the same bolt of fabric; those high-heeled sandals with clear plastic ankle straps were her trademark. The famous crystal blue eyes, flashing under the black slashes of her eyeliner, and the stony set of her crimson, butterfly-shaped lips could transform me into a pillar of salt.

I developed an especially close relationship with Marilyn Van Derbur, Miss America of 1958. One evening after a long, stressful afternoon of appearances, Marilyn, her official pageant traveling companion, and I decided to have dinner sent up to her suite in an Atlanta hotel. We ordered filet mignon, which arrived on a pink linen-skirted room-service table, along with a bouquet of pink sweetheart roses.

"Thank God this day is over!" I gasped as we kicked off our shoes and collapsed into chairs about the table.

"Why don't you do just that?" Marilyn urged.

"Just what?" I asked, trying to blink away the rum punches I had gulped down in the hotel bar before coming up.

"Thank God. Why don't you say grace, Sandy, so we can start on this gorgeous dinner!"

I was nonplused. I didn't know a grace to say. I couldn't remember the last time I'd heard one.

Then she rescued me. "That's okay, Sandy, I'll say it. You've had a rough day."

Softly Marilyn thanked God for his goodness, for his protection, for her responsibilities and privileges as Miss America. I suddenly wished I could talk to God as she just had. How many years had it been since I had gone to Sunday school or church? Five? More like ten.

What I couldn't understand was why I wasn't enjoying my life more. I was meeting glamorous and important people; I had a solid income (although never quite enough to cover my shopping flings) and all the travel and excitement I'd ever dreamed of. Yet I was empty and frustrated and needy and scared. Nothing was filling that void in my chest regardless of what I tried to stuff inside me. It was a hole so empty that the wind seemed to blow through it.

I was twenty-two and alone too much. Drinking by myself more and more. On lonely evenings my mind would travel wistfully the "white-cottage-and-rose-trellis" route. Maybe it was time for me to get out of the fast lane and settle down somewhere.

"[The Cinderella Complex] used to hit girls of sixteen or seventeen," writes Colette Dowling, "preventing them, often, from going to college, hastening them into early marriages. Now it tends to hit women after college—after they've been out in the world a while. When the first thrill of freedom subsides and anxiety rises to take its place, they begin to be tugged by that old yearning for safety: the wish to be saved, The Cinderella Complex."

But where is Prince Charming when you really want to find him?

For me he turned up in a most unlikely place: Billings, Montana. The Pepsi bottler there had arranged for a blind date for me.

"Oh, no," I groaned, recalling disastrous evenings set up for me in other cities.

"But he's Billings' most eligible bachelor!"

"Maybe the most eligible bachelor in the whole Northwest," the Pepsi supplier chimed in.

"And to top it all off, he's a *doctor*!"

Bells went off in my brain. Wedding bells. A doctor. That rose-covered cottage. Security. Prestige. A man to depend on. A man to love me. I had myself walking down the aisle in yards of white Chantilly before I had even met him.

And when I did, he was ruggedly handsome—a tanned, angular face, sandy blond hair, tall, athletic frame.

The evening flew by . . . a blur of cocktails at his apartment, dinner in a dimly lit Chinese restaurant, dancing at the Skyline Club atop the rimrocks that formed the northeast border of the city. My heart was dancing as fast as my feet.

Parked outside my hotel in the wee hours of the morning, Werner leaned an arm on the wheel of his Thunderbird convertible and looked me straight in the eye. "Young lady, I think I want to marry you."

Nine weeks later we were en route to Europe on our honeymoon.

Who is this stranger I married? I thought, waking in a Paris hotel to see a tousled head on the pillow beside me. We knew so little of each other. A flurry of phone calls, flowers, *I love you* letters. So little time together—maybe two weeks total, if that.

I was suddenly frightened. Marriage was such a big step and I was so ill-prepared. Maybe this isn't really happening. Maybe I'll be getting on a plane in a little while, on my way to some Pepsi promotion. But no, I was replacing one treadmill with another.

The honeymoon was a string of riotous days and nights. Afterward Werner stayed on for a radiology conference scheduled months before, while I went on ahead of him to New York.

A week later I met him at the International Arrivals Building at Kennedy Airport with some unexpected news. I felt sure I was pregnant.

His face dropped. So did the ever-present pipe in his mouth.

"All those people in Billings will think we *had* to get married," I wailed as we headed for home.

"That's okay, honey," Werner assured me. "Let 'em talk. You and I have got the world by the tail."

Wrong. I had a tiger by the tail. Its name was alcohol.

The invitations started as soon as we got back to Billings. Who was the beauty queen from the East who had snatched the town's most sought-after unattached male? Many seemed dying to know. Dinner parties, luncheons, summer barbecues—an endless flow of social engagements.

Usually parties were my forte. Not when I was pregnant, I soon learned. Would I ever be able to stop carrying my little bag of soda crackers?

Sitting on the lawn of our lovely new brick home on Rimrock Road during Werner's long days at the hospital, I'd look out at the college campus across the street, wrestling with the feeling of unreality that still swept over me. The collie dog at my side looked up at me with adoring moist brown eyes. Was this really me? The doctor's wife in Billings, Montana?

Nine months after our marriage our son was born. We named him Bradford, after Brad Frapart, the business manager of the Miss America Pageant who'd become a good friend.

Our Brad was adorable, a cuddly bundle. It was almost like playing dolls, only this doll cried and shrieked.

I'd never been around a baby before. Werner assured me that motherhood would come naturally. In his eyes, apparently, mothers were all-capable. Twenty minutes after his son and I got home from the hospital, he headed out the door to go bowling.

Brad was four months old when my doctor told me I was pregnant again.

To help me adjust to this news, Werner took me to Mexico. We left Brad in Billings with Werner's parents—strict, old-world German Swiss who still spoke with heavy accents. I was intimidated by my mother-in-law. She towered over me in every sense—a devout Christian always talking about "the good Lord." I couldn't remember what was so good about him.

"Bring me another Margarita," I said now to the hovering beach waiter.

Brent burst into the world feet first the following April and never stopped running. An active, cheerful, precocious baby, he kept me running, too. I was lifting him from his bath one morning when I caught sight of Brad grinding the contents of a can of coffee into the gold carpeting of the dining room with his little saddle shoe.

"I'm not cut out for this," I moaned as I raced to retrieve the can from Brad's chubby fist.

"I need a drink."

"I deserve a drink."

Brent was four months old when the doctor again had staggering news.

"I'm pregnant again, Polly," I told the woman who was living with us now to help care for the two little boys.

"That's wonderful!" she exclaimed. "Wouldn't you like to lie down and rest?"

Lie down? I wanted to flee—somewhere, anywhere. There was a Junior League meeting that afternoon. Or was it the Medical Auxiliary? An addict to volunteering, I belonged to every organization in town that could keep my mind off the growing silence between Werner and me.

Here is a description from Nancy Friday's bestselling *My Mother/My Self* of the kind of anxiety-ridden, angry, compulsive woman I had become: "The compulsive housekeeper, the lioness of the Anti-Porn Society, the nonstop charity-worker, the overprotective and critical mother who does it all for someone else's good—who can fault these people out loud? . . . Very often, these women are obsessive/compulsives—suffering from forms of behavior that seem to have nothing to do with anger. Unlike depressed people who turn their anger within, against themselves, the obsessive/compulsives express theirs outwardly—but in such an indirect way they never need face their furies at all."

My third pregnancy was the hardest of all. In my sixth month, regularly as clockwork at one in the afternoon, the premature labor pains would begin. Hospitalization was the only way to prevent the baby from being born too early. For six weeks I lay in a room on the maternity ward. And every afternoon at one the familiar pains would begin.

Lisa was a beautiful little girl with dark curls. Six weeks premature, her head was barely larger than a tennis ball. So fragile. So helpless. So in need of dedicated mothering.

With Lisa's birth I'd had three children in less than three years. Lying in bed in the hospital through the weeks of waiting had been a time for reflection. How little of this there'd been in my twenty-five years! I seemed to have careened through life with my motor racing. I couldn't seem to turn it off. *I want . . . I want . . . I want* had fueled it. "Anything worth doing is worth overdoing" seemed to be my motto.

But surely now, as a mother with three children, I could stop scrambling for whatever it was that kept eluding me. Now I would slow down, savor, devote myself to raising my family.

I returned home with my daughter in my arms and high resolve in my heart—and was soon driven as frenetically as ever. I didn't yet apply the word *compulsive* to my behavior.

Nor had I ever considered an observation like that of Stanton Peele, a social psychologist and probably the foremost expert on addictive behavior: "A person will be predisposed to addiction to the extent that he cannot establish a meaningful relationship to his environment as a whole, and thus cannot develop a fully elaborated life. In this case, he will be susceptible to a mindless absorption in something external to himself . . . his susceptibility growing with each new exposure to the addictive object [or experience]."

In fact, there were a succession of habits I seemed powerless to stop. The more I hated myself for them, the more I did them. The chain-smoking that had begun in lonely hotel rooms now launched the day: I couldn't get out of bed until I had a lighted cigarette in my hand. The four-letter words I'd acquired as "one of the boys" popped out increasingly when I least intended them.

What to do about my bulging waistline? I hated the flab and knew I needed to do something about it. Exercise! Jogging! I bought black tights and a leotard for workouts, a warm-up suit, and a pair of running shoes for jogging. At a women's program at the Y, I groaned and moaned through my first session. Agony! Next I donned my running gear and jogged around the wooden running track until cramps forced me to stop.

Day after day the same routine. Exercise, jogging, then I pummeled my fat on the wooden rollers and my hips with the canvas vibrating machine. My body began to revolt. Cramping, nausea, clouded vision. I simply didn't know when to stop.

"Jogging . . . can become addictive in its own right," writes psychotherapist Howard M. Halpern in *How to Break Your Addiction to a Person.* "I have seen people so obsessed with running and so uncomfortable and anxious about missing a planned run that the activity begins to interfere with other important areas of life." (See section on Compulsive Exercising, p. 231.)

Far from cutting down outside activities, however, I continued to volunteer for every civic cause that came along. I'd open my mouth to say no and out would come, "Of course! I'd be glad to."

Where was my backbone? But Polly was so competent with the children, so patient and steady . . . so unlike me. The only part of married life in which I felt confident was entertaining—and a doctor's wife did lots of that.

So the years slipped into a pattern: part-time mothering, full-time socializing. The drinks required to get me into a party mood grew in number. So did the awkward moments, the blackouts, the incidents I simply could not remember.

Like the turkey episode one Thanksgiving. Our guest list had grown to twelve. Preparation the day before had involved marketing, fixing dishes ahead of time, fussing over the table setting, arranging fresh flowers. Before dashing out the door for a luncheon date, I decided to stop at the supermarket and pick up a larger bird on my way home.

Four o'clock already! How I hated to pry myself away from those after-lunch coffee-and-brandies at the Golden Belle to face the teeming hordes at the grocery store.

The turkey department was a free-for-all. People pushing and elbowing one another to extricate the frosty birds from their refrigerated nests. A twenty-five pound frozen turkey isn't the easiest object to maneuver. As I lowered mine into my cart, waves of dizziness and nausea swept through me. Why did I drink so much? I didn't seem to be able to stop anymore. *I'll start cutting down tomorrow,* I promised myself.

Back at home I faced a new problem: Where was I going to thaw the turkey? *The clothes dryer! The perfect place!*

Thanksgiving morning I crawled shakily out of bed to get the turkey into the oven. A bird that size would take many hours. Now where was it? Not in the refrigerator, I quickly discovered. With increasing frenzy I searched the car trunk, bathtub, downstairs shower, outside barbecue, the roof of the tool shed. . . .

How many drinks had I had yesterday?

An attic-to-cellar search aided by all three children failed to unearth the elusive bird. Twelve guests arriving at three o'clock! I was in a panic. While making a last-ditch sweep through the laundry room, I saw hanging limply from the open dryer door a golden yellow tag: *Swift's Butterball.*

A scarier episode occurred many months later after a party at the Yellowstone Country Club. I didn't remember driving home. Around three A.M. I awakened to see lights glaring into the bedroom window.

Struggling to my feet and pushing back the drapes, I observed a peculiar scene in our front yard. There on the lawn sat the white Jeep Wagoneer I had driven alone to the party. (My husband had had to attend a special meeting and had gone in his own car.) The Jeep's headlights on high beam were blazing into my aching eyes. Both doors were wide open, an inside ceiling light illuminated the car's interior.

At first glance it looked like an errant UFO. I stumbled out the front door and through the thick grass to the lighted vehicle. Cautiously I backed the Jeep across the lawn, over the short curb into the street, then into our driveway.

Back in bed I noted gratefully that my husband had not awakened. *You lucked out this time, kiddo. When are you ever going to learn?*

The next morning I dragged myself out of bed, started the coffeepot, then headed out the front door to fetch the morning paper. As I passed by the Jeep, my glance turned into a stare of horror. Red stains covered the splash panels behind the front wheels. Long, ugly reddish streaks were splattered on the white door. The touch of a trembling finger confirmed my worst fears. It was blood.

What had I done? Had I run over someone last night? Had I killed someone? Oh, my God!

Dashing to the mailbox, I yanked the Sunday paper from the metal box with such intensity I skinned my knuckles. Tearing the rubber band from the paper, I searched the front page for a hit-and-run story, forgetting that of course there'd been no time to make today's news.

Nothing there. Frantically I spread the paper on the ground, tearing and flailing at the pages to find the item I didn't want to see. Still nothing. Gathering up the mangled newspaper, I headed back for the kitchen, my heart pounding. My head was splitting from front to back. What had I done?

"Lord God, I will never, ever drink again! Just tell me I haven't killed anyone and I'll go on the wagon for the rest of my life!"

My husband entered the kitchen and eyed the jumbled newspaper. "Did this thing get hit by a bus?" he asked, reaching for the sports section.

I was standing pressed up against the sink, taking short breaths so as not to faint from fear.

"Did you hear that dogfight this morning?" he went on. "I had to go outside and turn the hose on them. The setter across the street got bitten badly; his blood's all over the Jeep."

The relief that flooded through me made my knees buckle. "Gosh, no, I didn't hear a thing."

My vow never to drink again lasted exactly ninety minutes. As I fixed my children's breakfast I decided to treat myself to a Bloody Mary. I had something to celebrate!

These 1985 statistics from the National Council on Alcoholism are certainly nothing to celebrate: There are 18.3 million adult "heavy" drinkers in the U.S. (who consume more than fourteen drinks a week). Of these, 12.1 million are alcoholics (one-third of them women)—an increase of 14.3 percent since 1980.

New research indicates that women apparently metabolize alcohol differently from men—due, perhaps, to hormonal levels; the menstrual cycle; birth control pills; or even to women's lower percentage of water content and higher percentage of body fat.

Whatever the cause, observes *Ms.* magazine (February 1987), it adds up to the fact that "alcoholism and all its health consequences tend to 'telescope'—proceed at a much faster pace within a female body."

Researchers for the *Ms.* survey, moreover, found that as drinking increases, so does other addictive behavior.

Alcohol, drugs, tobacco and food, according to psychoanalyst Theodore Rubin in *Compassion and Self-Hate,* "are often used as sedative and anesthetic devices in an attempt to relieve self-hate. [Such people] put themselves into a temporary haze in order to escape their feelings. . . . This device is also unfortunately and nearly always unconsciously used as a form of slow suicide."

Are You an Alcoholic?

(The Johns Hopkins Questionnaire)

		Yes	No
1.	Do you lose time from work due to drinking?	___	___
2.	Is drinking making your home life unhappy?	___	___
3.	Do you drink because you are shy with other people?	___	___
4.	Is drinking affecting your reputation?	___	___
5.	Have you ever felt remorse after drinking?	___	___
6.	Have you gotten into financial difficulties as a result of drinking?	___	___
7.	Do you turn to lower companions and an inferior environment when drinking?	___	___
8.	Does your drinking make you careless of your family's welfare?	___	___
9.	Has your ambition decreased since drinking?	___	___
10.	Do you crave a drink at a definite time daily?	___	___
11.	Do you want a drink the next morning?	___	___
12.	Does drinking cause you to have difficulty sleeping?	___	___
13.	Has your efficiency decreased since drinking?	___	___
14.	Is drinking jeopardizing your job?	___	___
15.	Do you drink to escape from worries or trouble?	___	___
16.	Do you drink alone?	___	___
17.	Have you ever had a complete loss of memory as a result of drinking?	___	___
18.	Has your physician ever treated you for drinking?	___	___
19.	Do you drink to build up your self-confidence?	___	___
20.	Have you ever been to a hospital or institution on account of drinking?	___	___

If you answer yes to any one *of the questions, there is a definite warning that you may have a problem with alcohol.*

If you say yes to any two, *chances are you have a problem.*

If you answer yes to three *or more, you definitely have a problem with alcohol.*

5

The Cultist

Real life is harsh. It is constantly injuring our sensibilities.
The temptation to escape from it by flight is the stronger the
more sensitive we are: We run away in order to protect our
sensitivity, to escape the conflict which wounds it. The land
of dreams is close at hand, so that one can escape into it at
any moment, far from these painful realities. . . . It is a
secret treasure into which he pours the best of himself. It is
his way of turning the tables on harsh reality.

Paul Tournier, M.D.
The Healing of Persons

I DIDN'T WANT TO FACE MY FURIES. I WANTED SOMEONE ELSE TO DO IT FOR
me. Compulsive people are particularly vulnerable to the quick
fix of mind-bending fads and cults. We are dependency-prone. We
want to please. And from childhood I'd been attracted by the
invisible world.

"Have you noticed what a vivid imagination Sandra has?"
relatives would say of me. Being an only child in a houseful of
adults created companionship problems. So I created imaginary
playmates. The characters in my fairy tale books became real people
to me. Draped in lace curtains and tottering in Mother's high heels,
I was Cinderella swirling in the arms of Prince Charming at the
ball.

On warm, sunny days I'd scamper through the tall grass of our neighbor's pasture to my magic hideaway in the woods. It was a small mossy shelf to the right of the path, which I pretended was my majestic medieval bed. My headboard was an enormous Vermont maple with low hanging branches, my footboard a bush of wild roses.

Sometimes I'd bring along Ted, my lambskin teddy bear. Ted and I were great friends. I'd prop him up on my chest facing the rosebush, so he could see what I could see. His black silk eyes were far more perceptive than mine and he could spot an elf or a fairy at a hundred yards.

Once as we were sitting there, a yellow butterfly landed delicately on my chest. I hardly dared breathe for fear I'd frighten this glorious visitor. As the butterfly remained balanced there, I felt our souls touching at some mystical level. So real were these fantasies that it was often hard for me to return to everyday life.

Beautiful and innocent childhood fun, surely. Where and how does it begin to turn into something not so pure and good?

We often had a chicken wishbone at our house drying on the windowsill over the kitchen sink. Dad and I would wait till it was completely dried for the ritual of breaking. Whoever got the longer piece would have his wish granted.

Superstition was part and parcel of New England life:

Never walk under a ladder.

If you spill the salt, throw some over your left shoulder.

Never put your hat on the bed.

Never let a black cat cross your path.

Never open an umbrella in the house.

If you leave the house and have to go back for something, sit down and count to ten before proceeding on your way.

There were rabbit's foot keychains and horseshoes nailed over doorways. (Make sure to mount them properly or the luck will slip through.)

Then came a Ouija board craze. Great mysteries were revealed by this means, I was assured by one neighbor. She had special clairvoyant insights and could tell you where you had lost things. The police used to go to her to ask about missing persons. My mind whirled at such powers. In my early teens I made frequent visits to her house seeking answers to all kinds of problems.

Once as a seventh-grader I attended a magic show at the Barre Municipal Auditorium. My friend Betty Lou and I arrived early to get front-row seats. The magician, the Great Garlock, was a character right out of my early fairy tales. Tall and handsome (who wouldn't look that way in a tuxedo—the first I'd ever seen), he wore a magnificent floor-length black satin cape.

He needed twelve people to be hypnotized. Were there any volunteers? Betty Lou and I streaked to the stage. Perched on wooden folding chairs, we stared obediently into his intense blue eyes. "Count backwards with me," he told us. "One hundred . . . ninety-nine . . . ninety-eight. . . ." Somewhere in the eighties I lost consciousness. When I awakened it was to gales of laughter. Later friends told us that after being given hypnotic suggestions, we had scratched frantically as if covered by fleas and shivered violently from icy cold blasts.

Afterward we volunteers stumbled down the steep stairs from the stage. I crumpled uneasily into my seat. Something was wrong. My mind wouldn't focus. I felt confused, disjointed.

The Great Garlock spoke. "If any of you I have just hypnotized have any problems bringing your mind back into focus, I'll be here tomorrow morning in the director's office to help you readjust."

Next morning I made the mile walk back to the auditorium. The building smelled of varnish and perspiration. At my knock the door to the director's office was flung open and there stood the towering black figure from the night before. He was wearing the long satin cape, yet somehow it looked tawdry in the morning light.

"I'm one of the people you hypnotized last night," I told him. "I've felt strange ever since you woke us up. My mind seems fuzzy. Everything's all mixed-up."

"You must be one of the very sensitive ones," the Great Garlock replied. "Really, what I did last night was routine. Perhaps you went into a higher plane of consciousness than the others."

The man in the black cape fixed his eyes on mine and started the countdown from one hundred. I was aware of onions on his breath.

Suddenly I had the strangest sensation—as though something unknown, something dark and disagreeable, were trying to climb right inside me. My heart started pounding. "I don't want to do that again," I wailed.

"But you must if I am going to help you."

"Can't you do it any other way?" I pleaded.

"Well . . . perhaps."

He pulled a chair beside mine and explained that he would call upon a higher power to help me. I didn't understand the words he used after that. *Magicians must have their own language,* I thought.

Ten minutes or more passed. His voice trailed off into a chant. I was feeling very uncomfortable.

"You should have no further problems now, miss," he said at last.

I thanked him weakly and backed out of the room. Did I feel any better? I wasn't sure. A part of me felt violated that had felt safe and secure before that night.

Psychic phenomena, however, continued to fascinate me. It wasn't long after the Miss America Pageant that I visited a woman who told fortunes with a deck of cards.

"Your parents are divorced," she revealed. "They live in close proximity."

Quite true.

"You have just won a national honor," she went on. "It will carry

you into new horizons of job opportunities and influential relationships."

This woman is wonderful, I thought.

The shoe-buying orgy in Providence was my first look at my own
tendency toward excessive behavior. Alarmed by this lack of control
within, I started looking for control outside myself. Soon I was
searching regularly for the "Today's Horoscope" column in newspapers. If my horoscope said to beware of short trips, I'd hesitate to
cross the street for a cup of coffee.

When marriage to Werner failed to supply the needed external
control, I sought out a psychic in Billings. She called herself
Madame X—a pot-roast of a woman, solid, round, with watery
brown eyes and hair pulled into a tight bun at the back of her neck.
I began to depend on her for most of my decisions.

At one visit (fifteen dollars per session) she announced that we
had been joined by her "spirit guide" who also happened to be her
dead mother. Together they went into the previous lifetimes they
said I'd had, including one as the wife of a cruel Chinese war lord
who sold me as a prostitute. I was anxious to believe these
revelations, my imagination captivated by the intrigue of my
supposed past.

To expand my psychic awareness Madame X encouraged me to
attend the weekly class she taught. At these group sessions, held in
the basement of her modest home, she'd speak of members who
were absent, telling us what they were doing at the precise moment
we were meeting.

One mind exercise she taught was billet reading. We would
write things on pieces of paper, fold them up, and pass them around
in a basket. Picking one at random, we were to feel the vibrations
of the message and "read" it without opening it up. I got to be
pretty good at it.

One of my friends tried to warn me against all this. Influenced no
doubt by her Roman Catholic faith, Lois Ann a stately brunette

with compelling blue eyes, called such practices "occult." They were, she informed me, "an abomination to God." She even brought a Bible to my house one day and read me a passage out of Deuteronomy:

> Let no one be found among you . . . who practices divination or sorcery, interprets omens, engages in witchcraft, or casts spells, or who is a medium or spiritist or who consults the dead. Anyone who does these things is detestable to the Lord. . . .

It struck me as a little far out but I didn't say anything.

The person who brought the most stability into my life at this time was our cleaning woman, Hilda, an outgoing, energetic woman with copper red hair. (Polly had gone to be with her grandchildren.)

Hilda was more than an employee. She was a surrogate grandmother who had great strength, endurance, love, and tenderness. I often turned my responsibilities to my children over to Hilda so that I could focus on civic projects and social engagements.

Sometimes I would catch her looking at me sadly: "Sandy, you've got to spend more time with these kids. They need you. You don't have to volunteer for every committee in town. The years will slip away, the kids will grow up, and you'll have missed the most important time in their lives."

I knew she was right. And I loved my children dearly. But, compulsively driven as I was, I could only overwhelm them with gifts and affection in sporadic efforts to make up for lost time. What little I was able to pass along to them issued right out of my own compulsive traits.

My perfectionism where clothes were concerned, for example. I used my design training to see that the family's wearing apparel was color-coordinated. And one day I discovered that Lisa, age four, was changing her clothes several times a day. If her socks didn't match her dress or sweater, she went into a frenzy, tearing through her dresser drawers for just the right combination. The thought that my daughter was growing up like me was scary.

What I *didn't* give our children was time. My husband and I came home late from a country club party to find Brad, Brent, and Lisa asleep in the hall instead of their bedrooms. For solace—for companionship?—they'd wrapped themselves in their nylon comforters like three little quilted cocoons. Remorse tore at my heart. Why didn't I stay home more? What was I doing to these tender little lives?

Werner, too, was seldom available to them. Every daylight hour he spent at the hospital or tennis court. In addition, his practice took him to other towns in Montana. When I went to Madame X with a litany of complaints against my workaholic doctor husband and his absenteeism, she consulted her spirit guide and reported that we were not right for each other. I already knew that: at the ten-year point of our marriage I was rationalizing my heavy drinking as the result of our deteriorating relationship. Werner and I were two utterly unconnected people wandering in our own worlds. Strangers when we married, the passage of years had not brought us much closer.

What advice did Madame X have for improving my marriage? The psychic shook her head. "You and your husband are working out your karma from other lifetimes. Perhaps the next time around will be better for both of you."

Since I had suffered the trauma of my parents' breakup, divorce was the last thing I wanted for myself and our children. Nevertheless, it took place—legal separation in 1970, divorce the following year. I moved to our weekend home in Red Lodge, sixty-five miles from Billings, and entered the three children in school there.

It was a miserable time for us all. The children missed their father and their friends back in Billings. One fall morning my older son Brad, then ten, announced he was running away. He put on his corduroy jacket over his jeans and shirt, packed a pair of socks, two cans of tomato soup, a knife and fork, and a flashlight in a brown paper bag. Then he headed up the street, kicking the brown and yellow aspen leaves as he went.

I watched him from the living room window, set to jump into the car and follow him the moment he was out of sight. Where the road turned, however, he stopped. For a long while he stood there, head bowed. Then slowly he retraced his steps. Inside the house he emptied the contents of the paper bag onto the foyer floor. "I'm back," he said. I hugged him fiercely, his cowlick tickling my nose.

Brad's unhappiness with the current arrangement remained, however, and a few weeks after this episode he went to live with his father. Several years later Brent would join him.

Meanwhile, I married again. The answer to all my problems, I decided, was another husband. Perhaps this man could fix what was wrong with me, fill that empty place. The need for someone who could show me what to do, who could bring control and order into my life, was compelling.

"Too often," writes Dr. Sonya Friedman in *Men Are Just Desserts,* "women marry to escape their true selves, believing that marriage will make life work for them. Operating under the assumption that they are incomplete, unformed, lacking the capacity to take care of themselves financially or emotionally, they seek out a man who will be caretaker, benefactor, lover, and hero—'everything' to them."

Similarly, psychoanalyst Karen Horney in her classic *Feminine Psychology* referred to "neurotic women who feel unhappy, insecure, and depressed as long as they do not have someone devoted to them, who loves them or somehow cares for them."

My new husband, Randall, was a sharp Billings trial lawyer, a man of striking good looks. The children and I were glad to be back in Billings again, where we could see Brad more often, where Brent and Lisa could visit their father, where I could resume my hectic social schedule. In my obsessive busyness it didn't occur to me that no amount of outside activity, only a transformation inside, could satisfy. In my neediness I continued to cry out for answers from anyone and everyone.

One day I saw an advertisement in the newspaper that read something like this:

> Who Are You? Why Are You Here?
> Looking for Answers?
> Is inner contentment eluding you?
> Come Wednesday night to a lecture of
> *The International Serenity Society*[*]
> and revitalize your life.
> 8 p.m. Comanche Room, Warbonnet Inn.

I have a date with destiny tonight, I told myself as I pulled my car into the overflow parking lot of the hotel. I was disregarding the advice of Lois Ann who had warned, "Sandy, stay away from all that hocus-pocus! You're playing with fire."

I tuned out her words as I hurried up the concrete sidewalk and into the sprawling dark brown stucco building. Inside I found a registration table strewn with alluring color pamphlets of the Serenity Society. I grabbed a handful and headed for the crowded lecture room.

The evening's speaker was a stocky, handsome woman named Velda. She had short salt-and-pepper gray hair curled tightly about a strong square face, and bright dark eyes that snapped knowingly behind thick glasses.

---

[*] Not the real name.

"The International Serenity Society has totally revolutionalized my life," she began. "For years I suffered from depression, asthma, and painful arthritis, but this simple program has given me the tools to overcome these problems. Any one of you can change your lives this way, too."

The lecture lasted an hour. Facts, graphs, humor, even Scripture. Velda had a mixed bag of technical data and psychic techniques. I was captivated by her presentation, wanted to know more, and made a date with her for a special counseling session the following morning.

At 10:45 A.M. I swung into the driveway of the address she'd given me, a crisp twenty-dollar bill in my pocket. Velda greeted me at the screen door and invited me back to a book-lined study. A tall grandfather clock ticked in the shadows reminding me suddenly of Uncle Ralph. Feelings of helplessness, of the desire for some kind of external control, flooded me.

When I was seated Velda explained how she would help me contact my "spiritual guides" through her own guides, a process that involved much eyes-closed concentration.

Apparently sensing uneasiness on my part, Velda assured me, "You have nothing to be afraid of. These guides are spirits who've been with you ever since you were born. Even before that. They are committed to helping you as long as you are on this side."

Further revelation: I had nine guides, which supposedly meant I had a very important earthly mission. Most people have but four or five.

"You are a very old soul," Velda told me, "a master who has returned from many lifetimes. You didn't have to come back this time but *you chose to.*"

My head was spinning, the ticking clock setting the pace of my heartbeat. "What are you trying to tell me?" I asked.

"That you are a prophet," she answered, "with strong visionary capabilities—gifted in intuition, but confused in the feeling part of your psyche."

Before dismissing me, she urged me to attend the summer camp of the International Serenity Society, which would be held in Idaho at a place called Spirit Lake.

Should I go?

How I wished I had Madame X to advise me. She'd died recently of gall bladder trouble—a terribly grubby earthly ailment, I thought, for such an ethereal spirit.

In Madame X's classroom I'd heard about people who received answers via "automatic writing." Back at home I sat down at the kitchen table with pencil and legal pad borrowed from my new husband's desk. With pencil poised, I waited self-consciously for some message from the spirit world. "Should I go to this camp?" I wrote at the top of the page.

Now what? Would some unseen force seize my fingers and spell out the answer? Would the pencil write by itself? How did these discarnate spirits communicate?

For a long time nothing happened. Frustrated, I cried out, "Okay, if there are nine of you guides out there, or in here, or wherever you are, somebody please tell me something."

I felt my arm begin to shake with small tremors. Placing the pencil on the waiting pad, my hand scribbled, "YES. GO."

Thrilled with this outward sign of affirmation, I sent in my application.

I was a cauldron of conflicting thoughts and emotions when I returned from Spirit Lake. Part of my conscious mind was telling me it was all nonsense—maybe even dangerous nonsense, as Lois Ann had warned. Another part was telling me how fascinating this new knowledge was. Why, it even contained Scripture. Well, what sounded like Scripture.

What I didn't realize was that the compulsive woman unrecognized inside me was finding a "high" in these experiences. Psychic phenomena—offering experiences like altered states of consciousness, trances, perceptions of auras surrounding objects, even the exaltation of becoming divine—attract people seeking a mood change, and can deliver just as effectively (and addictively) as alcohol or drugs.

In fact, new research suggests chemical explanations for so-called transcendental states of consciousness ("Anatomy of Ecstasy," *American Health*, January/February 1987). Arnold Mandell, brain chemist and professor of psychiatry at the University of California, San Diego, theorizes that meditation inhibits the action of the neurotransmitter serotonin, ordinarily a brain-quieting hormone. The result: increased electrical discharges. In Dr. Mandell's words, "Affectual and cognitive processes characteristic of religious ecstasy."

Eugene d'Aquili, a psychiatrist and neuroscientist at the University of Pennsylvania, postulates that electrical stimulation of the parietal lobe of the brain corresponds with advancing states of transcendence, all the way to "ultimate mystic experience."

I knew nothing of such chemical explanations, of course, but was drawn by the intrigue and spiritual euphoria promised by the Serenity Society. Since I had agreed to be the Montana representative, our home soon became the destination of a steady stream of visiting ISS "counselors," each one stranger than the last. My new husband, Randall, had welcomed these visitors good-naturedly at first, but his attitude soon changed to frustration, then outrage at the constant intrusions, the endless long-distance phone calls. He was totally turned off by my new psychic vocabulary: chakras, auras, reincarnation, karma.

Desperate for help with my out-of-control drinking and the eating binges with which it alternated, I began calling these counselors for advice. To each I described my inability to concentrate; the mocking, haunting voices in my head; the ugly faces that zoomed in and out of my mind whenever I closed my eyes.

"You've picked up some angry souls from a past life who are out to get you, now that they have your attention," one told me.

"There is an astro-soul counselor in the Denver area," another said. "He could regress you through your former lives to find out just exactly who is harassing you." But the process, it seemed, would take months and be very expensive.

A third adviser suggested I try cold showers. "These dark spirits cannot stand the cold. Cold baths work well, too. You might want to throw in a couple of trays of icecubes." Later this same counselor called back long-distance (charges, of course, were always reversed). "We're having a conference here in Los Angeles this weekend. Friday night at ten o'clock sharp we will all send you our energy. Be standing under a cold shower so you can receive it."

At ten o'clock that Friday night (eleven o'clock my time) I was shivering in the shower stall. Was I receiving the promised energy? The only observable result was a miserable cold.

Days, weeks, months passed while the sinister voices, the hideous faces became more insistent. Nothing could shut them out—not alcohol, not the cakes and other sweets I'd slip into the kitchen to gorge on in the middle of the night.

My weight was now crowding two hundred pounds; coloring and setting my hair, taking time over my clothes—everything had become too much trouble. Once as I was standing in the checkout line at the grocery store, I overheard a woman behind me whisper to someone else, "She was in the Miss America Pageant? She couldn't win a livestock show the way she looks now!"

One day in desperation I remembered that my daughter possessed a two-inch silver crucifix on a black silk cord; I found it in her top bureau drawer and clutched at it for comfort, the sharp edges embedded in my frantic palms. But nothing seemed to help.

Nor any person. My husband was bewildered by the change in my appearance, and my enslavement to the bizarre practices of the Serenity Society. Brent and Lisa would come home from school and greet me with troubled faces. One day when I was out the two of them rifled through my desk drawers and threw out what they could find of my Serenity Society literature, explaining when I discovered the loss that it made me "act funny." I ached to be a real mother to them. Yet I had nothing to give. I was totally consumed with self— self-hatred and self-pity—and spent endless hours in bed with the covers pulled up over my head, the drapes closed to shut out any prying rays of the sun.

I had everything to live for and yet something inside me was pushing me straight into a dark pit.

These days "channeling"—men and women giving up temporary use of their bodies in order to channel the messages of spirits, ostensibly wise old "ascended masters"—has become a multi-million-dollar business. In California, according to the *New York Times* (May 10, 1987), consumers can consult a reincarnated "spirit" for as little as ten dollars or as much as $1,500 an hour. The best-known channels (formerly called mediums) charge admission fees of $200 to $400 at weekend seminars that attract hundreds of people.

The same *Times* article quotes Marcello Truzzi, professor of sociology at Eastern Michigan University who specializes in paranormal research, with this critique: "What we have is a tremendous democratization of religion, allowing many people to be the pathway to the almighty. Everybody has a pipeline, be your own guru; everybody is their own priest. It assuages guilt, tells people that what they are doing is all right. . . ."

Psychiatrist Scott Peck, on the other hand, in *The Road Less*

Traveled, writes tellingly of the attempt to escape the anxiety and pain of being responsible for one's self. It is this anxiety that drives the compulsive person to self-destructive acts and perilous dependencies:

> The difficulty we have in accepting responsibility for our behavior lies in the desire to avoid the pain of the consequences of that behavior. . . . Whenever we seek to avoid the responsibility for our own behavior, we do so by attempting to give that responsibility to some other individual or organization or entity. By this means we then give away our power to that entity. . . . In attempting to avoid the pain of responsibility, millions and even billions daily attempt to escape from freedom.

6

Why Live?

I do not believe a real urgency to die produces the suicidal act, so much as the feeling of not knowing what else to do to ease the Pain. The person is all out of struggles.

—Arthur Janov, Ph.D.
The Primal Scream

*I*T WAS NOT UNTIL I ATTENDED THE COMPULSIVITY CLINIC, YEARS LATER, that I gained true insight into my suicide attempt. Just as Peggy, in our small group there, had started me thinking systematically about my early years, so another group member helped me look into the depths of the pit I had finally reached.

Ginny was a small, thin brunette with a soft voice, eyes full of hurt, and an apologetic manner. At the Compulsivity Clinic she had listened to the lectures and small-group revelations with no sign of emotion. Confronted by our group leader, Maureen, for her passiveness, Ginny had opened up enough to say she loathed herself and had tried four times to commit suicide.

"You're full of anger, Ginny," Maureen informed her. "That's what's behind your suicide attempts. Suicide, you know, is the ultimate angry gesture."

The mousy little woman shook her head in shocked denial.

"Yes, you are angry, Ginny. You're angry at your father for abusing your mother. You're angry at your mother for putting up with it. And you're angry at them both for neglecting you. You've stuffed these feelings down for years. When they wouldn't stay down, you turned this rage on yourself."

Ginny again denied harboring such emotions.

"Everyone in this room is full of anger at someone or they wouldn't be here," Maureen persisted. "We're going to do something about yours right now."

With that she opened the closet in our small conference room and brought out a hollow plastic bat. Then she instructed the rest of us to make a pile in the center of the room of the cushions we were sitting on.

"Now, Ginny, your father is here, sitting there in the corner watching you. Go ahead and whack these pillows as you talk to him. Let it all pour out. You need to get rid of your rage if you're ever going to be healthy."

Protesting that it was silly, Ginny did it halfheartedly at first. Then something seemed to explode in her. Soon the room was reverberating with her fury. Quiet little Ginny had suddenly become the mouse that roared.

"I hate you, Dad!"

Whack! Splat!

". . . for your filthy, rotten mouth!"

Whack! Blap!

"For getting drunk all the time!"

Whack! Thump!

"For beating Mom all those times when she couldn't fight back!"

Thunk! Whap!

"For leaving us without money for food—and spending it on your creepy friends!"

Whack! Crack!

"For cheating on my mother!"

Whap! Klop!

"I hate you . . . I hate you. . . ."

Whack! Whack! Whack!

Ginny was so into it now that she began kicking the pillows right through the open door into the hall, all the while screaming, "I hate you, you rotten, miserable s.o.b.!"

We were drained just watching her. Ginny returned to the conference room red-eyed but peaceful, spent by her outburst of pent-up emotion.

"That sure felt good," she exclaimed. "Now I need some hugs." Soon she was in my arms holding onto me as if she would never let go, our tears running together.

I could identify with Ginny completely. For I was remembering the time several years before when I too had tried to end my life, and the tremendous store of repressed anger I myself had found. Therapy had helped me discover a lifetime of bottled-up rage—which was, Maureen insisted, the major factor in most suicides. I did not have the kind of traumatic memories Ginny acted out. But I had grown up in an environment that blocked the free expression of negative emotion, an environment that encouraged peace at any price.

There might be another reason for my anger, too. The echoes roused in me at the sight of Ginny's distorted face made me wonder suddenly: Did all of us share an inheritance of fear and rage, roots deep in the human past that I could have unwittingly tapped into when I opened myself to the visitations of "spirit guides"? By the time I arrived at the Compulsivity Clinic I no longer believed the Serenity Society's far-out theories about previous existences. But those rage-twisted faces, those shrieks and curses hounding me asleep and awake, had been real enough. Could I have invited Anger itself into my unconscious?

By the time of my second marriage I had also started seeing a psychiatrist, but we did little but spar with words. Several times I was a patient for a period of weeks on the psych ward of Billings' Deaconess Hospital. These served as brief drying-out times only. Back home each time I resumed my drinking to blot out the voices, the faces, the reality of my failure as a human being. One advantage of alcohol as an escape is that it occupies your mind even when you're sober. All my creativity went into subterfuges to disguise the amount I was consuming.

The Tuesday morning trash collection ritual, for example. The moment I heard the familiar grinding of the garbage truck down the street, I would speed out to the garage where sat our two green plastic trash cans. Stealthily I would lift a white dress box from under a dusty stack of discarded magazines nearby and place it into one of the containers.

A gentle shake of the box satisfied me. The bottles didn't rattle: I'd wrap each one in tissue paper and Scotch tape. Inside six empty Smirnoff bottles lay like silent soldiers, shrouded for burial.

Quickly I would open the garage doors, push the cart containing the bottles out to the street, then run back into the garage and fumble for the "door close" button. Whew! One more time I'd gotten the bottles out of the house before Randall had found them.

Getting rid of the empties had become an increasingly challenging ritual. They were always wrapped carefully so that the garbage men wouldn't see them. Heaven forbid these four faceless men (I never had the nerve to look out the window to see what they actually looked like) should know how much I drank!

An all-out commitment to soap operas was another way I drowned out the painful situation around me. The soaps had become my reality since it was too difficult to face my failure as a mother and wife.

At eleven A.M. sharp I'd be seated in the den waiting for *All My Children* to begin. I'd surround myself with a nest of pillows on the black naugahyde couch, make sure I had a fresh pack of cigarettes and sometimes a sixpack of Pepsi with ice bucket and vodka bottle. The phone came off the hook. I didn't want any interruptions.

As time went by, my repertoire of soaps expanded: *The Young and the Restless, The Days of Our Lives, Search for Tomorrow, The Edge of Night, Another World.*

The characters in the dramas became good friends. I talked about them as though they lived next door. Each tragedy I eagerly identified with, each triumph accepted reluctantly. For my own life was still in a shambles.

Even my grocery list was a problem. Why burden my mind with more decisions than I could cope with? List in hand, I'd drive to the small neighborhood grocery store, wrapping the paper around the steering wheel so as not to lose it. Once things got into my purse, they could be lost forever, and I couldn't risk losing anything as important as this. I had to get dinner. That was one function I still performed. Yet it was becoming increasingly hard to stir and sauté and chop and fry.

Grocery shopping would have been impossible without the woman at the checkout counter. Somehow Shelly seemed to look past my rumpled clothes, the dried vomit in my hair, my confused manner. If she suspected that the boxes of candy and cookies were not for "those hungry kids" but for myself, she said nothing. Sometimes she'd leave her checkout line and help me assemble each item on my list. *She cares about me,* I thought on more than one occasion. *I wonder why.*

One morning as I laced my steaming cup of black coffee with a healthy slug from the vodka bottle, I remembered suddenly that Lisa's sixteenth birthday was the following day. By now Brent had joined Brad at his father's; Lisa still lived with Randall and me.

Visions of a glorious birthday celebration suddenly danced in my head. Lisa, radiant and smiling, her bright-eyed young girlfriends seated about a candlelit table. Great baskets of field flowers everywhere. A spectacular concoction of marzipan, whipped cream, and candied violets ablaze with sixteen candles illuminating the contours of her beautiful face. "Make a wish and blow out your candles," I would urge her gaily. "*All of them,* or your wish won't come true!"

But it was only a vision. There wasn't time to invite guests. And anyway, Lisa's mother was . . . too sick to do it. None of Lisa's wishes were coming true. The smiling sixteen-year-old of my daydream was in reality a fretful, stressed young fawn, blinking shyly as she surveyed her disenchanted forest. Life in her stepfather's home was increasingly tense; my remarriage was already floundering under the strain of my progressing addictions.

Well, if it was too late to ask friends, at least we could have her brothers over—make it a warm and wonderful family celebration! At the grocery store Shelly greeted me courteously and helped me find the things I needed for the birthday dinner. Back in my kitchen, I would have just one beer before starting. Three beers and two hours later, I plodded through the motions of unpacking the groceries.

I must make tomorrow special for Lisa! After all, a sixteenth birthday is very important. I recalled how often as a tiny girl she'd stood by my bed with a bottle of Vicks syrup and a spoon in her little hands when she'd heard me coughing in the night.

Closing my mind to such memories, I tried to focus on the job at hand. The cake. The birthday cake. The cake for my child. The child who is taking care of me. Do something special for her, for God's sake!

I picked up the box of chocolate cake mix. *Add two eggs and one cup water.*

I put the box back on the counter, sat down in the middle of the kitchen floor, and wept. I couldn't cope with a cake mix. It was too hard.

A call to the bakery produced an angel food cake with pink icing.

The next day I muddled through a family birthday dinner that was strained and sad.

But not as sad as the following Mother's Day. On my breakfast plate was a card—*To the Most Wonderful Mother in the World*—with a verse that brought wrenching sobs to my gut. Late that afternoon my husband and I went to visit friends. There were many drinks.

At 11:30 P.M. we returned home. The dining room table had been set lovingly with our best dishes and gold-filled flatware. In the center of the table was a bouquet of hand-picked flowers from our yard arranged in my favorite crystal vase. Loving touches from the loving hands of a girl wanting to please her mother, to honor her mother on her special day.

I lurched woozily past the pan of dried-up barbecue ribs Lisa had tried valiantly to keep warm for the Mother's Day dinner. I lifted the lids from the pots on the cold stove. Rice . . . broccoli . . . carrots. I sampled each pot's wilted contents, wiped my mouth with the back of my hand, and headed for Lisa's bedroom.

She was still awake. She had been crying.

Weakly I tried to apologize. "Lisa, I'm so sorry. . . ." The excuse was threadbare by now.

"Where were you, Mom?" she asked, her voice anguished. "I've been so worried. . . ."

"Please forgive me, honey. It will never happen again." As I bent down to kiss her she turned her face into the pillow.

As the number of alcoholics has increased over the years, a new category of damaged people has emerged. According to statistics[4] there are now from 28 to 34 million children of alcoholics in the United States, of whom seven million are under the age of 18. One out of every eight Americans is the child of an alcoholic. Here are further facts:[5]

Alcoholism runs in families.

Sons of alcoholic fathers are four times more likely to become alcoholics.

Daughters of alcoholic mothers are three times more likely to become alcoholics.

Children of alcoholics are often grandchildren of alcoholics.

Daughters of alcoholics are more likely to marry alcoholics.

Many of us who have contributed to these statistics are trying to rectify the damage done to our children, to rebuild their sense of self-worth, to help them find fulfillment in life. It can happen, but not easily or quickly. Because of their upbringing, Adult Children of Alcoholics (ACOAs) develop the following tendencies:[6]

1. Adult children of alcoholics guess at what normal behavior is.

2. Have difficulty following a project from beginning to end.

3. Lie when it would be just as easy to tell the truth.

4. Judge themselves without mercy.

5. Have difficulty having fun.

6. Take themselves very seriously.

7. Have difficulty with intimate relationships.

8. Overreact to changes over which they have no control.

9. Constantly seek approval and affirmation.

10. Usually feel they are different from other people.

11. Are super-responsible or super-irresponsible.

12. Are extremely loyal even in the face of evidence that the loyalty is undeserved.

13. Are impulsive. They tend to lock themselves into a course of action without giving serious consideration to alternative behaviors or possible consequences. This impulsivity leads to confusion, self-loathing, and loss of control over their environment. In addition, they spend an excessive amount of energy on cleaning up the mess.

I was forcing my children, especially Lisa, into this life of misery. I despised myself. The taunting voices in my head were growing insistent: *Give everyone a break . . . kill yourself. Go ahead! Do it! Get out of this life!*

No question about it—everyone would be better off without me. The angry little men who inhabited my inner world had been pointing this out for some time. Sometimes I'd fondle the handle of Randall's hunting rifle. No, I couldn't possibly shoot myself. Or use a razor.

At the very back of the top shelf of the bedroom closet was my exit visa from the world: a cache of sleeping pills that I'd ferreted away in a fat orange plastic cylinder.

Clutching it in a shaking hand one late April afternoon in 1978, I headed for the cherry cabinet where stood a tall, clear bottle of vodka, almost full.

"You'll soon be where you can't do any more damage," I promised myself as I poured the liquor into a water glass at the kitchen sink. Opening the plastic container, I dumped the pills onto the black formica counter where they rolled about in a riot of color.

The yellow wall phone caught my eye. From far away something said, *Don't do this. Think of your children, your husband, your parents. For God's sake, don't do this. Call someone. Get help.*

No. Death would be a welcome relief. I was dead in so many ways already.

Scooping up the skittering capsules, I stuffed them into my mouth and washed them down with an enormous gulp of the bitter vodka. More pills . . . more vodka . . . till the capsules were gone. Then more vodka to kill the taste of the gelatin coating. Two cups of strong black coffee, half-coffee/half-vodka. I reasoned that the hot coffee would melt the capsules in my stomach faster and speed the whole process.

Outside, the gray Montana sky increased the sense of doom. Anyone glancing up at the brick ranch-style house with the white shutters would see a manicured lawn, majestic blue spruces, a glorious willow tree sweeping the ground. No one would suspect that the figure standing at the kitchen window in a red bathrobe was waiting for death.

My lips started forming words. In a quivering voice I began to sing, "Jesus loves me, this I know, for the Bible tells me so. . . ." How peculiar that I would think of that song at such a time! The happy Sunday school tune of years ago marched persistently through my mind. I could think of nothing else.

I placed my hand on the kitchen counter as if it were a ballet barre and practiced ridiculous leg positions, all the while singing "Jesus Loves Me."

Did everyone revert to childhood at a time like this?

Drowsiness was stealing over me. I had to get into bed before I collapsed. I didn't want Lisa or Randall to find me on the floor. Locking the bedroom door, I turned back the bed covers, lowered myself onto the cool sheets, and pulled up the blankets.

I plumped the pillow around my head, the way Mother used to tuck me into bed at night. My eyes scanned the familiar walls of our bedroom for one final time. On the dresser the chocolate brown digital clock stared back at me, its green fluorescent numbers blipping away the final moments of my life.

My eyes rested on a framed watercolor of a red barn. A Vermont barn. Then inky blackness. A howling wind. Nothingness.

Where was I?

I smelled adhesive tape and ether. A blinding light was shining from somewhere above.

Then the sound of my husband's voice: "Sandra, are you awake?" Randall's anxious face looked down at me.

I struggled to comprehend. The pills, the darkness . . . but I wasn't dead.

"Who found me?" I managed to mumble.

"Lisa," my husband answered. "She crawled through the bedroom window."

Self-loathing filled me. Lisa had found me. I had planned all this carefully so that she'd be spared needless horror. What kind of monster was I?

"You've been in Intensive Care for twenty-four hours," Randall was saying. "It took three medical teams to bring you around. They'd given you up—someone felt a faint heartbeat. You were lucky. . . ."

I didn't feel lucky.

I felt sick. Despairing. I couldn't even succeed at killing myself. I rubbed my nose and my fingers came away stained with dark gray crystals. Charcoal. They had used it to save my life. Why had they bothered?

I had reached the bottom of the pit.

Fully thirty percent of all suicides, according to the Department of Psychiatry at Cornell University, are committed by people suffering from severe depression mixed with alcoholism and drug abuse. Recent statistics on suicide, available through the National Center for Health Statistics, indicate that in 1985 there were 28,620 *successful* attempts at suicide. Many more people than that attempt to kill themselves every year—for a variety of reasons.

"It seems incongruous," writes Arthur Janov in *The Primal Scream,* "to say that the aim of killing oneself is to live, but my experience with the attempted suicides makes it difficult to reach any other conclusion. . . . As a rule, the attempt at death is one more neurotic plea to be loved. In this sense, the attempt at death is a cry for life."

7

Breaking the Cycle

*At the time any person comes for psychiatric help he is
lacking the most critical factor for fulfilling his needs, a
person whom he genuinely cares about and who he feels
geniunely cares about him.*

—William Glasser, M.D.
Reality Therapy

*I*T WAS AT THE BOTTOM OF THE PIT THAT CHANGE FOR ME BEGAN. I HAVE
since come to learn that this is typical of compulsive personalities.
So long as we can keep up the slightest pretense of normality, we
deny the seriousness of our problem. Nor, until a crisis comes, do
those around us confront us with our unacceptable behavior.

With my near-suicide all this changed. At the insistence of my
psychiatrist and my husband, I entered Montana's hospital for
mental disorders at Warm Springs, two-hundred-fifty miles from
home, and one of very few facilities in the state then available to
treat people with addictions.

I arrived at the hospital dazed, lethargic. There were perhaps
eighteen men and women on the ward where I was placed; addicts
at that time were mixed in with the mentally ill. The best way the
staff knew to keep their charges functioning and manageable was
through medication.

The turning point for me occurred in this hospital, but it did not

97

come through chemicals; it happened in another, totally unexpected way.

As one hopeless day slid into another, I sat staring through the greasy, nicotine-streaked windows at the dazzling blue Montana sky outside. How had I gotten myself into such a miserable state, locked up now like a criminal? I didn't want to answer that question, really. For whom could I blame but myself? Two husbands, my children, my parents, my friends had tried to help me. Lord knows how hard they had tried.

Family visits were infrequent because of the distance. Friends sent me helpful books. One, *Beyond Our Selves* by Catherine Marshall, I carried about for days, but never got beyond the dedication page: "To Len," whoever he was. I seemed to have a block about reading anything religious. At the words *God* or *Jesus* my eyes would simply refuse to focus.

One afternoon my roommate, "Jackie," a wispy, angular waif with sad, dark eyes, and I were sitting on our beds waiting for the dinner bell to ring—a signal for us to line up by the front door to be counted before being picked up by the asthmatic old bus that took us all to the central dining hall. Just then a nurse brought a new patient to the room adjoining ours. The young woman collapsed on her newly assigned bed, sobbing and plucking at the bed covers.

Jackie and I looked at each other uneasily. This show of raw emotion was not uncommon at the hospital, but the moans of this poor girl were unnerving. "Oh, Jesus! Jesus! Jesus!" she intoned over and over.

"Karen, try to pull yourself together," the harried nurse implored. "It's almost dinnertime!"

"I don't want to eat, I want to *die*," came the muffled sobs.

Catching sight of Jackie and me, the nurse came to our doorway. "Karen is very upset. She was to be married next week and her fiance has been killed in a car wreck. Perhaps you two can speak with her and persuade her to come to dinner with the rest of the unit."

Jackie got up swiftly from her bed and stepped into Karen's room. I shuffled self-consciously behind her, alarmed at this new patient's wailings and writhings. Karen was not to be consoled. "Jesus, help me!" she kept crying out. *"Please,* Jesus—help me!"

I was to hear these words hundreds of times in the days that followed.

When Jackie and I returned to our room after dinner, we were startled to discover Karen up and walking regally about the hall. The change in her appearance was startling. Before she'd been a crumpled, sobbing body in rumpled sweater and jeans. Now her short auburn hair was neatly combed, framing a gracefully beautiful oval face. Huge luminous brown eyes shone beneath thick lashes. She had changed into a long white bathrobe and white slippers, giving her an angelic appearance as she glided down the hospital corridor.

I was struck by her loveliness—such a powerful contrast to the other disheveled, vacant-faced patients. She fascinated me and frightened me. I wanted to reach out to her, but her constant calling on Jesus grated on my nerves.

As a little girl I had loved to hear Aunt Ethel tell us Bible stories and to stare at the picture on the Sunday school wall of Christ holding the lost sheep. Somewhere along the way I had lost that connection to him. So I felt a grain of envy for Karen's faith. Even through the personal torment I sensed within her a quality of grace.

Later that first week after Karen arrived I was alone in the room when I looked up to see her in the doorway. "May I come in and talk to you?" she asked shyly. "I'm scared of this place . . . of some of the men. . . ."

This was the first of endless visits to our room. Karen seemed to appear in a puff of smoke—suddenly she'd just be there. It soon became apparent that Karen had appointed me her special friend and protector. I never had to guess who was behind me in the food line, her beautiful brown eyes searching for assurance that it was okay for her to be around. She'd be waiting in the corridor when I got out of the shower room, by the door at the close of my therapy session.

Before long we became close friends. She shared her love for Jim, her deceased fiance, the dreams and plans they'd made for their lives together.

One sultry July night, tossing restlessly in the heat of the stuffy hospital room, I was aware of Jackie's deep, regular breathing in the bed next to me. How could she sleep in this oven?

Then I sensed another presence in the room. Half-sitting up in my bed, I saw a familiar white-robed figure. There was Karen standing in the doorway, her long robe startlingly bright in the moonlight.

As Karen approached my bed I could hear she was crying. "Oh, Sandy, does Jesus love me? Does Jesus *really* love me?"

The pleading in her voice sounded as though this was the only thing in life that mattered to her.

What to do? What to say? Some instinct in me longed to comfort this weeping child. I got up gingerly, not sure how to console this quivering soul—how to reassure anybody of anything. Taking Karen in my arms, I patted her damp hair. It had been a long time since I'd held anyone to offer comfort. I'd always been the one demanding comfort.

Clearing my throat awkwardly, I said, "Yes, Karen, Jesus loves you."

Her sobbing stopped in an instant.

My heart was beating furiously. I felt cold and warm at the same time.

Karen detached herself from my embrace, wiped her eyes with the back of her hand, thanked me in a voice of childlike gratitude, and slipped back to the adjoining room.

I lay back down, puzzling at a strange lightness, almost giddiness, that was pulsing through me.

The full moon dipped lower in the west. The room seemed filled with a fragrant coolness.

I slept peacefully until dawn.

As I write these words eight years later, I am filled with awe at how a fragile little event like this can change the direction of a life. We compulsives travel down one road after another, willfully driven on toward growing darkness and a dead end. In fact, road signs along the way warn that we proceed at our own risk. But pride and stubbornness compel us on.

Then something happens. Perhaps an encounter with another traveler, the breakthrough of a new idea. A change takes place—perhaps only a slight change, as in my case through Karen, but a change nevertheless. The traveler changes direction, hesitantly at first. And the way becomes lighter.

The turning point for me was no more than a flicker in my spirit. Shortly after her nighttime visit Karen was discharged, her leaving as sudden as her arrival. Lying on my bed one early morning a few days later, my eyes drifted to the room next door, resting on the rumpled bed that had been Karen's. Priscilla, a burned-out rock singer, was now camped there. Her bed was a shambles of posters and *Rock Star* magazines. A hand-tooled leather belt with thunderbolts etched around the word *rock,* hung limply to the floor like a fleeing snake.

A chill rushed over me. I recoiled at the thought of this violation to Karen's special place. She'd brought such light to those dreary surroundings.

Shifting to a sitting position on the side of my bed, I stared out the window into the small grassy courtyard. The morning sun had appeared over the building annex, exposing the drabness of our rooms. The windowpane was covered with dusty rivulets from last night's thunderstorm. How I longed to polish the window to crystal clarity. The dirty windows everywhere represented more walls—transparent walls, but *walls* further reinforcing my feeling of confinement.

Glancing down at my lap, I was astonished to see my hands in a prayer position. Across my skirt and onto the floor marched a shadow pattern from the slotted roof overhang—a pattern of *stripes.*

"By his stripes we are healed."

Where had those words come from? Of course! I'd heard them as a child in Vermont from Aunt Ethel. I didn't have any more idea what they meant now than I had then, except that they were somehow good words. Strong words.

My eyes went back to Priscilla's snake belt on what to me was Karen's bed. What if there really were two worlds at war, good and evil?

The breakfast bell jarred me back to the reality of hunger pangs. I really felt hungry! I hadn't felt anything for so long.

"Good morning, Gus," I chirped to our pudgy Scottish bus driver.

"Well, gud mawrnin' to you, Miss Sandy. An' if you aren't a bright-lookin' lass!"

After breakfast, another change. Somehow this morning the thought of gulping down my nine o'clock medication was repellent. The inevitable line was forming, patients clutching yellow Dixie cups to receive their juice and pills.

I inched forward at the end of the "meds" line, my eyes sweeping the dingy lounge strewn with old magazines and pots of pathetic scrawny plants, finally resting on the blaring TV set suspended from the ceiling (a precaution to keep the inmates from wrecking it). I saw NBC announcer John Chancellor appear:

"We interrupt this program to bring you a special news bulletin. The Pope has died in Rome." I felt a rise of tears burn my eyes. Why should I react? I wasn't even Catholic. I remembered with a pang the off-color stories I'd told about the Pope. Being funny had given me power. All at once I was repulsed by my "gutter humor" which, like foul language, slipped so readily from my tongue.

I had almost reached the cart where two nurses were mechanically filling the cups and dispensing the medications. I didn't want to swallow these pills anymore. What would happen if I didn't take them?

As the person in front of me moved away, I approached the nurses' station with newfound resolve. "Here are your meds, Sandy." One nurse filled my Dixie cup while the other proffered gray capsules in a small pleated cup.

Her tired blue eyes stared at me as I popped the pills into my mouth and swished them quickly under my tongue, at the same time swallowing the canned orange juice "chaser."

As they pushed their squeaky cart back to the nursing station, I slipped into the women's bathroom. My heart was pounding as I entered the wooden stall. Flushing the toilet, I spit the bitter pills into the swirling water.

No more pills. The words seemed to come from outside of myself. Suddenly it mattered what I took into my body.

"Going against medical advice can be dangerous," my first husband had said many times from hard-won experience as a doctor. True, if arbitrarily you discontinued medication for something like diabetes. But these pills were chiefly to pacify and control.

Leaning against the rough plaster wall, I felt a tremulous stirring of well-being in that squalid little stall.

Like many women alcoholics, I had become addicted to prescription drugs, creating a dependency I was hardly aware of. The addiction continued when I was institutionalized during the 1970s because the use of drugs was a standard procedure in the treatment of patients during this period. Today most treatment centers have patients go through a detoxification procedure before entering their program; drugs then administered are done only after careful evaluation of the patient's medical history.

Many of these treatment programs, moreover, see a good rate of success. Kitty Dukakis, for example, wife of the Massachusetts governor, announced in July 1987 that she had been treated successfully for a secret twenty-six-year addiction to amphetamines—diet pills. "I am now drug-free and I have been for five years," she was quoted telling an audience. "I'm very proud of that. . . . I am telling my story because I want to help others."

It was a sign of the times that her confession elicited not criticism but respect, and even sympathetic identification.

As knowledge has increased about cross-addiction (for example, a patient is freed from an addiction to alcohol only to become addicted to sweets), patients are treated for their basic compulsive-addictive personality disorder. Cross-addiction, for me, also meant that at one time I was addicted to several substances (alcohol, tobacco, sweets, etc.)

At the well-publicized Betty Ford Center in Rancho Mirage, California, only ten to fifteen percent require prior hospitalized detoxification, but it takes at least a week for the different drugs to leave a patient's system. Whether the problem being treated is alcoholism (their number-one problem), cocaine or prescription drug abuse, or often a combined addiction, that first week represents the hell of withdrawal—shakes, headaches, nausea, and exhaustion.

Even withdrawal, however, is only the first step. The person trying to break any addictive pattern is subject to an extraordinary degree of internal conflict. She wants to break the pattern and she doesn't want to. Symptomatic of this conflict: *dissociation,* a sense of separation from oneself, which sometimes results in a woman's feeling like a helpless spectator to her own self-indulgence.

"Dissociated feelings," write Drs. Hodgson and Miller in *Self-Watching,* "are linked with anxious and depressed states of mind in which willpower, planning, and reasoning are difficult to sustain. In helping people to overcome habits, then, it is not enough to identify why habits arise and how they are triggered. The individual must be equipped with the necessary skills to survive episodes of conflict, when morale and motivation are likely to be at their lowest ebb."

8

Do It Now

*To acknowledge {our necessary losses} and nevertheless find
our freedom, make our choices, recognize what we are and
what we might be, is what a responsible adult is all about.
Bowing to necessity, we must choose. This freedom to choose
is the burden and the gift that we receive when we leave
childhood, the burden and the gift that we take with us
when we come to childhood's end.*

—Judith Viorst
Necessary Losses

WHAT WAS THIS CHANGE INSIDE ME AFTER KAREN?
At first it was simply in my attitude. Less despair. A
glimmer of hope. And the resolve to take no more of the daily
medication.

When there was heavy traffic in the john, I would slip the pills
into an empty cigarette pack and hide them temporarily in my
suitcase. I was careful about this because I'd seen what happened to
patients who refused to take their medication. Off to the "Quiet
Room" to be strapped to a table and given their medication by
injection.

I couldn't risk discovery. My progress was slow—imperceptible
some days—but I rejoiced at the new freedom I felt. Freedom from

the inner fuzziness produced by the Quaaludes and the effect of the Thorazine, which seemed to fling my nerves against my body walls while I drifted in and out of reality. How could I ever get well in a psychedelic haze?

I knew that for some patients—the more violent—chemical stabilizers were the welcome alternative to physical restraint. Yet I sensed that in my case true recovery could not begin until I was free of artificial aids.

A second resolve was to regain my sense of personal dignity. My clothes had been confiscated for "special laundering" when I was admitted. There had been a forced shower and shampoo ordered by the impersonal admitting physician who inspected me like a side of beef, charting my scars, birthmarks, and tooth fillings. Even my wedding ring was taken from me, the last vestige of my "belonging" to somebody.

I felt like a faceless number among murderers, rapists, manic-depressives. Every conceivable type of mental illness was baking in an asphalt pressure-cooker. Helplessness and despair had all but swallowed me whole.

To restore my sense of dignity, I began spending more time on personal grooming, taking more interest in my crafts class, even standing straighter. I stuck all my greeting cards on the wall over my bed as a cheery reminder that I was loved.

As I lay on my bed during rest time one afternoon, my spirit felt lighter. I fell asleep contemplating a return home to my family. Then a nurse was shaking my shoulder. "Wake up, Sandy. The staff wants to see you at once."

I followed her apprehensively down the corridor. What could the staff want to see me for?

As I entered the conference room I saw nurses and doctors assembling in a circle of chairs ready for "report." They were sipping coffee, shuffling papers and patients' charts. My eyes fell on Harry, the hospital administrator, the ever-present unlit cigar jammed into the corner of his mouth. Today he looked particularly disgruntled. My heart sank. I was in trouble, but I wasn't sure why.

At a nod from the nurse I threaded my way past the outstretched feet and lowered myself into an orange plastic chair.

"It has been brought to our attention that you have not been taking your medications," Harry began. "Unswallowed capsules were discovered in your suitcase this morning. Not taking your prescribed medicine is a serious violation of hospital rules. Do you have anything to say for yourself?"

Panic gripped me. Visions of being strapped down in the Quiet Room almost paralyzed my voice. Then something happened. My voice acquired strength. Purpose. I requested formally to be taken off all medication. To my surprise I had moved suddenly from defense to offense.

"I also need a week at home with my family to see if I can adjust to the outside world. Please," I concluded, "just give me a chance."

Surprised looks. Clearly they had been caught off-guard.

"Reactions?" Harry queried his staff.

At first there was mild dissent. I pressed my point, stressing the progress I had made in recent weeks.

"I'll need to clear it with your doctor," Harry said uncertainly. "If she says you may go, I guess there's no reason a week at home wouldn't be all right. Okay, staff?"

There were reluctant nods of agreement around the circle. When queried, my doctor, a warm-hearted Filipino woman, was favorable. The only stipulation: stay on my medication. Before week's end I was on a bus to Billings.

My husband was waiting at the bus station. On the drive home our conversation was strained. Later I stood in my own kitchen for the first time in four months and looked about in childlike wonder. Was this really my home? Somehow everything looked strange. Different.

I was suddenly aware of the depth of my emotional and physical exhaustion. As tired as I was, however, I dreaded going to bed with this stranger I was married to. Randall must have felt it, too. A silent wall separated us that night. He, so vibrant, bright and productive; I, so frightened and uncertain, a failure at everything.

The temptation to stay in bed the next morning was nearly overwhelming. A late August breeze was puffing the green shantung drapes in languid little bursts. Why not just roll over and go back to sleep? It would be so easy to do that. I really wanted to.

Yet deep within a kind of inner knowing gnawed at my soul. If I didn't get started right this morning, my life might never get straightened out. Today was the first day of the rest of my life. With this realization came the practical message I most needed to hear: *Get up! Get moving! Do something to help yourself! Do it now.*

There had been countless mornings when I'd had this choice and had chosen to avoid the world, to hide in my bed, blankets pulled over my head. When I finally would get up, I would go from doctor to doctor, psychic to psychic, friend to friend, desperately hoping one of them could "fix" me, somehow transform me magically into a whole person, sound of body and mind. The answer over the years had become agonizingly obvious: no one else could do it for me. The effort to change, to get well, was going to have to start with me.

In describing this freedom to choose, Dr. Theodore Rubin in *The Winner's Notebook* writes: "The decision I arrive at is uniquely my own and born of my freedom to struggle through my feelings to either act or not act. . . . This kind of freedom to feel and to decide and if necessary, to experience conflict and to struggle through conflict to an answer, produces values. This kind of tapping of one's own feelings and arriving at one's own individual values produces a sense of self-responsibility and identity."

Now, from my bed, I gave myself a set of commands: "Get up, take a shower and get dressed!" My body obeyed reluctantly. These seemingly normal routines had been almost impossible during my periods of depression.

Wiping the steam from the bathroom mirror with the sleeve of my pink cotton robe, I peered at the anxious face that stared back at me. My appraisal:

Eyes: Apprehensive. Needed the usual help from a mascara wand and eyeliner. I hadn't bothered with eye makeup for months.

Eyebrows: A jungle growth. Get out the tweezers fast!

Skin: Ghastly! So dry. Like an alligator suitcase. Alcohol and cigarettes do a job on skin. I looked at broken spider-web veins around my nose. Quick, where's the face cream and liquid foundation?

Hair: A disaster area. Stubborn wisps of gray hair were spiraling through the tangled auburn mop like errant bits of barbed wire. It had been months since I'd cared about coloring my hair.

To signal the change that I hoped was taking place inside, I'd start today to make over the outside. I dressed carefully, then went across the hall to the den where I had a small desk. There I made a list of the things I wanted to accomplish that day. Simple things. Make a date at the hairdresser. Take my soiled dress and slacks to the cleaners. Buy nail polish. I came up with nine items.

As I searched for the hairdresser's number, the old temptations flooded back. *What's the hurry? You've been four months in a grubby hospital. Sit down and have a cigarette. Bet there's a cold beer in the refrigerator. You deserve a break. What are you trying to do—win a medal?*

For a moment it was an all-out battle. My new resolve vs. the old pattern. Oh, how I was tempted.

Do it now!

Those three words snapped me out of it. I found the number and reached for the telephone.

That nagging little voice pursued me all day. *Are you some kind of slavedriver? Take it easy.*

Then from inside the rebuttal: *You've had enough rest. Get on with your life. Do it now.* At the end of the day, to my astonishment, I'd completed all nine items on my list. I'd also made a decision *not* to take the tranquilizers given me by the hospital.

The high point came when I went to get my hair done. What is there about the sounds and smells of a beauty shop that rejuvenate even before the work begins? As Rod, my favorite hairdresser, snipped and whirled me about in the dance that hairdressers do, visions of a new me spun through my brain. For some reason my mind flashed back twenty-two years to the summer of 1956 before the Miss America Pageant. I had felt the same sense of adventure, of a life-changing journey. The clinging coat of depression was dropping away from me like hunks of hair from Rod's scissors.

Wow, what a difference, I thought when Rod finished. I couldn't believe my eyes. The "before" and "after" was staggering.

My husband did a double-take when he walked through the door that evening. "Can this be the same woman I said good-bye to this morning?" he asked with an astonished smile.

Settling for the week into a household routine after months of hospitalization, however, wasn't as simple as I'd thought. The second morning I wondered—should I dust? Should I iron? Should I bake something? Such mini-decisions seemed overwhelming.

I wandered from room to room trying to reacquaint myself with my surroundings. Gingerly I examined each object in the living room as though reintroducing myself to old friends. Why did everything look so strange? A sudden fear began to strip away the fragile self-confidence built up by the first day's small achievements. Would I be able to stick out the week?

Our house was full of old ghosts. Dreadful, painful memories. The chair where I did my heaviest drinking and planned my suicide seemed to menace me each time I passed it. Maybe it should be stored in the basement where I couldn't see it. No, that would be ridiculous. All the furnishings held memories of some sort.

Taking a deep breath, I entered Lisa's now-vacant room. She had moved to her father's house to live with him and her brothers during my hospitalization. I was grateful that the children had pulled together while their mother was falling apart. I wondered if they knew how much I loved them, how guilty I felt.

As my sickness had worsened it had become increasingly difficult to hug them, to show them warmth. My heart had become an icy lump sprouting from stainless steel ribs, my body home to miles of nerves that twisted and tangled around wooden bones. I had felt no life, just desperation.

Lisa's room still had her fragrance about it. The "Love" cosmetics popular with teenagers sat in a pristine row on a mirrored tray. Her dressing table was immaculate, each item in meticulous order. The stuffed animals she'd left behind stared up at me from her red plaid bedspread. Clutching an armful of them, I sobbed into their soft plush bodies. Lisa had often held them for comfort. "Oh, Lisa, what have I done to you? To all of us?"

In the hallway outside her room, the white stucco walls seemed to close in on me. Then they expanded like rubber bands stretching to some far-off horizon. Back and forth. Back and forth.

Perhaps I belonged back in the hospital. Apparently I wasn't as strong as I'd thought. It had seemed so easy in my daydreams at the institution. Was I becoming a robot like so many of the patients there? Had I developed an institutional mentality? Was I unable to make any decisions or do anything for myself?

An insistent inner voice shouted, *No! Get busy. Do something. Do it now!*

This was going to be the toughest battle of my life.

One night that week my husband took me out to dinner. He seemed so proud of the "new me" and scrambled to open the car door and help me with my chair at our favorite table at the Rex Hotel. For the first time in months, I felt special.

As I took dainty sips from my chilled glass of white chablis, I forgot the panic in the hallway. My husband was newly attentive, my self-confidence straining to break through the years of self-loathing. The rather attractive woman reflected in the bar mirror was really me. I tried not to stare at her.

From our table in the back room next to the wall, Randall liked to watch the stream of diners drift in and out. He had the lawyer's observing mind—every detail, every nuance. I admired him so. Yet our marriage had stretched on the brink of disaster for five years. It would take a miracle to breathe new life into it after so much damage.

I tried not to think back to only two years before when we'd sat at the same table on my fortieth birthday. I was on medication and had sat in this same chair in a fuzzy haze. My size eighteen dress did not cover the bulges from my binge eating. I'd felt like an overstuffed chair. A black-and-white print chair. The dress was hideous, but it was the only one I could still get into.

Now, while Randall ordered dinner, I took another sip of chablis to wipe out the memory. A little wine never hurt anyone. After all the heartbreak, I had still not faced up to my drinking problem. . . .

On the six-hour bus ride back to the hospital, I thought back over the ups and downs of the week just ended. The visits with my children had been too short and tense to be satisfying. They had stared at this "new" mother, doubtless wondering whether they dared trust the changes they saw.

What had been accomplished by these seven days? A start . . . and the latching hold of a three-word principle: *Do it now.*

When I arrived back at the Warm Springs Hospital, it was afternoon. Since the entrance door was always locked, I rang the buzzer for admittance. A nurse named Gretchen peered through glass at me. "May I help you?"

"Gretchen, it's me! Sandy. Don't you recognize me?"

"Good heavens, no! You look so . . . good. In fact, you look terrific! Come on in."

Patients and staff alike gathered in the smoky lounge foyer to survey the returning patient. Incredulous stares greeted me, as though I were an alien from outer space.

Harry almost bit through his cigar as he rounded the corner of the nurses' station. "Looks like Billings agreed with you, Sandy. We're about to staff. We'll want a report on your week."

My doctor's round face was wreathed in smiles as she spotted me. "You look wonderful," she declared in her thick Filipino accent. And to the rest of the staff: "We can all see the positive results of home visits!"

Harry was staring at me with questioning, "show-me" eyes. "Give us a report, Sandy."

The pressure was on, every eye in the room riveted on me.

"I-I got along fine," I began. "The hardest part was to walk back into a house that held so many memories of pain and failure—and to know my time there was an experiment only. Could I change old habits? Could I start over? In many ways I was like a baby who had to learn to crawl before she could walk.

"I knew I had to set a schedule for myself that I could follow. I've always put unrealistic goals on myself. I've been such a perfectionist. If I couldn't do something perfectly, I wouldn't try at all. That's been a real trap for me all my life.

"I decided to choose a few simple tasks and do them. Not to expect perfection, but to make progress—any progress—on functioning normally. I wasn't sure that I could, but I did do what I set out to do. I was able to relate to my husband and my children as an adult instead of a sick-o. They were all surprised about that. I got up each morning and showered and dressed and accomplished my housework.

"The first morning I decided to do something about the way I looked on the *outside,* to show that things were changing on the *inside.* I made an appointment to have my hair cut and colored. After coming out of a mental hospital, it took courage to walk back into that shop and face all those beauty operators I'd known so well. I was amazed at the warm way they all welcomed me! Since I'd let fear paralyze me for so long, it felt good to take a risk and have it work out. It's given me confidence to face the next hurdle."

Harry's bulldog face was set in rapt attention. The cigar was teetering in the corner of his mouth.

Gretchen seemed puzzled. "You make it sound so easy, Sandy. It's hard for me to believe you could adjust so quickly. You didn't show that kind of initiative here. . . ."

My heart sank. Did the rest of the staff feel this way, too?

"Let's let Sandy continue," urged my doctor. "I'm sure she has a lot more to tell us."

Now what? What could I add? Frantically my mind raced ahead trying to second-guess what would impress these staffers. I had never been in a situation like it—except the judges' interview at the Miss America Pageant. The thought of that experience in this setting was so ludicrous I almost laughed. It was the comic relief I needed.

"I don't know what else to say," I told them. "Obviously Gretchen finds my new resolve hard to believe. But I've had a lot of time to think while I've been a patient here. What do I want to do with the rest of my life? I want to get well. I want to have a good marriage and be a good mother. I want to be the best I can. Thus far I've been pretty much of a goof-off. I want to get on with the rest of my life."

"All good intentions," Harry interjected. "How do you plan to accomplish all this, Sandy?"

My heart was beating like a threshing machine. My eyes were stinging. What to say?

"I've made some progress. My husband is supportive and my children are anxious to have their mother back. That's a good start. I have a solid base to go home to. I'd like to find a job. I feel optimistic about my life in Billings . . . about my chances to get well there. Frankly, I don't believe I belong in this hospital or any hospital."

My doctor was smiling at me. Patting my clammy hand, she spoke softly. "Staff, I'm going to ask Sandy to leave the room while we process this. Just have a seat in the lounge, if you will."

I struggled to my feet and all but fled.

"Somebody give me a cigarette," I commanded in the lounge area. My roommate, Jackie, offered me an unfiltered one. The bitter jolt of raw nicotine almost spun me around.

"How can you smoke these things?" I gasped.

"I've always said if you're going to smoke, smoke a real cigarette," Jackie retorted. If she only knew how many nights I'd been awakened by her racking cough. Suddenly I felt very tender toward her.

It seemed like hours but it was probably only twenty minutes before I was readmitted to the conference room. Taking the vacant orange chair, I awaited the verdict with lowered eyes.

"It is the consensus of the staff," my doctor announced, "that you are capable of being released from this institution as soon as we can process your papers. We feel you have shown favorable initiative and sufficient resolve to adhere to a solid program of recovery. You've been a cooperative patient. I especially will miss you, and I wish you much good luck in your life outside this hospital."

Tears welled up in my eyes and slid down my cheeks as the staff applauded.

9

The Pain in Change

It is indeed possible for us to mature out of a belief in God. What I would now like to suggest is that it is also possible to mature into a belief in God. A skeptical atheism or agnosticism is not necessarily the highest state of understanding at which human beings can arrive. To the contrary, there is reason to believe that behind spurious notions and false concepts of God there lies a reality that is God.

—M. Scott Peck, M.D.
The Road Less Traveled

M Y HOSPITALIZATION AND RECOVERY PERIOD INTRODUCED ME TO A new word in the treatment of compulsive behavior: *enabler.* An enabler is the addict's spouse/parent/child who because of embarrassment or a sense of guilt attempts a cover-up to protect the family, *enabling* the addict to continue his destructive behavior.

An enabling wife is one who calls her husband's office on Monday morning and tells his boss that her hung-over spouse has the flu. A whole pattern of deceptive practices, involving all members of the family, is under way. The addict's sickness is all too obvious; the rest of the family's "sickness" is not so recognizable, yet it is just as real and needs to be treated.

"No matter what personality type you live with," writes Mary Ellen Pinkham in *How to Stop the One You Love from Drinking,* "all members of the family will react to the alcoholism, and as the alcoholic becomes more involved with his drinking, *you* become more involved with *him.* You will eventually experience identifiable and pathological behavior that is as predictable as the pattern of the alcoholism itself."

If, as the National Council on Alcoholism estimated in 1985, each of the 12.1 million alcoholics in the U.S. directly affects four other people, then there are at least sixty million people intimately involved with alcoholism.

Family members, through embarrassment and guilt, will try to cover up the destructive behavior of the addict. Husband and children will adjust their daily routines and even go through psychological change in their efforts to protect the addictive wife and mother. In doing this, they became enablers. They not only do not help the addict; they become sick, too. (Check your own co-dependence on p. 262.)

The addict's sickness is usually obvious to family and close friends; the rest of the family's "sickness' is not so recognizable, yet it exists and needs to be treated.

An enabling husband will often assume the role of peacemaker in the family when his wife is an addict. A family friend in his forties, for example, was married to an alcoholic for twelve years. When she died, he took his two young children quickly into a second marriage with a widowed woman and her teenage daughter. The result: tension and conflict in the home.

"When I tried to resolve these squabbles, they dubbed me "peacemaker,' " the friend revealed. "The term was often used contemptuously. It took an Al-Anon meeting to make me see that in my first marriage my role as enabler had, in a sense, made me sick too. My ability to act openly and forthrightly was impaired. I did seek peace at any price and my second family was calling me on it."

My own past is most painful to reflect on, when I see the effect of my compulsive behavior on my family. All tried valiantly to help me: my parents, two husbands, my children, my parents-in-law. All became enablers in one way or another in their efforts to protect me, doing damage in the process to themselves.

My husband Randall, for example, used to watch the liquor cabinet to see how much I consumed. I knew this, so one winter morning I conspired to outwit him. After he left for work I plucked a full bottle of vodka from the cabinet, plotting to use just one shot in my morning coffee. I planned to add a touch of water to fill it up, then restick the seal with glue. He'd never know. Besides, Randall never drank vodka in the winter anyway—just Scotch.

At 11:30 I was on my second pot of coffee and the bottle was half-gone. *I'll run out later this afternoon and get another bottle,* I promised myself. By four o'clock it was snowing and I was in no condition to drive anywhere. I had to sober up and fix dinner. When Randall arrived home at 6:30 the vodka bottle, filled with water, was back in the liquor cabinet, paper seal in place.

Randall sat down in his favorite chair and started to peruse the evening paper. "How about fixing me a vodka and tonic tonight?" he asked.

My heart pounded. I'd gotten caught. "There's no vodka," I murmured.

"What do you mean no vodka? There's a full bottle in there."

"I'm afraid it's full of water."

His eyes never left the paper. His tone of voice never changed. "Okay, then fix me a Scotch and water."

No confrontation. He had resigned himself to the hopelessness of the situation. I wondered how he could go through this little drama without blinking an eye. *No wonder he's such a good trial lawyer,* I thought to myself.

Like millions of other husbands with alcoholic wives, there were times when he did get angry at my heavy drinking, railed at the family upsets that resulted. But over the years he drifted into the role of enabler, protecting me as best he could from myself.

When I returned home from the Warm Springs hospital in the fall of 1978, I had made only the tiniest start on the road to recovery. At my departure my doctor had given me a list of medications to take, most of which I had already decided against using. As the months passed, I had no idea what further steps to take.

There had been some kind of spiritual change inside me, but I didn't know what to do about that either. I even sensed God had spared me—but why? I was still tormented at times by angry inner voices.

My deepest desire was to rebuild my home situation, become a good wife, and develop closer relationships with my children. But how to do that? Probably by working to conquer my destructive behavior patterns. Three areas especially concerned me: smoking, overeating (especially sweets), and drinking. (I was not ready to admit I could not drink at all.) How should I attack these problems? Willpower, I concluded.

A flutter of resolve stirred within me. I wanted to change. I knew I had to change. But how does change happen?

I decided to begin with nicotine, which had already been demonstrated scientifically to engender genuine drug addiction, not just an addiction to the activity of smoking (Edward Brecher, Consumers Union, 1972).

I'd first tried to quit eight years earlier, when a doctor warned me that smoking was damaging my lungs. I'd agreed. It was time to stop. Besides, I hated the spidery lines that were forming around my lips from my constant puffing.

I'd done it back then on sheer willpower. My first act of a morning had been to *not* light up as soon as my eyes opened, but reach for a Life-Saver. If I'd forgotten to leave these "saviour" packs by the bed, I'd fly into a frenzy. What to stick into my mouth?

Ballpoint pens, frayed toothpicks, paper clips, anything I could lay my hands on. Every pair of eyeglasses I owned soon had their bows chewed so badly that they scratched my temples.

What had happened then should have alerted me to the fact that it was not tobacco I was battling—or alcohol, or overspending, or any of my other excesses—but a compulsive personality beneath all the specific cravings. Eliminating cigarettes eight years before had simply brought about a switch in compulsions. Chocolate had then become my slavemaster. In any form. At any time. I'd stir from my bed at ungodly hours and bake a pan of brownies or struggle through the ritual of a devil's food cake mix. "Aptly named," I'd sigh as I stumbled around my kitchen in the darkness.

My clothes had gotten tighter and tighter, as the fibers strained to cover my ever-increasing thighs and derriere. My nocturnal baking sessions baffled my children at first, but soon they looked forward to fresh-baked "surprises" for breakfast. Brownies and cereal. Brownies and eggs. Brownies and pancakes.

After two years off tobacco, one day for no reason I had picked up a pack of cigarettes. "I merit a Merit!" I joked weakly to my drinking companions. The first puff slammed against my throat in a burst of welcome relief. Every dormant nicotine sensor screamed to first-alert: *Welcome back! We knew you'd give in someday.*

I had begun to smoke more than ever. Two packs a day. Three packs if I got up early and stayed out late. I'd have smoked in the shower if I could have figured out a way to keep the thing lit.

I had hated myself for caving in. What had happened to all the resolve? I had resigned myself to the fact that it was better to smoke than to be fat—just the opposite of what I'd told myself before as I'd waited those endless hours for my cakes to bake. I had thought willpower was the answer—if only I were *strong* enough. I know now why that is a typical, erroneous thought of a compulsive person: "Willpower as a pure act," writes Dr. Theodore Rubin in *The Winner's Notebook*, "invariably comes from compulsive drives and contracts and further contributes to compulsion. There is no real *self* involved in an attempt to overwhelm a disastrous situation by an act of 'strength' alone. It just doesn't work. Insight, on the other hand, involves real knowing of self and real self-involvement on the deepest level."

I had no such insight into the driving force of my own inner compulsions.

Today the hard evidence against smoking is overwhelming, connecting smoking with cancer and diseases of the heart, lungs, and circulatory system. Smoking is dangerous to one's own health, to nonsmokers around, even to persons not yet born. Smoking is a problem on the job. Each year smokers miss almost three days more work than the nonsmoker. Counting smoking damage, health insurance, and other factors, the smoker costs his/her company about $4,600 per year.

Despite the almost irrefutable evidence, however, about one-third of adults—54 million Americans—are still smoking, including 26 million adult women.

Dr. Virginia Ernster, associate professor of epidemiology at the University of California at San Francisco School of Medicine, observes that cigarette companies worldwide perceive "the working woman, under stress, as the ideal candidate for their product."

Nicotine is extremely addictive; its addictive characteristics are now being compared to heroin and cocaine. What's more, although individuals involved with other addictions such as alcohol or hard drugs sometimes take a break from their usage—from a few days to weeks and sometimes even a few months—smokers never take a break. They smoke every day, through all their waking hours. Some even have difficulty making it through the night without smoking.

Dr. Ellen Gritz, director of the Division of Cancer Control at UCLA's Jonsson Comprehensive Cancer Center, points out that "cigarettes are often used to control negative moods and stressful feelings. When a woman quits, she may start expressing these negative feelings, and people around her get upset. I've had lots of women tell me that their families begged them to go back to smoking."

Even if a woman can escape this pressure, and even survive the pain and discomfort of cold-turkey withdrawal, she is met with a psychological attachment that is extremely difficult to break. Some of the following might prove helpful:

Ways To Curb The Urge To Smoke[7]

- If craving a cigarette, distract yourself, change your activity, telephone an ex-smoker or an understanding friend until the feeling subsides.

- If cigarettes give you an energy boost, try modest exercise, a brisk walk, deep breathing exercises, and a balanced diet, avoiding foods high in sugar.

- Go places where you can't smoke.

- Keep a glass of water nearby and instead of smoking take sips through a straw.

- Don't linger at the table after a meal.

- If you do slip and smoke a cigarette or two, that doesn't mean you've become a smoker again. Decide why you succumbed to temptation and set a new goal of not smoking—and not slipping up.

Remember, the urge to light up lasts only five to ten minutes.

One day I was visiting with a friend going through a painful separation. We were commiserating with each other about the messes we'd made of our lives. I took out a pack of cigarettes, my third of the day, and struggled with the stubborn cellophane wrapping.

"I'll quit if you will," she challenged me suddenly. "Let's put money on it. The first one who smokes owes the other . . . fifty dollars?"

Realizing it wouldn't be possible to extract that much in secret from my household budget, I declined the contract. "We can do it without any bets. I know we can."

Enthusiastically we pumped each other's hands. We could kick this thing. Later, to reinforce my resolve, I rolled down the window of my car as I drove home.

"Farewell, evil weeds!" I intoned, tossing the fresh pack out the window. Suddenly it was as though Karen were sitting in the car beside me. I heard her voice as I'd heard it so many times in the hospital at Warm Springs: *Please, Jesus—help me!*

"If you really exist," I whispered, "and if you really do help people . . . will you help me quit smoking? *Please.*"

When I awakened the next morning, my eyes greeted the sunny morning with a strange new clarity. And an unaccustomed sense of peace. The frayed edges of my ragged nerves were somehow knitted together. The craving for tobacco was simply and amazingly gone. I stared wonderingly through the bedroom window at the dazzling blue Big Sky of Montana.

As before, however, doing without cigarettes seemed to activate my taste buds. My urge for chocolate returned stronger than ever. I tried to resist, but defeat followed defeat in my kitchen. The inner voice seemed to gloat, *Weak, hopeless, failure.*

At the time I didn't understand that if checked in one area, the compulsive nature will break out in another, that the sickness was not this addiction or that, but deep inside me. I was upset when I went to yard sales and came home with items I didn't need, or even want. Clothing sales drew me like a moth to a flame. When closets bulged with "bargains," I hid the overflow in bags under the bed.

Harvard psychiatrist George Vaillant has observed just this kind of cross-addictive behavior, reporting that former alcoholics often shift to new dependencies—candy, compulsive work, hobbies, gambling, etc. Indeed, in the groundbreaking *Ms.* survey, women confessed addictions to a large variety of behaviors, including shopping, walking, running, yoga, exercise, cleaning, sleeping, work, daily routines, credit cards, nail-biting, even using the phone.

For me there was always a monster lying in wait, ready to take charge again: my craving for alcohol. I still sipped wine at the dinner table and drank at parties—but no longer could I count on the numbing relief, the rush of exhilaration that had always accompanied the flow of alcohol into my system. More and more often now there was only a fearful gray fog whenever I took a drink. I longed to stop altogether, but lacked the willpower—or, as Dr. Rubin points out, the self-knowledge.

The answer came unexpectedly. It was Valentine's Day, 1980. That night I was hostess for a dinner party in my home.

The day began with feelings of nervous anticipation, a desire that the party be a dazzling success. I'd made a special quilted tablecloth, spent hours planning the food—even to colors that harmonized—and arranged elaborate floral decorations.

It would be a night of striving to win the approval and acceptance of my husband's friends and law associates. I'd be under the microscope. Being scrutinized wasn't new, but an ex-mental patient always seems to have more to prove. Could I pull the evening off?

As the guests arrived, I fluttered in the kitchen, hovering over gurgling pans and checking the oven obsessively. Somehow the meal materialized on my flower- and candle-bedecked table. There were so many decorations there was barely room for the food. Profuse compliments flowed as fast as the dinner wine. Then Randall tapped his wineglass to signal "toast time."

I grasped the stem of my goblet. As I did, the dark burgundy sloshed about, creating swirling purple rings in the crystal. And in those rings I saw, as clearly as if they had been etched in the glass, three words:

Poison
Death
Insanity

I wanted to scream. I stared incredulously at the telltale words. The others were raising their glasses, laughing, talking. Couldn't they see the message inscribed in wavering purple letters?

I don't want to drink this.

I don't want to drink anything alcoholic ever again.

A feeling of warmth coursed through my body from head to toe. A renewed sense of being protected. Was it Karen's God revealing his love to me on Valentine's Day, the day for lovers?

Days passed. As with cigarettes, the craving for alcohol was startlingly and totally gone.

For other women, of course, the battle is more drawn-out, especially when they are faced with social situations in which they are urged to have "just one" drink. The following suggestions, from Hodgson and Miller's *Self-Watching: Addictions, Habits, Compulsions,* help to develop skills for coping with those social situations likely to arise:

Social Coping Strategies

1. Stay for a half hour and then leave.

2. Get over my anxiety by just listening to people. Forget about trying to impress.

3. Drink tonic, because people might think it is vodka and tonic. They will then be less likely to pressure me into drinking.

4. If I feel a craving coming on, then I'll walk around the block until it disappears—that is, the craving, not the block!

5. I must remember how good I felt at Charlie's party two months ago when I successfully resisted the pressure to drink.

6. Be assertive. Tell all and sundry that I am not drinking and I will be very angry if they offer me a drink.

Despite the fact that I had suddenly, completely lost the desire for alcohol, I had *not* lost the desire for chocolate. Or the sudden yearnings to go shopping. And the pain was still in place.

In an effort to understand my compulsive tendencies, I started reading everything I could lay my hands on. One report, "The Nature of Craving,"[8] showed that monkeys and rats, even when hungry, chose cocaine over food. When given free access to cocaine, the animals "went into a frenzy of drug-taking activity."

The study suggested that some machinery for addiction is built into our brains. To combat this innate tendency, the author called for a joining of biological, psychological, and sociological forces. No mention was made of spiritual forces having any part to play.

As I read this report, I had a picture of all the antiseptic hospital halls I'd walked down, of intellectually determined and well-meaning medical men talking in scientific jargon about my problems, of pills prescribed and then more pills, and of a kind of emotional and spiritless sterility that surrounded it all.

This sterility of spirit is referred to in Scott Peck's *The Road Less Traveled*. "It is indeed tempting for psychiatrists to view themselves as knights of modern science locked in noble combat with the destructive forces of ancient religious superstition and irrational but authoritarian dogma," he writes.

Meanwhile I struggled with the volcano of compulsion inside me. Why did eating binges and shopping splurges so quickly follow my victories over tobacco and alcohol?

I asked this question of a neighbor. Kathy was about my age, mid-forties, with a pert nose and a short, chestnut page-boy haircut. She responded by inviting me to a prayer meeting. Because I was hungry for answers, I agreed to go.

So one bright June morning I walked into a living room filled with smiling women who welcomed me warmly. Nervously I perched on the edge of a green sofa. The pastor of the Methodist church was there, giving me a sense of assurance that I was not involved with spiritual oddballs.

At the prayer meeting someone suggested that because of my exposure to the occult, I should get rid of everything related to it. I went home and burned all my occult books and horoscope readings. It was amazing the amount of psychic material a scavenger hunt revealed. I even discarded items of my clothing that had signs of the zodiac and jewelry with arcane symbols. Part of me argued that the whole performance was nothing but superstition and fanaticism. Yet with these things out of the house I felt . . . lighter, somehow. Purged.

Was it my imagination, or in the days that followed were the angry voices in my head fainter, farther off—often silent for long periods.

But the craving for food, especially chocolate, still drove me. I still slept late too many mornings, had trouble getting myself organized. My needs were visible to everyone.

Kathy, however, was one of those caring people who sees a friend through the long haul. I especially remember the morning she appeared on my doorstep clutching a book. Eyes filled with concern, she thrust the book into my hands as I stood behind the slightly cracked door.

"Here, Sand, maybe *this* will help. . . ." Then she ran back to her idling car and sped off down the street.

Shutting the door, I thrust the book into the pocket of my

rumpled bathrobe. In the walnut-framed hall mirror I caught a look at myself.

Good grief! Who is that?

Backing up in disbelief, the leering image gaped back at me. That couldn't be me! It must be some beached whale wrapped in a chenille robe.

And those haunted eyes ringed with wilted mascara. Raccoon eyes!

A beached whale with raccoon eyes.

Tears flooded my eyes, splashing down my cheeks onto my robe. I was suddenly aware of the deep hollow in my chest. I knew how to fill it. There was a fresh half-gallon of chocolate ice cream hidden in the freezer under the Brussels sprouts. I could count on my dark, cool, sweet friend to bring me relief.

To the freezer! I'd need a serving spoon. Yes, a *big* spoon. For I intended to eat it all.

The just-delivered gift of love, Kathy's book, now rested forlornly on the dark pine kitchen table, its pristine newness smudged with brown dribbles from my chocolate binge. *I'll read it tomorrow,* I promised myself.

Several weeks later Kathy's voice on the phone sounded bright and enthusiastic as she told me about an upcoming workshop at her Methodist church. I wasn't so sure, except that since I'd stopped drinking I needed something to occupy my mind. There were so many raw emotions coming to the surface that I couldn't deal with: frustration, fears, anger, and—oh, God—the guilt.

"Sandy! Welcome!" Entering the church for the workshop I was smothered with hugs of well-wishers, many of whom I'd known socially over the years in Billings. I tried not to be preoccupied with the hug wrinkles on my meticulously ironed blouse and scarf.

The workshop leaders were a couple from Spokane, Washington. As the husband spoke I glanced at the shadows on the far brick wall—a syncopated pattern of stripes. I thought of the stripes I'd seen across my lap in the hospital.

The speaker was opening his Bible. "Turn with me to Isaiah 53, verses 4 and 5," he said. Then he began reading:

"Surely he [Jesus] hath borne our griefs, and carried our sorrows: yet we did esteem him stricken, smitten of God and afflicted. But he was wounded for our transgressions, he was bruised for our iniquities . . . and by his stripes we are healed."

I stared at him open-mouthed, stunned at the timing of the words, and felt a transfusion of hope.

"Are you coming to the healing service Sunday night?" Kathy asked later. "I'll be happy to pick you up."

I shook my head. "I'd better pass it up."

Sunday evening Randall and I ate dinner in silence. I tried not to look at the kitchen clock that indicated twenty-five minutes until the healing service began. While scraping the dishes, I wondered what my priorities should be. On the one hand, my husband's negative attitude toward my churchgoing was clear. Religion almost seemed more of a threat to our marriage than my drinking. On the other hand, something inside was pushing me toward the church. That, obviously, would be a mistake.

I changed into my faded blue jeans and slipped on a baggy gray sweater for an evening of TV-watching. When I entered the den, Randall was already settled in his black leather chair, the set tuned to the Sunday night movie. I sank into the couch.

A moment later I was back on my feet. "I have to go to church," I said lamely. "I don't expect you to understand why. I'm not sure I do, either."

I raced out the front door with the image of his puzzled stare following me. Was I being driven by yet another compulsion?

Organ music was filling the church with a mighty crescendo when I entered. Such joy flooded the sanctuary that the putty in the stained glass windows must have struggled to keep them from exploding outwards.

The memory of my husband's disapproving look was dissolved in the majesty of the music. When the invitation was given to come forward for healing, I rose from my seat and walked down the center aisle. People were streaming toward the front from all over the church. There was just enough room for me to squeeze in at the altar rail.

A large white cross hung from the ceiling over the marble altar. In the brilliance of the ceiling spotlights its whiteness was dazzling. My eyes fell on the enormous open Bible resting on the marble missal stand. Below it in brushed brass letters were the words *This Do in Remembrance of Me.*

At first, as I grasped the thick oak altar rail, my mind was racing. Scenes: the living room at Uncle Ralph's; wearing the flower crown of Miss Vermont; awaiting death at my kitchen window. Places: Atlantic City, Disneyland, Deaconess Hospital here in Billings. Faces: Brad, Brent, Lisa, my mother and father, Shelly at the checkout counter, Karen. Like whirling dancers they sped past. Then calm—a holy silence.

A few minutes later a woman minister joined me at the altar rail and listened to my litany of pain. Then she placed her hands on my shoulders and looked straight into my eyes, as the following words flowed with quiet authority from her lips: "If God has forgiven all your sins, how dare you not forgive yourself?"

My eyes smarting, my nose running, I offered up my prayers to God—and felt the deep-down happiness of being accepted for what I was. I was the object of a love greater than any I had ever known.

"To forgive your own self," writes Louis B. Smedes in *Forgive and Forget,* "is almost the ultimate miracle of healing! To forgive yourself is to act out the mystery of one person who is both forgiver and forgiven. You judge yourself: this is the division within you. You forgive yourself: this is the healing of the split."

Later, as I reflected on what happened at the church, I saw it as a major step toward health. Since compulsive behavior, by its very definition, entails acts we experience as involuntary—in which our wills are overwhelmed by a desire that feels as if it comes from outside ourselves—the remedy for such behavior lies in submitting ourselves to a countervailing positive force. Alcoholics Anonymous call this force a Higher Power. Many therapists construct other ideals "outside" the patient.

A skeptic might argue that by this procedure the compulsive person merely exchanges addictions. I don't agree. Every sufferer knows the difference between pain and release from pain. As Dr. Stanton Peele writes in *Love and Addiction:*

"The difference between not being addicted and being addicted is the difference between seeing the world as your arena and seeing the world as your prison. . . . If what a person is engaged in enhances his ability to live—if it enables him to work more effectively, to love more beautifully, to appreciate the things around him more, and finally, if it allows him to grow, to change, and expand—then it is not addictive."

Though other compulsive women may find other "Higher Powers" that release them from enslavement to detested but irresistible urges, I can speak authentically about only one. For me, Christian conversion and faith was the necessary outside force to break the grip of patterns that held me in thrall most of my life.

A sociologist might say that compulsive individuals in our culture are predisposed toward a Judeo-Christian solution to their behavior. Whatever reasons may be given, I can only say personally that it worked for me. My compulsive lifestyle was reordered by a power outside myself, which since that night in the church I continue to experience and call Jesus Christ.

IO

Intervention

For some reason, I can tell you where each person in that room was sitting; the floor plan is burned into my brain. . . . And they all proceeded to confront me with a second intervention. Only this time, they meant business. . . . All of them hurt me. I collapsed into tears. But I still had enough sense to realize they hadn't come around just to make me cry; they were there because they loved me and wanted to help me.

—Betty Ford
The Times of My Life

As I probe back into my recovery, and that of other compulsive people, and see how the sick and defeated are transformed into healthy and productive people, one central fact comes through: *Recovery seldom comes about through one or two experiences; recovery is not an event, it is a process.*

Encountering Karen at Warm Springs Hospital was a beginning, the activation of a long-buried desire to respond to the hurt and need of someone else. Explains John Schwarzlose, executive director and vice-president of the Betty Ford Center: "Alcoholics and addicts have isolated themselves for years. We want them to form relationships again."

The discovery of those three little words *Do it now* was also a step to healing, the coming to life of a part of me that wanted to take responsibility. It too was part of the process.

After throwing my cigarettes from the car window and uttering what might have been the first real prayer of my life, I was loosed from bondage to nicotine. When months later I was released from the desire to drink at the Valentine's Day party, I thought I was now free from all addiction. (Far from it. My compulsions to overeat and go on shopping binges were to reemerge stronger than ever.)

And after the beautiful cleansing experience at the Billings Methodist Church, the mental and physical listlessness brought on by years of abusing my body was replaced by a powerful infusion of energy. I felt more alive than I had in twenty years. Yet this healing was also only a step on the long road back to health.

During the recovery process, I encountered attitudes that were troubling. Some new church friends took the position that I would find all the healing I needed through prayer alone. God's work in me might be endangered, they said, if I got involved with any secular-scientific treatment. The medical world, on the other hand, expressed indifference and even hostility toward any healing that came about through "religion," saying it came either from mass hysteria or a kind of self-hypnosis.

Yet I could see value in what both camps offered.

In any case, there were few effective medical treatment centers for addictive people until the 1970s. Before then alcoholics and drug addicts were often institutionalized, as I had been, right in with the mentally disturbed. Once separate facilities were set up to help addiction sufferers, a new era began. These medical centers usually worked closely with Alcoholics Anonymous (AA), the one approach to alcoholism that had proven effective statistically since it was started in 1935. A significant discovery was that the basic Twelve-Step program of AA worked not only for alcoholics, but for other compulsive behavior problems, too. (See p. 209.)

Recovery begins, counselors discovered, when patients face reality—as required by the all-important First Step of the program. But oh, how hard it is for the addict to change years of practiced deception and self-delusion. Our emotions are defensive, self-protective. Facing truth can be like pulling teeth without anesthesia . . . as I was soon to discover.

For weeks after my healing at the Methodist church, Bible study and prayer groups became the doors to a new life, while I tried not to look at the wreckage of two homes.

My three teenage children were living with their father and had their own lives and activities, where I did not fit. Randall and I were growing farther and farther apart. Many months had passed since my last drink. My resolve was intact, but my body was behaving strangely. Sometimes I talked like a machine gun. I raced from the supermarket to a prayer meeting to back home again at a frantic pace.

"Are you sure you're okay?" friends would ask. "You seem so revved up. Slow down and catch up with yourself!"

Any sense of peace had lit momentarily like the butterfly that had enchanted me in my childhood hideaway, then flitted off elusively. A restless gnawing often filled my heart. I couldn't seem to focus my mind anymore. Blaming the symptoms on the stress of my personal life, I didn't realize I was heading straight for a "dry drunk" condition when a recovering alcoholic exhibits deceptive, unrealistic or "hyper" behavior without the use of alcohol. (See Checklist of Symptoms, p. 214.)

Thinking a change of scene would help, I decided to drive out to a seminar in Seattle. On the way I could spend the weekend with my new friend Cathy and her husband, Dirk.

At their home in Red Lodge, Montana, Cathy and Dirk welcomed me warmly. Feeling exhilarated by our evening of discussion, I lingered in the cozy living room of their log cabin lodge long after Cathy and Dirk went off to bed.

Classical music from an FM station set a dreamy mood. I drifted about the room, rolled back the braided rugs, and danced barefoot on the smooth varnished floor.

The sound of a male voice fractured my reverie. It was Dirk. "What in the world are you doing at this ungodly hour?"

Startled, I just stared at him.

"Sit down, Sandy. I want to talk to you," he exclaimed as he tightened the tie of his terrycloth bathrobe. "You may not like what I'm going to say, but I have to say it anyway."

He studied me for a moment in the soft light. "I know how much progress you've made since Cathy and I first met you and how fragile you are right now, but I have to tell you that your behavior is absolutely bonkers. You are on one heck of an emotional binge, kiddo. A dry drunk. If you don't do something about it, it may turn into a wet drunk and God knows what would happen to you then.

"You are in absolutely *no* condition to drive to Seattle by yourself. Or anywhere else for that matter. You need to go to a treatment center. And fast. I mean tomorrow. Before the sun goes down.

"Meanwhile, quit prancing around like a princess and get to bed. You need rest. We'll call St. Mary's when the office opens at eight o'clock and see if we can get you in. You've got to go, Sandy. Your life depends on it. You're a lot sicker than you think you are."

I hated him. I was fine . . . just on a slight roll. I argued, stormed, wept, but deep down I knew he was right. His words pierced through all my denial. I couldn't run any longer. My life was still out of control. It was time to face my sickness head-on. Dirk helped me face the truth—that I needed professional help.

The next day I was on my way to St. Mary's Treatment Center in Minneapolis.

The "dry drunk" is a common experience for recovering addicts if there has been no inner healing of the emotions. The message to me was pointed: "You may have stopped drinking, Sandy, but you are still binging emotionally." My compulsive nature was still in control. Turn off tobacco, turn on sweets; turn off alcohol, turn on a "spiritual" high from music or overtalk.

What Dirk had done for me was a spontaneous form of an increasingly popular treatment approach called *intervention*. (See p. 258.) The purpose: to get the sick person to face up to reality. The method: confrontation. "Your behavior is bonkers, Sandy. Your very life's at stake. Get to treatment—fast."

Intervention is "a move initiated out of love and concern by the people who care about the alcoholic," writes Mary Ellen Pinkham in *How to Stop the One You Love from Drinking.* "It involves their getting together to tell the alcoholic the facts about his disease and how it is affecting him. It's the only kind, gentle, and caring way to help a chemically dependent person. It's the only thing that works, the key to stopping someone whose life is in danger."

If too many family members have been "co-dependents" with the addict for too long a period, they lose their ability to be honest with each other, to share true feelings. An intervention reverses this process of denial and deception by the family and facilitates their facing up to truth—and dealing with their loved one—in a loving, caring way.

Since family and close contacts are too involved emotionally to lead an intervention, a specialist is needed. Such a professional can usually be found through a local drug or alcohol council, Alcoholics Anonymous, or a mental health department.

Interventions are structured carefully, with as many as six or more people involved. The ideal combination is the spouse, a parent, one or more children, a doctor, the employer, and the family pastor.

Preparation for an intervention calls for a series of meetings between family members and the intervention professional, usually at a location other than the addict's home. The professional explains the process and rehearses the concerned persons as to how they will present their facts. Very often this is the first time the family has actually sat down together and discussed what is going on in the home. All those involved make a list of events in which the addict's behavior has hurt and embarrassed them. Then they practice their presentation. Intervention works for drug abuse, bulimia, anorexia, gambling, and other compulsive behaviors.

Other suggestions:[9]

Timing is crucial. Most successful interventions take place early in the morning when the addict is most vulnerable. It is not advisable to do an intervention when the addict has had time to fortify herself with alcohol or drugs. This is when her denial and defenses are highest.

Firmness of resolve. The spouse and family should have a plan for separating themselves from the addict if she refuses to go for treatment. The employer should be ready with an ultimatum: treatment or loss of job. Often the threat of the loss of one's salaried position is the most persuasive factor.

Who to exclude from an intervention. Anyone who would be too legalistic or moralistic; anyone whose mental balance is questionable; family members too full of hate to perceive the addict as sick and in need of help.

Have a specific treatment plan ready. If the addict agrees to go for treatment, have a time and place firmly set. If there is too much delay, the addict will change her mind.

If the intervention fails. Sometimes the addict will storm out of the meeting. If possible, try it again. Remember that there is tremendous anxiety inside the addict, who is involved in all-out denial. What doesn't work at one setting, will at another. Also the intervention, even if it fails, can start a healing process in the family by bringing members together to face the truth of their situation.

Is there any type of person for whom intervention won't work? None that I know of. When I went to a treatment center, I met doctors, pastors, two lawyers, and a judge, all of whom were patients. Addiction grips people in the highest and lowest job classifications—which is why Betty Ford in *A Glad Awakening* calls alcoholism an "equal-opportunity disease."

There is new hope for all these people in that ninety-seven percent of alcoholics, given the intervention procedure by a specialist, go to treatment within forty-eight hours. The process is so simple that few can believe it works—but it does.

I hated being confronted by Dirk just as much as I had three years before by my friend Lois Ann. For this was the second (not the first) time someone had cared enough to play this uncongenial but necessary role in my life. Three years earlier, at the height of my involvement with the Serenity Society, when each new "spiritual counselor" sent me spiraling deeper into craziness and depression, Lois Ann had organized her own version of intervention.

One day she'd invited me to her house for morning coffee to meet a special friend. The friend turned out to be a vivacious blonde who had just gotten out of an alcohol rehabilitation center in Minneapolis. Her sky-blue eyes danced as she excitedly related her twenty-eight day experience there. "I feel like a new woman," she rhapsodized, "like I have a second chance in life. I can't believe how much better I feel."

I took an instant dislike to this lovely creature. She looked too happy, too put together. I suddenly felt terribly tacky in the tired black polyester pantsuit I'd had on for several days. My head itched from need of a shampoo; the runners in my pantyhose looked like the Los Angeles Freeway. *What a slob you are,* I had thought to myself.

Lois Ann cleared her deep voice and began in halting phrases. "I've invited you here today for a very specific reason, Sandy. I don't know much about alcohol, but perhaps this is your problem, too. Perhaps you need treatment. I can't bear to see what you're doing to yourself. . . ." Taking a deep breath as though to muster a new burst of courage, she added painfully, "Have you looked at yourself in a mirror lately?"

Her words burned into my soul. She had hit a raw nerve. But alcohol wasn't my problem! I drank to escape my problems.

"I'll be glad to phone and make arrangements for you," the friend volunteered. "I know a marvelous counselor there who can answer any questions you might have."

Soon I was chatting with a pleasant-voiced older man. "We'll take good care of you here, Sandy," he said. "When you get out, you'll be the woman your husband fell in love with."

That challenge registered. I promised Lois Ann I'd speak with my psychiatrist and my husband. At my doctor's appointment that afternoon, I broached the subject. He thought it was worth a try. The sessions with him were clearly not working.

Randall was more skeptical. The last three years had diminished his faith for my restoration. He saw such devastation and hopelessness in me. He lived with it and in it. Nevertheless, he agreed it was worth trying.

One January morning in 1977 I was on a Northwest jet headed for Minneapolis.

The intervention set up by Lois Ann had succeeded to the extent that it got me into a treatment center. In the majority of cases today, these specialized facilities get the addict turned around. I was one of their failures. The twenty-eight-day treatment, like my short stays on the psychiatric floor of Billings' Deaconess Hospital, removed me temporarily from my destructive lifestyle and started me on new disciplines. But when I returned home and tried to deal with the old problems, the old pitfalls were too many. I chose to ignore the "aftercare" plan that had been set up for me. I'd been confronted with the truth, but at that period in my life I had had no resources to undergird me and I couldn't cope with it. I had opted for the "out" of suicide and begun squirreling away sleeping pills on a closet shelf.

Perhaps, though, it was that first intervention by Lois Ann in 1977 that prepared me for this second one, in June 1980, which got me into a treatment program that worked.

Facing Truth

*Contrition . . . is not an American virtue, and, indeed,
mere contrition could admit everything, and change nothing. To find culprits is more our style; but culprits, in
taking their punishment, take our part of the guilt with
them. Liberation can come only from insights into the
relevance of past guilt and into the place of ethical choice in
the reformation of identity.*

Erik H. Erikson, M.D.
Dimensions of a New Identity

*L*OOKING BACK, I SOMETIMES THINK DIRK'S INTERVENTION, UNSTRUC-
tured as it was, saved my life. I had been trying to put up a
good front with Randall, my children, and my friends; underneath
I was confused and frightened. What to do about my marriage?
Though Randall had supported me during six bad years, I had
sensed his rejection in a number of ways. Now that I'd stopped
drinking and was on the road to recovery, he expected me to fit back
into his lifestyle. I couldn't do it. It was this social scenario that had
kept me in trouble for so long.

"In our society," writes Betty Ford in *The Times of My Life*, "we
get to know one another over drinks, we associate feasts and
celebrations with liquor. We think we have to drink, that it's a

social necessity. . . . It's romantic as long as you can handle it—for years I could and did—but it's misery when you become addicted."

Randall didn't understand this, or why my new religious faith was suddenly important. Since I was no longer the wife he married, and since we were going in different directions, we agreed to separate.

My children were completely bewildered by my decision to go to a treatment center. To them, I was more stable than they could ever remember me. Why did I have to go back to the hospital? I couldn't explain to them how desperately insecure I was, how close to the breaking point.

In mid-June 1980, I entered St. Mary's Rehabilitation Center, a twenty-eight-day treatment facility for alcohol and drug-related addictions in Minneapolis (a different facility than the one I'd gone to three years earlier).

The three-story treatment center contains, in addition to patients' rooms and counselors' offices, a number of small meeting lounges, a large lecture room, a small chapel with stained glass windows, nurses' stations, and a large recreation area with pool tables and a piano.

I had a small single room with cream painted walls, a hospital bed, and built-in dresser and desk. The daily schedule given us:

Breakfast, 8:00 A.M.

Morning lecture, 9:00 A.M.

Group therapy, 10:00–11:45 A.M.

Lunch, 12:00 noon

Afternoon lecture, 1:00 P.M.

Group therapy, 2:00–4:30 P.M.

Free time/ relaxation therapy, 4:30–6:00 P.M.

Dinner, 6:00 P.M.

Evening lecture, 7:00 P.M.

Free time/alcohol support group meetings/reading/homework,
    8:30 on

At intake I was given a physical, a blood test, and psychological testing (Minnesota Multiphasic Personality Inventory—the "MMPI"). I also met with a staff psychiatrist who suggested Lithium therapy for my mood swings. For the first few days my blood pressure was monitored frequently.

For me, group therapy would be the cutting edge of the program. Six of us met together twice a day for close sharing led by a staff counselor. In our group there was Gwen, our counselor, in her late forties; Max, a stockbroker, maybe sixty; Carol, fiftyish, a clothing saleswoman; Larry, a balding, middle-aged businessman; Sue, a tense, depressed girl barely twenty; and myself, now forty-four.

We met in Gwen's office, a plain room with a desk pushed into the corner and six plastic chairs placed in a circle. On one wall hung a chart of the Twelve Steps of Alcoholics Anonymous. I got as far as the First Step—"We admitted we were powerless over alcohol, that our lives had become unmanageable"—and stopped reading. *Powerless. Unmanageable.* Tough words.

Gwen passed out a worksheet to each of us. Homework to be done in our rooms that evening. In response to a series of questions we were to write out our drinking history. I did not look forward to that. "You need to get the garbage in your lives out on the floor and sort through it," Gwen explained. "You will know if you're in touch with how it really was, because it will hurt. So I wish you a lot of pain, because then something is happening to you."[10]

After two hours of sharing and teaching, Gwen closed the session. Holding hands in a circle, we recited Reinhold Niebuhr's Serenity Prayer (a staple in many treatment programs): "God grant me the serenity to accept the things I cannot change, the courage to change the things I can, and the wisdom to know the difference."

That night I sat down to tackle the homework. *The sooner I get going,* I told myself, *the sooner I'll get it over with.* At the little formica-topped desk, I began reading the sheet of questions.

"Effects on character. List thirty values important to you and give examples of how you have compromised them as a result of your usage."

Suddenly my mind was swirling with indictments—ignoring people's feelings, lying, wasting money, forgetting my children's needs, taking advantage. . . . Now the whirlpool was sucking me down toward unbearable horrors. I flipped the sheet of paper over and slapped my hand down on top of it. "I'll do it later."

I wandered into the big lounge and joined Carol, the fiftyish clothing salesperson, and Sue, the depressed twenty-year-old. "It's so awful to be a woman and an alcoholic," Carol was saying. "The hiding you have to do, the denying—it really grinds your insides."

Sue nodded bleakly.

"What made me really mad was the unfairness," Carol continued. "It was okay for the men to be at the bar having fun. I was stuck at home. My husband and I had equal status till we got married, and then all of a sudden, *plop!*"

I nodded, remembering my days at Pepsi Cola: "I wanted to drink like a man so I could be with the men."

Our group sessions, while the cutting edge of the program, soon became the most difficult part of treatment for me. There was always a knot in my stomach as I approached the door to our counselor's room. How could I escape Gwen's penetrating green eyes? I admired her, but feared she could make mincemeat of my carefully cultivated poise if she probed too close. I would sit in the circle with my best Miss America training: knees and ankles together, one foot tucked behind the other. And my Miss America smile intact. I'd learned to smile early. "Put on a happy face," my mother would tell me.

When my turn came to give a brief biography, I described my hospital experiences in Billings and Warm Springs, and how I'd since stopped smoking and drinking. I touched lightly on my healing that night at the Methodist church, trying hard not to come across as a religious fanatic. Most of the group looked impressed with my progress. Gwen's eyes were expressionless.

"You paint a positive picture of yourself, Sandy. Just why are you here?" Gwen asked.

"My friends think I'm on a dry drunk."

"Do you agree with them?"

"I guess so."

"But you're not sure?"

"My life is sort of a mess. My marriage is breaking up; that is, my second marriage. My three children are living with their father, my first husband. And"—to my disgust, tears were filling my eyes—"and I'm . . . well, not sure of myself at all."

"In short, you could fall off the wagon tomorrow."

"I guess so. I came here to Minneapolis for treatment back in 1977. Stayed sober for two months afterwards, then took that one drink. I know I shouldn't drink."

"Correction. You know you can't drink, but you're not sure you won't."

"I'm pretty sure."

"Sandy, I'll be blunt with you. In some ways you're the sickest person in this room. You spout pious phrases, you hold people off with your sense of humor and your light approach, but you're not in touch with your feelings. I've yet to hear you say how you feel."

"Right now I feel like I've been kicked in the butt."

"Good."

"And I'm miserable underneath all these smiles." The tears were flowing again. "And I'm scared. And I hate myself for what I've done to my family."

"Much better, Sandy. For the first time you come across as real." She turned to others in the group. "What is your feedback to Sandy?"

"Likable, but too pious," ventured Carol. "I felt she was determined to show us she didn't belong here."

"Trying too hard," offered Max. "She was out to win us from the start. A people-pleaser. A lot of froth on top to cover up something underneath she didn't want us to see."

"Hear that, Sandy." Gwen's eyes were boring into me. "Because you've been to treatment before and because you've been dry for a while, you felt you were above the others."

Devastating. Carol handed me some tissues. I felt naked before these people.

Inner healing had begun.

The purpose of these group sessions was to get us to open up, be honest, be vulnerable, express what we felt, not what we thought we ought to feel. At the next session, Gwen zeroed in on my relationship to Randall. "How did he react to your drinking?"

"Frustration at first. Apathy at the end. As a lawyer it bugged him that he couldn't persuade me to stop. He's used to being able to control people and situations."

"So you showed him that he couldn't control you by drinking more than ever."

I shifted uneasily in my chair. "My drinking was a problem before I married him."

"Would you have drunk so much if he had been less controlling?" Max asked suddenly.

Startled, I thought a moment. "Maybe not," I admitted.

Max kept pressing, "Why?"

I jammed my hands under my thighs. "Well, I got so mad . . . maybe there was some revenge mixed in there."

"I just heard something honest," Gwen said, "and I congratulate you. What was your reward for getting mad?"

My mind swam. My mouth was dry. Leaning forward, I stared at the toes of my shoes. Maybe if I leaned far enough the floor would open and swallow me. "I don't know. Maybe I was getting something out of my system."

"There was a great big reward," Gwen said, "and I'm not sure you want to give it up yet."

I could feel the circle of eyes watching me. Finally I said tentatively, "Maybe part of the reward was an inner permission to drink more."

"Part?" asked Gwen, cocking an eyebrow.

"A lot," I said.

"Do you see," Gwen said, "that your anger has been one of the dynamics of your alcoholism?"

There was another long pause. I felt a fear I could not explain. "But sometimes I drank because I was happy."

Max asked, "What would make you so happy you'd take a drink?"

I laughed. "Not taking a drink."

Gwen was not smiling. "I don't know whether you do that in all your relationships, but humor is a way of getting off the hook and stopping communication. As I see it, Max was trying to help and you made a joke. Then he's down and you're up. Take a look at that."

Gwen spoke again. "I urge you to accept what has been said, Sandy. I don't see you making any progress toward accepting the disease concept and the fact that you are powerless over alcohol— which tells me that you are not working on your First Step. You will not really get into treatment until you begin focusing on *you*, your addiction, and how it has affected you."

At the close of the session I hurried away to an isolated chair in the second-floor lounge. I replayed the last exchange—Gwen's voice zapping me for that joke. I felt marooned in a hot funk of embarrassment, like a little girl caught red-handed.

Max's voice broke into my trance. "Sandy, don't look so down. It happens to the best of us."

Looking up, I smiled ruefully. "It's always darkest before it's totally black." Max shrugged and left me alone.

I felt a flush like a prickly rash spreading up my throat and across my face. I had just done it again, made a quip to keep someone at arm's length.

My time came as it did for everyone in our group to read aloud the first homework assignment: a comprehensive look at how addiction had affected every area of my life. Afterward, I waited confidently for the group's approval. No one could accuse me now of covering up: I'd bared my very soul!

But the others disagreed. Some thought I'd minimized the effects on myself and my family, others that I "skated away" from talking about real issues.

And I was totally unprepared for Gwen's response. She told me calmly that I was one of the angriest women she had ever had in her group and that I'd better get in touch with that anger or it would surely sabotage my recovery. "When you finish your treatment here," she said, "I think you should consider going to a women's halfway house for continuing recovery."

She added that I'd been so ill for the past twenty years, I hardly knew what planet I was on, and that going to Billings could be disastrous. "And from now on," she concluded, "I want your outsides to match your insides! No more hiding behind your smile."

I was stunned that she detected such anger in me. I hadn't lost my cool even once in the group. Was I really so angry? I wasn't sure I wanted to find out.

After this session, I slipped down to the chapel on the second floor of the treatment center. It was my special place of peace and refuge, an eye of calm in the storm all around me. Kneeling in the serenity of that place, I started to search my life for clues to my aborted anger.

As I meditated, I saw I was indeed angry, and that it had begun when I was very young. I had picked up people's feelings and moods, known what was acceptable behavior and what was not.

Observing adult responses to my actions, I'd discovered it was not all right to be angry. My home was not a healthy emotional climate where feelings were expressed frankly. So I learned to mask anger and annoyance, smile sweetly, say nothing. I felt one way and acted another. Pretty soon I didn't know how I felt. Apparently this pattern was still in effect, refined by years of practice. My denial system protected me like a bulletproof vest.

What Gwen said, then, was true. Beneath the placid exterior I was angry. In fact, I was mad as hell! A childhood episode came back to me. Once when I was angry at my grandmother I'd covered my whole body with big white adhesive-tape Band-Aids. Then I'd stood in the lawn sprinkler so the Mercurochrome on the pads would run down my body like blood. It was a pathetic attempt to get people to notice my feelings—and won me no attention at all.

As an adult I became a door-slammer. On three occasions, when angry at my husband, I'd thrown pots through a kitchen window. The man at the glass repair shop chuckled the third time he replaced the pane: "It'd be cheaper to kick a tire, lady."

I had never learned to express feelings appropriately. I knew I couldn't blame my parents. They were victims of victims and I realized that I, too, had made victims of my children.

Was it this pattern of denied emotions, I wondered, generation after generation, that had made me such a ready receptor for those "angry little men" who'd tormented me so long? I only knew there was an avalanche of rage inside that wanted to come out.

A similar pattern of repressed anger shows up again and again in compulsive individuals like me—smiling people-pleasers who are covering up years of suppressed anger and hurt.

"No matter how 'grown-up' one acts in therapy or in life," writes Arthur Janov in *The Primal Scream,* "it must be an act which has little bearing on one's maturity until the 'little girl' is felt. . . . We must feel the anger fully in order to eradicate it. When a person can feel himself, instead of acting out his feelings symbolically, he will be unlikely to act either impulsively or aggressively. The dialectic of anger, as with Pain, is that when it is felt, it disappears, when it is not felt, it remains waiting to be felt."

As the days passed and I opened up haltingly to the group, some of the long-buried feelings came out. Memories surfaced that had festered unacknowledged for years. But always, it seemed, more pain lay underneath.

The third week of my treatment was called "family week," made memorable for me by a visit from my son Brent, at nineteen a handsome six-footer. My middle child, Brent has always been creative, athletic, popular with his peers. The day he joined our group, Gwen placed our two chairs in the center of the circle face-to-face, then asked Brent to describe how it felt to grow up in an alcoholic home.

He shifted about uncomfortably and said he hadn't noticed anything was wrong until he had visited the homes of his friends and seen that their mothers didn't drink as I did.

Gwen explained to him that children of alcoholics blank out the pain and have almost an amnesia about their parents' drinking.

As Brent talked, I looked into his guileless eyes and felt such a wrenching pain in my stomach that I thought I would be sick. The sense of lost years with him, Brad, and Lisa was almost unbearable.

"Stop crying, Sandy," Gwen ordered. "You're manipulating him with your tears."

It was a hard time, I know, for Brent, as it was for me—yet so very good to have him there.

After kissing him goodbye as he left for the airport, I returned to my room and found a note propped up against my pillow. It was neatly printed with a black felt-tip pen on a paper towel:

Dear Mom, I am sorry that my stay had to be so short. I hope that we have cleared up some problems that you have had! I learned a lot while I was here. The people are beautiful. I want you to know I *love* you very much and I don't use the term loosely. I'm sure Brad and

Lisa feel the same. Please give my best wishes to all the nice friends of yours. I send them all the willpower in the world and my very best wishes. Take care and if you ever have a problem, just give us a call. We will help.

> Love, Brent
> & God bless

I weep seven years later upon reading this. The message has been framed and matted in sunny yellow and hangs on my kitchen wall. It's a precious prized treasure from the heart of my son.

During treatment I was served with divorce papers. Though I knew they were coming, the reality devastated me. More guilt, remorse, defeat. For two days I barely functioned. The lecture by a counselor named Jessica was life-restoring.

Jessica had been a Roman Catholic nun, then an alcoholic. She'd found sobriety through the AA program and was now dedicated to carrying the message of restoration to others. Her very presence inspired confidence. The serenity of her spirit washed over me as she began to speak.

"An alcoholic can be sober," Jessica was saying, "but still the most miserable, God-forsaken person on two feet. There has to be some rebuilding of the spiritual values destroyed by chemicals: honesty, humility, forgiveness, trust, love, courage. This process begins with surrender. It is saying 'I give up!' I surrender to the powerlessness and unmanageability of my life. The chemical controlled me. I said and did things while drunk that were hurtful, painful, devastating, destructive.

"In recovery," she continued, "the hardest thing for me to accept was the fact that kind, gentle, caring Jessica, while drunk, was capable of doing terrible things. I knew I could be forgiven for those things. But as long as I was unable or unwilling to forgive myself, it was difficult to feel their forgiveness in my gut. I still carried the burden of my past around like a big boulder on my back."

As Jessica spoke my thoughts went back to that night at the Methodist church. The words of the woman minister rang in my head: "If God has forgiven all your sins, how dare you not forgive yourself?" It sounded so simple, but I saw now that a lack of self-forgiveness had continued to be the biggest stumblingblock in my recovery.

Jessica continued: "So I finally faced the reality that I was a failure at running my own affairs. Then the question: Where am I going to get help outside myself? Is there anything in this program that I can grab hold of and hang onto very, very tightly that will make me become a healthier, happier person? Is there anything that will give me a deep sense of forgiveness? That brought me to a further stage of surrender—surrender to God as I understood him—which, surprisingly, I had never really done.

"I know now," Jessica concluded, "that God will give me the grace, the strength, the courage, the people that I need to get through today without drinking. For that I am very grateful."

Powerlessness. Acceptance. Surrender. Gratitude. Great words to say, but how to own them, to integrate them into my life? I suddenly saw with new eyes the unmanageability of my life.

I could take Step One of our recovery program and put any number of things where the word *alcohol* appears: cigarettes, food, relationships, shopping sprees, the occult, caffeine, anger. . . .* The list seemed endless. I was powerless over my whole life. That was what was unmanageable.

Step Two was equally crucial: "Came to believe that a power greater than myself could restore me to sanity."

"Developing your spirituality," writes Robin Norwood in *Women Who Love Too Much,* "no matter what your religious orientation, basically means *letting go of self-will,* of the determination to make

---

* The Twelve Steps can be applied to any self-help group or program.

things happen the way you think they should . . . believing that you alone have all the answers . . . becoming willing to hold still, be open, and wait for guidance for yourself. It means learning to let go of fear (all of the 'what ifs') and despair (all of the 'if onlys') and replacing them with positive thoughts and statements about your life."

At the end of her talk, Jessica instructed us to stand and grasp the hands of the people next to us while we sang "Amazing Grace." At my right was a ruddy-faced young man whose mother, Carol, was in my treatment group. At my left was Veronica, a tiny, birdlike woman in treatment for her ninth time. I was struck by the difference of handclasps. One so powerful, the other so tremulous. The words we sang pierced my soul: "I once was lost, but now am found, was blind, but now I see."

Soon people were sobbing openly. Veronica leaned against me, her tears wetting the sleeve of my blue cotton shirt. I doubt there was a person in that room who was not grappling with that reality. There was new purpose in faces that before had been vacant. The air was charged with electricity. I felt safe and cared for and loved. But most of all, I felt forgiven.

Self-forgiveness without honesty, writes Louis B. Smedes in *Forgive and Forget,* "is psychological hocus-pocus. The rule is: we cannot really forgive ourselves unless we look at the failure in our past and call it by its right name. When you forgive yourself, you rewrite your script. What you are in your present scene is not tied down to what you did in an earlier scene. . . . You release yourself today from yesterday's scenario. You walk into tomorrow, guilt gone."

12

Anger and Male Dependency

At our worst, we women who love too much are relationship addicts, "man junkies" strung out on pain, fear, and yearning. . . . We use relationships in the same way that we use our addictive substance: to take our pain away. . . . As long as we are bent on escaping ourselves and avoiding our pain, we stay sick. The harder we try and the more avenues of escape we pursue, the sicker we get as we compound addictions with obsessions.

> Robin Norwood
> *Women Who Love Too Much*

A S MORE AND MORE IS LEARNED ABOUT ADDICTIVE BEHAVIOR, THERAPISTS are urging patients to continue their recovery programs beyond the twenty-eight-day average stay at a treatment center, preferably in a halfway house. If for one reason or another, often financial, this is impossible, the alternative is a support group in the patient's hometown using the Twelve-Step program.

At the suggestion of Gwen, my counselor at the treatment center, I agreed to enter a halfway house. Twenty years of addictive behavior, she said, could not be changed in a month's program. I hated to be away still longer from Billings where I could see my children several times a week, but my prime responsibility to my family was to get well.

My interview at the Jane Dickman House (about twenty miles outside of St. Paul) was a surprise. The words *halfway house* had always conjured up a vision of cracked plaster walls, leaky ceilings, and dead flies on the windowsills. In contrast, the ride up to Dickman House coursed along a winding driveway, passed a tennis court and manicured lawn, and came to a halt beneath the portico of a sprawling wood-and-stone structure. It looked more like a country vacation resort than a facility for chemically dependent women.

Inside I was led past groups of women talking over coffee around small tables and into a dining room with a chalet window that offered a panoramic view of a lake. My interviewer asked me probing questions about my life and my goals for recovery, noting my answers on a yellow pad. At the end of our time, she offered a treatment plan for me: I needed to work on building trust levels, improving family relationships, understanding my feelings and emotions. The cost of living there came to about $1,100 a month. All participants were encouraged to find jobs locally or in nearby St. Paul, not only to help pay expenses, but to build a new life of independence.

The first few weeks were spent in "Feelings Groups," large and small house meetings, one-on-one counseling, exercise periods, and alcohol support group meetings. There were kitchen duties, special weekend projects, and social events with our brother halfway house, Team House, in nearby St. Paul.

Each woman at Jane Dickman was given a "verbal" by her counselor. Before we were allowed to speak, we had to use our special verbal and say how we felt. Mine, for example, was, "I need to share with you on a meaningful level. I feel sad [or embarrassed, or angry, or whatever]." By doing this, I would be forced to get in touch with my feelings.

After one group session my counselor, a no-nonsense, authoritative woman named Betsy, called me into her office for a one-on-one.

"Sandy, your steady smile tells me that you're a good-natured person. Are you really that happy on the inside or have you gone through life in a smiling depression?"

"Perhaps."

"Then that happy smile must be a mask to cover up how you're really feeling."

I nodded, recalling how my group at St. Mary's had called me on this.

"Some of your smiles seem spontaneous and natural. Others I suspect are cover-ups."

"Cover-ups for what?" I asked, half-afraid to hear her response.

"Your deep-rooted anger. We're going to deal with that in the next few weeks."

With that, Betsy instructed the other women to confront me every time I smiled and ask what I was smiling about. As an exercise to get my insides to match my outsides, I was to pay a small fine whenever I used my smile as a defense. I was also to be penalized if I employed exaggerated words like *itsy-bitsy, teeny, humongous, gigantic.* Such words distorted communication, Betsy said. It was a shock to discover how often these exaggerations popped out in my everyday conversation.

Betsy also assigned me individual "anger work." I was to spend five minutes a day in the indoor racquetball court "screaming." At first this exercise seemed ridiculous. Self-conscious at first, my screams were little more than squeaks, but as I got into the routine, the emotion poured out. Using the ball as the object of my anger, I blasted at it with my racquet. Soon the squeaks became roars. I discovered I was not merely angry, but as Gwen had predicted, I was full of buried rage.

If the resident had an automobile, as I did, those of us with anger work were encouraged to use driving time for screaming. Once, on my way back to Dickman House from doing an errand, I was idling at a stoplight and decided it would be a good place to let out some feelings. I didn't realize my car window was open until a woman in the lane next to me scrambled from her car to come to my aid. That cured me from screaming at stoplights, but not on interstates.

Betsy suggested I make an anger diary going back as far as I could remember, noting events, people, and situations that made me angry. What a revelation that was! I'd had emotional gangrene most of my life and never realized it.

I'd always been one of those "don't-make-waves" people who shied away from confrontations. In our sexual abuse group one day I was urged to deal with my unexpressed anger against Uncle Ralph for his molestation of me when I was five.

"Go back to that place and that episode," the counselor instructed. "Tell your uncle how it was for you. You're not the helpless little girl now. Tell him whatever you need to." She gave me several pillows to use.

Closing my eyes for concentration, I went back in time to Uncle Ralph's living room. I could smell the Sir Walter Raleigh tobacco he rolled into homemade cigarettes . . . hear the sound of ticking clocks from the hallway.

Then I saw Uncle Ralph sitting in his squeaky wooden rocker. Felt his hands on me, heard him wheezing, clicking his teeth. I started to sob and beat my thighs.

"Use the pillows," the counselor ordered.

"I loved and trusted you, Uncle Ralph, and you took advantage of me. I was little and couldn't fight back. You hurt me! You scared me! I hate you for that!"

I was shouting now, my voice high and shrill. The five-year-old Sandy was doubled over, pounding the pillows with both fists.

During these sessions I realized that in the past my anger had erupted all right, only in indirect, inappropriate ways. Example: *overeating.* You could never have convinced me when I was binging on chocolate that I was really acting out my inner rage. Not just at Uncle Ralph, but at all the times I'd swallowed my feelings and said nothing. It made no difference that my dress size was headed for the twenties, that I was totally revulsed at myself and nauseated physically by food. The raging dragon inside demanded to be fed. Or placated with cigarettes. Or booze. Or a new outfit.

One day the staff counselor at Dickman House jolted me by saying, "Sandy, do you realize how male-dependent you are?"

Anger in me was now very near the surface; *available* was the staff's approving term. It welled up in me. "You make me sound like a streetwalker!" I flared.

"I'm not talking about that kind of dependency. Your thoughts, your actions, your needs are centered on men. You require their approval to be fulfilled."

"How can you say that?" I argued. "I've been hurt by men all my life. Now at long last I'm free of them."

The counselor shook her head. "You only think you're free. Let me explain what I mean." She tapped a paper on her desk.

"The results of your psychological testing confirm your hostility and dependency on men. You have probably been dependent on every man in your life, starting with your father. The problem with being male-dependent is that a woman ties all her feelings of self-worth into what men think about her, what they do and say. You need to begin to become responsive to yourself and your own needs. You are a 'people-pleaser' like most alcoholics—and the people you try hardest to please are men."

For several moments I was silent, devastated by this appraisal that I knew deep-down to be true. "How do I get free?" I finally asked.

"For the next four weeks you will be on a 'male restriction' program. This means you will not have anything to do with men. You can write or call one male member of your family once a week, but you're to avoid conversations with men, even eye contact with men on the street. You need to learn to trust women and the feedback they have for you."

At first this program seemed peculiar and unfair. Four weeks without talking to a man except my father, Brent, or Brad once every week or so? Impossible.

But it wasn't. I discovered how automatically I sought to make eye contact with men—in restaurants, at meetings, anywhere—even with total strangers. Somehow the approval of these nameless outsiders mattered. I'd be buoyed by a flicker of interest, dejected by indifference. It was a searing discovery.

"The notion that men are absolutely vital to any value we may have," writes Nancy Friday in *My Mother/My Self,* "is so woven into feminine reality that most women think to reject it would be like trying to reject the law of gravity."

Friday recalls in her book that "it was the promise of men, that around each corner there was yet another man, more wonderful than the last, that sustained me. You see, I had men confused with life. . . . It was a religion of a god who gave and took away life. . . ."

Psychologist Sonya Friedman in her book *Men Are Just Desserts* points out one of the most deeply ingrained messages that daughters receive from their mothers: *A man is the measure of your worth.*

To break the cycle of male dependency, then, it was apparent that I needed to enhance my sense of self-worth completely apart from men. And, in fact, after the first few days of my male restriction program, it became a little easier. Each time I resisted looking at a man for approval represented a victory. I was greatly encouraged. My self-esteem was growing in little flutters, but growing. By the end of the four weeks, I sensed a new strength in this area.

Other revelations: Male dependence had strangled my development as a person, kept my maturing process on hold. I'd often given up decision-making and goal-setting to comply with what the "he" in my life dictated. I had not learned to make responsible choices.

It was disconcerting to realize how early I'd begun to depend on male approval of my behavior, my appearance, my plans. An occasional desire for this kind of approval is normal and good, of course, but needing it constantly had long since become an unhealthy way of life.

Robin Norwood explains in *Women Who Love Too Much* that "a woman who uses her relationships as a drug will have fully as much denial about that fact as any chemically addictive individual, and fully as much resistance and fear concerning letting go of her obsessive thinking and high emotionally charged way of interacting with men. But usually, if she is gently but firmly confronted, she will at some level recognize the power of her relationship addiction and know she is in the grip of a pattern over which she has lost control."

You can test yourself for "Male Dependency" with the quiz on page 238.

An important aspect of my halfway house program was to reach a point where I could go out into the world and not only acquire a job, but succeed in it. Before I was ready for this step, my counselor felt I needed special preparation.

"Sandy, it's time for you to attend the assertiveness class," Betsy told me one day. She explained that the recovering addict needs to learn how better to handle confrontational situations without waffling or being dishonest. These four everyday situations, for example:

1. A salesclerk won't refund your money.

2. You ordered a steak medium-rare and it comes to the table well-done.

3. Your car wasn't repaired the way you specified.

4. A door-to-door salesman persists in trying to sell you something you don't want.

In the assertiveness class we were taught to "hang in there" for our viewpoint. Here is a typical role play:

Clerk: "May I help you?"

Me: "Yes. I'd like a refund of $85.99 on this vacuum cleaner."

Clerk: "We don't give refunds."

Me: "I understood that if I brought in the receipt, you would refund my money. Here is my receipt. I'd like my money back."

Clerk: "I'm not supposed to give refunds. I'll get in trouble."

Me: "I'm sorry for you if that happens, but I still want my $85.99 refunded."

Clerk: "Why don't you take the vacuum cleaner home and try it out for another week? Get used to it."

Me: "I want my $85.99 or your name and the name of your supervisor."

Clerk: "I'm not supposed to do this, you know," as he takes the receipt and refunds the money.

In the above exchange I was instructed to state persistently what I wanted and avoid being sidetracked onto irrelevant issues. (The person playing the clerk was told to resist in every possible way.) My ace in the hole was what I had been told initially about the store's general policy regarding refunds.

Learning such basic life skills was essential before we recovering alcoholics were ready to enter the rough-and-tumble of the job market. Even with this training, the thought of having to interview for employment paralyzed me. My work as an artist at Disneyland and my public relations position with Pepsi Cola had been over twenty years ago. Who would want to hire a forty-four-year-old has-been? Was I employable?

For two days at the Office of the Civilian Employment Training Agency (CETA), five of us from Jane Dickman House underwent intensive schooling on how to conduct ourselves at a job interview. Then weeks passed and the only work that became available for me was through an office temporary service. Stuffing envelopes for mailings didn't pay much, and at the end of the day my fingers were covered with Band-Aids to cover the paper cuts. "I'll never get a decent job," I moaned. "How am I ever going to support myself?"

Then CETA phoned. "The Minnesota Museum of Art is looking for an assistant preparator of exhibitions. Call and set up an interview . . . and good luck!"

What do you wear for an interview with three museum directors? I had visions of three dour faces peering at me from behind a mahogany, skating-rink-sized conference table. What a shock to find three laid-back, obviously creative, no-nonsense professionals in tweeds and corduroys chatting merrily, drinking coffee.

The business administrator asked most of the questions. I liked her immediately. Her pale blue eyes danced in a thin, angular face. She'd be enjoyable to work with. "Do you have any carpentry skills?" she asked. "You'll need to be able to do a little bit of everything around here."

"My father taught me how to build and paint and wallpaper," I offered. "Even how to do simple plumbing and electrical work."

The director's eyes lit up. "I had pictured giving this job to a man," he said, "but if you think you could handle the physical demands, you might be the one for it. We have a number of others to interview today before we decide. Thanks for your time."

I was waiting for him to say, "Don't call us, we'll call you," but he didn't.

Back at the halfway house I lunged for the phone each time it rang. Hours later the administrator called, "We've reviewed all the applications and have narrowed it down to two. I need to ask you a crucial question: do you know how to drive a truck?"

My mind was racing. I really wanted that job. Could I drive a truck? Of course! But my conscience was saying, *You've driven only a pickup truck.* Clearing my throat, as if to convince myself first, I replied, "I can drive a truck just so long as it isn't an eighteen-wheeler."

"Great," she responded. "The job is yours."

I held the job for seven months until my counselor felt I was ready to go back home to Billings. It was a valuable experience, bolstering my sense of self-worth and rekindling my creativity. It felt so good to be productive again.

A sign of my walk toward wholeness was the interest I began taking in other women and their problems. A seed was growing inside me of love for people. The capacity to reach out had withered during twenty years of addiction, only to sprout anew that night in the Warm Springs Hospital when I comforted Karen.

One of the patients at the halfway house with whom I developed an almost mother-daughter relationship was a seventeen-year-old named Sophia. She was a pretty girl with brown hair and a face that didn't show her drug and alcohol abuse. Sophia had started drinking when she was in the third grade. In the sixth grade she was introduced to marijuana; two years later she began using hashish, speed, and LSD.

At fifteen Sophia moved out from her family and in with a boyfriend, got a cleaning job at a bar, and was soon drunk morning, noon, and night. She'd recently spent a month in treatment, then entered Jane Dickman House.

I was attracted to Sophia because she was close to the age of my daughter Lisa (then eighteen) and so needy for love and attention. Treatment had given her some handles on her disease, but her counselor and friends wondered if these would be broken when she returned to her old environment and faced both chemically active friends and a male-dependent relationship.

The issue came to a climax one March afternoon. Her boyfriend—I'll call him Nick—rolled into the parking lot on his motorcycle and bellowed for his "woman." Sophia hadn't seen Nick in six months.

Her roommate and I went outside to talk with him. Nick measured about six-two and looked at us with sullen, half-closed eyes. "Where's Sophia?" he demanded.

"She says she doesn't want to see you," her roommate told him.

"I want *her* to tell me that."

Reluctantly Sophia came outside and faced the past. Several of us formed a protective semicircle behind her while Sophia stared at Nick in silence. We could all feel the power he held over her. Bluntly he ordered her to come with him.

I knew well what was going on inside of Sophia. On the one side, a pull toward sex, drugs, alcohol; on the other, freedom from the cravings, the beginning of a new self-worth. The choice: Hop onto Nick's bike and return to her old life, or stay with us and continue being healed.

She turned and looked at us, the people who had befriended her. No one spoke, but something clicked. A decision. She turned to the biker: "No, I don't want to see you ever again." His eyes intensified, bore hard into hers to test her resolve. Then, with a shrug, he got onto his bike and roared away.

Each woman who goes through the program at Jane Dickman has a personal graduation ceremony. Mine was highlighted by a visit from Lisa, generous tributes from the staff, other patients, and friends I'd made in the area. First steps had been taken in leaving anger and male dependency behind. It was time, as Sonya Friedman writes in *Men Are Just Desserts,* to reassess my skills, my personality, my self-esteem.

"The more you are," she says, "the more you possess yourself without getting caught up with pleasing others and the more you can understand that no one's going to make you happy, or complete, but yourself. The more you *are,* the more you will realize that a man can detract from or enhance your happiness, but he can never be responsible for answering all your needs."

13

Deception and
Other Little Monsters

*The key word in [self-cure] is self: taking charge of your own
problem. Some psychologists call this self-mastery; others,
self-efficacy; others, the belief in free will. It translates into
three components necessary for change: an urge to quit, the
belief that you can quit and the realization that you must
quit—no one can do it for you.*

—Stanton Peele, Ph.D.
"Out of the Habit Trap"
American Health

RECOVERY IS NOT ONLY A PROCESS; IT'S A PROCESS THAT TAKES TIME. A lot of time.

Treatment programs—whether they last a month or a year—are only a beginning. A turnaround. The compulsive person is given a temporary sanctuary, a direction to go, guidelines to follow. He's then released into the world, at which point the real battle begins. One chemical dependency specialist estimates that fifteen percent of recovery occurs in treatment, the other eighty-five percent in the outside world.

When I came out of nearly eight months of treatment at Jane Dickman I asked myself, "What have you learned?"

A great deal. I knew, for example, that one drink—just one—could start an avalanche inside me that would propel me down, down, down to destruction. This was not theory. When I emerged from twenty-eight days of treatment in Minneapolis that first time, back in 1977, I abstained for two months, then decided to have a single drink. What followed was disaster.

Later I had well-meaning church friends tell me I was now free of my bondage and that an occasional drink would not trigger a relapse. I consider that deadly advice.

Besides, even if it were true that I could take a drink without ill consequences, I wouldn't do it. I've come to love the way I feel alcohol-free. I like the clear head, the aliveness. One drink would bring on the dullness I remember too well. What I thought was stimulation was the very reverse. The seduction of alcohol is that you feel you are getting sharper, brighter, wittier, while the exact opposite is occurring. You are getting duller, more sluggish, merely silly. I want no part of that second-class existence now that I've lived first-class for years since that Valentine's Day 1980.

I'd also learned that *recovery means civil war*. Back home I would literally be going to war with myself and my old destructive habit patterns. After nine months of treatment the battleground was clear to me. It involved change—change across-the-board.

Fortunately, most treatment centers offer an "aftercare" plan. Mine covered the obvious things I'd already been working on:

Anger

Male dependency

Food issues

Shopping/spending

Perfectionistic behavior

To help me abstain from chemicals, I was to be involved with a continuing alcohol support group.

I was to talk about and express my feelings with someone daily.

I was to get regular exercise.

I was to watch my nutrition carefully.

As I picked up the routines of living, I discovered that the danger was not going to be so much from the big monsters that had nearly destroyed me, as from a lot of little ones. Reentry into Billings, Montana, where I had been so sick, was painful. There were old relationships to sort through and mend, new ones to contemplate. Most importantly, my grown children lived and worked there. My dearest wish was to reestablish warm, healthy relationships with them. They were so mature in some ways, self-reliant from years of fending for themselves. Yet also hurting and vulnerable, watching me with guarded enthusiasm. Is this really Mom? Is she going to be okay? In some ways we were almost strangers.

Sometimes at night as I lay sleepless in the small apartment I'd moved into, I tried to piece together the fragments of lost years with them. What had happened during their junior and senior high school years? Those were the years I was mostly out-of-it. I felt robbed of so many milestones in their lives. In my remorse I tried to think of ways to make up these losses to my children. It wasn't possible, of course. The damage done was real and could not be erased by guilty efforts at compensation. In fact, my counselor had warned me that if I focused too much on trying to undo the past, it would not only sabotage my recovery but confuse my children in unhealthy ways.

So each day I tried to deal with this little monster of *if-only*. If only I hadn't . . . whatever. The best method was to focus on today and be grateful for how far I had come. I tried to start each day in this frame of mind, dressing quickly before six A.M., bounding down the stairs of my small third-floor apartment, and walking a three-mile route I'd laid out around the city, before digging into my work of costume-and-doll designing for a Boston firm.

There was something therapeutic about being out in the crisp morning air—more so than the compulsive morning exercising at the Y that had been so unproductive. I'd read that walking was good for patients suffering from depression and now I could understand why. All body systems seem to tune up when you're walking. The senses expand to enfold everything about you.

As I passed the Deaconess Hospital on my route, I offered prayers for the patients on the psych ward where I had spent several "drying-out" periods back in the mid-1970s. Looking up at the fluorescent-lighted ceilings on the second floor, I recalled the countless hours I stared at those very light fixtures, and watched forlornly out the window at people bustling up and down the same streets I now walked in health and growing freedom.

Another of the little monsters I sought to overcome was the monster of *lying*. This was an especially difficult part of my recovery program—to change my deceitful nature into an honest one. The problem is that lying becomes a way of life for the addict. We start by lying to ourselves: "I couldn't have done that. I just *wouldn't* behave that way."

Later my behavior in blackouts had to be covered with lies because I couldn't remember what I'd said or where I'd been. I lived in a constant state of fear because I couldn't remember large blocks of time—what I'd done, how I'd gotten home. The blood spattered on our white Jeep, for example, that had caused me such apprehension. Many were the mornings I raced to the garage to see if my car was in its usual spot.

All of life thus becomes a lie. Even my sober times were colored with various shadings of the truth. I was wound about like a mummy with layers and layers of deception. My ears were deaf to the truth; my eyes saw only a miniscule slice of reality.

When I started working my recovery program, I knew I had to get honest with both myself and other people. Especially with myself. My conscience became newly activated. As soon as I told a lie, a searing stab of conviction would hit me.

Once, counting my change outside the grocery store, I realized that the checker had mistaken a ten-dollar bill I'd given her for a twenty. This came at a time when I was short of funds. But I went back into the store to return the money. It was a small act, but represented growth.

Cash-register honesty came more easily than more subtle challenges. At the beginning of my rehabilitation, I promised myself I wouldn't lie for one whole day. It was interesting to see how quickly little fibs and exaggerations tended to creep into my conversation. A friend asked me over the phone how I liked the book she had loaned me. "I'm getting a lot out of it" slipped off my tongue. A white lie, but still deceptive. The truthful reply should have been, "I'm looking forward to reading it this weekend."

I was interested much later to note a similar push toward honesty in an article by Dr. Sirgay Sanger in the newsletter of the National Council on Compulsive Gambling (Winter 1985). He identifies even accepting too much change in a store as a serious ethical problem that often leads to behavioral relapse.

"I have yet to see compulsive gamblers who have been lying and cheating not fall back into gambling," he observes. "What I usually recommend is a complete dedication to honesty and integrity in as many areas as possible."

My own daily effort at truthfulness showed me how inclined I was to deny unpleasantness, always to paint the rosy picture. The most staggering realization was how I minimized or lied about my feelings. As my time of sobriety lengthened, real feelings that I had medicated for years started emerging. Unwrapping those endless layers of cover-up was agony. Lies had been my armor, my protection. Now I stood shivering in naked vulnerability with no place to escape.

An especially nasty little monster was *profanity*. I had started swearing in high school because it seemed sophisticated, and I progressed to the point where bad language was an automatic knee-jerk reaction to things that went wrong—or even right. Once

I overheard a woman tell her husband in hushed tones what a foul mouth I had. I dismissed it as the utterance of a prude.

Now I felt uncomfortable saying, or even hearing, four-letter words. Yet they still slipped out—sometimes at the most inopportune times.

Though I've begun to make progress in this area, I don't kid myself. Lurking in my compulsivity is a little monster that has been exposed, rebuked, and reduced to a whimper. But it hasn't left the premises.

My behavior is often at war with my will. I want to be disciplined, but it's as though my desire world has metastasized, with each tiny fragment capable of spawning a cancerous growth of its own.

Another monster with which I've had to deal is *shopping*. Like so many hurting women, I used spending binges to fill the emptiness in my life. In 1976, for example, my work as a sales clerk in Billings' largest department store was a disastrous experience economically. Each day I bought at least one item, rationalizing I was saving money with my employee's discount. At month's end my store bill far exceeded my salary.

Somehow loading my arms with bundles and boxes relieved my sense of low self-worth, made me feel important, cared for. What I didn't realize was that this is addictive behavior as surely as drinking and drug-taking.

"It is well known," wrote Erich Fromm in his *Anatomy of Human Destructiveness*, "that . . . compulsive buying is one attempt to escape from a depressed mood . . . a symbolic act of filling the inner void and, thus, overcoming the depressed feeling for the moment."

After the well-publicized spending excesses of Imelda Marcos, it is interesting that Tammy Faye Bakker, in the height of the so-called "holy war" among television evangelists, confessed on ABC's *Nightline* to prodigious shopping and bargain-hunting because it "helps my nerves. It's cheaper than a psychiatrist."

During my recovery period I saw my own shopping binges for what they were— saw the shallowness of them, saw the disastrous outcome in domestic strife and economic setbacks.

Back in Billings I put myself on a budget. I'd always moaned that this was too hard, that I couldn't do figures. I found, of course, that anyone can do figures if she tries. But I still have to be careful when I'm tired or upset; at such moments shopping can become my fix.

Today when I pass stores advertising *Sale!* I ask myself, "Do I need this?" If I start to enter a store I ask, "Why am I going in here?" The temptation to spend always begins with the thought *I want this.* I'm gradually learning to counteract this thought with the question of need. If the desire won't stand cold, hard scrutiny, then I don't really want it at all.

In fact, all my problems, it seems, begin in my thought life: *I'll eat just this one cookie, I'll just browse at this sale and not buy anything. I'll take just one drink.* These thoughts and a myriad of others have to be brought under control.

Do's and Don't's for Compulsive Shoppers
Do's

1. Work out a systematic budget and stay with it. Be aware of where almost every penny goes.

2. List all your debts on a large wall calendar as a constant reminder.

3. Set a goal to get out of debt. The benefits, such as peace and delight, will be well worth it.

4. Stay with whatever plan you devise. You will often want to stop. Don't rationalize by saying, "I can skip a month; it's too much trouble to keep records."

5. Always pay bills before spending money on other things.

6. Use the income from a secondary source or from a working spouse basically for savings, investments, or paying off existing bills and loans.   From *Money: How to Spend Less and Have More* by David J. Juroe

Don't's

1. When you see a sale sign, you don't always have to stop.

2. Remember that if you don't need something, it is not a bargain at any price, even if it is on sale.

3. Limit the cash you take with you on trips. If you have more, you may spend it.

4. Be careful about setting dates for entertainment or events where you know you will overspend, if you can't afford it.

5. Don't add new debts. This is very important. Why not call for a family gathering and make definite plans to cut spending?

6. Don't use credit for small items. Concentrate on paying cash for everything, even if you're in debt.

7. Don't throw away "junk." Much of it may be useful to someone else. So why not consider a sale at your house, like a yard or garage sale? Then use the money to pay off old debts.

Procrastination was another little monster that threatened the recovery process. "I'll do it tomorrow" was deeply ingrained. I'd rail at my daily schedule, want to stare out the window or chat on the phone. The *Do it now!* philosophy was helpful in this area. Slowly but surely I watched my life taking on healthy structure.

Each morning I made a list of the things that needed to be accomplished that day, trying to prioritize the three most important items and get them done before noon. I also included in my schedule times for recreation and rest. As one who had wasted so much time, rest was hard for me to take. I felt I needed to make every waking moment count until I realized my body couldn't physically meet those kinds of demands.

Whenever I attacked a compulsive pattern in my life, the little creepy crawler monsters would start to undermine my progress. *Food* and *shopping* continued to be booby traps, probably because I couldn't simply eliminate these areas of my life. Unlike alcohol or cigarettes, where the best—the only—answer for the compulsive woman is total abstinence, we all have to eat and we all have to go into stores. For the compulsive personality, moderation is the hardest achievement of all.

For a while I'd do fine on a reasonable regimen of eating. Then—most often in the late afternoon—I'd be attacked by what I called the "hungry horrors." Stricken, I'd dash to the refrigerator or out to a nearby convenience store for a pound bag of chocolate-covered peanuts, one of my choice binge foods. This would in turn trigger a desire for more sugar, more pastry, anything with white flour. I'd been warned at Dickman House that I was a "wheataholic." (*Why not,* I had thought. *I seem to have been every other kind of "aholic" there is.*)

The tendency to rush to the refrigerator when things go wrong can be compulsivity at its worst. Fortunately, I had friends now to help me face down the food monster. They steered me to a group of singles in Billings who met for meals and fellowship often during the week. This accomplished three things. It made me: (1) eat on schedule; (2) choose nutritious foods; (3) retain the companionship I needed to strengthen my self-discipline.

Several of us in the singles group who had similar eating problems benefited from a list of alternatives to food-binging. Here are some steps we learned to take.

When the Urge To Binge Is Overpowering:[11]

1. Call a group member or friend. Keep calling until you reach someone.

2. Write the binge down instead of eating.

3. Take a bath or shower.

4. Take a walk.

5. Do a non-food-related activity outside the kitchen. Stay out of the kitchen.

6. Go to an eating disorder support group meeting.

7. Do a relaxation exercise or meditation.

8. Distract yourself with a craft project, book, or TV program.

9. Read something inspirational or positive.

10. Run or jog.

11. Take a nap.

12. Engross yourself in something.

13. Go to a concert, play, etc.

14. Think the binge through—"what I'll get out of it."

15. Put the binge off five minutes at a time.

16. Write down the things you want out of life.

17. Write down the things you've missed because of binging.

The following guidelines to good eating habits can be helpful:

1. Eat slowly and chew well—especially when emotionally upset.

2. When eating, only eat. No other activities such as TV, radio, reading, or driving.

3. Eat sitting down at a table.

4. Clear the table immediately when through eating.

5. Know what you're going to do after a meal—have a plan.

6. Throw leftovers away. It's okay!

It was also helpful to remember that it takes twenty minutes for our stomachs to register a "full" feeling. I tried to stop eating *before*

I felt full. The best defense I found against the hungry horrors and other assaults was to begin each day with an admission of my helplessness and dependence on God.

My religious faith has played a growing role in my overcoming these and other "monsters." A verse from the New Testament book of Romans is interesting, in this regard: "I do not understand what I do. For what I want to do I do not do, but what I hate I do."[12] This internal warring describes the compulsive woman to a T, and I am as dependent as the writer of these words in finding success by turning to Jesus Christ, my Higher Power, when I am overwhelmed by the temptation to succumb to one of my former compulsions.

The same biblical writer talks in another place about bringing "every thought captive" to Christ.[13] Is this God's suggestion to those of us who are dealing with compulsivity?

Many women, of course, do not choose this way of dealing with it. I understand. Regardless of a person's religious orientation, it is imperative only that she practice some form of quieting herself, of centering down, of broadening her perspective on life.

"Develop your spirituality through daily practice," advises Robin Norwood in *Women Who Love Too Much.* "Whether or not you have a belief in God, and if you do, whether or not you're on speaking terms with Him, you can still practice this step. . . . Even if you are a 100-percent atheist, perhaps you get pleasure and solace from a quiet walk, or contemplating a sunset or some aspect of nature. Whatever takes you beyond yourself and into a broader perspective on things is what this step is all about."

Along the way to recovery I found it necessary to break off relationships with old drinking friends or those who had "enabled" me when I was ill. As I expected, some heaped scorn on me as "self-righteous" or "judgmental" or "a lousy friend." Later, when I'm stronger, perhaps I can seek them out to try and establish relationships on a new basis.

Other good advice that came to me along the way:

"Stay in the present! Yesterday is a canceled check. Tomorrow is a promissory note. Today is ready cash. Spend it wisely. Enjoy life where you are right now."

Whenever I forgot and started to dwell on the past, I was dragged down into a numbing state of depression. Actually, I thought of it as a "depressionetta," a mere niggle compared to the crashing bottoming-out of the past. What helped me was having a meditation time while I walked in the morning and a prayer time when I took my personal inventory before retiring for the night. As I struggled through a succession of difficult choices day by day, I was chasing the little monsters out of my life.

"It takes time, effort, and faith to mature out of an addictive disposition," declares Stanton Peele, one of the foremost authorities on addiction. ". . . Therapy or no, the ultimate responsibility is still our own" [*Love and Addiction*].

In taking responsibility for my own recovery, and in breaking the pattern of negative thinking I've engaged in for most of my life, I'm learning to get my feelings out on the table, look them over, and realize they can be changed. One procedure is through simple positive statements such as the affirmations:

Changing the Negative to Positive[14]

1. I [your name] like myself. I am a lovable person.

2. I have the right to say no to people without losing their love.

3. Other people have the right to say no to me without hurting me.

4. I am building a perfectly functioning body.

5. I affirm health, harmony, peace, and abundance.

6. I am giving my subconscious mind a new blueprint for my life.

7. I am calm, relaxed, serene, and confident.

8. Smoking no longer appeals to me.

9. I am developing a taste for non-fattening foods.

10. Every day I am becoming more aware of things for which I can be thankful.

11. I have now enough time, energy, wisdom, and money to accomplish all my desires.

12. I have an abundant supply of energy and draw upon it at will.

13. I have an excellent memory and it is getting better every day.

14. I am well-organized in every phase of my life, giving me time for leisure.

15. I am able to relax as deeply as I wish at any time.

16. It is safe for me to love and trust people and to accept the love and trust that is my birthright.

17. I see myself in my right job, performing it completely and easily.

Learning to Like Yourself

Learning to fulfill our needs must begin early in infancy, and continue all our lives. If we fail to learn we will suffer, and this suffering always drives us to try unrealistic means to fulfill our needs. A person who does not learn as a little child to give and receive love may spend the rest of his life unsuccessfully trying to love.

—William Glasser, M.D.
Reality Therapy

*F*OR YEARS I'VE ASKED MYSELF WHY SOME PEOPLE CARRY AROUND SUCH A low self-image when they're as richly endowed with gifts and talents as anyone else.

In my case I've identified some partial answers dating to childhood. An early episode of sexual abuse produced in me a sense of shame because I felt somehow it was my fault that it happened. The silent, unhappy home where emotions were not acknowledged soon made me ashamed of any strong feelings. When eventually my parents divorced I felt still more shame, believing that undoubtedly this was my fault, too.

The root of compulsive behavior, as we have already seen, is shame. To compensate for my own shame, I became an overachiever and people-pleaser. This way I didn't have to face my own pain, anger, fear, and guilt. My constant attempts to win approval led me into a pattern of obsession about my appearance and the neatness of my surroundings. If everything looked impeccable on the outside, no one would ever know that inside there was such a mess.

Because I couldn't love myself, I searched for others to love me, especially men, even though subconsciously I didn't trust them. I was desperate for the reassurance that I was lovable. When these relationships didn't work out, I sought my reassurance from alcohol and food. My search for some sense of worth and meaning led me into a cult that left me haunted with more self-hate and condemnation than before. Soon all my compulsive behaviors and dependencies became woven together in a spiderweb trap. I'd break through in one area only to be strangled in another.

In thinking back to when my suicidally low self-image began a turnaround, I've identified some early steps:

1. Karen singling me out in the hospital as her friend. Her need compelled me to give instead of take.

2. Making a list of simple things to do my first day at home from the hospital—and then getting them done.

3. Making a successful case before the staff for my discharge from the hospital.

4. Stopping smoking.

5. Stopping drinking.

These action-steps may not even have been as important as the corresponding changes that took place in my mind and spirit. These changes, harder to trace, began at that magical moment in the hospital when I remembered a Scripture verse learned as a child: "By his stripes we are healed. . . ." I knew then my mind was not damaged beyond recall. The changes that followed revolved around the fundamental—and astonishing—awareness that I didn't have to prove anything to God. To my amazement he loved me unconditionally.

Despite my insights into the origins of a poor self-image, and how this can change, developing a sense of self-worth was a painfully slow process. It's a strange thing to encounter the real you for the first time in middle age. Strange and frightening. What if I didn't like me, let alone love me?

I did love the new freedom—freedom not to have secrets any longer. Freedom to be open and honest. Being able to share in groups, learning to have my own opinions instead of parroting those around me, helped self-esteem grow. Gradually I began to feel more comfortable with myself. For years I had been running and hiding from myself, searching for answers everywhere but inside.

At the four-year mark of my sobriety I felt a sense of peace, of being on target. I had moved in March 1984 back to my home state of Vermont, taking a small house in Montpelier next to my mother's even smaller one. (My stepfather had died the previous spring.) I hadn't wanted to move so far from my children, but they were all in their twenties, out in the working world, driving their own cars, busy with their own friends. We had loving relationships though not intimate.

So I settled into my little house in Vermont, quick to commit to an alcohol support group. I also converted the raised hearth of my living room fireplace into a makeshift altar. I laid a white lace cloth on the bricks and placed on it a pair of my Aunt Ethel's candleholders with white candles. It was here I spent much time in quiet prayer and reflection.

Sometimes my mind went back to the people I'd hurt—used and abused—and to situations I had tried to forget. As I repented of my sins against husbands, children, parents, friends, I asked God to show me where amends were possible and where restoration had to lie with him alone; where trying to clear my own conscience publicly would only lay further burdens on those I had injured.

Still other times I thought of people I needed to forgive, of anyone against whom I had nursed a grievance, starting with Uncle

Ralph. I'd write the name on a scrap of paper, say a prayer releasing that person from my judgment, and ask God's blessing on his or her life. Then I'd touch the paper to the nearest candle and watch old resentments turn to ashes in the fireplace.

What lightness and exhilaration of spirit followed! One by one the closed doors of my life were being opened, as I did what in effect amounted to a personal housecleaning.

Along the way I discovered ten exercises that have helped me begin to find the creativity I had lost. Since people recovering from addictive behavior have to face up to their need for personal disciplines, I offer them to you:

Ten Disciplines to Restore Creativity

1. Go "lean" one day a week. This is not necessarily a fast. Some who use this discipline reduce their food intake to juices, clear soups, and a few crackers.

2. Write a letter complimenting someone—or make it a telephone call. Be specific: "I admire the stand you took for that minority housing project," etc.

3. Once a week do something you've very seldom (if ever) done before. Go to the ballet, walk through a museum, try out a new recipe, plant some flowers, attend a church service.

4. Be completely honest for one full day in everything you say or do. If you can't be honest about your boss's expansion plans or your friend's new outfit, for example, say nothing.

5. For one hour think or pray on one subject. Or divide the hour into two separate periods, each devoted to one concern.

6. Express a heartfelt regret or ask forgiveness for something negative you have said or done fairly recently to a friend, co-worker, relative, etc. Do this through a letter or telephone call.

7. Spend one day being totally concerned about other people. This can be accomplished through volunteer work, through visits to

a hospital, through helping a friend with housework, through intercessory prayer. Avoid talk about yourself, your ideas, your plans.

8. For a set period of time—at least a day, perhaps a week or longer—keep your conversations with close friends or acquaintances or chance encounters on his/her interests solely. Focus on drawing the other person out. Learn what he/she thinks, feels, is experiencing.

9. Plan your activity in minute detail for one whole day and then live with this plan unless emergency situations arise. Try to anticipate everything that will happen and schedule time for telephone calls, for rest, recreation, eating, etc. See how close you can stick to your plan.

10. Set aside one day for obedience. As best you can let God and/or others determine what you do (within reason, of course). Consider yourself a total servant for this day. See yourself as a willing tool or instrument to bring joy and encouragement to others.

In the course of my own recovery, I decided the single life must be what I was now called to. I'd attended a number of retreats and workshops on how to find fulfillment as a single. I discovered I could help hurting single women, especially the ones with alcohol or drug problems, and felt drawn toward this work.

Sometimes I thought about marrying again, but always dismissed the thought. Two failures there had battered my self-image as a desirable person. And yet . . . something deep within me yearned to be a genuine partner. Not the needy, confused Sandy of the past, compulsively seeking a man to solve my problems, but a real wife, able to give as well as take. Could I hope to believe I had become, in a real sense, a new woman, clean and pure as the freshly fallen snow on my Vermont rooftop? I thought about this often, that first winter back East.

As I began telling my story here and there, a publisher contacted me and suggested I write a book. My newly won self-confidence quailed before such an assignment. I borrowed a typewriter and spent long, frustrating hours in front of it. When it was obvious I didn't know what I was doing, the publisher suggested I attend the *Decision* Magazine Writer's School to be held in St. Paul, Minnesota, in August 1984.

Once out there, I pored over the week's schedule, wondering what courses to take. On Monday afternoon there was to be a workshop on Creative Ideas by a longtime *Guideposts* editor named Leonard LeSourd. Hmmmm. I needed creative ideas for sure.

Monday morning there was talk at breakfast about the LeSourd workshop and about the death of his wife Catherine. "He must be awfully lonely," one woman said. "They were so close." Everyone seemed to know this Catherine and said her name with reverence.

Catherine who? I wondered to myself, not wanting to show my ignorance. "I've read *Christy* seven times!" someone gushed. Finally someone said Catherine Marshall.

Beyond Our Selves! I'd carried her book around for weeks at the Warm Springs Hospital. I had flipped through the pages thinking, "This woman has it too put together for me." Several times I had stopped at the dedication page—*To Len*—wondering who he could be.

That afternoon I arrived at the auditorium early and found a seat directly in front of the speaker's podium. Soon a handsome gray-haired man wearing a blue-and-white striped seersucker jacket and light blue trousers stepped up to it. Why, as Len LeSourd began to speak, did my heart do a ridiculous flip-flop? I didn't know this man at all.

With so many people crowding around him after the talk, I felt shy about introducing myself. I walked out of the lecture hall regretting that I would never exchange even a word with him.

At dinner, however, Len chanced to sit at the same family-style table where I was. Somehow I found myself telling him about my struggle with alcoholism. To my amazement, tears formed in his slate-blue eyes. "I have a niece who is battling that problem," he said. "Would you be willing to write to her?"

He gave me her address and took mine. Noting that I lived in Vermont, he mentioned that he would be driving through New England later that month. "Maybe I'll give you a call."

Three weeks later in Vermont, my telephone rang. Len was in the area; could I make a room reservation for him somewhere nearby for Saturday night? He'd become such a workaholic since Catherine's death, he explained, that his family had needled him into taking this vacation trip through New England. "I'm supposed to stop regularly and smell the flowers."

I took that as a personal mission. I reserved a room at the Montpelier Tavern Inn, a historic spot where stagecoaches used to stop. Now for a surprise welcome.

Margaret, a creative friend of mine, and I borrowed the key to his room. We pinned a newsprint banner—*Welcome to Montpelier, Len!*—to the top of the drapes. On one of the twin beds, we placed a large black teddy bear, decked out in an antique lace collar and black hat trimmed with violets. Nestled next to the bear was a straw basket labeled *First-Aid Kit for the Weary Traveler.* In it was a box of Vermont maple candy, a clump of red grapes, imported crackers and cheese, and a bottle of aspirin.

On the small table by the picture window was a bouquet of black-eyed Susans. I smiled recalling how I'd picked them the day before in a drenching rain. Was my compulsive nature showing? Well, Len had admitted to a compulsive side, too.

Late in the afternoon the telephone rang again. Len was chuckling. "There seems to be a bear in my room. Does she have a name?"

"Yes. 'Golly.' "

"I see." A pause. "Is she a good roommate?"

"Oh, yes. She almost never snores."

After our first dinner date at the Trapp Family Lodge in nearby Stowe, Vermont, Len and I began to see a lot of one another. As the weeks passed and he kept discovering reasons to come to Vermont, we acknowledged that we were falling in love. At the same time, both of us were impressed by a principle we chose to govern our relationship: *The best comes out of self-denial.*

I'd known that with my mind all my life. Even as my compulsivity drove me to indulge every passion—whether for chocolate, clothes, booze, cigarettes—I'd known that a saner, healthier existence meant saying no to these things. What I'd never been able to do was make my *no* stick.

Now, because of the psychological, chemical, and spiritual healing taking place in me, I found a bracing kind of joy in self-denial. By forgoing a sexual relationship, Len and I became friends first, learned how to laugh together, got to know each other at a deeper level.

As weeks turned into months and the desire for marriage grew in us both, we set out to visit all members of our two families. The visit that showed me much about my recovery was when I joined Len for a weekend at his farm in Virginia, forty-five miles west of Washington. Living with him in her own wing at Evergreen Farm was his mother-in-law, Leonora Wood, whose exploits as an eighteen-year-old schoolteacher in the Great Smoky Mountains back in 1912 formed the basis for Catherine's novel *Christy.* Mother Wood, then 93, was the beloved and respected family matriarch. How would she receive me? And how would Len's friends and business associates respond to the new woman in his life?

After the Sunday morning service at Len's church, one woman with piercing gray eyes grilled me in a polite way, drawing out that I had been twice married and twice divorced and was presently unemployed because I was trying to write a book. Hardly a success story.

Nor was my time with Mother Wood encouraging. Though frail

and bent in body, Mrs. Wood was a towering personage with an active mind, mixed with the loneliness of a mother and grandmother who had said premature good-byes to a husband, two children, and three grandchildren. She was kind and courteous to me, but I sensed underneath a steely opposition. And why not? To her I must have seemed a brash outsider with designs on taking Catherine's place.

Wherever I went in the nineteen-room farmhouse, Catherine's presence preceded me. She smiled at me from dozens of photos about the home and office. Her serene gaze from a magnificent oil portrait in Evergreen's formal parlor met my own each time I came through the front door.

Only a few years earlier, I would have fallen into the trap of comparing myself with her. Shame-ridden people—compulsive people—do that. Finding no worth in themselves, they make other people the standard. Other people's achievements, other people's virtues.

I learned, happily, that I was far enough along in my recovery to realize that of course I could not take Catherine's place, or the place of anyone else. I was me. I'd spent the past few years getting to know me—and, wonder of wonders, I was beginning to like me.

Still, there came a bleak moment when I just wanted to flee. Clearly I didn't belong among these productive, successful people. In my despair I sought out Len and suggested I return early to Vermont. He looked at me, smiled, and shook his head.

"It's rough for you, Sandy, but you'll make it."

"But your family is so . . . put together. I'm still struggling, and I'm a failure as a wife and parent."

"You are not a failure. You're an overcomer. That's even better than being a success."

I knew for sure at that moment why I loved this man.

Other family get-togethers followed over the next few months—

with Len's three children and their two spouses, his stepson and family, my three children, and my parents.

The final green light for me came after the Mother's Day church service one May Sunday in Virginia. Len and I had taken Mother Wood there, packing her wheelchair into the trunk of the car. When I leaned down to release the brake before wheeling her out, she drew my face very close to her own and looked into my eyes with her incredibly intense blue ones. "I love you, Sandy," she said softly. "I'm so grateful you're going to be part of our family."

Len and I were married on June 22, 1985, at the Trapp Family Lodge, in Stowe, Vermont—ten months after our first date there the previous August. As we began to adjust to each other in marriage, we both took a hard look at compulsive behavior persisting into the present—mine and his. Len had been a workaholic and a sportsaholic. Forty years of meeting publication deadlines, often working past midnight and over the weekend, had produced an imbalance in his life. Often his change of pace came through a more-than-casual involvement in televised sports, especially pro football.

Len's emotional involvement with the Dallas Cowboys was a revelation. "To root for a team you need to read up on the players, coaches, get all the local color," he told me by way of explaining the pile of sports magazines by his chair.

"But why does losing a game take on more importance than a nuclear accident or a disastrous earthquake?" I asked.

Len looked reflective. "I'm powerless over my sports addiction and my life has become unmanageable," he said with a grin. Then, more seriously, he confessed to disturbance over the intensity, even destructiveness, of fans absorbed with a team, the ridiculous salaries of the players which often lead to drug use, the obsession with winning.

He admitted that involvement in a late-night game on television often rendered him sleepless for hours afterwards, wiping him out for most of the next day. Sunday afternoon games often assumed such importance, he further revealed, that he would duck social engagements, even family responsibilities, to watch his team play.

"Next Sunday I won't watch the game," he declared suddenly. "We'll go for a drive, smell the autumn leaves."

Next Sunday afternoon we did go out for a couple of hours. Upon our return he fidgeted miserably about the living room, then switched on the TV. Soon he was glued to the action. I watched him with bemused understanding.

For I'm still battling certain compulsions in my life. Shopping, for one. Sometimes I still come out of stores with more items than I planned to buy, and rail at myself later.

Then there was the time I made a special greeting card to celebrate the birth of one of Len's grandchildren. It started out as a simple card. Four hours later it had grown into a huge eight-color poster announcing *The First Annual Mary Catherine Lader Golf Classic.* The following day, playing golf with friends, Len and I displayed the poster on the back of our golf cart and sent photos of the "event" to Len's daughter and son-in-law.

It was this spontaneous "golf classic," silly but fun, that helped me understand something about compulsive behavior.

It's not all bad!

Along with certain native gifts and abilities, we often have an inner drive that helps us channel gifts into a successful career. We need the tenacity, the determination, the focused energy to achieve worthwhile things. Len's compulsion for work made him a topflight editor; my compulsion for quality—whether in dress design or floral displays—is also an exercise of my gift. The all-out effort poured into a project can make that project shine.

This was an important discovery for me. I'm not to crush my zealous nature, or scorn it. It's a part of me, a kind of inner dynamo given me for a purpose. Only for years I misused it. I let this driving quality inside, the "I-want-what-I-want-when-I-want-it" part of my nature, take over my life.

Now I'm striving to bring this compulsive part of me, like the rest of my being, under control. There are times when I try to take charge again, which we're all free to do. But I'm learning to catch myself.

In my early mornings, for example. As soon as we got married, Len and I began praying first thing in the day that God would take the inner drive we both have and guide it. This seems to be happening.

I also find continuous healing as I shift my attention away from myself to other people, focusing on the words *serve, give, teach, share.* As parents and grandparents, this involves Len and me with more than forty people in our family alone. But it doesn't stop there.

Len and I have begun conducting team workshops on the subject of compulsive behavior. Researching the subject has taken us to treatment centers around the country. What troubles me is that medical and religious programs do not work more closely together, since I received such solid help from both disciplines. The main differences stem from definition. The scientific world regards compulsive behavior as a disease—chemical or psychological or both. Christians consider it a sin.

It was a lift to find one treatment center that combines both approaches.

When we drove into the Dunklin Memorial Camp thirty miles west of Stuart, Florida, the spacious grounds were alive with activity: men on tractors, or wielding shovels, or hoisting furniture into the back of a mud-spattered pickup truck. This alcohol and drug treatment center was clearly a busy place.

We parked and entered a low stucco office building to receive a warm welcome from Mickey Evans, who over a twenty-three-year period has built a sizable complex out of eight hundred acres of Florida swamp. He eased his powerful frame into a desk swivel chair and got quickly to the facts:

"This is a center for male alcoholics and drug addicts," he began. "We can house about thirty. Most of the men are poly-addicted; we don't get 'simple' alcoholics today except a few older men. We don't detox here. That's done down at the center in Fort Pierce. The men come to us sober. They're here to work and learn. I tell each man, 'There's a waiting list to get into this place. If you want to stay here, you must earn the right. If you don't, I'll give your bed to someone who'll make better use of it.' "

Mickey went on to describe excruciating difficulties with cocaine-users, calling this drug "deadly beyond our understanding; it can stay in the system for up to ten months."

Then came words that elated me: "Some Christian programs treat addiction as a sin, which it obviously is. Sin simply means 'off-the-mark'—and these men's lives are certainly that. But some of these places go further and take the stand that alcoholism and drug addiction are *not* physical diseases. They shun all medical helps, including the Twelve-Step program. After twenty-three years, I've concluded that chemical dependence is both sin and sickness. We treat addictions as a disease and use the Twelve-Step program that stresses commitment to a Higher Power. Here the Higher Power is Jesus Christ.

"We insist each man have a quiet time first thing in the morning," Mickey continued. "He also must make a daily moral inventory of the past twenty-four hours. This helps him get in touch with the attitudes that are motivating him. Addicts have to change their attitudes before they can change their behavior. All the men keep a personal journal to record their insights into themselves. Also, some of them never knew prayer is a two-way street. I feel the quiet time—learning to listen as well as to speak—is the key to the whole program."

The work program is also crucial to the addict's recovery, Mickey explained. This includes kitchen duty, laundry, painting, ranch work, gardening, caring for the horses. Residents grow most of their food and raise their own beef.

Weekends are devoted to family programs, when wives and children come out to participate in various activities. Even spouses are asked to do a daily moral inventory. Mickey considers addiction a family disease: "Sometimes the wife and children are sicker than the addict himself."

The Dunklin Camp has seen some remarkable improvements in families on these weekends. "Often it's the first time they've been able to sit down and be honest with each other," says Mickey. "Also, the first time the patient has been thinking clearly enough to hear what his family has to say to him. We won't take a man unless his family will agree to be part of every weekend program."

At first addicts were taken in without charge. But as time passed Mickey became aware of the human tendency to take lightly what we get for nothing. Though the program is still financed largely by contributions, the fee is now set at a thousand dollars for each three months of treatment. Each family pays fifteen dollars for the weekend program.

If a man is too poor to pay, but does have a television set, a gun, or some garden tools, Mickey will accept these as payment. He is convinced that unless a man has some kind of material investment in his treatment, he tends to drift through it. For those who stay in treatment for one year, there is a ninety percent recovery rate.

When I asked Mickey about a comparable program for women, he said that one Dunklin graduate and his wife had recently started a program in the Orlando area, based on Dunklin procedures.

People helping people. That's the message I receive as I look back on all I've learned over the past ten years. Karen; my Filipino doctor at Warm Springs; my friend Lois Ann; Dirk, who intervened when I was flying without chemicals; my counselor Gwen. . . . The list goes on and on.

* * *

July 9, 1986, was an extraordinary day, as well as a traumatic one. Len and I had traveled to Billings, Montana, to visit my children and meet with certain groups. But I was apprehensive about a speech I was to give before two hundred women at the Warbonnet Inn.

As our hostess for the week drove me to the meeting, I looked at my old hometown with new eyes. So many familiar landmarks, most filled with painful memories. The Warbonnet Inn itself: twelve years before I'd come to this same hotel ballroom for that first Serenity Society conference. How dazed and confused and frightened I'd been back then! And how much worse after my involvement with that cult. Now I felt alive, filled with enthusiasm.

As the audience started arriving my excitement—and nervousness—mounted. Many of the women had been dear friends during the twenty-one years I had lived in Billings.

Kathy, my former neighbor, who had led me to the seminar and church where I received my healing.

And Hilda, the woman who had been more of a mother to my children as our housecleaner for twenty years than I had.

And the grocery store clerk, Shelly, who had helped me with my grocery list when I could barely function—who had loved me when I couldn't love myself.

I was delighted to greet my former mother-in-law who visited me faithfully when I was in the state mental institution and encouraged me during my dark years.

Best of all, my daughter, Lisa, who had taken the afternoon off from her work at a video store.

Never before had there been assembled in one room so many people I loved, so many who had touched my life: the women from the Thursday prayer group, some of my tennis and bridge club friends; friends from the singles group; even former babysitters.

After the introduction I moved up to the podium before these people, opened my mouth to speak . . . and instead broke down and wept. When I regained my composure, I told the story of my compulsive behavior, addictions, hospitalization and recovery, having a strange sense of being at one point or another *every woman* in the room.

Looking back on my life, I was overwhelmed with gratitude for the patience, love, and support of so many people: family members who always believed in me somehow during the darkest of times; close friends who never quit praying that a miracle would occur in my life; and a loving and forgiving God who brought me back from the pit of hopelessness. Now I could say with total conviction that there are no hopeless situations. A helping hand awaits anyone, everyone who reaches out for it.

For I knew only too well the frustration, the pain, the sense of failure, the depression, the desire to self-destruct that compulsive women feel at one time or another. I had been through it all and discovered there are no hopeless cases. There is a way through the darkness into the light. We compulsive women can be freed from our bondage.

The way is long but it's possible. It begins with a frank acknowledgment of the areas of our addiction, all of them—a surrender to the reality of the problem. Critical are the steps of self-forgiveness and forgiving others, going back as far as we can remember. Face any long-buried emotion; walk through it, not around it. A "feelings journal," like my anger diary, may be helpful in this. A support group is invaluable. Developing a relationship with a Higher Power is crucial.

Then come the building-up steps. Set a succession of reachable goals. Maybe the admonition *Do it now* will be as helpful to you as it is to me. Every small victory raises our self-esteem, lets us know we can succeed, that we can do something even better. At last we will be ready to move beyond focusing primarily on ourselves and reach out toward those around us.

What a great feeling it is to know we have stopped being takers—that at last we have something to give!

PART TWO

HANDBOOK
OF
SPECIAL
HELPS

CONTENTS

BOOK TWO—HANDBOOK OF SPECIAL HELPS

Contents

Contents

Contents

Introduction:

How Do I Get Back on Track?

While both men and women are prone to compulsive behavior, the problems of women especially concern me—because I have been there. Correction, I am still there because I will be coping with my compulsive nature the rest of my life.

The good news, for me, is that I am on the recovery road. I know what I have to do to keep on that road. I can't do it on my own power; primarily it is surrender to the Higher Power that keeps me on track. But there are other guideposts that give me direction every day of my life.

This Handbook of Special Helps, the result of months of research, is a compilation of some of the resources and tools available for addictive/compulsive people. Though far from being a complete listing, it can chart a course of where to go in finding the recovery road that is right for you. Suggested action: Go through the listing of helps on the contents page and focus on the areas of compulsivity to which you relate.

My hope for you is that if you are being defeated by behavior you can't control, as I was for so many years, you will decide today that it is time to do something about it.

SSL

I. Self-Help Programs

1. ALCOHOL ADDICTION

The Twelve-Step Program of Alcoholics Anonymous (AA)

These steps are the cornerstone of most treatment programs. Alcoholics Anonymous is the pioneering group that established the basic principles to guide the addict back to health.

AA was founded in Akron, Ohio, by two men, publicly identified as Bill W., a New York stockbroker, and Dr. Bob S., a surgeon. Both had long histories of irresponsible drinking. Both had been considered hopeless alcoholics.

In the fall of 1934, Bill W., hospitalized for alcoholism, experienced a sudden spiritual "awakening" that seemed to free him of the desire to drink. He tried to persuade other alcoholics that they could experience the same transformation, but none recovered.

The following spring in Akron, after the collapse of a business venture, Bill was seriously tempted to drink again. Fearful of the inevitable consequences of taking the first drink, Bill recalled that he had had no desire for liquor during the preceding months while he had been working with alcoholics in New York. In desperation, he sought a similar contact in Akron and was led to Dr. Bob. The latter, impressed by Bill's recovery story and by the opportunity to share his own drinking problems with an admitted alcoholic, achieved sobriety shortly thereafter.

More important, the two men discovered that their own sobriety was strengthened when they offered to share it with others, stressing their own practical experience as recovered alcoholics. By the fall of 1935, a small group of sober alcoholics was meeting regularly in Akron, known as the Fellowship of Alcoholics Anonymous.

The following two-paragraph definition is now read at many AA meetings:

> Alcoholics Anonymous is a fellowship of men and women who share their experience, strength and hope with each other that they may solve their common problem and help others to recover from alcoholism.
>
> The only requirement for membership is a desire to stop drinking. There are no dues or fees for AA membership; we are self-supporting through our own contributions. AA is not allied with any sect, denomination, politics, organization or institution; does not wish to engage in any controversy, neither endorses nor opposes any causes. Our primary purpose is to stay sober and help other alcoholics to achieve sobriety.

Preamble printed
with permission of
The AA *Grapevine,* Inc.

Step One: *We admitted we were powerless over alcohol—that our lives had become unmanageable.*

Step Two: *Came to believe that a power greater than ourselves could restore us to sanity.*

Step Three: *Made a decision to turn our will and our lives over to the care of God as we understood Him.*

Step Four: *Made a searching and fearless moral inventory of ourselves.*

Step Five: *Admitted to God, to ourselves, and to another human being the exact nature of our wrongs.*

Step Six: *Were entirely ready to have God remove all these defects of character.*

Step Seven: *Humbly asked Him to remove our shortcomings.*

Step Eight: *Made a list of persons we had harmed, and became willing to make amends to them all.*

Step Nine: *Made direct amends to such people wherever possible, except when to do so would injure them or others.*

Step Ten: *Continued to take personal inventory and when we were wrong promptly admitted it.*

Step Eleven: *Sought through prayer and meditation to improve our conscious contact with God as we understood Him, praying only for knowledge of His will for us and the power to carry that out.*

Step Twelve: *Having had a spiritual awakening as the result of these steps, we tried to carry this message to alcoholics, and to practice these principles in all our affairs.*

The Twelve Steps reprinted with
permission of Alcoholics Anonymous
World Services, Inc.

How You Can Apply the Twelve Steps

Here are suggested guidelines for adapting the Twelve-Step program to your compulsion/addiction. These comments are observations of the author and not of Alcoholics Anonymous.

Step One: This is perhaps the most difficult step for the addict who does not want to concede weakness and helplessness, who says, "I can stop any time I choose to." Taking this first step means conceding that there has been a long period of self-deception. But for progress to begin, the ego must topple off the throne. Then the addict can admit, "I'm no longer in control."

Step Two: The addict is faced with a second momentous decision. Previously she admitted her life was out of control; now she admits she needs help, not from a husband or friend, but from that area of a mysterious Higher Power. Most addicts have trouble acknowledging this Higher Power because self has been their higher power for years. Now comes an agonizing shift—a transferral from a power that's broken down to a power that's new and different, a threat to all that was comfortable and familiar.

Step Three: The progression of decisions the addict must make continues. First, an admission of powerlessness; second, an acknowledgment of strength greater than our own; third, a decision to surrender to the greater strength. How one resists that idea! Yet inner release comes through giving up that hard-core area of self-reliance. Letting go brings peace. You give up something that's been destructive to get something that promises health.

Step Four: This is a most painful step for the addict who would prefer to blot out of her consciousness all the terrible things she has done to herself and others. Making a searching, fearless moral inventory means *writing down* people, places, events, dates with brutal candor and incisiveness. Spare nothing. This is the way toward recovery.

Step Five: Looking on paper at the specifics of our moral inventory has to raise the question "What can I do about all this?"

Try to forget it? That's the road back to chemical dependency.

Confession? Yes. To God and to another person.

What person?

Someone you trust, who will keep what you say in confidence.

Step Six: After confessing their wrongdoing, many women leave it there, figuring they've done all that's necessary. God does forgive, doesn't he? Now we can go on with our lives.

But wait! What about those character defects? Pride, anger, lust, jealousy, resentment, and so on. They have become "old friends." Are we ready for God to change these things? Are we willing to do what he asks to bring about the change?

We need to make a conscious act of setting our wills in a state of readiness so that we can receive any instructions.

Step Seven: After an act of the will that says to God, "I'm ready for you to change me," then comes the next step, asking God to take action. We have moved ahead steadily from unbelief or indifference to a relationship with God. Now comes the expectation of a miracle! Those who see their Higher Power as human destiny or nature or some other impersonal force may struggle with these steps. If so, they may want to rethink what or who the Higher Power, for them, really is.

Step Eight: The key words here are *became willing*. The act of making a list will be difficult because of painful memories, some of which may have been blotted out. A good procedure is: (1) Take pencil and paper, go back in time, and write down in some chronological order with dates, the names of people harmed and what the offenses were; (2) Pray that God will unblock your mind and reveal the people and events he wants you to include; (3) Ask him to help you *become willing* to make amends.

Step Nine: In this crucial and painful step of the recovery process, there is need for sensitivity and discernment as to whom we contact. At an alcohol family support meeting one man whose problem was lust admitted that attempts to make restitution to a woman with whom he had had sexual encounters years before backfired on his current marital situation. Consider each person on your list, seeking wisdom about what action to take.

Step Ten: The addict has lived in a world of self-indulgence for so long that a formidable defense system separates her from the rest of the world. The road to recovery involves tearing down this defense system. Coming to the point where the addict can admit a mistake, which also may mean an apology, is a big step toward health. "I was wrong. I am sorry. I made a mistake. Please forgive me." There's healing every time these words are uttered.

Step Eleven: Moving into prayer and meditation is a major step for the addict because it means the building of a relationship with God, a process that could take months, even years. On top of that the addict is to pray for power to follow God's will. For some, Bible study classes and prayer are essential to make Step Eleven work.

Step Twelve: This last step is a clarion call to reach out to other addicts. Unlike the previous steps, most of which involve pain, this one flows almost irresistibly from the newfound joy and purpose of our lives. The transition from compulsive self-centeredness to being "others-centered" releases undreamed-of energy into daily living.

Twelve Rewards of the Twelve-Step Program

1 Hope instead of desperation.
2. Faith instead of despair.
3. Courage instead of fear.
4. Peace of mind instead of confusion.
5. Self-respect instead of self-contempt.
6. Self-confidence instead of helplessness.
7. The respect of others instead of their pity and contempt.
8. A clean conscience instead of a sense of guilt.
9. Real friendships instead of loneliness.

10. A clean pattern of life instead of a purposeless existence.

11. The love and understanding of our families instead of their doubts and fears.

12. The freedom of a happy life instead of the bondage of a drugged obsession.

Remember, the task ahead of us is never as great as the power behind us.

Drugs Alcoholics Should Avoid[1]

The following is a partial list of drugs demonstrated to be hazardous to alcoholics and other chemically dependent people.

- All sedatives, including barbiturates and synthetic drugs, barbiturates such as Nembutal, Seconal, Tuinal, etc., and synthetic sedatives such as Doriden, Quaalude, Dalmane, Placidyl, etc.

- All narcotics, including opium derivatives such as codeine, morphine, heroin; and synthetic narcotics such as Demerol, etc.

- All tranquilizers, including the newest ones. Of special danger are Valium, Xanax, and Librium due to their wide usage and addictive capabilities.

- Most pain-relieving medications such as Darvon, Talwin, etc. Darvon seems to act as a tranquilizer, and Talwin has characteristics of a narcotic. Both these drugs are capable of producing severe addictions.

- All antihistamines.

- Drugstore medications containing antihistamines or scopolamine, such as Nytol, Sominex, Contac, Dristan, NyQuil, and even Miles Nervine.

- Antidepressants and stimulants such as Elavil, Ritalin, amphetamine compounds, etc.

- Cough medicines and other medications containing narcotics, alcohol, or antihistamines. This means almost *all* cough syrups and *many* liquid vitamin preparations.

- Weight control tablets.

- Reserpine compounds, which are basically tranquilizers. Preparations containing reserpine prescribed for hypertension should be used with caution and only when absolutely necessary.

Danger Signals for Women

There are numerous checklists of danger signals—most of them based on what is known about male drinkers. This one, prepared by the National Council on Alcoholism, is one of the few aimed specifically at women.

- Do you drink when you're feeling depressed, in the hope that it will make you feel better?

- Do you regularly use alcohol as medicine—to relieve menstrual cramps, help you sleep, calm your nerves?

- Do you talk a lot about drinking?

- Do you need a drink to feel sociable?

- Do you feel more witty or attractive when you are drinking?

- Do you drink when under pressure, or after an argument? Do you drink to drown out angry feelings or to relax?

- Do you try to get someone to buy liquor for you because you are ashamed to buy it yourself?

• Do you buy liquor at different places so no one will know how much you purchase?

• Do you hide the empty bottles and dispose of them secretly?

• Do you plan in advance to reward yourself with a little drinking bout after you've worked hard in the house or on the job?

• Are you permissive with your children because you feel guilty about the way you have behaved while you were drinking?

• Do you have "blackouts"—periods about which you remember nothing?

• Do you ever phone the hostess of a party the next day and ask if you hurt anyone's feelings or made a fool of yourself?

• Do you find cigarette holes in your clothes or the furniture but can't remember when you made them?

• Do you take an extra drink or two before leaving for a party, though you know liquor will be served there?

• Do you wonder if anyone knows how much you drink?

• Do you feel panicky when faced with nondrinking days, or when you are without money to purchase alcohol?

• Do you invent social occasions for drinking, such as inviting friends for lunch, cocktails, or dinner or arranging business appointments around mealtimes or after work?

• Do you ever carry liquor in your purse?

• Do you become defensive when someone mentions your drinking?

• Do you become irritated when unexpected guests reduce your liquor supply?

- Do you try to cover up when you can't remember promises and feel ashamed when you misplace or lose things?

- Do you drive your car though you've been drinking, feeling certain you are in complete control of yourself?

- Do you have prescriptions for sleeping pills or tranquilizers that you use along with alcohol?

- Do you use alcohol to engage in or avoid sexual activity?

Any woman who answers yes to more than five of these questions may have an alcohol problem—but even a few affirmative answers may be a sign of serious trouble.

Which One Describes You?

Woman to Woman, a women's alcohol-awareness group, defines three levels of alcohol consumption.

- Light drinker: one or two drinks a month.

- Moderate drinker: one or two drinks a few times a week.

- Heavy drinker: two or more drinks every day.

A drink is defined as five ounces of wine, a twelve-ounce can of beer, or one and one half ounces of liquor.

From *New Woman,* Sept. 1988
Holly G. Atkinson, M.D., M.S.J.

The Dry Drunk[2]

When an alcoholic is not drinking but the out-of-control behavior and attitude problems continue.

(Checklist of Symptoms Leading to Relapse)

1. Exhaustion. Allowing yourself to become overly tired or be in poor health. Some alcoholics are also prone to work addictions; perhaps

they are in a hurry to make up for lost time. Good health and enough rest are important. If you feel good, you are more apt to think well. Feel bad and your thinking is apt to deteriorate. Feel bad enough and you might begin thinking a drink couldn't make it any worse.

2. Dishonesty. This begins with a pattern of unnecessary little lies and deceits with fellow workers, friends, and family. Then come important lies to yourself. This is called rationalizing—making excuses for not doing what you do not want to do, or for doing what you should not do.

3. Impatience. Things are not happening fast enough. Or others are not doing what they should or what you want them to.

4. Argumentativeness. Arguing small and ridiculous points of view indicates a need to always be right. "Why don't you be reasonable and agree with me?" Looking for an excuse to drink?

5. Depression. Unreasonable and unaccountable despair may occur in cycles and should be dealt with—talked about.

6. Frustration. At people and also because things may not be going your way. Remember, everything is not going to go just the way you want it.

7. Self-Pity. "Why do these things happen to me?" "Why must I be alcoholic?" "Nobody appreciates all I am doing."

8. Cockiness. Got it made. No longer fear alcoholism. Going into drinking situations to prove to others you have no problem. Do this often enough and it will wear down your defenses.

9. Complacency. "Drinking was the farthest thing from my mind." Not drinking was no longer a conscious thought either. It is dangerous to let up on disciplines because everything is going well. Always to have a little fear is a good thing. More relapses occur when things are going well than otherwise.

10. Expecting Too Much from Others. "I've changed; why hasn't everyone else?" It's a plus if they do—but it is still not your problem if they do not. They may not trust you yet; may still be looking for

further proof. You cannot expect others to change their lifestyles just because you have.

11. Letting Up on Disciplines. Prayer, meditation, daily inventory, alcohol support group attendance. This can stem from either complacency or boredom. You cannot afford to be bored with your program. The cost of relapse is always too great.

12. Use of Mood-Altering Chemicals. You may feel the need to ease things with a pill, and your doctor may go along with you. You may never have had a problem with chemicals other than alcohol, but you can easily lose sobriety starting this way—about the most subtle way to have a relapse. Remember, you will be cheating! The reverse of this is true for drug-dependent persons who start to drink.

13. Wanting Too Much. Do not set goals you cannot reach with normal effort. Do not expect too much. It's always great when good things you were not expecting happen. You will get what you are entitled to as long as you do your best, but maybe not as soon as you think you should. "Happiness is not having what you want, but wanting what you have."

14. Forgetting Gratitude. You may be looking negatively on your life, concentrating on problems that still are not totally corrected. Nobody wants to be a Pollyanna, but it is good to remember where you started from—and how much better life is now.

15. "It Can't Happen to Me." This is dangerous thinking. Almost anything can happen to you and is more likely to if you get careless. Remember, you have a progressive disease, and you will be in worse shape if you relapse.

16. Omnipotence. This is a feeling that results from a combination of many of the above. You now have all the answers for yourself and others. No one can tell you anything. You ignore suggestions or advice from others. Relapse is probably imminent unless drastic change takes place.

Summary: Clearly, the time to prevent a relapse is long before the irrational thinking has reached the final insanity of taking the first drink, pill or fix.

See the AA listing in your local telephone directory or newspaper schedule of events or write:

Alcoholics Anonymous
World Services, Inc.
475 Riverside Drive
New York, NY 10115
(212) 870-3400

Suggested Reading

Alcoholics Anonymous. *Alcoholics Anonymous, The Big Book,* 3rd ed. New York: Alcoholics Anonymous World Services, Inc., 1976.

Alcoholics Anonymous. *Twelve Steps and Twelve Traditions.* New York: Alcoholics Anonymous World Services, Inc., 1952.

Meryman, Richard. *Broken Promises, Mended Dreams.* Boston, Mass.: Little, Brown & Co., 1984.

Spickard, Anderson A., M.D. and Thompson, Barbara. *Dying for a Drink.* Waco, Tex.: Word, Inc., 1985.

DeJong, Alexander. *Help and Hope for the Alcoholic.* Wheaton, Ill.: Tyndale House Publishers, 1982.

Dunn, Jerry G. *God Is for the Alcoholic.* Chicago, Illinois: Moody Press, 1965.

Sandmaier, Marian. *The Invisible Alcoholics: Women and Alcohol Abuse in America.* New York: McGraw-Hill Book Company, 1981.

Manning, Brennan. *A Stranger to Self-Hatred.* Denville, N.J.: Dimension Books, 1982.

2. DRUG ADDICTION

Today the main focus of drug rehabilitation seems to center on cocaine, including crack and "ice." Yet there are eight substances that have destroyed the lives of millions of people. Here is information about them:[3]

Facts about Eight Deadly Drugs

Cocaine

- Causes heart palpitations, which can become chronic and can cause death by cardiac arrest. Cocaine acts directly on the heart, and also on the area of the brain that controls the heart and lungs.

- Increases the pulse rate and blood pressure by constricting the blood vessels and accelerating the heart. This can result in stroke.

- Causes epileptic seizures.

- Causes chronic nausea or vomiting.

- Causes chronic fatigue and exhaustion.

- Causes chronic mood swings, including depression, paranoia, and irritability.

- Brings about suicidal tendencies.

- Causes chronic sleep problems.

- Impairs the appetite by fooling the brain into thinking the user has eaten. Users lose weight and develop vitamin deficiencies.

- Brings on a hard-hitting "crash" as the drug's effect wears off, causing a strong desire to take more cocaine for relief.

- Anesthetizes the vocal cords, causing chronic sore throat and voice problems.

- Causes chronic nosebleeds and runny nose through its effects on the nasal passages. Large ulcers can result, followed by eventual loss of the septum—the skin that separates the nostrils. Causes sinus problems, resulting in headaches.

- Invites other addictions. Cocaine abusers often depend on alcohol, marijuana, or heroin to help them sleep or to combat the jittery feeling that characterizes the cocaine high.

- Causes sexual problems. Habitual cocaine use causes a chronic loss of interest in sex, as well as impairment of sexual performance.

- Causes compulsive behavior, such as constantly straightening a tie or licking the lips.

Alcohol

- Causes birth defects. Babies of mothers who drink during pregnancy are likely to be small and have facial deformities; those of fathers who drink heavily during the six months prior to conception are likely to be small.

- Causes liver damage.

- Changes the metabolism of some heart cells, which can cause fibrillation (uncontrolled fluttering of the heart), arrhythmias (disturbances in the heart's rhythm), and possibly heart attack.

- Damages the pancreas, which hinders digestion and upsets blood sugar balance.

- Impairs absorption of nutrients in the intestine, causing malnutrition. Deficiency of vitamin B1 resulting from poor absorption can cause neurological damage to the brain. The liver's failure to absorb vitamin A causes night blindness.

- Impairs immune system through its interference with the production of white blood cells.

- Enlarges red blood cells, causing high blood pressure.

- Alters the hormone balance so that the body is in a state of permanent stress.

- Disrupts menstrual cycle.

- Interferes with sexual performance in males by interfering with the production of the hormone testosterone. Shrinks the testicles and decreases fertility by lowering the sperm count.

- Causes slurred speech, disorientation, lack of coordination, and impaired memory, perception, and judgment.

LSD

- Alters perception and can cause sensory distortions.

- Impairs judgment.

- With long-term use, can cause "flashbacks": periodic distortions of vision or time perception, as well as periods of emotional imbalance and the intrusion of dreamlike states while awake. Presumed to be due to permanent damage to certain brain systems.

PCP

- PCP (phenylcyclohexyl piperidine) may cause, in large doses, permanent impairment of brain function, including motor control, memory, concentration, and the ability to think clearly. The possibility of permanent brain damage is currently being studied.

- Causes visual, auditory, and motor disturbances in babies born to mothers who have used PCP. Damage may be permanent.

• Brings on a psychotic state resembling schizophrenia, characterized by delusions and hallucinations. Behavior is unpredictable and often violent. Macabre murders and mutilations have been committed by those under PCP's influence; users are also prone to injury or death from drowning or jumping from buildings.

• Distorts sense of time and distance; some users have drowned in the bathtub, as if they thought it was a much larger body of water.

• Decreases sensitivity to pain. Users run the risk of serious and sometimes fatal injuries (such as by sticking a hand in a fire), because they don't feel pain.

• Induces a catatonic state, in which the user stares mutely into space, seemingly oblivious to others and unable to communicate.

Marijuana

• Causes behavior and reproductive problems, delayed puberty and birth defects in the offspring of parents who smoke it.

• Weakens the immune system. Researchers are now investigating whether those who smoke marijuana may be more vulnerable to AIDS if exposed to the virus.

• Causes lung damage similar to that from cigarettes; contains powerful carcinogens.

• Impairs psychomotor function, such as driving a car or piloting a plane.

• Impairs short-term memory, learning ability.

Heroin

- Slows down breathing. In the case of an overdose, this can result in death.

- Depresses the central nervous system, causing slurred speech, clumsy movement, drowsiness.

- Overdose causes convulsions and coma.

- Increases risk of infections such as AIDS, skin abscesses, endocarditis (inflammation of the heart), hepatitis—from contaminated needles (the drug is almost always injected).

Amphetamines

- Increase blood pressure and heart rate, which strains the cardiovascular system and could result in heart attack or stroke.

- Prompt production of a toxin that kills nerve cells in the brain. This may make a person more susceptible to Parkinson's disease later in life.

- May cause "mini-strokes" on the brain's surface, in which small portions of the brain die—particularly when the drug is injected.

- Kill the appetite; the drugs fool the brain into thinking the user has eaten.

- Cause insomnia.

- Cause a condition known as "amphetamine psychosis," similar to paranoid schizophrenia. It's a result of overstimulation of the same brain systems that cause insomnia. The person may hear imaginary threatening voices and can commit violent acts to defend himself.

- Bring on a severe crash when the drug's effects wear off, characterized by depression and irritability.

Barbiturates

- Cause lethargy and sleep in mild doses; overdoses lower body temperature, cause lungs to fill with fluid, and can bring about coma and death.

- Result in serious addiction. Withdrawal from barbiturates can be fatal, probably because barbiturates interfere with the brain's ability to coordinate many different functions.

- Combine synergistically with both alcohol and antihistamines, causing a loss of concentration, coordination, and control, and increasing the chance of overdose death.

- Cause liver damage.

- Cause anemia, probably because of toxic effects on the liver.

- Prompt rapid tolerance, requiring larger and larger doses to get the same effect, though the lethal dose remains constant.

Before Taking a Drug

If you are currently on any mood elevators, tranquilizers, diet pills or anti-depressant drugs, I urge you to make the effort to ask your physician about the side effects and addictive patterns of the drug. More than that, check it out for yourself.

Discuss these things with your doctor:

- How necessary is this drug?

- Why is it prescribed for this length of time?

- Why is the dosage prescribed?

- What are the drug's possible interactions with food, alcohol and other drugs?

- What are the possible side effects?

- Is it psychologically or physically addictive?

- Are there any alternatives to taking the drug?

From *Virtue* magazine, March 1987

Narcotics Anonymous (NA)

This fellowship of men and women is for those for whom drugs have become a major problem. It is a program of complete abstinence from all drugs. There is only one requirement for membership: the desire to stop using. Those who enroll in the NA program make the following admissions:

We admit we could not manage our own lives. We could not live and enjoy life as other people do. We had to have something different and we thought we had found it in drugs. We placed their use ahead of the welfare of our families, our wives, husbands and our children. We had to have drugs at all costs. We did many people great harm, but most of all we harmed ourselves. Through our inability to accept personal responsibilities, we were actually creating our own problems. We seemed to be incapable of facing life on its own terms.

Most of us realized that in our addiction we were slowly committing suicide, but addiction is such a cunning enemy of life that we had lost the power to do anything about it. Many of us ended up in jail, or sought help through medicine, religion and psychiatry. None of these methods was sufficient for us. Our disease always resurfaced or continued to progress; until in desperation, we sought help from each other in Narcotics Anonymous.

After coming to NA we realized we were sick people. We suffered from a disease from which there is no known cure. It can, however, be arrested at some point, and recovery is then possible.

If you want what we have to offer, and are willing to make the effort to get it, then you are ready to come to grips with the Twelve-Step program used by Alcoholics Anonymous.

What can defeat us in our recovery is an attitude of indifference or intolerance toward spiritual principles. Three of these that are indispensable are honesty, open-mindedness and willingness. With these we are well on our way.

Anonymity is the spiritual foundation of all our traditions, ever reminding us to place principles before personalities.

From Narcotics Anonymous booklet
© 1986 by World Service Office, Inc.

For further information write:

World Service Office, Inc.
Narcotics Anonymous
P.O. Box 9999
Van Nuys, CA 91409
(818) 997-3822

Pills Anonymous
P.O. Box 248
New York, NY 10028
(212) 874-0700

Cocaine Anonymous World Services
3740 Overland Avenue, Ste. C
Los Angeles, CA 90034
(310) 559-5833

National Drug Abuse
Information and Referral Line
1-800-662-4357

Cocaine Hot Line
1-800-COCAINE

Suggested Reading

Ellis, Dan C. *Growing Up Stoned*. Deerfield Beach, Fla.: Health Communications, Inc., 1986.

Kirsch, M. M. *Designer Drugs*. Minneapolis, Minn.: CompCare Publishers, 1986.

Weiner, M. *Getting Off Cocaine: 30 Days to Freedom*. New York: Avon Books, 1984.

Strack, Jay. *Drugs and Drinking: What Every Teen and Parent Should Know*. Nashville, Tenn.: Thomas Nelson, 1985.

Hazelden Collection for Addicts, Center City, Minn.: Hazelden Educational Materials, order no. 5957. 1986.

Hafen, Brent Q. Ph.D., and Frandsen, Kathryn J. *Marijuana*. Center City, Minn.: Hazelden Foundation, 1979.

3. EATING DISORDERS

Anorexia Nervosa and Bulimia

Anorexia nervosa and its associated syndrome, bulimia and bulimarexia, are extremely widespread and dangerous problems. The chief symptoms are self-induced starvation and/or binge eating and purging. For many, this is a compulsive addiction analogous to alcoholism. Thousands of cases report ill health, psychological impairments, shame, guilt, withdrawal and isolation—all leading to devastated lives. The illness is also highly destructive to other family members.

Many physicians and other health professionals have not been trained to recognize or treat anorexia and bulimia. Parents and families do not have basic information concerning eating disorders, including recognition of symptoms, psychological insights or nutritional requirements. Thus, the immense value of early detection and treatment is often lost. The illness is not diagnosed until it reaches an advanced state when it is more difficult to treat. Recognizing and coping with anorexia is still in a pioneering state with an enormous need for public education and the training of health professionals.

Other facts:

- There may be 6,000,000 or more victims in this country alone. It is estimated that six percent of serious cases die.

- Ninety to 95 percent are women.

- Male cases are being reported with increasing frequency.

- The illness can lead to death or life-long problems in those of normal weight who compulsively binge and purge and in the self-starver, but it can be cured.

- Although most anorexics or bulimics start in their teens, a significant number are now in their upper twenties, thirties, forties or older. More cases are being reported in the eight to eleven age bracket.

- Many people think that in the "war on fat" binge and purge eating keeps you thin; in fact, it keeps you at average weight or above.

Compulsive Eating—A Case Study

As a child, I ate butter sticks like they were carrot sticks and would even search through the trash for leftover Easter candy my mother had carefully hidden from me. As a result I was called "Butterball." I've kept the "five-to-ten pounds overweight" image of myself most of my life.

At home we only had sit-down meals on holidays and special occasions. The rest of the time we ate only when we were hungry. I believe this erratic eating pattern was at least partially responsible for the establishment of some of my very strange eating habits. My mother, although a very thin woman on the outside, seemed to be "fat in her head." She apparently was afraid to cook for fear of regaining the childhood chubbiness she once was known for.

At boarding school our hall became known for its "pig-outs" which occurred with almost daily frequency. It was then I discovered the thrill of "eating buddies" who would plot with me to raid the candy machine at 3:00 A.M. or "chow down" on the remaining pie from dinner. Food became my friend when I was lonely, and even when I wasn't.

My college eating buddies and I joked about fat and did strenuous exercises to "keep the fat at bay," but inside we ached for help from our common bondage. At 5'2½" and 139 pounds I was rather chunky but fortunately I did not elicit the kind of stares really fat people receive, which would have further wounded my already negative self-image.

By this time I had already gone the gamut of weight reduction pains: Behavioral Modification, Weight Watchers, and finally, Overeaters Anonymous. How thankful I was to find OA, a group of people who finally were willing to help me get to the root of the problem and who could understand this compulsion that was driving me to eat. The constant fear of another pig-out, the sickening feeling of waking up with horrible breath from a late-night binge, the useless feeling of "why bother to try?"— all these emotions were shared by and with my comrades in OA. Together we learned to pray to a "Higher Power."

The weight began to leave me as only the proper amount of food was allowed in. Since that momentous occasion I have felt more joyful and free than ever before. The destructive desire to be a human garbage pail left.

I drink six to eight glasses of purified water daily, run two-and-a-half miles a few times a week and work out at the gym two or three times weekly. These are all areas of wisdom God instructed me to partake in so that I would not be only thin, but healthy as well. I also eat lots of "health foods."

Evelyn S.

Danger Signals for Eating Disorders

1. *Changes in eating behavior:*
   Alternating between feasting and fasting, loss of appetite, rapid eating, obsession with dieting or with one particular food.

2. *Changes in general behavior:*
   Obsessive weighing, changes in bathroom habits, menstrual irregularity, complaints of constipation, overexercising, impulsive behavior that might indicate drug or alcohol abuse, complaints of chills, use of laxatives or diuretics.

3. *Physical changes:*
   Gradual but constant weight loss, skin rash, loss of hair, swelling of cheeks, chronically sore throat, distended stomach, broken facial capillaries, a red face or watery eyes upon leaving the bathroom.

4. *Psychological changes:*
   Depression, sudden withdrawing or antisocial behavior, extreme concern with achievement or perfectionist goals.

5. *Constant talk about food:*
   Collecting of recipes, counting of calories—but avoidance of eating when anyone else is present.

6. *Development of rituals around eating:*
   Such as organizing the food on the plate, cutting it into little bits, dawdling over meals and eating little.

7. *Consumption of diet sodas:*
   To the exclusion of all other drinks, sometimes to the point of drinking a case daily.

8. *Compulsive exercise:*
   Such as refusing to eat unless they have run five miles or more and done hundreds of sit-ups before mealtime.

9. *Increasing social isolation:*
   Withdrawing from friends and family to concentrate on fasting.

Overeaters Anonymous (OA)

Overeaters Anonymous, so helpful to Evelyn, is a fellowship of men and women from all walks of life who meet in order to help solve a common problem—compulsive overeating. The only requirement for membership is a desire to stop eating compulsively.

This organization was founded in January 1960 when three people living in Los Angeles, California, began meeting for the purpose of helping each other with their eating problems. They had tried everything else and failed. The program they followed was—and continued to be—patterned after the Alcoholics Anonymous program. From that first meeting OA has grown until today there are thousands of meetings in the United States and other countries.

The concept of abstinence is the basis of OA's program of recovery. By admitting inability to control compulsive overeating in the past, and abandoning the idea that all one needs to be able to eat normally is "a little willpower," it becomes possible to abstain from overeating—one day at a time. OA offers the newcomer support in dealing with both the physical and emotional symptoms of compulsive overeating. For weight loss, any medically approved eating plan is acceptable. The diagnosis of a compulsive overeating disorder, like the diagnosis of alcoholism, must be self-declared if treatment is to be effective. In our do-it-yourself society, where weight control is a billion dollar business and a national pastime, no matter how obese the candidate, treatment is not possible unless the individual is sick of being driven to overeat. Otherwise, it is just a dissatisfaction with excess weight for which the individual feels he still has some tricks up his sleeve for self-control. That has to be left alone, unless there is a genuine despair about the compulsion.

Nor is overweight the sole criterion for turning to OA. People are recognizing their food disorder earlier in life, with only a minimal amount of excess weight, just as more and more alcoholics are able to recognize their addiction in its earliest stages and are seeking help. Extreme excess weight is no longer the criterion for many new entrants. Recognition of the compulsion is.

Variants of the disorder include the food abuser who has no apparent weight problem and is often quite underweight but who maintains this by eating and vomiting, a practice called bulimia. Another extreme is a form of self-starvation which results in anorexia.

Overeaters Anonymous has no religious requirement, affiliation, or orientation. The twelve-step program of recovery is considered "spiritual" because it deals with inner change. OA has members of many different religious beliefs as well as some atheists and agnostics.

©1979. Overeaters Anonymous, Inc.

To contact Overeaters Anonymous, or other eating disorder support groups, look in your local telephone directory and/or your local newspaper's social or calendar section. Or write:

> Overeaters Anonymous, Inc.
> World Service Office
> 8075 West Third Street, Ste. 405
> Los Angeles, CA 90048
> (213) 936-6252

> National Assoc. for Anorexia and
> Associated Disorders
> Box 7
> Highland Park, IL 60035
> (847) 831-3438

Suggested Reading

Hollis, Judy. *Fat Is a Family Affair,* Center City. Minn.: Hazelden Foundation, 1985.

Rowland, Cynthia Joyce. *The Monster Within: Overcoming Bulimia.* Grand Rapids, Mich.: Baker Book House, 1985.

Stein, Patricia M. and Unell, Barbara C. *Anorexia Nervosa: Finding the Life Line.* Minneapolis, Minn.: CompCare Publishers, 1986.

Hall, Lindsey and Cohn, Leigh. *Bulimia—A Guide to Recovery: Understanding & Overcoming the Binge-Purge Syndrome.* Santa Barbara, CA: Gurze Books, 1986.

Kano, Susan. *Making Peace with Food: A Step-by-Step Guide to Freedom from Diet/Weight Conflict.* New York: Harper and Row, 1989.

McFarland, Barbara and Baker-Baumann, Tyeis. *Feeding the Empty Heart.* San Francisco: Harper/Hazelden, 1989.

Jensen, Judy W. *Dieting Can Be Fattening.* Center City, Minn.: Hazelden Education Materials, 1988.

Roth, Geneen. *Breaking Free from Compulsive Eating.* New York: Signet Books, 1989.

Minirth, Dr. Frank, *et al. Love Hunger: Recovery from Food Addiction.* Nashville, Tenn.: Nelson, 1990.

Miller, Caroline Adams. *My Name Is Caroline.* New York: Doubleday, 1988.

Bryan, Nancy. *Thin Is a State of Mind.* Minneapolis, Minn.: CompCare Publishers, 1982.

Roth, Geneen. *Feeding the Hungry Heart: The Experience of Compulsive Eating.* New York: Signet Books, 1983.

Chapian, Marie and Coyle, Neva. *Free to Be Thin.* Minneapolis, Minn.: Bethany House, 1979.

Barrile, Jackie. *Confessions of a Closet Eater.* Wheaton, Ill.: Tyndale House Publishers, 1983.

4. EMOTIONAL DISORDERS

Emotions Anonymous

Emotions Anonymous (EA) was formed by a group of individuals who found a New Way of Life by working the Twelve-Step Program of Alcoholics Anonymous as adapted for people with emotional problems. Their statement of purpose:

> There is but one ultimate authority—a loving God as He may express Himself in our group conscience. Our leaders are but trusted servants; they do not govern.
>
> The only requirement for membership is a desire to become well emotionally.
>
> We respect anonymity—no questions are asked. We aim for an atmosphere of love and acceptance. We do not care who you are or what you have done. You are welcome.
>
> We do not judge—we do not criticize—we do not argue. We do not give advice regarding personal or family affairs.
>
> Part of the beauty and wonder of the Emotions Anonymous Program is that at meetings we can say anything and know it *stays there*. Anything we hear at a meeting, on the telephone, or from another member is confidential, and is not to be repeated to anyone.

From Emotions Anonymous, Inc.

"Just for Today"—The EA Credo

JUST FOR TODAY I will try to live through this day only, not tackling my whole life problem at once. I can do something at this moment that would appall me if I felt that I had to keep it up for a lifetime.

JUST FOR TODAY I will try to be happy, realizing that my happiness does not depend on what others do or say, or what happens around me. Happiness is a result of being at peace with myself.

JUST FOR TODAY I will try to adjust myself to what is—and not force everything to adjust to my own desires. I will accept my family, my friends, my business, my circumstances as they come.

JUST FOR TODAY I will take care of my physical health; I will exercise my mind; I will read something spiritual.

JUST FOR TODAY I will do somebody a good turn and not get found out—if anyone knows of it, it will not count. I shall do at least one thing I don't want to do, and will perform some small act of love for my neighbor.

JUST FOR TODAY I will try to go out of my way to be kind to someone I meet; I will be agreeable; I will look as well as I can, dress becomingly, talk low, act courteously, criticize not one bit, not find fault with anything, and not try to improve or regulate anybody except myself.

JUST FOR TODAY I will have a program. I may not follow it exactly, but I will have it. I will save myself from two pests—hurry and indecision.

JUST FOR TODAY I will stop saying "If I had time." I never will "find time" for anything. If I want time I must take it.

JUST FOR TODAY I will have a quiet time of meditation wherein I shall think of God *as I understand Him* and of my neighbor. I shall relax and seek truth.

JUST FOR TODAY I shall be unafraid. Particularly, I shall be unafraid to be happy, to enjoy what is good, what is beautiful, and what is lovely in life.

JUST FOR TODAY I will accept myself and live to the best of my ability.

JUST FOR TODAY I choose to believe that I can live this one day. The choice is mine!

For further information about Emotions Anonymous write:

Emotions Anonymous
International Services
Post Office Box 4245
St. Paul, Minnesota 55104
(612) 647-9712

Other helps:

Recovery, Inc.
The Association of Nervous and Former
Mental Patients
802 North Dearborn Street
Chicago, IL 60610
(312) 337–5661

Neurotics Anonymous International
3636 16th Street
Washington, DC 20010

Do You Need Help?

Here are general guidelines to judge whether you could use a therapist. If you're troubled by any of the following symptoms it may be time to seek help. Of course, if you have any of the *physical* symptoms listed, you should also have a medical evaluation:

- Severe anxiety, panic or fear.
- Frequent feelings of depression, unhappiness, hopelessness, despair.
- Abuse of drugs or alcohol.
- Sharp mood swings.
- Recent changes in appetite or sleep patterns.
- Extreme weight gains or losses.
- Excessive worrying.
- Loss of parent, spouse or other close relative or friend.
- Recurring sexual difficulties.

- Vague physical problems, such as headaches or stomach pain, or a preoccupation with physical illness.

- Personal or professional crisis.

- Any change, including a positive one, such as marriage, moving or the birth of a child.

- Seek *immediate* help if you're having hallucinations, hearing voices, have out-of-control feelings of violence or are experiencing such severe depression you're considering suicide.

American Health, June 1986

Suggested Reading

Dobson, Dr. James. *Emotions—Can You Trust Them?* Ventura, Calif.: Regal Books, 1984.

Bradshaw, John. *Healing the Shame That Binds You.* Deerfield Beach, Fla: Health Communications Inc., 1988.

Minirth, Frank B., M.D. and Meier, Paul D., M.D. *Happiness Is a Choice.* Grand Rapids, Michigan: Baker Books, 1978.

Seamands, David. *Healing for Damaged Emotions.* Wheaton, Ill.: Victor Books, 1981.

Sandford, John and Paula. *Transformation of the Inner Man.* So. Plainfield, N.J.: Bridge Publishing, Inc. 1982.

Rubin, Theodore Isaac, M.D. *The Angry Book.* New York: Collier (subsidiary of Macmillan Publishers), 1970.

Learner, Harriet G., Ph.D. *The Dance of Anger: A Woman's Guide to Changing the Patterns of Intimate Relationships.* New York: Harper & Row, 1985.

Rosellini, Gayle and Worden, Mark. *Of Course You're Anxious.* Center City, Minn.: Hazelden Educational Materials, 1990.

Rosellini, Gayle and Worden, Mark. *Here Comes the Sun: Dealing with Depression.* Center City, Minn.: Hazelden Educational Materials, 1988.

Peck, Scott. *The Road Less Traveled.* New York: Simon and Schuster, 1978.

Bozarth-Campbell, Alla, Ph.D. *Life Is Goodbye/Life Is Hello.* 2nd ed. Minneapolis, Minn.: CompCare, 1983.

Jampolsky, Gerald. *Good-Bye to Guilt.* Toronto: Bantam Books, 1985.

5. COMPULSIVE EXERCISING

Exercise is good for you when done under proper guidance and controls. Therapists and physical education people can help you find a balanced program of walking, jogging, and/or use of gym equipment.

When you turn exercise from a "want-to" into a "have-to," you take the healthy part out and you take the joy out. Watch out.

It becomes compulsive exercising when you stop listening to your body, how you're feeling, and drive yourself with an urgency that has little to do with reality. Compulsive exercising is when you're afraid that your looks, your well-being, your relationships all hinge on going to exercise class six days a week.

Warning Signs

- You get so used to your exercise routine that even very important events are intrusions. You start fitting your life into your classes instead of fitting your classes into your life.

- What you eat or don't eat depends on whether you are exercising or not.

- You don't feel "right" or "complete" or "good" unless you exercise.

- You exercise even when you feel sick or tired.

- It's beginning to be hard to drag yourself to exercise class. You think of ways to get out of it; you hope you'll get pneumonia; you don't like the people who stand next to you in class; you want to punch the teacher in the mouth.

When any or all of these warning signs apply to you, here are some things to do.

1. Listen to them. They are a sign that something has gone wrong.

2. Don't go to your class for a day or a few days. Take a walk instead, or sit in a rocking chair for an hour and do nothing, or read a book.

3. The next morning after you skip a class, notice that although you didn't burn off 500 calories the day before, you have not suddenly gained ten pounds. Keep noticing.

4. Remind yourself of all the things you are besides your body. Make a list. Begin it with "I am . . ." and don't allow any negative judgments about your body to creep in or on. In case you forget, you are worthwhile, you are caring, you are growing. To name just a few attributes.

5. Eat when you are hungry, eat what you want, stop when you're satisfied. Remember that your body *does not want to destroy you* and will not go haywire as soon as you let down your guard. Trust that the two of you are working for the same end—your health, your happiness, your peace.[4]

6. COMPULSIVE GAMBLING

News of the Wall Street scandals touched me in a personal way. I remembered Fred at the Compulsivity Clinic, the heavy-set man in his thirties who was a stockbroker. Fred admitted that Wall Street was spawning a new breed of gambler, the compulsive investor, and that he had been infected. As a result he had become involved in the Gamblers Anonymous program.

Compulsive gambling is a disease many people don't believe exists. On the surface gamblers seldom show symptoms of their disease, as do alcoholics and drug addicts. It is a progressive behavior disorder in which an individual has a psychologically controlled preoccupation and urge to gamble that compromises family, job and other pursuits. Studies show that close to ten percent of the population have a gambling problem. These addictive people usually begin to gamble at an early age (96 percent start before the age of fourteen) and gamble to compensate for anxiety, anger, and the deprivation of their early years.

Approximately one third of compulsive gamblers are women, of whom 75 percent gamble to escape problem situations. About half of all women gamblers have a drug or alcohol addiction, too. Frequently, the compulsive gambler who has exhausted all credit sources and the savings of family members will resort to crime.

Reports Arnie Wexler, executive director of the New Jersey Council on Compulsive Gambling and a former compulsive gambler himself: "It's an invisible disease. People can understand what happens to drug addicts and alcoholics when they withdraw. But not many know that a compulsive gambler can develop stammering, eye twitches, bloody noses, and other problems when going through withdrawal."

Warning Signs

The following twenty questions may help you decide whether compulsive gambling is a problem for you or for someone you know:

1. Do you lose time from work due to gambling?
2. Is gambling making your home life unhappy?
3. Is gambling affecting your reputation?
4. Have you ever felt remorse after gambling?

5. Do you ever gamble to get money with which to pay debts or to otherwise solve financial difficulties?

6. Does gambling cause a decrease in your ambition or efficiency?

7. After losing, do you feel you must return as soon as possible and win back your losses?

8. After a win, do you have a strong urge to return and win more?

9. Do you often gamble until your last dollar is gone?

10. Do you ever borrow to finance your gambling?

11. Have you ever sold any real or personal property to finance gambling?

12. Are you reluctant to use "gambling money" for normal expenditures?

13. Does gambling make you careless of the welfare of your family?

14. Do you ever gamble longer than you had planned?

15. Do you ever gamble to escape worry or trouble?

16. Have you ever committed, or considered committing, an illegal act to finance gambling?

17. Does gambling cause you to have difficulty in sleeping?

18. Do arguments, disappointments or frustrations create within you an urge to gamble?

19. Do you have an urge to celebrate any good fortune by a few hours of gambling?

20. Have you ever considered self-destruction as a result of your gambling?

Most compulsive gamblers will answer yes to seven or more of these questions.

From "Compulsive Gambling,"
Christopher News Notes, 12 East 48 St.,
New York, NY 10017

Gamblers Anonymous (GA)

Gamblers Anonymous is the most effective self-help organization available to compulsive gamblers. Modeled along the lines of Alcoholics Anonymous, GA was founded in California in 1957. It now has 300 chapters in the United States, a total of 450 world-wide. It uses the Twelve-Step Program as its basic tool. For further information about Gamblers Anonymous or Gam-Anon (for families) or Gamateen (for teenagers) write:

> Gamblers Anonymous
> Post Office Box 17173
> Los Angeles, CA 90017
> (213) 386–8789

> Gam-Anon/Gamateen
> Post Office Box 570157
> Whitestone, NY 11357
> (718) 352-1671

The National Council on Compulsive Gambling, Inc., was established in 1972 to disseminate information and education on compulsive gambling as an illness and public health problem. Their address:

> 445 West 59th Street
> New York, NY 10019
> 1–800–522–4700

Suggested Reading

Galski, Thomas. *The Handbook of Pathological Gambling.* Springfield, Ill.: Charles C. Thomas, 1987.

Braidfoot, Larry. *Gambling: A Deadly Game.* Nashville, Tenn.: Broadman Press, 1985.

Pamphlets. *Understanding Compulsive Gambling* order no. 5497; *Early Signs of Compulsive Gambling* order no. 5587; *What Is G.A.* (*Gamblers Anonymous*) order no. 1393. Center City, Minnesota: Hazelden Educational Materials.

Moore, Robin. *Compulsion: The True Story of an Addictive Gambler.* New York: Doubleday, 1981.

7. OBSESSIVE-COMPULSIVE DISORDER

The man who has to wash his hands five times before each meal or the woman who checks the locks on her front and back doors exactly eight times each night before bedtime probably has obsessive-compulsive disorder (OCD). Aside from this unusual behavior, most OCD's act so normally that close friends are unaware that they are ruled by fears and repetitive, repellent thoughts.

The more bizarre forms of this behavior include such situations as the young father who won't mail a letter without checking to make sure his daughter isn't sealed inside. Or the woman who saves *everything,* including the fuzz that comes off her carpet, although she has no explanation as to why she does this.

Recent studies show that at least ten times more Americans have OCD than previously estimated, or 2.5 out of every 100 adults, with an even male-female ratio (about five million people).

Most people described as compulsive do not have OCD. Some successful people in demanding fields often show signs of OCD, with their preoccupation with dirt, time, and money. Though such people are inclined to be miserly, workaholic and perfectionist, they are only somewhat more likely to have OCD than others. Nor is the OCD person likely to be addicted to alcohol, sex, gambling, or food—which all include an element of real enjoyment. In contrast, the obsessive-compulsive gets no pleasure from the dreary, often despised rituals he's driven senselessly to perform.

Only in recent years has behavioral therapy emerged as the OCD's best avenue of help. The therapist makes the patient confront what he fears over and over again, while preventing him from lapsing into the ritual acts. This breaks the circuit between obsession and compulsion. Certain drugs also help reduce the patient's fear. What was once considered incurable behavior can today be treated. The possibility of spiritual treatment for OCD is an untapped area.[5]

Most-Frequently Asked
Questions about OCD

1. What is Obsessive-Compulsive Disorder (OCD)?
   OCD is characterized by recurrent unwanted and unpleasant thoughts (obsessions), and/or repetitive ritualistic behaviors, which the person feels driven to perform (compulsions). People with OCD *know* that their obsessions and compulsions are irrational or excessive, yet find they have little or no control over them.

   Typical Obsessions:
   Dirt and contamination; fear of acting on violent or aggressive impulses, feeling overly responsible for the safety of others (i.e., unreasonable fear of having run someone over); abhorrent religious (blasphemous) and sexual intrusions; inordinate concern with order, arrangement or symmetry; hoarding, etc.

   Typical Compulsions:
   Washing (particularly handwashing) and cleaning, checking, touching, repeating, counting, arranging and ordering, saving; ritualistic behaviors that lessen the chances of provoking obsessions (i.e., putting all sharp objects out of sight); superstitious-like acts that reduce obsessional fears (i.e., only wearing certain colors), etc.

   A person can have a few or a multitude of these symptoms.

2. What are some of the other symptoms of OCD?
   People with OCD may become demoralized or develop depression. Feelings of intense anxiety are common.

3. What is the age of onset of OCD?
   The disorder usually begins in adolescence or early adulthood, but it may also occur in childhood.

4. What is the course of OCD?
   If not treated appropriately, the disorder is often chronic, with waxing and waning of symptoms. In some cases, people may outgrow the disorder; in others, it may follow a progressively deteriorative course.

5. How disabling is OCD?
   Impairment ranges from minimal to severe. Sometimes the symptoms are crippling; frequent hospitalizations may become necessary and regular employment impossible. On the other hand, many successful doctors, lawyers, engineers, educators, homemakers, businessmen/women, factory workers, performers and entertainers continue to succeed despite symptoms of OCD. For the majority of people who lead otherwise normal lives, life would be even more productive and fulfilling if they were free of symptoms. The emotional and economic costs of OCD to the individual, the family, and society are enormous.

6. Are people with OCD "crazy"?
   No. The behaviors may seem "crazy" but the person performing them is not. In fact, an OCD sufferer is acutely aware of the excessiveness or irrationality of his/her fears or behaviors yet is unable to control them. This self-awareness creates a new fear for the person with OCD: the fear that others will think he/she is weak or crazy. People with OCD are often very secretive about their symptoms and thus afraid to seek treatment. This may account for why the incidence of OCD was previously underreported.

7. What are the possible causes of OCD?
   The exact causes of OCD are still unknown. Researchers strongly suspect, however, that a biochemical imbalance is involved. Alterations in one or more brain chemical systems that regulate repetitive

behaviors may be related to the cause of OCD. Psychological factors and stress may heighten symptoms.

Family Guidelines

Learn to recognize these twelve signals that indicate a person is having problems. Remember, it is not "just their personality." Changes are gradual yet significant. They include:

1. Withdrawal.

2. Doing things again and again—repetitive behaviors.

3. Constant questioning of own judgment; need for constant reassurance.

4. Simple tasks taking longer than usual.

5. Increased fatigue.

6. Perpetual tardiness.

7. Increased concern for minor things and details.

8. Severe and extreme emotional reactions to small things.

9. Inability to sleep properly.

10. Significant change in eating patterns.

11. Daily life becomes a struggle.

12. Avoidance.

For further information on Obsessive-Compulsive Disorder and its treatment, write:

The OCD Foundation
Post Office Box 70
Milford, CT 06460

Suggested Reading

Jenike, Michael A., M.D.; Baer, Lee, Ph.D; Minichiello, William E., Ed.D. *Obsessive Compulsive Disorders: Theory and Management.* St. Louis, Mo.: Mosby-Year Book, Inc., 1990.

Rapoport, J. Dr. *The Boy Who Couldn't Stop Washing.* New York: Plume Books, 1989.

8. RELATIONSHIP DEPENDENCIES

Relationships Anonymous

If you feel you have a tendency toward unhealthy relationships, *Relationships Anonymous* is a self-help organization that uses the Twelve-Step recovery program of Alcoholics Anonymous to break the pattern of addictive and destructive relationships. Support is provided during painful break-ups. The meetings emphasize the importance of confidentiality; only first names are used. For further information, write to Relationships Anonymous, P.O. Box 40074, Berkeley, CA 94704.

How Male Dependent Are You?[6]

If you wonder to what degree you are dependent on men to satisfy your emotional needs, the following test will give you some clues. Answer by checking Yes or No in the designated spot.

1. You come from a dysfunctional home in which your emotional needs were not met. ____Yes ____No

2. Having received little real nurturing yourself, you try to fill this unmet need vicariously by becoming a care-giver, especially to men who appear, in some way, needy. ____Yes ____No

3. Because you were never able to change your parent(s) into the warm, loving caretaker(s) you longed for, you respond deeply to emotionally unavailable men whom you can again try to change, through your love. ____Yes ____No

4. Terrified of abandonment, you will do anything to keep a male relationship from dissolving. ____Yes ____No

5. Almost nothing is too much trouble, takes too much time, or is too expensive if it will "help" the man you are involved with. ____Yes ____No

6. Accustomed to lack of love in personal relationships, you are willing to wait, hope, and try harder to please. ____Yes ____No

7. You are willing to take far more than 50 percent of the responsibility, guilt, and blame in any relationship. ____Yes ____No

8. Your self-esteem is critically low, and deep inside you do not believe you deserve to be happy. Rather, you believe you must earn the right to enjoy life. ____Yes ____No

9. You have a desperate need to control your men and your relationships, having experienced little security in childhood. You mask your efforts to control people and situations under the guise of "being helpful." ____Yes ____No

10. In a relationship, you are much more in touch with your dream of how it could be than with the reality of your situation. ____Yes ____No

11. You are addicted to men and to emotional pain. ____Yes ____No

12. You are predisposed emotionally and often biochemically to becoming dependent on drugs or alcohol and/or certain foods, particularly sugary ones. ____Yes ____No

13. By being drawn to people with problems that need fixing, or by being enmeshed in situations that are chaotic, uncertain, and emotionally painful, you avoid focusing on your responsibility to yourself. ____Yes ____No

14. You may have a tendency toward episodes of depression, which you try to forestall through the excitement provided by an unstable relationship. ____Yes ____No

15. You are not attracted to men who are kind, stable, reliable, and interested in you. You find such "nice" men boring.

    ____Yes____No

Note: If you answered 12–15 "yes," you are strongly male addicted; 9–12, you have a definite problem; 6–9 there is instability in your life.

The Woman Recovering from Loving Too Much

1. She accepts herself fully, even while wanting to change parts of herself. There is a basic self-love and self-regard, which she carefully nurtures and purposely expands.

2. She accepts others as they are without trying to change them to meet her needs.

3. She is in touch with her feelings and attitudes about every aspect of her life, including her sexuality.

4. She cherishes every aspect of herself; her personality, her appearance, her beliefs and values, her body, her interests and accomplishments. She validates herself, rather than searching for a relationship to give her a sense of self-worth.

5. Her self-esteem is great enough that she can enjoy being with others, especially men, whom she accepts just as they are. She does not need to be needed in order to feel worthy.

6. She knows that a relationship, in order to work, must be between partners who share similar values, interests, and goals, and who each have a capacity for intimacy. She also knows that she is worthy of the best that life has to offer.

What Women Want Most[7]

A recent survey of 300 women of all ages revealed that it's not sex, not money, not good looks that women want most—it's *intimacy*. A similar survey of men was done the previous year. Here are the comparisons:

- In their 20s, women want love and romance, but also want to be respected for their brains and talent. Men want a beautiful, sexy woman.

- In their 30s, women want helpmates. "They would rather have someone who will take the kids to the orthodontist than have a candlelight dinner once a week." Men want a woman with outside interests and a good income.

- In their 40s, women want it all—men who are cooperative, caring, attentive, and sexy. Men focus again on beauty, sex—and younger women.

- In their 50s and 60s, women and men want companionship. "They do more things together."

How to Distinguish Between
Addictive and Authentic Love

Addictive love says:

1. I can't live without you. I can't make it on my own. Only you give my life meaning.

2. I need for you to be a total part of my life, and for me to be a total part of yours.

3. I can't bear to think of you sharing your thoughts and feelings with someone else. You are the only one who has ever understood me.

4. If you really care, you will treat me the way I need to be treated to be happy.

Authentic love says:

1. I trust you to have other close relationships.

2. Though I can make it on my own, having you as a part of my life makes life richer and better.

3. I encourage you to pursue your interests and I will pursue mine. This kind of space and diversity is good for us.

4. I believe love should seek the other's highest good. To the best of my ability, I will do that for you.

Adapted from *Please Don't Say You Need Me*
by Jan Silvious (Zondervan, 1989)

Suggested Reading

Wegscheider-Cruse, Sharon. *Coupleship: How to Build a Relationship.* Deerfield Beach, Fla.: Health Communications, Inc., 1988.

Norwood, Robin. *Women Who Love Too Much.* Los Angeles: Jeremy P. Tarcher, Inc., 1985.

Schaeffer, Brenda. *The Healthy Relationship Series: Power Plays, Signs of Healthy Love.* Center City, Minnesota: Hazelden Foundation, 1986.

Peele, Stanton and Brodsky, Archie. *Love and Addiction.* New York: Taplinger Publishing Company, Inc., 1975.

Halpern, Howard. *How to Break Your Addiction to a Person.* New York: Bantam Books, Inc., 1982.

Colgrove, Melba, et al. *How to Survive the Loss of a Love.* New York, New York: Bantam Books, Inc., 1976.

Schaef, Anne Wilson. *Escape from Intimacy—Untangling the "Love" Addictions: Sex, Romance, Relationships.* San Francisco: Harper and Row, 1989.

Cruse, Joseph R., M.D. *Painful Affairs: Looking for Love Through Addiction and Co-Dependence.* Deerfield Beach, Fla.: Health Communications, Inc., 1989.

Covington, Stephanie and Beckett, Liana. *Leaving the Enchanted Forest: The Path from Relationship Addiction to Intimacy.* New York: Harper and Row, 1989.

Mowday, Lois. *The Snare: Avoiding Emotional and Sexual Entanglements.* Colorado Springs, Col.: NavPress, 1988.

Jambolsky, Gerald. *Love Is Letting Go of Fear.* New York: Bantam Books, Inc., 1970.

Larsen, Earnie. *Stage II Recovery—Life Beyond Addiction.* New York: Harper & Row, 1985.

9. SEXUAL ADDICTION

Sex addiction refers to the thinking and behavior patterns of a person who uses sex to cope with life and to defend against low self-worth and a shameful identity. For the addict, sex is not a fulfilling experience that enhances a primary relationship and life itself, but a compulsive, often highly ritualized activity that ultimately adds to the pain and loneliness the addict is already battling.

The Progression Toward Sex Addiction

In his newspaper column "Six Deadly Addictions," Joseph A. Pursch, M.D., invited his readers to examine themselves with these statements. Do you see yourself anywhere in this progression?

1. I like sex. I keep thinking about it.

2. It's like a pleasant preoccupation.

3. I seem to want to do it more and more, even from men I don't particularly like.

4. My husband (boyfriend, date) says it's getting to be a problem.

5. How come every date leads to this?

6. Sometimes I don't even enjoy it. Often I wish I hadn't done it.

7. This is getting me into bad situations.

8. (Waking up in a strange place:) I can't believe this—I don't even know these people; they look crummy. I'd better get out of here before they wake up.

9. If my (husband, friend, boss, pastor, parents) knew about this, they'd put me in an institution.

10. That's it! I'm stopping! This is not normal! I feel driven.

The scenario is the same for gamblers (from the first bet to bankruptcy), for overeaters, bulimics and anorexics (binging, starving), for workaholics (deadlines, ulcers, miserable "family" vacations).

The common dynamic is a compulsion which continues in spite of all "common sense" resolutions and repeated negative consequences.

Sex Addicts Anonymous (SAA)

This is a group of men and women who share their strength, hope and experience with each other so they may overcome their sex addiction and help others to recover. They describe themselves as follows:

"We were sexually compulsive people. Despite our most heroic efforts and solemn promises, we were unable to turn away from behaviors and obsessions that were ruining our lives. We interpreted our lack of control as proof that we were bad or defective people, so we sought comfort by justifying our behaviors (and sometimes reveling in them), or by denying our sexuality, and hiding in our shame. Our compulsions were at once our worst enemies and our most familiar sources of comfort.

"We came to SAA because we could no longer deny the pain that our compulsive sexual behaviors had caused in our lives. Many of us experienced divorce, disease, jail, or financial ruin before seeing that our lives had become unmanageable. Others among us were confronted about our behavior by family, friends, or counselors, and were given a choice to seek help or face yet more loss in our lives. When we learned of SAA, we began to hope again that our lives could be freed from our sexual compulsivity.

"Our recovery began when we attended SAA meetings. We heard stories similar to ours, and we heard how others in SAA were abstaining from their compulsive behaviors. We learned of the twelve suggested steps of recovery, and when we began to apply them in our lives, we discovered that we, too, could abstain from our compulsive behaviors, with the help of our fellow addicts. We acquired the faith and courage to make appropriate changes in our lives, and to accept our daily problems as stepping stones for spiritual growth. As we continue in our recovery from sexual addiction, one day at a time, we are developing healthier sexuality, a stronger sense of personal integrity, and an ability to truly enjoy our lives."

Most sex addicts using the Twelve-Step Program choose to rebuild the boundaries in their lives through some form of abstinence. One woman's progress report:

"I see my abstinence as dynamic. It changes as I do. It is not a rigid list based on prohibiting certain behaviors, but a positive affirmation of my program. It is grounded in my attitude and my relationship with my Higher Power, which includes the humility and joy of knowing I am not alone anymore. There's a real lightness I find when I'm centered in my Higher Power.

"When I slip—as I do—I try to be gentle with myself, recognizing my powerlessness over my addiction and sharing my pain with others. Then I start again with the love and support of my own self, my group, and, above all, my Higher Power, who has given me the wonderful gift of my recovery."

Ask Yourself—A Quiz

If you answer "yes" to three or more of the following 15 questions, you may want to seek help for an addiction to sex.

1. Has your sexual behavior caused you either to seek help or made you feel scared or different—somehow alienated from other people?

2. Do you keep secrets about your sexual or romantic activities from those important to you? Do you lead a double life?

3. Have your needs driven you to have sex in places with people you would not normally choose?

4. Do you find yourself looking for sexually arousing articles or scenes in newspapers, magazines or other media?

5. Do you find that romantic or sexual fantasies interfere with your relationships with others or are controlling you?

6. Do you frequently want to get away from a sex partner after having sex? Do you frequently feel remorse, shame or guilt after a sexual encounter?

7. Does each relationship continue to have the same destructive patterns which prompted you to leave the last relationships?

8. Have you ever tried to leave a specific person or a destructive relationship and found yourself returning?

9. Do you obsess about sex or romance even when it interferes with your daily responsibilities or causes emotional discomfort?

10. Does the time you spend reading pornographic magazines or watching films interfere with the demands of your daily activities and relationships with people?

11. Is it taking more variety and frequency of sexual and romantic activities than previously to bring the same levels of excitement and relief?

12. Are you in danger of being arrested because of your practices of voyeurism, exhibitionism, prostitution, sex with minors, indecent phone calls, etc.?

13. Does your pursuit of sex or romantic relationships interfere with your spiritual development?

14. Do your sexual activities include the risk, threat, or reality of disease, pregnancy, coersion, or violence?

15. Has your sexual or romantic behavior ever made you feel hopeless or suicidal?

From the booklet "From Shame to Grace"

Also write or call:

> Sex and Love Addicts Anonymous
> Glendale, CA 93062
> (213) 259-6549

> International Service Organization of SAA
> P.O. Box 70949
> Houston, TX 77270
> (713) 869-4902

For those who are/have been in a relationship with a sex addict write:

> Co-Sexaholics Anonymous
> P.O. Box 111910
> Nashville, TN 37222
> (615) 331-6230

> Sex and Love Addicts Anonymous
> P.O. Box 650010
> Newton, MA 02165
> (617) 332-1845

Suggested Reading

Hope and Recovery: A Twelve-Step Guide for Healing from Compulsive Sexual Behavior. Minneapolis, Minn.: CompCare Publishers, 1987.

Carnes, Patrick, Ph.D. *Out of the Shadows: Understanding Sex Addiction.* Minneapolis, Minn.: CompCare Publishers, 1985.

Carnes, Patrick, Ph.D. *Contrary to Love: Helping the Sexual Addict.* Minneapolis, Minn.: *CompCare Publishers, 1989.*

Hunter, Mic. *The First Step: For People in Relationships with Sex Addicts.* Minneapolis, Minn.: CompCare Publishers, 1989.

Earle, Ralph, Dr. and Crow, Gregory, Dr. *Lonely All the Time: Recognizing, Understanding, and Overcoming Sex Addiction for Addicts and Codependents.* New York: Simon and Schuster, 1989.

Kasl, Charlotte, Ph.D. *Women and Sex Addiction.* Minneapolis, Minn.: Castle Consulting, 1984.

10. SHOPAHOLICS

Check Your Spending Habits[8]

1. Is shopping your major form of activity?

2. Do you put off meetings with friends because you prefer to go shopping?

3. Do you buy new clothes that sit in the closet for weeks or even months before you wear them?

4. Do you frequently throw out clothes you've never worn?

5. Do you spend more than twenty percent of your take-home pay to cover your loans and credit cards?

6. Do you ever pay one line of credit with another?

7. Do you pay only the minimum balance on your charge accounts each month thereby incurring substantial interest charges?

8. Do you ever hide your purchases in the car or lie about them so your spouse doesn't know you were shopping?

9. Do you ever lie about how much something cost so your spouse or friends think you were just after a great bargain?

10. Do you buy something just because it's on sale even though you have no use for it?

11. Are you unable to enter a store without buying something, even if it isn't what you were looking for?

12. When out with friends for dinner, do you offer to put the check on your credit card so you can collect the cash?

13. Do you feel nervous and guilty after a shopping spree?

14. Do you feel anxious on days when you don't go shopping?

15. Is your paycheck often gone on Tuesday when the next payday isn't until Friday?

16. Do you borrow money from friends, even though you know you'll have a hard time paying it back?

17. Do you frequently have to charge small purchases, such as toiletry items and groceries because you don't have enough in your pocket?

18. Do you think others would be horrified if they knew how much money you spent?

19. Are you within $100 of your credit limit on all your credit cards?

20. Do you often feel hopeless and depressed after spending money?

If you answered "yes" to five or more of these questions, the experts say you have a spending problem and should seek help.

Suggestions for Problem Shoppers

1. Reduce temptation by reducing the number of your credit cards. Better yet, use only cash.

2. Live on a budget, allowing so much each month for spending.

3. Families should discuss spending problems together, agree on what to buy.

4. When you shop, shop alone. Friends tend to encourage each other to buy.

5. Shop only with a list and buy only the items on it. This helps establish some control over your spending. Plan a nonspending reward for sticking to your list.

6. Shop with a calculator. This keeps you in touch with the reality of how fast your purchases are adding up.

7. Avoid sales! Many people buy things impulsively at sales they don't need or even want just to get a bargain. Sales can be seductive to compulsive shoppers.

8. Throw out catalogs immediately. Go directly from the mailbox to the trash can. Catalogs have a way of tempting a person in a weak moment as does the TV Shopper's Channel. Don't touch that dial!

9. If you go into debt from shopping, don't hide. Communicate with creditors, explain your debt situation, seek a schedule of payments mutually acceptable.

10. Reward yourself by saving. Put aside money for something you really want and when you have the cash, go buy it. Note the sense of freedom you feel, the lack of guilt, the joy of not having to pay for it later.

Where to Find Help

Several cities have chapters of *Debtors Anonymous* (P.O. Box 400, Grand Central Station, New York, NY 10163-0400), an organization for compulsive spenders modeled after Alcoholics Anonymous. If your area has a chapter, it will be listed in your local telephone directory.

National numbers:
Rotary: (212) 642-8220
Debtors Anonymous Hotline: (212) 969-8111

Shopaholics, Limited
(212) 675–4342
(active in the NYC area)

Suggested Reading

Wesson, Carolyn. *Women Who Shop Too Much: Overcoming the Urge to Splurge*. New York: St. Martin's Press, 1990.

Damon, Janet. *Shopaholics: Serious Help for Addicted Spenders*. Los Angeles, Calif.: Price Stern Sloan, 1988.

Witkin, Georgia, Ph.D. *Quick Fixes & Small Comforts*. New York: Villard Books, 1988.

Mundis, Jerrold. *How to Get Out of Debt, Stay Out of Debt and Live Prosperously*. New York: Bantam Books, 1988.

11. SMOKING ADDICTION

The evidence is overwhelming . . . smoking is dangerous to one's health, to the non-smokers around the smoker, and even to persons not yet born. Yet the facts are that most smokers are motivated and would like to quit . . . but have given up to some extent on their ability to succeed and on the value of outside assistance.

Guidelines for Quitting
---

1. Set this phrase solidly in your thinking: "Smoking is a threat to my life. I must quit."

2. The urge to smoke lasts five to ten minutes. Wait it out by exercising, reading, meditating, etc. The first 24 hours without a cigarette are the hardest.

3. See yourself as a non-smoker, enjoying food more, being more congenial, healthier.

4. Stay in areas and situations where smoking is forbidden.

5. Set a goal for doing without smoking. If you backslide, don't be depressed. Start over. You can do it!

6. Tell your friends of your desire not to smoke. Ask them to pray that you'll be strong enough to quit.

Smokenders

One avenue of help is Smokenders, the oldest, largest and most successful program of its kind in the world. It has been in operation for over seventeen years, and is taught throughout the United States, Canada, Great Britain, Australia and Japan.

Smokenders is not a quick fix, but a comprehensive six-week program designed to deal with the addiction and to break the psychological connectors. The two-hour sessions are taught by former smokers who have quit successfully with Smokenders, then were trained to become instructors. For further information call or write:

Smokenders

1-800-828-HELP

Quit and Stay Quit

Terry A. Rustin, M.D.

9731 Greenwillow

Houston, TX 77096

The American Cancer Society

19 W. 56th Street

New York, NY 10019

(212) 382-2169

Their Fresh Start program consists of two-week programs.

Smokers Anonymous meets in many places. Check local paper for information.

Suggested Reading

Casey, Karen. *If Only I Could Quit: Becoming A Non-Smoker*. Center City, Minn.: Hazelden Educational Materials, 1987.

Walker, Ellen. *Smoker: Self Portrait of a Nicotine Addict*. Center City, Minn.: Hazelden Educational Materials, 1990.

Jenne, E. *12 Steps for Smokers*. Pamphlet. Center City, Minn.: Hazelden Educational Materials, 1987.

12. WORKAHOLISM

Have you ever wondered how much of a workaholic you are? We have found the following inventory to be useful in that determination. Complete it as quickly as you can! Your first response is often your most honest answer.

Workaholism Inventory[9]

1. Once I start a job I have no peace until I finish. _____True _____False

2. Whereas most people are overly conscious of their feelings, I like to deal with facts. _____True _____False

3. I sometimes become so preoccupied by a thought that I cannot get it out of my mind. _____True _____False

4. I have periods in which I cannot sit or lie down—I need to be doing something. _____True _____False

5. My mind is often occupied by thoughts about what I have done wrong or not completed. _____True _____False

6. I feel irritated when I see another person's messy desk or cluttered room. _____True _____False

7. I am more comfortable in a neat, clean, and orderly room than in a messy one. _____True _____False

8. I cannot get through a day or a week without a schedule or a list of jobs to do. ____True ____False

9. I believe that the man who works the hardest and longest deserves to get ahead. ____True ____False

10. If my job/housework demands more time, I will cut out pleasurable activities to see that it gets done. ____True ____False

11. I frequently feel angry without knowing what or who is bothering me. ____True ____False

12. I think talking about feelings to others is a waste of time. ____True ____False

13. I like always to be in control of myself and to know as much as possible about things happening around me. ____True ____False

14. I feel that the more one can know about future events, the better off he will be. ____True ____False

15. I rarely give up until the job has been completely finished. ____True ____False

16. I often expect things of myself that no one else would ask of himself. ____True ____False

17. I sometimes worry about whether I was wrong or made a mistake. ____ True ____False

18. I would like others to see me as not having any faults. ____True ____False

Now go back and count the number of "True's" you checked. A score of 5 or less reflects a fairly relaxed person. A score of 6 to 10 is average. A score of 10 or more reflects a definite tendency toward workaholism.

I. Self-Help Programs

Suggested Reading

Minirth, Frank B., M.D., et al. *The Workaholic and His Family: An Inside Look.* Grand Rapids, Mich.: Baker Book House, 1981.

Smith, Carol Cox. *Recovery at Work: A Clean and Sober Career Guide.* Center City, Minn.: Hazelden Educational Materials, 1990.

Woititz, Janet G., Ed.D. *The Self-Sabotage Syndrome: Adult Children in the Workplace.* Deerfield Beach, Fla.: Health Communications, Inc., 1989.

Robinson, Bryan E. *Work Addiction: Hidden Legacies of Adult Children.* Deerfield Beach, Fla.: Health Communications, Inc., 1989.

Berry, Carmen R. *When Helping You Is Hurting Me: Escaping the Messiah Trap.* San Francisco: Harper and Row, 1988.

13. OTHER COMPULSIONS[10]

An Evaluation

Use the following profiles as an evaluation tool. How many "position statements" can you identify with in each of the four categories? Check those statements that apply to you, then take a look at the scoring.

CARETAKER

_____ I generally feel responsible for the happiness of others.

_____ I have often "bent the rules" to bail people out of trouble that they brought on themselves.

_____ Sometimes I wonder why so many people lean on me without being sensitive to *my* need to lean once in a while.

_____ I find it easier to take care of others than to take care of myself.

_____ I never have enough time to accomplish all my tasks.

_____ I am more interested in talking about other people's problems than in talking about my own.

PEOPLE PLEASER

_____ I have trouble saying no even when I know I should.

_____ I often say "It doesn't matter," when it really does.

_____ I seldom feel angry, but often feel hurt.

_____ In the name of peace, I try to avoid talking about problems.

_____ I usually feel that other people's needs and opinions are more important than my own.

_____ I often apologize.

_____ I would rather give in than make someone mad.

MARTYR

_____ I am usually willing to do without so others can have what they want.

_____ I feel I have terrible luck.

_____ It feels natural to worry a lot about other people.

_____ My first impulse is to say no when something fun comes up.

_____ When life runs smoothly for a while, I begin to anticipate disaster.

_____ I believe life is a struggle and I accept suffering as my lot.

TAP DANCER

_____ I find it difficult or impossible to tell anyone the whole truth.

_____ I would rather end a primary relationship than make a binding commitment.

_____ Figuring out "what I can get away with" is exciting to me.

_____ I have an abiding fear of being "caught" or "cornered."

_____ I always have "Plan B" in mind in case I need to escape.

_____ To avoid feeling lonely, I have to run faster than I used to.

Remember, no one is perfect. Everyone faces some of these obstacles. Even though we may shake our heads and say, "My God,

I'm all of it," the issue is that we can deal with anything we can name. This is not an exercise to see how broken we are, but to understand that if we can identify the obstacles and are willing to work through them, we will increase our ability to "soar like eagles."

Are You a Perfectionist?

Check the following statements that apply to you.

_____ If I can't do a thing exactly right, I won't do it at all.

_____ I often start things I don't finish.

_____ It's hard for me to relax even after my work is done.

_____ I am often amazed at the incompetence of others.

_____ I can't stand it when things are out of place.

_____ I find unpredictability vexing, if not intolerable.

_____ I have a burning need to set things right.

_____ I worry a lot about why I haven't done better.

_____ Any kind of personal failure is the worst thing I can think of.

_____ It seems to me that standards are slipping everywhere.

If you checked more than three of the above, you tend to be a perfectionist, which means you are subject to procrastination, problem-filled relationships, low self-esteem. Extremes of perfectionist behavior can lead to anorexia, bulimia and psychosomatic behavior.

Ways to overcome perfectionism include:

1. Begin by acknowledging your mistake-prone nature. No one is perfect. Relax and accept yourself just the way you are; not the way you think you should be.

2. Make a list of the advantages and disadvantages of requiring flawlessness in yourself. You'll be surprised at how few advantages there are to rigid thinking.

3. See the difference between perfectionism and the healthy pursuit of excellence.

4. Adjust your thinking to reduced goals. Dare to be average for a time.

5. Don't be driven by others' expectations of you. "The way to be perfect is to be perfectly you."

6. Be willing to experience anxiety about loose ends. These feelings will pass if you let some things slide.

7. Say, "I can concentrate on hearing my own voice, my own needs, my own feelings." That is when healing begins.

8. For the extreme perfectionist, therapy is recommended.

How to Help a Compulsive Friend

- Sometimes we wonder if a friend or relative is compulsive. Keep in mind that it's sometimes difficult to diagnose a friend's compulsion unless she's told us her inner feelings.

- Confront. Talk to her about it in a gentle way. Give her a book or pamphlet about the problem and ask her if she identifies with it. If you're dealing with the same problem, share your experiences.

- Don't be discouraged if she doesn't respond at first. One overweight person visited a self-help group once a year for five years before she began working on her overeating problem.

- Locate help. If your friend is aware of her problem, encourage her to get help. Investigate professional counselors or self-help groups. Accompany your friend on her first visit.

- Don't preach. Understand your role as a sounding board, not an advice giver. It's easy to give poor advice. For example, when friends of a bulimic advised her to exercise more instead of throwing up, she did and became a compulsive exerciser as well as bulimic. A "quick fix" solution often does not deal with root issues.

- Listen. Remember that compulsions often come from childhood pain and that people need to deal with this pain. Try not to be shocked by anything your friend tells you. Keep confessions confidential.

- Pray for and with your friend. Pray for her impaired thinking as well as her external behavior. Ask God to help you understand the problem and do whatever is needed.

- Don't tempt. Don't suggest another doctor to the prescription drug addict. Don't offer the overeater "just one little piece" of cheesecake.

- Be patient. "It may get worse before it gets better." Counselor's advice: "Depression may be a good sign in compulsives because they're getting in touch with their feelings instead of avoiding them through their wrong behavior."

- Accept her. Your love is invaluable. As your friend finds she doesn't have to hide her true self around you, she'll accept herself more. And you'll find the joy of being a mirror of God's love to her.

From Virtue magazine, March/April 1989

Suggested Reading

May, Gerald G., M.D. *Addiction and Grace.* San Francisco: Harper and Row, 1988.

Schaef, Anne Wilson. *When Society Becomes an Addict.* San Francisco: Harper and Row, 1987.

Smalley, Gary and Trent, John, Ph.D. *The Language of Love: A Powerful Way to Maximize Insight, Intimacy, and Understanding.* Pomona, Calif.: Focus on the Family Publishing, 1988.

Lasater, Lane. *Recovery from Compulsive Behavior: How to Transcend Your Troubled Family.* Deerfield Beach, Fla.: Health Communications, Inc., 1989.

Burka, Jane B., Ph.D., and Yuen, Lenora M., Ph.D. *Procrastination: Why You Do It, What to Do About It.* Reading, Mass.: Addison-Wesley Publishing Company, 1983.

Stoop, Dr. David. *Hope for the Perfectionist.* Nashville, Tenn.: Thomas Nelson Publishers, 1989.

Viorst, Judith. *Necessary Losses: The Loves, Illusions, Dependencies and Impossible Expectations That All of Us Have to Give Up in Order to Grow.* New York: Simon and Schuster, 1986.

MacNutt, Francis, and MacNutt, Judith. *Praying for Your Unborn Child.* New York: Doubleday, 1989.

Timmons, Tim. *Anyone Anonymous.* Old Tappan, N.J.: 1990.

14. TREATMENT CENTER INFORMATION

Lifeworks Clinic

(Also known as The New Life Family Workshop)

Started in 1983 as a special four-and-a-half day program designed to help compulsive/addictive people discover and work through the family-of-origin roots of their self-defeating pattern of living.

Terry Kellogg, Director of Lifeworks Clinic, is a family systems therapist and has founded several mental health programs in recent years. For further information about location of these clinics and types of programs available, write to:

Inquiries/Referrals

Friel Associates/Lifeworks/ClearLife

P.O. Box 26097

St. Paul, MN 55126

(612) 628-0220

Addiction Treatment Centers

For information about the location of more than 1,600 centers offering various programs and services for recovery write:

Health Communications and Journal Directory
Customer Services
3201 S.W. 15th Street
Deerfield Beach, FL 33442
1-800-851-9100

15. OTHER RESOURCES FOR PUBLICATIONS, FILMS, TAPES, VIDEOS, ETC.

Hazelden Publishing and Education
RW 15 P.O. Box 176
Center City, MN 55012
1-800-328-9000

Recovery Publications, Inc.
P.O. Box 44
Curtis, WA 98538
(360) 245-3386

Johnson Institute
7205 Ohms Lane, Ste. 200
Minneapolis, MN 55439
(612) 831-1630

National Self-Help Clearinghouse
25 West 43rd Street, Room 620
New York, NY 10036
(212) 354-8525

Health Communications and Journal Directory
3201 S.W. 15th Street
Deerfield Beach, FL 33442
1-800-851-9100

For information about workshops, treatment and educational
materials for adult children and co-dependents, write:

Onsite Training and Consulting, Inc.
Nurturing Networks
Joseph R. Cruse, M.D.
 and Sharon Wegscheider-Cruse
2455 West Chicago Street
Rapid City, SD 57702
(605) 341-7432

Kelly Productions
530 South Philadelphia Boulevard
Aberdeen, MD 21001
1-800-638-5430

II. Help for Families and Friends

OPEN LETTER TO THE FAMILY[11]

"I am an alcoholic. I need help. Don't allow me to lie to you and have you accept it as the truth, for in doing so you encourage more lies. The truth may be painful, but get at it.

"Don't let me outsmart you. This only teaches me to avoid responsibility and to lose respect for you at the same time.

"Don't let me exploit you or take advantage of you. In doing so, you become an accomplice to my evasion of responsibility.

"Don't lecture, moralize, scold, praise, blame, or argue when I'm drunk or sober. Don't pour out my liquor; you may feel better, but the situation will be worse.

"Don't accept my promises. This is my method of postponing pain. If an agreement is made, keep it.

"Don't allow your anxiety to tempt you to try to do for me what I must do for myself.

"Don't lose your temper with me; it will destroy you and any possibility of helping me.

"Don't cover up the consequences of my drinking; it reduces the crisis but perpetuates my illness.

"Above all, don't run away from reality as I do. Alcoholism, my illness, gets worse as my drinking continues. Start to learn now. Understand. Plan for my recovery. I need help from professionals who deal with my illness. I cannot help myself. To do nothing is the worst choice you can make for me."

1. INTERVENTION

How It Gets the Addict to Treatment

During my period of alcoholism I had two experiences where loving people tried to make me face up to my problem. These confrontations now have a specific name—*intervention*. The purpose: to get the sick person to face up to his/her problem and, preferably, go into a treatment center—or if this cannot be financed to seek help through a local support group.

The first effort on my behalf succeeded in getting me to a treatment center. After coming home from this 28-day program, I was dry two months before "falling off the wagon." I was one of the small percentage of failures of this particular treatment center.

The second intervention also got me to a treatment center and probably saved my life.

Careful planning is essential. It can work with serious drug, alcohol, gambling problems, plus other life or family-threatening addictions. You can see how carefully the following intervention must have been planned and rehearsed beforehand:

Intervention—A Case Study

Late one Sunday morning Paul Taylor dragged himself out of bed with a groan. He was sick to his stomach, his head hurt, and his hands were shaking. He wished he hadn't had so much to drink the night before, and he was looking forward to a strong cup of coffee.

When Paul came downstairs, he was surprised to find his wife and children sitting in the living room with the family doctor and the vice-president of the insurance company where he was a salesman. The doctor explained to Paul that they wanted to talk with him about his drinking problem, and he asked Paul to take a seat.

It was Paul's wife who spoke first, her voice shaking. "Three weeks ago you came home drunk in the middle of the night, yelling and swearing. You threw my mother's antique china through the window, and the children and I hid in one of their bedrooms. We were so afraid of what you might do, we locked the door."

Paul glared at his wife and shook his head in amazement. He turned to the vice-president, who was his immediate supervisor, and explained that his wife was a nervous woman who frequently became hysterical for no reason. "I may have a little too much to drink now and again, but my wife is really sick. Maybe she needs to see a psychiatrist."

"Dad," Paul's oldest son interrupted hesitantly, "when I played football in high school, I was always afraid of how you would act at my games. One time when you were drinking, you ran out on the field and tried to slug the referee. Last month I brought my fiancée home to meet the family and you were sitting in the rocking chair, drinking. When we were alone you said that you could take her any time you wanted, and that she would like an older man."

Paul was furious. "You're a liar," he shouted at his son. "If I have a few too many drinks once in a while, it's none of your business."

Next to speak was Paul's employer. "You're one of our best salesmen," the vice-president said warmly. "And we go back a lot of years. But lately you've cost us three major clients because of your heavy drinking. We want to keep you in the firm, but as long as you are drinking, we can't afford to have you with us."

After the vice-president listed examples of Paul's inappropriate behavior, Paul grew quiet and grim-faced. He slumped down into his chair and listened impassively while his seventeen-year-old daughter told her father how much she loved him, and how much it hurt that he did not keep his promises. "On my sixteenth birthday, you were going to take me out for dinner, but you came home from work drunk and passed out on the floor. I spend a lot of time at my girlfriend's house, but I never bring her here anymore. I'm afraid she might see you drunk, and I don't know what you will say to her."

The family doctor spoke last. He explained to Paul the physical consequences of his heavy drinking, starting with the damage to his brain and descending to his throat, heart, stomach, and liver. "Your high blood pressure makes you a likely candidate for a stroke," he concluded. "And you are fast becoming impotent because of the shrinking of your testicles. If you continue to drink alcohol, your chances of living another five years are not very good."

When the doctor finished speaking, Paul threw up his hands and looked helplessly at his boss. He admitted that he had been drinking a bit too much and that he was worried about his health. "I promise I've had my last drink, and you won't see me drunk again."

The doctor reminded Paul of all the previous times that he had promised to quit drinking and had failed. He explained that alcoholism is a disease that does not respond to will power or good intentions. It was highly improbable that Paul would ever stop drinking on his own. But there was a local treatment center that could give him the help he needed. A room was waiting for him, and he could leave in the morning for a 28-day stay.

Paul admitted that maybe he did need help, but he was offended by the suggestion that he leave immediately. He appealed to his boss to explain that it would take at least a month to find a substitute for his job. The vice-president told Paul that his job was covered, and he was not expected back at work until he completed treatment. This news startled Paul, who protested that he was being railroaded, that he would think it over, and if it seemed like a good idea, he would go when he got ready.

There was an uncomfortable moment of silence, and then Paul's youngest child, a thin, shy five-year-old girl, walked over to her father and put her hand in his. "Daddy," she pleaded, "it's now or never." Paul looked at his daughter and without warning burst into

tears. By the next morning he was on his way to a treatment center.
Note that the core of this intervention was *truth*. No persuasions,
except by the five-year-old at the very end. Medical facts. Facts
regarding family events. On such-and-such a date, this happened.
Paul's work performance spelled out by his employer. All carefully
planned ahead of time.

Families in Crisis

For an intervention specialist, write: Families in Crisis, Inc.,
5200 West 73rd Street, Edina, MN 55439, (612) 893-1883, or
contact local support groups or health professionals for further
information in your area.

Suggested Reading

Pinkham, Mary Ellen and Staff of Families in Crisis, Inc. *How to
     Stop the One You Love from Drinking.* New York: Putnam
     Publishing Group, 1986.
Ford, Betty, with Chris Chase. *Betty: A Glad Awakening.* New
     York: Doubleday Company, Inc. 1987.
Spickard, Anderson, M.D. and Barbara Thompson, *Dying for a
     Drink.* Waco, Tex.: Word Books, 1985.

2. CO-DEPENDENCY

"Codependency is a pattern of painful dependency on compulsive
behaviors and on approval from others in an attempt to find safety,
self-worth and identity. Recovery is possible."

From The National Conference on
Co-Dependency, Scottsdale, Ariz.
September 7–9, 1989

Co-dependents, often without being aware of it, are in bondage to a drinking or drug-using family member. Or to a close friend who is an addict. You can measure the degree of your co-dependency by the number of the following statements that apply to you.

Test Yourself

_____ My good feelings about who I am stem from being liked by you.

_____ My good feelings about who I am stem from receiving approval from you.

_____ Your struggles affect my serenity. My mental attention focuses on solving or relieving your pain.

_____ My mental attention is focused on pleasing you.

_____ My mental attention is focused on protecting you.

_____ My mental attention is focused on manipulating you to "do it my way."

_____ My self-esteem is bolstered by solving your problems.

_____ My self-esteem is bolstered by relieving your pain.

_____ My own hobbies and interests are put aside. My time is spent sharing your interests and hobbies.

_____ Your clothing and personal appearance is dictated by my desires because I feel you are a reflection of me.

_____ Your behavior is dictated by my desires because I feel you are a reflection of me.

_____ I am not aware of how I feel. I am aware of how you feel. I am not aware of what I want. I ask you what you want. If I am not aware of something, I assume.

_____ The dreams I have for my future are linked to you.

_____ My fear of rejection determines what I say or do.

_____ My fear of your anger determines what I say or do.

_____ I use giving as a way of feeling safe in our relationship.

_____ My social circle diminishes as I involve myself with you.

_____ I put my values aside in order to connect with you.

_____ I value your opinion and way of doing things more than my own.

_____ The quality of my life is in relation to the quality of yours.

Letting Go—Freeing Oneself from Co-Dependency

To "let go" does not mean to stop caring, but that I can't do it for someone else.

To "let go" is not to cut myself off, but to realize that I can't control another.

To "let go" is not to enable, but to allow learning from natural consequences.

To "let go" is to admit powerlessness, which means the outcome is not in my hands.

To "let go" is not to try to change or blame another, but to make the most of myself.

To "let go" is not to care for, but to care about.

To "let go" is not to fix, but to be supportive.

To "let go" is not to judge, but to allow another to be a human being.

To "let go" is not to be in the middle arranging all the outcomes, but to allow others to affect their destinies.

To "let go" is not to be protective, but to permit another to face reality.

To "let go" is not to deny, but to accept.

To "let go" is not to nag, scold or argue, but instead to search out my own shortcomings and correct them.

To "let go" is not to adjust everything to my desires, but to take each day as it comes, and cherish myself in it.

To "let go" is not to criticize and regulate anybody, but to try to become what I dream I can be.

To "let go" is not to regret the past, but to grow and live for the future.

To "let go" is to fear less, and love more.

For more information write:

Co-Dependents Anonymous, Inc.
(602) 277-7991

Suggested Reading

Beattie, Melody. *Codependent No More.* San Francisco: Harper/ Hazelden, 1987.

——. *Beyond Codependency: And Getting Better All the Time.* San Francisco: Harper/Hazelden, 1989.

Wegscheider-Cruse, Sharon. *Choicemaking: For Co-Dependents, Adult Children and Spirituality Seekers.* Deerfield Beach, FL: Health Communications, Inc., 1985.

Mellody, Pia. *Facing Codependence: What It Is, Where It Comes From, How It Sabotages Our Lives.* San Francisco: Harper and Row, 1989.

Rinck, Dr. Margaret J. *Can Christians Love Too Much? Breaking the Cycle of Codependency.* Grand Rapids, Mich.: Zondervan, 1989.

Hemfelt, Dr. Robert; Minirth, Dr. Frank; Meier, Dr. Paul. *Love Is a Choice: Recovery for Codependent Relationships.* Nashville, Tenn.: Thomas Nelson Publishers, 1989.

Ells, Alfred. *One-Way Relationships—When You Love Them More Than They Love You: Healing the Codependency in All of Us.* Nashville, Tenn.: Thomas Nelson Publishers, 1990.

Schaef, Anne Wilson. *Co-Dependency: Misunderstood-Mistreated.* San Francisco: Winston Press, 1986.

Woititz, Janet. *Struggle for Intimacy.* Deerfield Beach, Fla.: Health Communications, Inc., 1985.

Silvious, Jan. *Please Don't Say You Need Me.* Grand Rapids, Mich.: Zondervan, 1989.

3. AL-ANON

Al-Anon is a fellowship for the families and friends of alcoholics who need help in understanding and dealing with the alcoholic person. Al-Anon meetings are held weekly in most communities throughout the country. Participants give and receive comfort and encouragement through an honest and open exchange of experiences, strength, and hope. Such groups are bonded together by a policy of anonymity.

An Overview

In Al-Anon sessions people learn:

- not to suffer because of the actions or reactions of other people;
- not to allow themselves to be used or abused in the interest of another's recovery;
- not to do for others what they should do for themselves;
- not to manipulate situations so others will eat, go to bed, get up, pay bills, etc.;
- not to cover up for another's mistakes or misdeeds;
- not to create a crisis;
- not to prevent a crisis if it is in the natural course of events.

This kind of detachment is neither kind nor unkind. It does not imply evaluation of the person or situation from which one is detaching. It is simply a means for individuals to recover from the adverse affects on their lives of living with someone afflicted with the disease of alcoholism. Detachment helps families look at their situations realistically and objectively, thereby making intelligent decisions possible. For further information, write to:

Al-Anon Family Group Hdq., Inc.
1600 Corporate Landing Parkway
Virginia Beach, VA 23454
(757) 563-1600

Suggested Reading for Families and Friends of Alcoholics

Wegscheider, Sharon. *Another Chance: Hope and Health for the Alcoholic Family.* Palo Alto, Calif.: Science and Behavior Books, Inc., 1980.

Costales, Claire and Barack, Priscilla. *A Secret Hell—Surviving Life with an Alcoholic.* Ventura, Calif.: Regal Books, 1984.

Spickard, Anderson A., M.D. and Thompson, Barbara R. *Dying for a Drink.* Waco, Texas: Word, Inc., 1985.

Drews, Toby R. *Getting Them Sober: A Guide for Those Who Live with an Alcoholic, Volume 1 and Volume 2.* Los Angeles, Calif.: Bridger Publications, Inc. 1980 (Vol. 1) and 1983 (Vol. 2).

Al-Anon Staff. *Al-Anon Faces Alcoholism.* 2nd ed. New York: Al-Anon Family Group Headquarters, Inc.

Staff of Family in Crisis, Inc. and Pinkham, Mary Ellen. *How to Stop the One You Love from Drinking.* New York: Putnam Publishing Group, 1986.

Larsen, Ernie. *Stage II Recovery: Life Beyond Addiction.* San Francisco: Harper and Row, 1985.

4. FAMILIES ANONYMOUS

Families Anonymous is a fellowship of relatives and friends of people who are involved in the abuse of mind-altering substances or exhibiting related behavioral problems such as running away, delinquency, underachieving, etc. Any concerned person is encouraged to attend meetings—even if there is only a suspicion of a problem. It is a self-help organization whose program is based upon an adaptation of the Twelve Steps and Twelve Traditions first formulated by Alcoholics Anonymous.

Group discussions are built upon a specific theme: such as expectations, anxiety, overprotection, or better communications.

As members share their own experiences—successes and failures—those going through a particular crisis find understanding and emotional support. Attention is focused upon the feelings, attitudes, actions, and reactions of family members; not upon trying to change the person involved in the unacceptable behavior. Experience has shown that help for the family means important help for the chemically dependent individual.

Those wishing to obtain information about the Families Anonymous group in their area or to start a new group may contact:

> Families Anonymous, Inc.
> P.O. Box 3475
> Culver City, CA 90231
> 1-800-736-9805
> (310) 313-5800

To help defray costs (including postage) FA charges $2.00 for a packet of informational material.

> National Domestic Violence Hotline
> 1-800-799-7233

Suggested Reading for Adult Children from Addictive and Other Dysfunctional Families

Bradshaw, John. *Bradshaw On: The Family: A Revolutionary Way of Self-Discovery.* Deerfield Beach, Fla.: Health Communications, Inc., 1988.

Whitfield, Charles L., M.D. *Healing the Child Within: Discovery and Recovery for Adult Children of Dysfunctional Families.* Deerfield Beach, Fla.: Health Communications, Inc., 1987.

Whitfield, Charles L., M.D. *A Gift to Myself: A Personal Guide to*

Healing My Child Within. Deerfield Beach, Fla.: Health Communications, Inc., 1989.

Friends In Recovery. *The 12 Steps for Adult Children from Addictive and Other Dysfunctional Families.* San Diego, Calif.: Tools for Recovery, 1988

Friends In Recovery. *The 12 Steps—A Way Out: A Working Guide for Adult Children from Addictive and Other Dysfunctional Homes.* San Diego, Calif.: Tools for Recovery, 1988.

Ross, Ron. *When I Grow Up . . . I Want To Be An Adult.* San Diego, Calif.: Tools for Recovery, 1990.

Friends In Recovery. *The Twelve Steps for Christians: From Addictive and Other Dysfunctional Families.* San Diego, Calif.: Tools for Recovery, 1988.

Friends In Recovery. *The Twelve Steps—A Spiritual Journey: A Working Guide for Adult Children from Addictive and Other Dysfunctional Families.* San Diego, Calif.: Tools for Recovery, 1988.

Wegscheider-Cruse, Sharon. *The Miracle of Recovery: Healing for Addicts, Adult Children and Co-dependents.* Deerfield Beach, Fla.: Health Communications, Inc., 1989.

Wholey, Dennis. *Becoming Your Own Parent.* New York: Doubleday, 1988.

Buhler, Rich. *Pain and Pretending: You Can Be Set Free from the Hurts of the Past.* Nashville, Tenn.: Thomas Nelson Publishers, 1988.

5. ADULT CHILDREN OF ALCOHOLICS (ACOA)

Test for Family Members of Alcoholics

1. Do you lose sleep because of a problem drinker?

2. Do most of your thoughts revolve around the problem drinker or problems that arise because of him or her?

3. Do you exact promises about the drinking that are not kept?

4. Do you make threats to a drinker in the family and not follow through on them?

5. Has your attitude fluctuated toward this problem drinker (alternating between love and hate)?

6. Do you mark, hide, dilute, and/or empty bottles of liquor or medication?

7. Do you think that everything would be okay if only the problem drinker would stop or control the drinking?

8. Do you feel alone, fearful, anxious, angry, or frustrated most of the time? Are you beginning to feel dislike for yourself and to wonder about your sanity?

9. Do you feel responsible for and guilty about the drinking problem?

10. Do you find *your* moods fluctuating widely—as a direct result of the problem drinker's moods and actions?

11. Do you try to conceal, deny, or protect the problem drinker?

12. Have you withdrawn from outside activities and friends because of embarrassment and shame over the drinking problem?

13. Have you taken over many chores and duties that you would normally expect the problem drinker to assume?

14. Do you feel forced to try to exert tight control over the family expenses with less and less success? And are financial problems increasing?

15. Do you feel the need to justify your actions and attitudes and, at the same time, feel somewhat smug and self-righteous when you compare yourself to the drinker?

16. If there are children in the house, do they often take sides with either the problem drinker or the spouse?

17. Are the children showing signs of emotional stress, such as with-drawal, having trouble with authority figures, or rebelling?

18. Have you noticed physical symptoms in yourself, such as nausea, a knot in the stomach, ulcers, shakiness, sweating palms, or bitten fingernails?

19. Do you feel utterly defeated in that nothing you can say or do will move the problem drinker?

20. Where this applies, is your sexual relationship with a problem drinker affected by feelings of revulsion? Do you "use" sex to manipulate, or refuse sex to punish him or her?

A yes to any five of these questions probably indicates that alcoholism exists in the family and is producing negative changes in the person answering them.

The Bill of Rights for Adult Children of Alcoholics

I have the right . . .

1. To have numerous choices in my life beyond mere survival.

2. Not to be responsible for others' behaviors, actions, feelings, or problems.

3. To say no to anything or anyone when I feel I am not ready, it is unsafe or violates my values.

4. To be uniquely me without feeling I'm not good enough.

5. To make mistakes and not have to be perfect.

6. To terminate conversations with those who put me down or humiliate me.

7. To change, grow, and be healthier than those around me.

8. To set limits, make my own decisions, honor my own priorities.

9. To get angry, even at someone I love, without fearing that I, the other person, or the relationship will dissolve.

10. To feel all of my feelings, to get in touch with the wounded Inner Child.

11. To grieve over what I didn't get that I needed or what I got that I didn't need or want.

12. Not to smile when I cry or feel hurt.

13. To my own personal space and time needs.

14. To have my needs and wants respected by others.

15. To change my mind at any time.

16. To be relaxed, playful and frivolous. It's O.K.!

17. To grieve over actual or threatened losses.

18. Not to be ashamed for what I don't know or can't do.

19. Not to be molested by fear.

20. To forgive others, to forgive myself and to give and to receive unconditional love.

Adult Children of Alcoholics can obtain help by attending Al-Anon and ACOA (Adult Children of Alcoholics) meetings if they need to understand more about their relationship to alcoholics. A telephone directory or local newspaper can provide local numbers to call for further information.

Suggested Reading

Woititz, Dr. Janet G. *Adult Children of Alcoholics*. Deerfield Beach, Fla.: Health Communications, Inc., 1983.
Black, Claudia. *It Will Never Happen to Me: Children of Alcoholics As Youngsters*. Denver, Colorado: M.A.C. Printing and Publications Division, 1982.

Gravitz, Herbert L. and Bowden, Julie D. *Guide to Recovery: A Book for Adult Children of Alcoholics.* Homes Beach, Fla.: Learning Publications, Inc., 1985.

Ackerman, Robert J., Ph.D. *Perfect Daughters: Adult Daughters of Alcoholics.* Deerfield Beach, Fla.: Health Communications, Inc., 1989.

Deutsch, Charles. *Broken Bottles, Broken Dreams: Understanding and Helping the Children of Alcoholics.* New York: Teacher's College Press, 1982.

Seixas, Judith S. and Youcha, Geraldine. *Children of Alcoholism: A Survivor's Manual.* New York: Harper and Row, 1986.

Kritsberg, Wayne. *The Adult Children of Alcoholics Syndrome from Discovery to Recovery.* Deerfield Beach, Fla.: Health Communications, Inc. 1983.

Curtis, Nancy. *Beyond Survival: The New Testament Solution for Adult Children of Alcoholics.* Lakeland, Fla.: Accord Books, 1990.

Martin, Sara Hines. *Healing for Adult Children of Alcoholics.* Nashville, Tenn.: Broadman Press, 1988.

6. ALATEEN

Alateen is a fellowship of young Al-Anon members, usually teenagers, whose lives have been affected by someone else's drinking. These young people come together to share experiences, strength and hope with each other and thus learn effective ways to cope with their problems.

The Twelve Traditions of Alateen

1. Our common welfare should come first; personal progress for the greatest number depends upon unity.

2. For our group purposes there is but one authority—a loving God as He may express Himself in our group conscience. Our leaders are but trusted servants; they do not govern.

3. The only requirement for membership is that there be a problem of alcoholism in a relative or friend. The teenage relatives of alcoholics, when gathered together for mutual aid, may call themselves an Alateen Group provided that, as a group, they have no other affiliation.

4. Each group should be autonomous, except in matters affecting other Alateen and Al-Anon Family Groups or AA as a whole.

5. Each Alateen Group has but one purpose: to help other teenagers of alcoholics. We do this by practicing the Twelve Steps of AA ourselves and by encouraging and understanding the members of our immediate families.

6. Alateens, being part of Al-Anon Family Groups, ought never to endorse, finance or lend our name to any outside enterprise, lest problems of money, property and prestige divert us from our primary spiritual aim. Although a separate entity, we should always cooperate with Alcoholics Anonymous.

7. Every group ought to be fully self-supporting, declining outside contributions.

8. Alateen 12th-Step work should remain forever nonprofessional, but our service centers may employ special workers.

9. Our groups, as such, ought never to be organized; but we may create service boards or committees directly responsible to those they serve.

10. The Alateen Groups have no opinion on outside issues; hence our name ought never to be drawn into public controversy.

11. Our public relations policy is based on attraction rather than promotion; we need always maintain personal anonymity at the level of press, radio, TV and films. We need guard with special care the anonymity of all AA members.

12. Anonymity is the spiritual foundation of all our Traditions, ever reminding us to place principles above personalities.

Used with permission from Al-Anon Family Group Hdq., Inc. © 1969
1600 Corporate Landing Parkway
Virginia Beach, VA 23454

The Twelve Traditions of AA

1. Our common welfare should come first; personal recovery depends upon AA unity.

2. For our group purpose there is but one ultimate authority—a loving God as He may express Himself in our group conscience. Our leaders are but trusted servants; they do not govern.

3. The only requirement for AA membership is a desire to stop drinking.

4. Each group should be autonomous except in matters affecting other groups or AA as a whole.

5. Each group has but one primary purpose—to carry its message to the alcoholic who still suffers.

6. An AA group ought never endorse, finance, or lend the AA name to any related facility or outside enterprise, lest problems of money, property and prestige divert us from our primary purpose.

7. Every AA group ought to be fully self-supporting, declining outside contributions.

8. Alcoholics Anonymous should remain forever nonprofessional, but our service centers may employ special workers.

9. AA, as such, ought never be organized; but we may create service boards or committees directly responsible to those they serve.

10. Alcoholics Anonymous has no opinion on outside issues; hence the AA name ought never be drawn into public controversy.

11. Our public relations policy is based on attraction rather than promotion; we need always maintain personal anonymity at the level of press, radio, and films.

12. Anonymity is the spiritual foundation of all our traditions, ever reminding us to place principles before personalities. Used with permission of Alcoholics Anonymous World Services, Inc.

Suggested Reading

Hornik-Beer, Edith Lynn. *A Teenager's Guide to Living with an Alcoholic Parent.* Center City, Minn.: Hazelden Foundation, 1984.

DiGiovanni, Kathe. *My House Is Different (For Children of Alcoholics Age 6 and Up).* Center City, Minn.: Hazelden Foundation, 1986.

Ackerman, Robert J. *Growing in the Shadow—Children of Alcoholics.* Deerfield Beach, Fla.: Health Communications, Inc., 1986.

Hipp, Earl. *Fighting Invisible Tigers: A Stress Management Guide for Teens.* Minneapolis, Minn.: Free Spirit Publishing, 1985.

Smith, Ann. *Grandchildren of Alcoholics: Another Generation of Co-dependency.* Deerfield Beach, Fla.: Health Communications, Inc., 1988.

For further information:

> Children of Alcoholics Foundation
> 33 West 60th Street
> New York, NY 10023

7. PARENTS OF CHILDREN ON DRUGS

Seven Do's and Don't's

1. *Be patient.* Don't rush into one-on-one confrontations and conflicts with the youngster. You are dealing with a competitor (drugs) that is a wily adversary.

2. *Don't feel compelled to act as a parent should.* Parent/child rules don't apply during this time. You are dealing with a sick person who is in a frenzied emotional state. Normal parental rules and patterns usually don't work.

3. *Don't use or listen to negative messages.* Detach yourself. Don't participate in name-calling. It's destructive and weakens everyone's self-image. Resist the normal impulse to defend yourself against accusations the teen makes about you.

4. *Don't be angry when your child doesn't show love and concern.* During this time, your child is incapable of displaying genuine emotions. Be responsible first for your own behavior. Don't return useless anger, judgmental resentment and name-calling. Show concern and sympathy but don't try to cover up or aid the drug-user's addiction. The individual is sick. Don't become sick along with him/her.

5. *Don't give the teenager anything destructive.* Don't give financial or emotional support if it will be used in a negative way. Be tough in your loving.

6. *Take care of yourself.* Set goals and achieve them. Don't let your teenager be an excuse for your own poor achievement and laziness. Maintain your own health and mental and spiritual well-being.

7. *Go outside the family for help.* City, township and county groups, your local hospital or substance-abuse treatment center, schools and clergy can provide information and support.

For further information:

> The National Clearinghouse for Alcohol and
> Drug Information
> P.O. Box 2345
> Rockville, MD 20852
> (301) 468–2600

Parents Anonymous

Parents Anonymous is a program for parents who already have or are afraid they might physically abuse their children. Not a twelve-step program. For further information send $2.00 donation to:

> Child Help USA
> 1345 El Centro Ave.
> P.O. Box 630
> Hollywood, CA 90028
> (213) 465–4016

Suggested Reading

Dobson, Dr. James C. *Love Must Be Tough.* Waco, Tex.: Word, Inc., 1983.

Halpern, Howard M., Ph.D. *Cutting Loose: An Adult Guide to Coming to Terms with Your Parents.* New York: Bantam Books, Inc., 1978.

Nilsen, Mary Y. *When A Bough Breaks: Mending the Family Tree.* Center City: Minn.: Hazelden Foundation, 1985.

Hodgson, Harriet. *A Parent's Survival Guide: How to Cope When Your Kid Is Using Drugs.* New York: Harper and Row, 1986.

Kaufman, Gershen. *Shame, The Power of Caring.* Cambridge, Mass.: Schenkman Publishing

Satir, Virginia. *Peoplemaking.* Palo Alto, Calif.: Science and Behavior Books, Inc., 1972.

8. CHILD ABUSE/INCEST/SEXUAL ABUSE

In recent years there has been a shocking new awareness of the magnitude and destructiveness of child abuse. As I revealed my own experience (see page 34) of childhood molestation by an uncle in behavior workshops, workshops, seminars, and discussion groups, women have opened up, often with an explosion of tears, to tell how it happened to them. "All these years I've kept it hidden," they will almost always say. "I've never been able to tell anyone before."

It is painful for them to open up old wounds, yet many, many healings have resulted when they do. Sexual abuse, incest survivors, and battered women support groups are forming all over the country.

Child abuse is often sexual, incestuous. It can be physical, verbal, mental, emotional, spiritual as well. Deprivation abuse occurs when the parent(s) are in the home but are emotionally unavailable to the child. There are more and more cases of parents beating their children to death. As drug abuse has increased, child abuse has increased. Recent studies reveal that one in three women will be sexually molested by her eighteenth birthday and usually by someone she knows.

Incest Survivors Anonymous

For help write:

Incest Survivors Anonymous
P.O. Box 17245
Long Beach, CA 90807
(562) 428-5599

National Domestic Violence Hotline:
1-800-799-7233

Suggested Reading

Gil, Eliana. *Outgrowing the Pain: A Book For and About Adults Abused as Children.* San Francisco: Launch Press, 1984.

Woititz, Dr. Janet G., Ph.D. *Healing Your Sexual Self.* Deerfield Beach, Fla.: Health Communications, 1989.

Bass, Ellen and Davis, Laura. *The Courage to Heal: A Guide for Women Survivors of Child Sexual Abuse.* New York: Harper and Row, 1988.

Bass, Ellen and Davis, Laura. *The Courage to Heal Workbook: For Women & Men Survivors of Child Sexual Abuse.* New York: Harper and Row, 1990.

Forward, Susan and Buck, Craig. *Betrayal of Innocence: Incest and Its Devastation.* Los Angeles: Jeremy P. Tarcher, Inc., 1978.

Jannsen, Martha. *Silent Scream.* Philadelphia, Penn.: Fortress Press, 1983.

McNaron, Toni and Morgan, Yarrow. *Voices in the Night: Women Speaking about Incest.* Pittsburgh, Penn.: Cleis Press, 1982.

Sandford, Paula. *Garlands for Ashes: Healing Victims of Sexual Abuse.* Tulsa, Okla.: Victory House Publishers, 1988.

Kunzman, Kristin A. *The Healing Way: Adult Recovery from Childhood Sexual Abuse.* New York: Harper and Row, 1990.

Ackerman, Robert J. *Abused No More: Recovery for Women from Abusive or Co-dependent Relationships.* Blue Ridge Summit, Penn.: HSI/TAB Books, 1989.

Miller, Kathy C. *Out of Control: A Christian Parent's Victorious Struggle with Child Abuse.* Waco, Tex.: Word, Inc.

Rutter, Peter. M.D. *Sex in the Forbidden Zone: When Men in Power—Therapists, Doctors, Clergy, Teachers and Others—Betray Women's Trust.* San Francisco: Jeremy P. Tarcher, Inc. 1990.

Martin, Jessica. *How Our Family Coped with Incest.* Avon-by-the-Sea, N.J.: Magnificat Press, 1989.

Allender, Dan, Ph.D. *The Wounded Heart: Hope for Adult Victims of Childhood Sexual Abuse.* Colorado Springs, Col.: Nav-Press, 1990.

9. SUICIDE

Before you finish reading this page, someone in the United States will try to kill himself. At least 60 Americans will have taken their own lives by this time tomorrow. More than 25,000 persons in the United States killed themselves last year, and nine times that many attempted suicide. Many of those who attempted will try again, a number with lethal success. And here's the irony: Except for a very few, all of the people who commit suicide want desperately to live.

A *USA Today* poll of 11,000 eighth, ninth, and tenth graders revealed that eighteen percent of girls and eleven percent of boys have tried suicide. As many as one out of seven teens may have tried to end their lives.

No single group, nor color, nor class of people is free from self-inflicted death. Rich or poor, male or female, Christian or Jew, black or white, young or old—to some extent every category of man suffers death by suicide.

The most typical American suicide is a white Protestant male in his forties, married with two children. He is a breadwinner and a taxpayer. The sorrow his untimely, preventable death brings to his family cannot be totaled, but the financial burden on his family and community is considerable. Costs begin with the city or county ambulance fee. The cost of the coroner's time and facilities soon follows. Widow's and survivors' benefits and insurance must be added. Recent studies indicate that the surviving children of suicide victims frequently require mental health care.

Over the years a suicide can cost his community at least $50,000. Counting all the taxes that he would have paid over the next quarter century, in the end, a suicide may cost the community a great deal more.

From "Suicide—It Doesn't Have to Happen," by Edwin S. Schneidman, Ph.D. and Philip Mandelkorn. Prepared by the American Association of Suicidology in cooperation with MSD Health Information Services.

As a parent, relative or friend of a troubled loved-one, here are some of the warning signals that indicate he/she might be thinking about committing suicide:

Warning Signals.

- A previous suicide attempt.
- Extreme depression, which could include sadness, anxiety, and other personality and behavioral changes.
- An unexplained drop in quality of work.
- Clear changes in sleeping or eating habits.
- The abuse of drugs or alcohol.

- Sudden withdrawal from spouse, family, close friends.

- Taking unnecessary risks.

- Major decline of energy and interests.

- Verbal expression of suicidal thoughts, threats, or other statements indicating a desire to die.

- Giving away of prized possessions.

- Extreme neglect of appearance.

- Preparations for death such as putting affairs in order, making a will.

Ways to Help the Person Who Might Be Considering Suicide

- Understand the basic facts, that most suicide attempts come from intense feelings of loneliness, worthlessness, helplessness, depression, or from drug and alcohol abuse, or from disease.

- Take his/her problems, feelings and statements seriously, assuring the person that something can be done for him or her. Encourage professional help.

- Listen and ask concerned questions.

- Don't ever challenge the person to "go ahead." He/she often could call your bluff.

- Help the person dispose of any means he/she might use to end his/her life. Dispose of the pills or guns, for instance.

- Stay with the depressed person. Do something together.

- Don't analyze motives or offer advice such as: "Think how much better off you are than many people. You have so much to live for. Be grateful for what you have. Pull yourself together and keep a stiff upper lip."

- Don't argue or try to reason.

The cardinal rule of suicide prevention is this: *DO SOMETHING*.

If someone you know has attempted suicide and has not received professional care: *GET HELP*.

If someone you know threatens to end his/her life: *GET HELP*.

If someone you know has undergone a drastic change in his/her life and begins preparing wills or giving away personal possessions: *GET HELP*.

Don't wait to see if other signs develop.

Don't decide to consider it for a while. Do it today. Tomorrow may be too late.

Your friendship, concern, and actions could save a life.

Give him/her a crisis number to call. Most communities have local crisis line numbers and information listings. Other sources of help: Suicide prevention centers, crisis intervention centers, mental health clinics, hospitals, family physicians, clergymen.

The American Association of Suicidology is devoted to research and service in the field of suicide prevention, crisis intervention and life-threatening behaviors. The Association sponsors a journal, *Suicide and Life-Threatening Behavior* and a newsletter, *Newslink*. An annual meeting is held in a different city each year during which research papers and clinical seminars are presented. The Association encourages organization as well as individual members and conducts a certification program for organization members. Membership applications from interested professional and lay persons are welcome.

American Association of Suicidology
4201 Connecticut Avenue NW, Ste. 310
Washington, DC 20008
(202) 237-2280

Sugested Reading

Before It's Too Late: What to Do When Someone You Know Attempts Suicide. Pamphlet: The American Association of Suicidology (see address above).

Hipple, John, Ph.D. and Cimbolic, Peter, Ph.D. *The Counselor and Suicidal Crisis.* Springfield, Ill.: Charles C. Thomas, 1979.

Hipple, John, Ph.D. *Preventing Suicide.* Pamphlet. Center City, Minn.: Hazelden Educational Materials, 1988.

For information on the workshop: "Suicide—The Preventable Tragedy" contact:

John Hipple, Ph.D.
North Texas State University
P.O. Box 310968
Denton, TX 76203
(817) 565-2741

III. The Spiritual Dimension

1. ALCOHOLICS FOR CHRIST

Alcoholics for Christ (AC) is a non-denominational, non-profit Christian fellowship, founded in 1981, for alcoholics and their families. It is dedicated to the propagation of the gospel of Jesus Christ, as well as the sharing of his burden for lost and hurting individuals. This fellowship uses the Word of God as its primary source of direction. Its statement:

> We agree that drunkenness is a sin and we believe that alcoholism is a disease with spiritual origins. We rejoice that Jesus forgives us of our sin and heals us of our diseases. Both Scripture and science indicate that there can be an inherited *trait* in the alcoholic.
>
> This "trait" may be triggered in some by persistent rebellious abuse of alcohol (drunkenness) while in others, relatively casual use is all that is needed to set it in motion and, whether we describe it as a *predisposition to alcoholism* or the results of *a curse* ("visiting the iniquities of the fathers upon the children to the third and fourth generation . . . Ex. 20:5), the cure is to be found in *total abstinence* through Jesus Christ.
>
> We are learning that the Lord delivers some persons immediately from the compulsion and desire to drink, for others He does it gradually. In either case, the requirements for *maintaining* deliverance are total abstinence and an ever increasing relationship with the Lord. We believe that God wants us "chemically free" and that it is not His purpose to make "social drinkers" out of drunks. God heals us by removing the compulsion and desire and restoring us to Himself.
>
> The alcoholic and family members who attend local AA or

Al-Anon groups are encouraged to remain active in them and, where possible, to continue to worship within their own body of believers. However, we do recommend where no strong denominational ties exist, regular attendance in a Bible-believing church of their choice.

While the references deal primarily with alcoholism and the alcoholic, the spiritual principles set forth in AC are applicable to all persons and their families who are, or have been, chemically dependent, regardless of the nature of the addiction.

For further information write:

Alcoholics For Christ, Inc.
1316 North Campbell Road
Royal Oak, MI 48076
1-800-441-7877

2. PRAYER OF A RECOVERING ADDICT

Thank you
for setting me free.
Free to yellow my nose in buttercups,
catch a firefly to see his light,
pick the first wild strawberry,
count the stars,
talk to ladybugs,
chase a thistle.

Thank you for setting me free.
Free to see you in
sunlight dancing on the water,
dogwood smiling at the sky,
willows curtseying to the river,
azaleas flaming across the land,
rainbowed cobwebs,
drifting leaves.

Thank you
for setting me free.
Free to play with,
wonder at
and love
all that you have given me.
And free, as well,
to give it back.[13]

Sue Garmon
Souvenirs of Solitude

3. CULTS

Occult Practices

Those who are finding healing through Scripture and the Lordship of Jesus Christ need to be aware that occult practices can get them off track, as they did me (see chapter 5). God warned the Israelites as follows: "Let no one be found among you . . . who practices divination or sorcery, interprets omens, engages in witchcraft, or casts spells, or who consults the dead. Anyone who does these things is detestable to the Lord" (Deuteronomy 18:10–12, NIV).

Other occult practices to avoid:

Fortune telling	Channeling
Ouija boards	Eastern Meditation (TM)
Clairvoyance	Reincarnation
Yoga (Hinduism)	Karma
Automatic writing	Hypnosis/Self-Hypnosis
Astral projection	(trance inducement)
Psychic reading	Mantra Chanting
Psychic healing	Guided Imagery (spiritual
Table tipping	guides)
Biofeedback	Reflexology

Satanism	Pyramid power
ESP	Black/White Magic
Seers	Parapsychology
Metaphysical healing	Nature worship
Satanic music	Astrology
Auto-suggestion	Telepathy
Horoscopes	Voodoo
Tarot Cards	Levitation
Mind control	Cabala
Mind expansion	Seances
Telekinesis	Palmistry
Water-witching	Fantasy games (Dungeons and
Numerology	Dragons)

Information on Cults

Fight back! For information on Satanism and other cults write:

Spiritual Counterfeits Project
P.O. Box 4308
Berkeley, CA 94704
(510) 540-0300

International Cult Education Progra
P.O. Box 2265
Bonita Springs, FL 34133
(212) 533-5420

Suggested Reading

Russell, Harold L. *Unholy Devotion—Why Cults Lure Christians.* Grand Rapids, Mich.: Zondervan Publishing House, 1983.

Enroth, Ronald, et al. *A Guide to Cults and New Religions.* Downers Grove, Ill.: InterVarsity Press, 1983.

Martin, Walter. *The Kingdom of the Cults.* Minneapolis, Minn.: Bethany House Publishers, 1985.

Smith, F. LaGard. *Out on a Broken Limb*. Eugene, Ore.: Harvest House Publishers, Inc., 1985.

Geisler, Norman L. and Amano, J. Yutaka. *Reincarnation Sensation*. Wheaton, Ill.: Tyndale House Publishers, 1986.

Larson, Bob. *Larson's Book of Cults*. Wheaton, Ill.: Tyndale House Publishers, 1982.

Hunt, Dave. *The Cult Explosion*. Eugene, Ore.: Harvest House Publishers, Inc., 1980.

Groothuis, Douglas. *Confronting the New Age*. Downers Grove, Ill.: InterVarsity Press, 1988.

Chandler, Russell. *Understanding the New Age*. Irving, Tex.: Word, Inc., 1988.

Marrs, Wanda. *New Age Lies to Women*. Austin, Tex.: Living Truth Publishers, 1990.

Baron, Will. *Deceived By the New Age: The Story of a New Age Priest*. San Jose, Calif.: Pacific Press, 1990.

4. CHRISTIAN TREATMENT CENTERS

As the compulsion/addiction problem reaches crisis proportions in America, more and more Christian churches and groups are setting up treatment centers throughout the country. Specific information can be obtained through local churches. Here are names and addresses of a few treatment centers.

Rapha—Christ-centered in-hospital counseling care units, treating psychiatric, substance abuse, and other addiction problems for the Christian community. Has numerous locations nationwide.

Rapha
Box 580355
Houston, TX 77258
Nationwide number 1-800-227-2657

Teen Challenge—national ministry devoted to "soul saving and life saving." For information about drug and alcohol treatment write to:

> Teen Challenge, Inc.
> 444 Clinton Ave.
> Brooklyn, NY 11238
> (718) 789–1414

New Life Clinic—Comprehensive mental health care services, substance abuse, eating disorders, and other addiction treatment. Numerous locations nationwide.

New Life Clinic
820 West Spring Creek Parkway, Ste. 400
Plano, TX 75023
1-800-639-5433

Dunklin Memorial Camp (see report on p. 194)
3342 S.W. Hosannah Lane
Okeechobee, FL 34974
(561) 597-2841

3D—A twelve-week program offering help in diet, discipline, and discipleship.

> 3D
> P.O. Box 897
> Orleans, MA 02653
> 1–800–451–5006

Others:

Rapha
1-800-383-4673

Ephesians 5:18 Life Ministries
1620 Elton Road, Ste. 204
Silver Spring, MD 20903
(301) 439-7191

Fresh Start
P.O. Box 720907
Orlando, FL 32872

New Life Treatment Center
P.O. Box 38
Woodstock, MN 56186

Lost and Found
9189 South Turkey Creek Rd.
Morrison, CO 80465

Open Homes Fellowship, Inc.
1831 Central Park Avenue
Orlando, FL 32807
(407) 849-9888

Faith Farms
9538 Highway 441
Boynton Beach, FL 33437
(561) 737-2222

House of Hope
1010 West 30th Street
Orlando, FL 32805

The Anchorage, Inc.
P.O. Box 112
Albany, GA 31702
(912) 435-5692

Liberty Lodge
4050 Coquina Ave.
Titusville, FL 32780

5. CHRISTIAN SELF-HELP GROUPS

Alcoholics Victorious
National Headquarters
P.O. Box 10364
Portland, OR 97236
(503) 245-9629

Overcomers Outreach
520 North Brookhurst, Ste. 121
Anaheim, CA 92801
(714) 491-3000

Pressing Onward Support Groups
1731 Hamilton Street, SW
Palm Bay, FL 32909

Homosexual Issues

Spatula Ministries
(Parents of homosexuals and children with AIDS)
Barbara Johnson, founder/director
2230 Lake Forest Circle
La Habra, CA 90631
(562) 691-7369·

Exodus International
(For homosexuals and their families;
also for sexual addiction)
P.O. Box 2121
San Raphael, CA 94912

Survivors of Violence and Sexual Abuse

Jan Frank
P.O. Box 1491
Placentia, CA 92871

Christian Recovery International
Dale Ryan, executive director
P.O. Box 11095
Whittier, CA 90603
(562) 947-5140

VOICES in Action, Inc.
(Victims Of Incest Can Emerge Survivors)
P.O. Box 148309
Chicago, IL 60614
(773) 327-1500

Post-Abortion Recovery

> WEBA
> (Women Exploited By Abortion)
> Kathy Walker, director
> 3553-B N. Perris Blvd., Suite 4
> Perris, CA 92370
> (714) 657–0334

Ministry to Singles

> The Tear Catchers
> Harold Ivan Smith
> P.O. Box 24688
> Kansas City, MO 64131
> (816) 444–5301

6. HOW TO START A CHRISTIAN TWELVE-STEP SUPPORT GROUP OR STUDY GROUP

A Twelve-Step Support Group outline is contained in *The Twelve Steps—A Spiritual Journey* and available from:

> Recovery Publications, Inc.
> P.O. Box 44
> Curtis, WA 98538
> (360) 245-3386

Guidelines for Christ-centered study groups based on *When I Grow Up . . . I Want To Be An Adult* are available from:

Recovery Publications, Inc.

(see address on previous page)

FOOTNOTES

Book One

[1] Martha Janssen, *Silent Scream* (Philadelphia, Penn.: Fortress Press, 1983), pp. 13, 83. Used by permission.

[2] From a lecture by Terry Kellogg at the Compulsivity Clinic.

[3] Isaiah 53:5.

[4] From a pamphlet by Children of Alcoholism Foundation, Inc., 200 Park Avenue, New York, N.Y. 10166.

[5] Ibid.

[6] Janet G. Woititz, *Adult Children of Alcoholics* (Deerfield Beach, Fla.: Health Communications, Inc., 1983).

[7] John M. Leighty, "Smoking: How to Wrap It Up," *Washington Post* (November 19, 1986).

[8] Margaret Hamburg, M.D., "The Nature of Craving," *Vogue* (August 1986).

[9] Anderson A. Spickard, M.D., and Barbara R. Thompson, *Dying for a Drink* (Waco, Tex.: Word Books, 1985).

[10] Some materials in this chapter adapted from *Broken Promises, Mended Dreams* by Richard Meryman (Little, Brown & Co.). The anonymous woman in this book was a composite of several women, including Sandra Simpson LeSourd.

[11] From materials distributed by Rogers Memorial Hospital, Oconomowoc, Wisconsin.

[12] Romans 7:15.

[13] 2 Corinthians 10:5.

[14] Affirmations by Ann Larson from Compulsivity Clinic materials.

Book Two

[1] Anderson Spickard, M.D. and Barbara Thompson, *Dying for a Drink* (Waco, Tex.: Word Books, 1985).

[2] Charles W. Crewe, *A Look at Relapse* (Center City, Minn.: Hazelden Literature, 1974).

[3] From *USA Today,* September 16, 1987.

[4] Geneen Roth, *Breaking Free from Compulsive Eating* (New York: Bobbs-Merrill Co., Inc., 1984).

[5] Winifred Gallagher, "High Anxiety," *Rolling Stone* (March 12, 1987).

[6] Robin Norwood, *Women Who Love Too Much* (New York, New York: St. Martin's Press, Inc., 1985).

[7] Lois Leiderman Davitz and Joel Davitz, *Living in Sync: Men and Women in Love* (New York: Bergh Publishing, Inc., 1986).

[8] Susan Jacoby, "Compulsive Shopping," *Vogue* (April 1976).

[9] Frank B. Minirth, et al., *The Workaholic and His Family* (Grand Rapids, Mich.: Baker Book House, 1981).

[10] Ernie Larsen, *Stage II Recovery: Life Beyond Addiction* (New York: Harper and Row, 1985).

[11] From booklet about Families In Crisis, 7320 Ohms Lane, Edina, Minnesota 55435.

[12] Christine Adams, "Parenting the Drug-affected Youth," *Marriage and Family Living* (Abbey Press, March 1986).

[13] Brennan Manning, poems by Sue Garmon, *Souvenirs of Solitude* (Denville, N.J.: Dimension Books, 1979). Used by permission.

WITH GRATITUDE

The writing of *The Compulsive Woman* has been a long—and sometimes painful—journey. Without the loving care and concern of countless people, it could never have been birthed. As for any journey, there was a plan to follow, then detours, missed turns, stops for advice, pauses to recheck the road signs and a learning process all the way.

This book would never have happened without the undergirding love, support and direction of my husband and editor, Leonard LeSourd. His unflagging belief in my ability to put my thoughts on paper stretched me beyond any limits of creativity I thought I had. He believed in the face of my unbelief. He took my outpourings—always excessive, sometimes compulsive—and wove together a combination of personal stories, case histories, and a vast collection of facts and figures.

My deepest thanks go to Elizabeth (Tib) Sherrill for her

penetrating analysis and sensitive editing of the manuscript. To Jane Campbell for her creativity in compiling research and for her steady enthusiasm for the project. And to Richard Meryman for his incisive suggestions for manuscript development, plus words of encouragement. (Note: Through 1981–1982 Dick had interviewed me for countless hours in developing his book *Broken Promises, Mended Dreams* about a recovering woman alcoholic.)

There were many along the way who encouraged me to record my story. I wasn't sure I wanted to. It was so private, so personal, so painful to tell. And all the parties in the stories were still alive. Standing in a dinner line at a weekend retreat in the mountains of Montana one July evening, I told my story to Dr. William E. Berg of Minneapolis, who was the retreat leader. His response was simple and direct: "Sandy, write a book and tell your story. It will be used to ignite people's hope, to give them faith to struggle on, to assure them that no situation is too hopeless for the healing power of God."

My experience at The Compulsivity Clinic in 1985 helped me discover new aspects of myself. I am indebted to Terry Kellogg's teaching and to Mic Hunter, who so graciously read the manuscript and gave me helpful advice and additional material.

I'd like especially to thank Brennan Manning, whose tapes and books ministered hope to me in my early recovery and the reality of God's unconditional love and forgiveness when I didn't feel lovable or forgiven. We met at a week of renewal in Billings in 1982, at which time he too encouraged me to tell my story.

These people were also invaluably helpful in reading and making suggestions and corrections on early drafts: Phillip Bandt, Marjorie Switzer, June Qualy, and Phil McCarty.

Extra special thanks to the indefatigable Regina Trollinger, a word-processor wizard who typed and retyped endless manuscript changes and additions; to Jeanne Sevigny whose wisdom, encouragement, and typing skills were invaluable; to Elaine Brink, so helpful with research and special assignments; and to Pat Dowell, our bookkeeper, who is teaching me new disciplines in many areas of my life.

And to all those family members, friends, doctors, counselors, pastors and fellow travelers, too many to list, whose love, dedication, prayers, time and sacrifice have been crucial factors in my journey to recovery . . . to them my everlasting gratitude.

Sandra Simpson LeSourd
Evergreen Farm
Lincoln, Virginia 22078
April 19, 1987

The
Not-So-
Compulsive
Woman

To
Len

With Special Thanks . . .

To all the members of my family for your love, encouragement, support and dedication.

To those people who write and telephone me and undergird me with their love and prayers; to my friends at the Catherine Marshall Center and the Billings Thursday morning prayer group; to Charlsie Byrd and countless others who have attended my workshops; my heartfelt thanks.

To Yvonne Burgan, Mary White, Elaine Brink, Pat Dowell, Virginia Payne and Ann Moran, who have contributed blood, sweat and tears to the production of this book. You're such blessings to my life!

To Drs. Neil Solomon and Richard Layton for your help and expertise in my physical recovery. You've been lifesavers!

And to those specialists for their editorial genius—Elizabeth Sherrill, Jane Campbell, Ann McMath and my husband, Len. You do make something beautiful out of my compulsive outpourings!

CONTENTS

Contents

There's Healing in Art

The drawings in this book are a joyous expression of my gratitude to God for sticking with me through much denial, anger and misbehavior. What talent I have with art was His gift to me at birth. It emerged during my early schooling, was shaped during two years at the Rhode Island School of Design and was put on display one summer when I did character sketches at Disneyland in California.

As this book began to take shape, I felt an urge to depict some of the people and events: my children, Brad, Brent, and Lisa; the tennis fiasco; Karen; my grandchildren's tea party; "Mother's Day Mary." Putting my experiences on paper stirred deep emotions; my tears often streaked the page. Likewise, drawing people I care about has in some strange way made me feel closer to them and deepened my own healing.

I believe God is using my words and drawings to pour out His love to them, and to the people—you!—reading this book.

Sandra Simpson LeSourd
Evergreen Farm
Lincoln, Virginia
April 19, 1992

Turning Point

Recovery Principle # 1
SEEK PRAYERS OF OTHERS

---

*I*T IS SIX A.M. AND STREAKS OF GRAY ARE BREAKING THROUGH THE night's darkness. My husband, Len, is still sleeping. Quietly I slip out of bed and stand at the window, taking in the green lushness of this early morning in May 1991 at Evergreen Farm. Patches of yellow forsythia like bright sentinels line the driveway. Lilacs nod their fragrance from giant bushes swaying gently. Brilliant clumps of azaleas—fuchsia, coral, lavender, magenta—dot the sweeping front lawn before me.

"Lord, You are indeed the Master Artist," I reflect. "How beautiful is Your world! How blessed I am!"

Suddenly tears sting my eyes. How this view contrasts with the view from another bedroom window thirteen years ago! As memories flood over me, my body begins to tremble. . . .

In August 1978 I was a patient in the Warm Springs, Montana, State Hospital. My weight hovered near 200. Totally defeated by addiction to alcohol and prescription drugs, I had attempted suicide a few weeks before, was rescued at the last moment by my daughter, Lisa, and put into this institution.

As one hopeless day slid into another, I had settled into a routine of sitting in my chair, staring vacantly through my dingy, nicotine-streaked window, chain-smoking three packages of cigarettes a day. At age 42, I felt my life was over.

I would have been surprised to learn that in my hometown of Billings, Montana, 150 miles away, a group of women were praying for me. These women met every Thursday in the Methodist church to intercede for hurting people. They kept a special file of desperate situations, which they labeled their "Ten Most Wanted List."

I was on that list.

Not being a believer in much of anything, I would probably have shrugged off their special request for me: "Lord, send someone to help Sandy!"

Yet this particular prayer was answered in a most unusual way. I told this story in *The Compulsive Woman*, but in the five years since that book was written, an element of mystery has been added.

The episode began when a nurse brought a new patient to the room that adjoined mine. My roommate, Jackie, and I were sitting on our beds waiting for the dinner bell to ring. We looked through the connecting door and saw a young woman collapsed on her newly assigned bed, sobbing and plucking at the covers.

Jackie and I looked at each other uneasily. A show of raw emotion was not uncommon in the hospital, but the moans of this poor girl were unnerving. "Oh, Jesus! Jesus! Jesus!" she intoned over and over.

"Karen, try to pull yourself together," the harried nurse was imploring. "It's almost dinnertime!"

"I don't want to eat, I want to die," came the muffled sobs.

Catching sight of Jackie and me, the nurse came to our doorway. "Karen is very upset. She was to be married next week and her fiance has been killed in a car wreck. Perhaps you two can speak with her and persuade her to come to dinner with the rest of the unit."

Jackie and I went reluctantly into Karen's room. I was repulsed by this new patient's religious wailings. "Jesus, help me!" she kept crying out. "Please, Jesus—help me!" She did not respond to our invitation to dinner.

When Jackie and I returned from the dining room, we were startled to discover Karen up and walking regally about the hall. The change in her appearance was startling. Her short auburn hair was combed neatly, framing an oval face. Huge, luminous brown eyes shone beneath thick lashes. She had changed into a long, white bathrobe and white slippers, giving her an angelic appearance as she glided down the hospital corridor.

I was struck by her loveliness—such a contrast with other disheveled, vacant-faced patients. But her constant calling on Jesus disturbed and frightened me.

The next day, alone in my room, I looked up to see Karen in the doorway.

"May I come in?" she asked shyly. "I'm scared of this place."

This was the first of endless visits to our room. Karen seemed to appear in a puff of smoke; suddenly she would just be there. It soon became apparent that she had appointed me her special friend and protector. I never had to guess who was behind me in the food line, her beautiful brown eyes searching for assurance. She would be waiting in the corridor when I left the shower room, by the door at the close of my therapy session.

One sultry July night, I tossed restlessly in the heat of the stuffy hospital room, listening to my roommate's deep, regular breathing in the bed next to mine. How could she sleep in this oven?

Suddenly I sensed another presence in the room. Half sitting up in bed, I saw a familiar figure. There was Karen standing in the doorway, her long, white nightgown startlingly bright in the moonlight.

As Karen approached my bed I could hear her crying. "Oh, Sandy, does Jesus love me? Does Jesus really love me?"

How to respond? Some instinct told me I had to comfort this weeping child. I got up gingerly, not sure how I could reassure anybody of anything. Awkwardly I gathered Karen in my arms and patted her damp hair. It had been a long time since I had held anyone to offer comfort. I had always been the one demanding attention.

SANDY, DOES JESUS LOVE ME...?

Clearing my throat, I said, "Yes, Karen, Jesus loves you."

Her sobbing stopped in an instant.

My heart began to beat furiously. I felt cold and warm at the same time.

Karen detached herself from my embrace, wiped her eyes with the back of her hand, thanked me in a voice of childlike gratitude and slipped back to the adjoining room.

Now, thirteen years later, I marveled again at how that fragile event had begun a fundamental change in my life. What had happened?

The Billings women had prayed that God would send someone to me. I believe today that Karen was that God-sent person. My holding her in my arms, saying the words she needed to hear, had not only comforted her but had stirred something deep within me. In an instant I had changed from a totally self-centered individual to one with the tiny beginnings of a caring heart for others.

Not that in some supernatural way I suddenly became an others-centered person. That had to take place over a period of time. But there had been a supernatural change of attitude in my spirit.

Nor did I produce this change. It had come from outside myself. The only way I can explain it is that it resulted from the prayers of the Billings intercessors.

How did they pray for me?

As a group, I learned, they met Thursday mornings, began with songs of praise, then offered general prayers of thanksgiving for answers already received. Thanking God for His healing touch in the lives of their prayer subjects is crucially important, they had discovered, not only to open lines of communication with the heavenly Father, but also to lift and energize the spirits of the intercessors themselves.

They used Scripture prayer regularly, inserting my name into selected verses: "Strength and dignity are [Sandy's] clothing. . . . [Sandy] opens her mouth with wisdom, and the teaching of kindness

is on her tongue. . . . Her children rise up and call her blessed . . ."
(Proverbs 31:25, 26, 28).

Often the prayer went along this line: "God did not give [Sandy]
a spirit of fear but of power and of love and of a sound mind" (2 Tim-
othy 1:7). "And with His stripes [Sandy] is healed" (Isaiah 53:5).
Over and over they prayed, "[Sandy] can do all things through Christ
who strengthens [her]" (Philippians 4:13).

As I have learned more about prayer through my association with other intercessory prayer ministries, I understand more
about the intense dedication and persistence and patience of those
Billings intercessors. For years they prayed for me without seeing
any results at all. When my life turned around dramatically and
I began the long recovery process, they continued to intercede for me. They prayed specifically for God to send one of His
emissaries across my path to help me. Karen was certainly that
person.

How does prayer work?

There is a great element of mystery here, but we are told in
Scripture that because Jesus lives forever, He has a permanent
priesthood. . . . He lives to make intercession for us (see Hebrews
7:25).

Christ, therefore, is our chief Intercessor. He receives our prayers
and lays them before the throne of God. To receive and handle these
millions of prayer requests, God must have a tremendous heavenly
communications network, a system that would make our most complex computer program look like a child's toy.

Also important: God's angelic help. "And the number of [angels]
was ten thousand times ten thousand" (Revelation 5:11, KJV). That
adds up to one hundred million angels ready to take action as God
commands.

Seeing this picture helps me understand a little of how God can
hear and answer the prayers of even a tiny child.

After publication of *The Compulsive Woman,* I set about making a
list of the people I wanted to send gift books to. Countless people

were used by God along the journey: family, friends, doctors, pastors, priests, counselors. But in thinking about those involved, I realized Karen and the Billings women probably topped the list.

We had no difficulty in getting books to the group in Billings— but how to track down Karen? I got off a letter to the Montana state institution with the dates when Karen and I had been patients, the ward we had been on and any other facts I could recall.

Several weeks later a letter arrived from the institution.

> *Dear Mrs. LeSourd:*
> *Thank you for your inquiry. We have no record of*
> *the patient you mentioned in your letter.*

My first reaction had been one of annoyance at their dismissive attitude. Then, as I reread the letter, absorbing the implications of its terse contents, my body was flooded with chills.

If there was no record of such a patient . . . could Karen have been . . . an angel? She had certainly looked like one. At times her physical beauty had taken my breath away.

But it was her love. Her grace. Her indefatigable pursuit of Jesus, and of me. A hound of heaven? . . .

I turned from the window to see that Len was awake and sitting up in bed. He looked at me quizzically.

"Memory time?"

I nodded. "I was thinking again about Karen. Could she really have been an angel?"

"If she isn't, Sandy, you'll hear from her. You've told the Karen story on national television, in your book, in articles, at dozens of conferences. Sooner or later, if she lives on this earth, she'll hear about your recovery and get in touch with you."

"Please don't use *recovery* that way."

"What way?"

"As if it were final and complete."

Len grinned at me. "O.K. You are in a recovering situation; you always will be. Recovery is a process that will go on until you die. How's that?"

"Much better."

As we began our morning prayer time together, I was overwhelmed with gratitude at how far on the recovery road I had traveled. But I wasn't kidding myself. I was still on a journey, along with millions of others, with much to deal with. One day I listed all the addictions I had been dependent on at some time in my life:

1. Alcohol and prescription drugs

2. Work, achievement and success

3. Money addictions, such as overspending

4. Control addictions, especially if they surfaced in personal, sexual, family and business relationships

5. Food addictions

6. Approval dependency (the need to please people)

7. Rescuing patterns toward others (codependency)

8. Dependency on toxic relationships (relationships that are damaging and hurtful)

9. Physical illness (hypochondria)

10. Exercise

11. Cosmetics, clothes, trying to look good on the outside

12. General perfectionism

13. Materialism

14. Tobacco

15. Television

Fortunately I could now cross out drugs, alcohol, smoking, hypochondria, exercise. Other addictions were pretty much under control, while food issues, shopping, perfectionism, people-pleasing and over-spending were a continuous struggle.

But I was learning more and more how to build up my spiritual resources, how to deal with temptations when they assaulted me, and always how to keep my eyes on the One whose name Karen had called from the pit of despair.

2

The People-Pleasing Trap

Recovery Principle # 2
SAY NO

---

*T*HE KAREN EXPERIENCE BEGAN THE HEALING PROCESS INSIDE ME. A few weeks later I was released from Montana State Hospital to go back to my family. But I was far from well. In June 1980 I spent 28 days at St. Mary's Rehabilitation Center in Minneapolis. After this came a period of six months at the nearby Jane Dickman Halfway House—all of this described in some detail in *The Compulsive Woman.*

It was at the halfway house that a staff counselor jolted me by saying, "Sandy, do you realize how male-dependent you are? Your thoughts, your actions, your needs are centered on men. You require their approval to be fulfilled."

"How can you say that?" I argued. "I've been hurt by men all my life."

The counselor tapped a paper on her desk. "The results of your psychological testing show you've been dependent on every man in your life. The problem with being male-dependent is that a woman ties all her feelings of self-worth onto what men think about her. You need to begin to become responsive to yourself and your own values."

She paused a moment. "Like most alcoholics, Sandy, you're a 'people-pleaser.' And the people you try hardest to please are men."

For several moments I was silent, devastated by this appraisal that I knew deep-down to be true.

"How do I get free?" I asked at last.

"For the next four weeks you will be on a male restriction program. This means you will not have anything to do with men. You can write or call one male member of your family once a week, but you're to avoid conversations with men, even eye contact with men on the street. You need to learn to trust women and the feedback they have for you."

At first this program seemed peculiar and unfair. It wasn't. I discovered how automatically I sought to make eye contact with men—in restaurants, at meetings, anywhere. Somehow the approval of these nameless males mattered. I would be buoyed by a flicker of interest, dejected by indifference. It was a searing discovery.

To break the cycle of male dependency, it was apparent that I needed to enhance my sense of self-worth completely apart from men. And, in fact, after the first few days of my male restriction program, it became a little easier. Each time I resisted looking at a man for approval represented a victory. My self-esteem was growing—in little flutters, but growing. By the end of the four weeks, I sensed a new strength in this area.

As I worked at relating to women, I became doubly aware of what a people-pleaser I really was. Especially with someone like Lauren, a younger dorm mate in the program. How she would rail at the "feelings group" we were all required to attend once a week. She would plop down into her chair muttering, "How I hate this place," and spend the meeting staring out the window, mindlessly twirling a long strand of her red hair in her fingers.

Many nights Lauren would tap on my door and want to talk. A life of wealth and privilege had not prepared her for the rigors of a regimented halfway house. She groused and wailed especially over being placed on a male restriction program.

"Oh, Sands," she gushed one night, "I know I'm not supposed to look at guys, but there's this adorable blonde lawyer I met at the treatment center who wants to see me. I don't know how his letter got through the gestapo at the front desk, but it did."

"Lauren," I cautioned her, "you've already violated your male restriction by reading his letter at all."

"Please don't tell on me, Sands. You're the only person around here I can trust. I really must see Mark, and I need you to cover for me."

"Lauren, I don't *believe* you! If you're daydreaming about some guy, you're not working your program. You're just switching addictions from booze to men."

Her lovely ivory complexion flushed a deep crimson. "Don't be like the old bags around here. I have this really deep need. Please help me."

Sleep eluded me for many hours. Having been on male restriction for four weeks myself, I knew how valuable it was. I was learning to trust women with my feelings. This was a surprise and a delight since my female relationships had always been superficial and competitive. Would a conspiracy with Lauren now rob me of my serenity and deprive her of growth she desperately needed?

I should say no to her. But somehow I couldn't.

Lauren sought me out at the breakfast table. "I called Mark very late last night when everyone was asleep. He's agreed to meet me this afternoon when we go into town for our job interviews."

"You'll never get away with this," I warned her.

She just smiled and tossed her mane of red hair into a swirling cloud about her shoulders.

And so I unwillingly became her partner-in-crime. On our job-hunting foray into nearby St. Paul, I fibbed to the counselors that she had been with me, that we had had lunch together and walked the pavements looking for work, even though I hated the deception. It chipped away at my self-worth, so fragile to begin with.

"Why do I let Lauren manipulate me like this?" I would rail at myself. "I know better." But the raging people-pleaser in me was still driving my bus, so I covered for Lauren whenever she slipped out to see Mark on the sly. Meanwhile, she continued to "play halfway house," plodding listlessly through the motions of our feelings meetings, counseling sessions and other required activities.

I wondered if others knew what was going on. The counselors were pros and would surely find out. Would I be unmasked as a confidante and enabler?

One night Lauren burst into my room to announce that Mark had asked her to marry him. "Oh, Sands, I love him so much. He wants me to meet his parents!"

I knew there was nothing I could do to dissuade this headstrong young woman; I saw myself in her, ten years earlier, as impetuous and bullheaded as she was now.

"No one can make me stay in this awful place," she continued. "I'll be gone before breakfast. Mark is picking me up. Thanks, Sands, for being my friend. Here—this is for you."

Lauren placed into my hand a small pewter figurine of a young girl in a swirling dress flying a kite.

"Mother sent it to me when I graduated from the treatment center. She thought it looked like me as a little girl on the beach at the Cape. 'You're free to fly,' her card said, 'unencumbered by the demons of alcohol.' She wouldn't mind my giving it to you—you're the one who helped me fly free from this place. Goodbye, Sands, I'll call you soon."

The door slammed shut behind her. I sat on the edge of my bed staring at the figurine, feeling miserable. I also sensed I would get caught for my role in this episode. The consequences would not be pleasant—and for Lauren they could be catastrophic.

Why was I such a people-pleaser? I knew better. *Honesty.* How tough that word was for me; how tough to walk it out as an addict whose life had been a mesh of lies. An honest person would have taken a stand, refused to go along.

The next morning the house was abuzz over Lauren's hasty departure. My worst fears were confirmed at breakfast.

Lauren's counselor, Robin, entered the dining room stone-faced.

"Lauren has left the program," she announced, "and I fear for her sobriety and her recovery. Even more disturbing are her plans to marry a young man she met in treatment. Neither of them has three months' sobriety."

Then her blue eyes focused on me. "Sandy, I understand you knew about Lauren's male restriction violation from the beginning and covered for her. You have been the enabler, and by so acting you have not only jeopardized your friend's recovery, but you may have jeopardized her life.

"Enabling is a very serious thing, Sandy. The other counselors and I will decide on the appropriate disciplinary action to take in your case. . . ."

Having my male restriction program extended was painful, but much worse was the concern I felt for Lauren. Then, several months later, when I had completed my program and was working at the Minnesota Museum of Art in St. Paul, I got a call from Lauren. She and Mark had indeed gotten married and already she regretted it. Mark was drinking again, having an affair.

"Lauren, what are you doing for yourself? Are you going to your alcohol support group meetings?"

"Sure, Sands," she breathed into the phone, "I'm taking care of Number One."

I suspected she was lying and also that she had been drinking.

Years later, still haunted by my guilty role in Lauren's tragedy—knowing that by trying to please her I had hurt her—I told Len the story. It resulted in a spirited discussion, not about male dependency (which, thank God, isn't much of a factor with me anymore), but about people-pleasing and the damage it does in other lives as well as our own.

"I still have trouble saying no," I conceded.

"Especially with your children," Len added.

"You have trouble saying no to anyone and everyone," I shot back.

Len looked rueful. "You have a point. We're both people-pleasers but in different ways."

"How 'different'?"

"You became a people-pleaser as a little girl out of fear that others wouldn't like you if you didn't meet their expectations. I want people to like me, sure, but that isn't the reason it's hard for me to say no. I like to think of myself as able to solve any problem that comes along, especially in my work. To me a request is a challenge to my self-image. Saying yes is an ego thing."

"How do people like us learn to say no?"

"Let's take a hypothetical case," Len suggested. "Let's say you get a phone call from a close friend asking to borrow $300. What do you say?"

This was hard for me. "I'd probably loan her the money," I said.

"Even though you know she can't or won't repay it, and will probably come back later with still another request for money?"

I squirmed. "If she was really hurting—yes. How would you handle it if it came from one of your close friends?"

Len thought a moment. "If we were really close, I guess I would tell my friend that I never made a decision on something like that without praying about it first."

His eyes lit up. "That's it, Sandy! That's the way you and I should make every decision. Never agree to anything on the spur of the moment. Tell the person asking us to do something, or to give to a good cause, or whatever, that we'll pray about it and get back to him or her with an answer."

"That sounds like a delaying action," I objected.

"Not at all. We pray for God's answer, not ours."

"What if we get no answer?"

"Then we do nothing until we get an answer."

I was not satisfied. "Let's go back to my friend on the phone. She's desperate. I tell her we'll pray about it. We do, but get no clear answer. So I tell her—what?"

"The truth—that we prayed and did not get the green light to loan her the money. We're sorry."

"She'll probably think we're just using prayer as an excuse to say no."

"She may. And she may be angry with you for saying no. But you're missing the real point here, Sandy. When we go to the Lord in prayer, we don't know what the answer will be. It could be yes or no. Or not yet. But the key is this—*we go to Him in faith.*"

A few weeks after this discussion Len and I had a chance to put this new approach into action. I had been letting myself get stressed out by taking on too many speaking engagements. The call came one night from my good friend Sherry.

"Sandy, the women of our church are having a retreat the first weekend of next October. Will you be our speaker?"

"Let me check my schedule," I answered.

That particular weekend was free, and I started to give her a quick yes. But I did have several other major engagements that month. Then I remembered Len's and my discussion.

"Sherry, there are some complications. Let me get back to you."

Len and I talked it over, then prayed about it. I wanted to do it for Sherry, but had a slight check in my spirit. The next day the inner check was stronger in both of us.

My no to Sherry did not please her, but it was a small victory for me. Nor did my friendship with Sherry suffer. I came up with the name of someone free to do the speaking and who turned out to be just the right person for that particular women's group.

I was learning. The Lauren episode was a watershed experience. It showed me the weakness of people-pleasing, that giving in to Lauren's demands had not been being a good friend to her. As a good friend I wanted the best for her. What was best for Lauren? To stay with the treatment program because she wasn't ready to be a healthy, responsible wife and mother.

It may be that saying no would not have stopped Lauren from fleeing the halfway house to an ill-advised marriage; but then again, it might have. She would have been angry with me, called me names and I would have felt bad. But if I had said no lovingly, she would still have wanted my friendship. She would have needed my friendship and probably would have respected me more.

As I have thought and prayed about the weakness of being a people-pleaser and the strength of saying no, I suggest these guidelines when you are faced with a Lauren kind of situation:

1. Pray about your response, seeking God's direction. Ask Him, "Am I doing this because it's the right thing to do?"

2. If saying no is your inner conviction, do it gently, lovingly, but firmly.

3. Be prepared for a negative or even angry response, keeping in mind that your no is actually a positive response because you are overcoming a people-pleasing weakness and are thinking of what is right in the situation.

4. If possible, follow up your no with helpful suggestions and loving concern for the other person.

More often than not, saying no will benefit both parties. The person saying no will experience an inner strengthening of his or her self-worth. The person refused will often discover in time that this was not a rejection, but for his or her own good and growth. And God will have His way in the situation.

3

The Great Matchmaker

Recovery Principle # 3
TRUST GOD'S LOVE FOR YOU

M^Y SIX MONTHS AT THE HALFWAY HOUSE MARKED A CRUCIAL stage in my recovery. For one thing, I saw clearly for the very first time that I could not for the rest of my life take even one drink of alcohol. For me, that first drink would lead to many, then to bondage. Even death.

Male dependence, however, was more subtle and therefore harder to deal with. I could look back over my life and see a painful pattern: the breakup of my parents' marriage, which I blamed (perhaps unfairly) on my father, then two failed marriages of my own.

For years drinking had helped to anesthetize my feelings of defeat as a wife and mother. But sobriety, plus therapy, forced me to a realistic appraisal of the liabilities I had brought to marriage. The following became clear:

My immaturity
Gamesmanship with men (based on deception)
Fear of intimacy
Fear of responsibility
Inability to share my feelings at a meaningful level
Selfishness

My turning point experience with Karen had begun to work on my basic selfishness. At the halfway house the teaching on male dependency convinced me that a lot more had to change inside me before I should even think about marrying again. And Lauren's disastrous experience convinced me that no male relationships were better than bad ones. I was learning that I didn't have to have a man in my life to feel worthwhile. That was progress!

Deep down inside me was the desire to be, at last, a real wife to someone. But I was learning to turn this area of my life, like all the rest, over to the "Higher Power" of twelve-step programs. Especially helpful was a short essay, "His Plan for Your Mate," given to me at a singles' meeting. Here are excerpts:

Everyone longs to give him or herself completely to someone—to have a deep soul relationship with another, to be loved thoroughly and exclusively. But God says to the Christian, "Not until you discover that only in Me is real satisfaction will you be capable of the perfect human relationship that I have planned for you. . . .

"Don't be anxious. Don't worry. Don't look around at the things others have. . . . You just keep looking up to Me, or you will miss what I want to show you. . . .

"And when you're ready, I'll surprise you with a love far more wonderful than any you would ever dream of. . . ."

These words became guidelines. When on a Sunday night in March 1980 I made a total surrender of my life to God, I felt that if it were just He and I for the rest of my life, that would be O.K. with me. Perhaps I was called to be single. Perhaps to work with other single women, especially women addicts.

Often I would slip into an open church for prayer, such as Billings' St. Patrick's Cathedral where I would kneel up front before the crucifix. I found much comfort in this cool, darkened sanctuary. The hushed holiness washed over me and bathed my wounds. The Lord was indeed a husband to me as He promised in Isaiah 54.

I didn't need or want a man in my life at that time. I wasn't healed enough to have a healthy, meaningful relationship with any male.

Yet one morning as I was taking my brisk two-mile walk by the rimrocks, I found myself praying this prayer: "Thank You, Lord, for the relationship You and I have together. It's all I need. Yet I'm aware it could be Your plan for me to share my life with a special man You have picked out for me.

"If so, Lord, hold him close and meet his needs today. Bless him. Heal him. Draw him closer to You. . . ."

The months passed. My three children were in their early twenties now, grateful for a sober mother but cautious, clearly afraid I would go off the deep end again, adding to the hurts of past years. I ached for them, wept inconsolably at night over the damage I had done to them and so many other people.

Perhaps out of this sense of indebtedness, I determined to help hurting people wherever I could. I began to speak out more in alcoholic support groups. As I began telling my story here and there, a publisher contacted me and suggested I write a book. Though my embryonic self-confidence quailed at such a thought, I borrowed a typewriter and spent long, frustrating hours in front of it.

The result was a most unusual-looking manuscript. Someone advised me to keep a small spiral notebook tucked into my purse for jotting down ideas. Naturally I carried this idea to extremes! I scribbled ideas on anything handy—matchbook covers, paper napkins, brown paper bags, envelope flaps—then assembled these various remnants and stapled them to blank sheets of paper. These were interspersed among my pages of typed notes.

The total package was large, lumpy and unwieldy, with napkins and matchbook covers jutting out from all sides—more like something destined for the trash compactor than for the scrutiny of Ken Petersen, the Tyndale editor I was to meet with at the *Decision* Magazine Writers Workshop in St. Paul, Minnesota.

Something had to be done to transform the tottering tower of papers before me into something more presentable for my appointment. What could I do to make it more attractive? My eyes spied a yard of kelly green polka dot ribbon. Just what I needed for dramatic effect! Excitedly I bound my manuscript with the colorful ribbon, topping it with an elaborate bow.

The interview took place on the first day of my arrival in St. Paul. Ken was warm and friendly as he extended his hand in greeting. Why had I feared this man?

"You have a manuscript to show me, perhaps?"

Nervously I drew my creation from the depths of my shoulder bag and thrust it across the table into Ken's waiting hands. My beautiful bow drooped pitifully, mashed during the long flight from my new home in Vermont.

Ken's handsome face crinkled into a smile. I marvel now at his equanimity faced with such a hodgepodge of material. He stroked the ruffled edges of my offering thoughtfully, then untied the bow and leafed through the pages, making suggestions on the development of the material.

Elated at being treated like an actual writer, I pored over the week's schedule, deciding what classes to attend. On Monday afternoon I decided to attend a talk on creative ideas by a longtime *Guideposts* editor named Leonard LeSourd.

In *The Compulsive Woman* I told briefly how Len and I met at this workshop and the courtship that followed. Here is the story in more detail.

I arrived at the auditorium that afternoon early and found a seat directly in front of the speaker's podium. Soon I was joined by a pretty brunette from Watford City, North Dakota, who introduced herself as Polly Damaska. Her husband pastored a church and she had always wanted to write more than church bulletins.

She grabbed my arm. "That must be Leonard LeSourd now. He was married to Catherine Marshall, you know. He must miss her terribly since her death."

As the attractive gray-haired man stepped up to the podium, something inexplicable happened. A voice inside me said, *There he is.*

Excuse me, Lord, I thought. *Is this You? Are You telling me this is the man I've been praying for for so long?*

Impossible! I was imagining things.

Len finished his talk and gathered up his notes as the applause broke the quiet of the large lecture hall. I sat there strangely paralyzed.

Polly broke my trance with an insistent tap on my shoulder, her eyes wide with wonder. "Sandy, the Lord has something very special for you and Leonard LeSourd."

I blinked in amazement at hearing my own thought in the mouth of this total stranger.

As she joined the others gathered about Len, asking questions, I felt a sudden shyness, almost as if I were still on the male restriction program, and walked out of the lecture hall.

Entering the front door of the college cafeteria that night for dinner, I heard my name: "Sandy, come over here!" It was Fred Bauer, a former editor at *Guideposts* magazine whom I had met that afternoon. With him was Len LeSourd. Fred introduced us and Len and I sat next to each other at dinner, then again at the auditorium, where I found myself telling him of my long struggle with alcoholism.

To my surprise, tears formed in his slate-blue eyes. "I have a niece struggling with that problem," he said. "Would you be willing to write to her?"

He gave me her address and asked for mine. Noting that I lived in Vermont, he mentioned that he would be driving through New England later that month. "I'll give you a call."

It's the sort of thing people say. But sure enough, three weeks later my telephone rang. Len was in the area; could I make a room reservation for him somewhere nearby for Saturday night?

He had become such a workaholic since Catherine's death, he explained, that his children had needled him into taking this vacation trip through New England. "I'm supposed to stop regularly and smell the flowers."

I took that as a personal challenge. I reserved a room at the Montpelier Tavern Inn, a historic spot where stagecoaches used to stop. Then Margaret Guilmette, a creative friend of mine, and I went to work. Saturday morning we filled his room with the largest bouquet of flowers we could get through the door. Was my compulsive nature showing?

Across the top of the drapes that framed a large picture window, Margaret and I pinned a newsprint banner, *Welcome to Montpelier, Len!* Onto one of the twin beds we placed a cuddly black teddy bear, decked out in a hat trimmed with violets. Nestled next to the bear was a straw basket labeled *First Aid Kit for the Weary Traveler.* In it we put a box of Vermont maple candy, a clump of red grapes, crackers and cheese, assorted newspapers and magazines and a bottle of aspirin.

Finally Margaret and I taped Scripture posters to the wallpaper: *Our God Reigns* and *Let Everything that Has Breath Praise the Lord!* We giggled aloud imagining what the maid would make of our redecorating efforts.

Late in the afternoon the telephone rang. Len was chuckling. "There seems to be a bear in my room."

I made arrangements to pick Len up at the hotel that evening in my little brown Toyota. He had been driving all day, I reasoned, and would be delighted to be chauffeured to dinner. Or would he be turned off at the possibility that I was a "take-charge" woman?

I was acutely aware of his eyes on me as I threaded my car through the winding curves leading to the Trapp Family Lodge atop a majestic mountain overlooking the town of Stowe. Parking the Toyota, I glanced at my watch: thirty minutes till our dinner reservation. Another of my compulsions was always to be early.

Len suggested good-naturedly that we walk around the grounds while waiting. The evening sun was setting, brushing the mountains before us with rainbow hues of purple and mauve. I thought to myself, *God is really showing off His creation! He must have a special plan for us this evening.*

We stopped briefly at the small family cemetery where Baron von Trapp and other family members were buried beneath scrolled wrought iron crosses. Pansies, larkspurs and snapdragons bordered each small plot. As we turned to walk across the lawn to the main building, Len reached for my hand, his grasp warm and firm.

During dinner he drew out the story of my life. At first I held back the defeats and failures, wanting him to see only the good. Then something inside said, *Be honest.* I had come so to hate my past deception that it was a great relief simply to tell the truth. Len's warm response further reassured me.

"Would you like to have dessert at my house?" I asked him impulsively.

Arriving at my small yellow house in Montpelier, the first thing Len saw was a huge brown teddy bear sitting in the front hall, this one wearing a lace dress with a large printed label running diagonally across her chest: *Housemother.*

Len stared at the bear for a moment, then chuckled.

"Housemother is my ferocious protector," I informed him.

Then came a quick tour. As we went from room to room—lace curtains, quilts on the walls, stuffed animals and old dolls everywhere—I was uneasily aware that it looked like the dream house of a ten-year-old.

"What's this?" Len exclaimed as he approached the fireplace. I had covered the low stone hearth with a white linen cloth on which sat twin silver candlesticks, with my Bible in the center. "Looks almost like an altar."

"It is an altar. I spend a lot of time here each day on my knees talking to the Lord. This is also where I have Communion."

"Communion—by yourself?"

"Yes, most of the time. Sometimes with one of the women I'm praying with." I told him how the Lord had been using me more and more to reach out to hurting women.

Taking a deep breath, I blurted, "Would you like to have Communion here with me now?"

Surprised, Len's eyes searched mine. Then he nodded.

I returned from the kitchen with a goblet of grape juice and two round wafers on a small glass plate. We knelt together and Len read from 1 Corinthians 11:23–26: "The Lord Jesus in the night in which He was betrayed took bread; and when He had given thanks, He broke it. . . ." We served each other "the bread of life," then "the cup of salvation."

Afterward Len took my hand and prayed, "Lord, we are Your children, committed to You, eager to have You in charge of this relationship." Something deep and important happened to us as Len said those words.

And so God was there with us from the start. At my invitation Len returned to my house the next morning for breakfast, handsome in a navy cotton shirt and red, white and blue checked slacks.

Noticing a third place setting at the table, he asked: "Are you expecting someone else for breakfast?"

"That's the place I always set for the head of this house," I replied. When Len looked startled, I explained, "Jesus is my husband and the head of my home."

"That's great, Sandy. I love it." His eyes were misty as he spoke.

We had lunch at Peacham Pond with my friends Margaret and Frank—she of the hotel room refurbishing. After eating I asked Len if he would like to go for a walk in the birch-strewn woods. "Ah—a chance to smell the flowers," he said.

The August sun warmed us as it filtered through the canopy of leaves. Hand in hand we laughed and talked together. How I had longed for such a relationship!

Suddenly Len spied a patch of lady's slippers growing among a lush bed of ferns. He bounded playfully toward the flowers, knelt down and buried his head in the lavender blooms.

"Hey, no smell," he said, disappointed. Then he turned to me with that reflective look I was getting to know. "My mother used to tell me I needed to take time to fill my soul with beauty. She'd be pleased that I'm doing just that today."

His 92-year-old mother, he told me, was comatose in a nursing home in Gaithersburg, Maryland.

Now came the moment I had been waiting for. Pointing to a large birch tree by the side of the path, I exclaimed, "Look, Len, there's something sticking out of that tree."

Len went over to investigate, retrieved a zip-lock baggie tucked beneath a protective layer of silver bark.

"Open it up and see what it is."

Len gave me an inquiring look, undid the small plastic bag and read aloud the note inside: "Welcome to Peacham Pond, Len. Blessed is the man whose trust is in the Lord."

He was clearly dumbfounded. "You did this. But how did you know I'd be here today? I didn't know myself until last night."

"I didn't, either. But I hoped—and planned this surprise for you."

"You do indeed major in surprises." Len took both my hands in his, leaned forward and kissed me lightly on the lips.

Len had an appointment the next day in upstate New York, but promised to return to Montpelier Tuesday evening before heading south again.

Late Tuesday afternoon he phoned to say he was back at the Montpelier Tavern Inn—exhausted with a headache. "I'll be as good as new after a nap," he assured me.

Another challenge! I decided to prepare another first-aid kit, but this time deliver it myself—as a nurse.

I pressed a white cotton dress quickly, donned it, then took stock. What to do for a hat? Out of a piece of white construction paper I fashioned a nurse's cap, adding a black stripe and a large red cross in the front.

Needing a nametag such as nurses wear, I cut a three-inch heart from the same construction paper and printed on it *Nancy Nice Nurse.* That should do for a start, I laughed to myself, surveying the white figure staring back at me from the bathroom mirror. I did look like a nurse!

The first-aid kit consisted of band-aids, athlete's foot spray, aspirin and other medications in a small basket. I concealed basket and cap in a shopping bag and slipped a raincoat over my strange white outfit. In the hotel lobby I rang Len's room.

"O.K. if I come up? I've got something to help your headache."

Len opened the door to my knock and stared in disbelief. "Nancy Nice Nurse? I can't believe this!" He laughed until tears ran down his cheeks.

The idea of God as a matchmaker transformed our courtship into high adventure. From the beginning, starting with that Communion service, we prayed together. After get-togethers all the way from Vermont to Florida, we asked this of God: "Lord, if it is Your plan for us to marry, open every door along our way. If it is not Your plan, close the door."

So trust in God and His instructions about our future became the cornerstone of our courtship.

How different this was from the get-my-own-way atmosphere of the courtships prior to my first two marriages!

Early on Len revealed that his first marriage was to a beautiful New York City model named Eve. After trying for nearly ten years to help Eve overcome her bondage to alcohol, in great agony and with a sense of total failure Len filed for divorce and was given custody of their three small children. Then, feeling helpless and inadequate as a single parent, he turned to God for help in finding a new mate.

God responded in an amazing way. In 1959 He led Len to a woman whom, on his own, Len would never have considered approaching—Catherine Marshall, a bestselling author and Christian celebrity. Len and Catherine had a fulfilling and productive marriage for 23 years.

When Catherine died in 1983, Len was 64. After a year and a half as a widower, he turned once again to God, praying, "Lord, You know how I need a partner! I will accept every invitation, keep on the move so that You can direct my steps to the woman You choose for me."

Only a few weeks later Fred Bauer introduced the two of us.

Early on, I could sense in Len a wariness about my alcoholism—understandable after the agony of his first marriage. During our courtship he kept asking God, "How can Sandy and I be sure that this marriage is Your plan for us?"

His answer came in two words:

Trust Me.

Over and over in the weeks and months that followed: *Trust Me.*

Sometimes there were additional instructions.

Make yours a scriptural romance.

We interpreted this to mean that first we were to get to know each other spiritually, mentally and emotionally, and to get to know each other's families. The sexual relationship would be blessed after marriage.

Learn to have fun together.

For Len this bit of guidance was a surprise. A workaholic type, he admitted he had much to learn in this area.

Both of us were amazed at the joy and deep fulfillment to be found in courtship on God's terms. Those drawn together through physical attraction alone miss the heights and depths a romance can have. For after all, the God who created love knows how to tune two human hearts to thrilling harmony.

When you ask God to be a matchmaker, here are a few guidelines to help bring you into contact with the mate He has for you:

1. Accept that it will happen in His timing, not yours.

2. Go to places where your future mate might be (church, social gatherings, community meetings, sports events, etc.). It's unlikely you'll meet him or her in a bar.

3. Pray before turning down an invitation you ordinarily wouldn't accept. You may need to widen your acquaintances, broaden your interests before God can act.

4. If you meet someone you like but to whom you are not attracted physically, give it time. It is possible to fall in love with inner qualities more than outer.

5. Overeagerness is often a turn-off. When you meet someone you like, ask the Holy Spirit within you to take control. He will, in surprising ways, if you let Him.

6. Trust God as your best possible matchmaker. Trust Him to bring you and your future spouse together. Trust Him to guide you through a time of courtship. Trust Him to tell you both the right time to become engaged, the right date for your marriage. Most important of all, trust Him for the rest of your marriage.

Scripture always says it best: "Trust in the Lord with all your heart, and lean not on your own understanding; in all your ways acknowledge Him, and He shall direct your paths" (Proverbs 3:5–6, NKJV).

4

The Perils of a Perfectionist

Recovery Principle # 4
ACCEPT YOURSELF

---

*I*DON'T KNOW HOW OR WHEN I BECAME A PERFECTIONIST. PERHAPS it was hereditary; my mother has always been one, especially about cleanliness. Or perhaps perfectionism is just one of many faces of compulsiveness.

In any case, I remember back in junior high deciding I wanted to be a majorette. I practiced for hours with the baton, whacking at my knobby elbows in my spastic attempts to twirl like the big girls. My arms and legs were such a welter of bruises I might have been taken for a victim of child abuse! Never mind. I was dogged in my determination to master the spins and whirls and figure eights I had seen real majorettes execute.

That summer I enrolled in the school playground program. Our instructor, Shirley, was a majorette at Spaulding High School. I had seen her march and thought she was as glamorous as any Hollywood star. I spent hours in front of the mirror in my bedroom trying to do my hair just like Shirley's. I begged Mother for white canvas shoes like hers.

Shirley graduated and I switched my hero worship to Greta, who lived next door. Greta was also a majorette at Spaulding and often practiced on the front lawn. Shy, I watched her at first from behind closed curtains. She was poetry in motion. One day I mustered enough courage to ask Greta if I could twirl my baton along with her. She graciously consented and became a loving mentor and friend, the older sister I never had.

In my freshman year at Spaulding High I was a nervous wreck for days before tryouts to replace four graduating majorettes. I could barely eat. My studies suffered. Everything suffered. I suffered most of all.

Tryout day arrived. My palms sweated as I clutched the baton. The rubber ball and tip almost glowed; I had coated them with white shoe polish and buffed them to a blinding brilliance. My baton, after all, had to be perfect.

Whether it was my gleaming baton or the marathon practice sessions, I was one of the four selected. I floated home shouting, "Mummy, I made it! I made it!"

Near the end of the football season new uniforms were ordered for the majorettes. What an exciting day when they arrived just before the final game. We giggled and preened in our shiny new maroon satin outfits. They featured epaulets with silver fringe on the shoulders, satin bands around the cuffs, modest short circle skirts. And for our heads, tall fur hats with brilliant maroon feather plumes!

The last game of the season was with our arch-rival, Montpelier High School. Emotions were at fever pitch, and we majorettes had a new routine to outdazzle the Montpelier majorettes.

Game day came with not a cloud in the azure Vermont sky. We gathered with the band an hour before game time for the traditional march from our high school to the football field. Our new uniforms shimmered in the early afternoon sun as we marched and pranced past the hundreds lining the parade route. My heart was leaping with excitement despite the blisters my new white boots were raising on my heels. We took our places on the front row of bleachers, and the first half of the game passed in a riot of noise and action.

Half-time! Spaulding was ahead by a touchdown. Everything was going right for us.

As the visiting band, Montpelier performed first, while we appraised their routine confidently. We had to admit it was pretty good. But stand back, Montpelier! Prepare to be dazzled.

Our turn had come. Our drum majorette, Joan Plotner, blew her whistle and raised her baton. We were off strutting down the field. Pa dum ta dum. Pa dum ta da da da da dum ta dum. The staccato of the drums cracked like rifle fire through the autumn afternoon. The band separated in neat rows off to the side of the field. Zero hour.

The seven of us stood at attention in our familiar "V" formation, my position last on the left. The crowd roared its approval as we moved into our half-time routine. Batons spun in perfect precision like silver sparklers on the Fourth of July.

On we pranced and danced and spun and leapt. Now for the *pièce de résistance* of our spectacular new routine: the final high toss into the air. The drums rolled, our batons whirled in seven brilliant pinwheels before us. And now the toss. Up, up, up into the air went seven batons.

Looking skyward I caught aglimpse of six spinning silver sticks rising to dizzying heights, then spiraling earthward. But where was *my* baton? I squinted desperately into the afternoon sun.

Thunk! I felt as though a pile driver had slammed the top of my head. The bright afternoon went black, the roar of the crowd faded. I'd gone blind! Deaf! Maybe I was dead. . . .

Looking down, I saw the trampled grass of the football field. Then I knew. Hurtling back to earth, my baton had landed squarely on the top of my tall fur-plumed hat, driving it down over my eyes and ears.

Pa dum ta dum. Pa dum ta dum. The signal to march off the field came while I was staggering around in a circle trying to dislodge the hat wedged over my eyes. It was like prying a bucket off a basketball.

Finally, after what seemed an eternity, I wrenched it off and retrieved my baton from the ground. Utterly mortified, I dared not look at my fellow majorettes—or anyone else. Perhaps the 50-yard line would unzip and the earth would swallow me up.

Joan Plotner blew her whistle. Pa dum ta dum. Pa dum ta dum. Off the field we marched. The crowd was applauding—and laughing. Laughing at me. The perfectionist. The flawless performer.

It was the end of the world. It was worse. The world would go on, and I would have to go on living in it, revealed in all my weakness and imperfection.

In the second half Spaulding won the game and the town went wild with joy. The whole town, that is, except for one girl to whom nothing mattered—not the victory, not the overall excellent performance of the majorettes, not the graciousness and understanding of the others, nothing except that she had failed to live up to the order she had given herself somewhere along the line: Be perfect or be nothing.

By Monday, however, my despair was beginning to lift. One of the star players who had not noticed me before asked me out on a date. What to wear? My outfit had to be just perfect. . . .

As I have continued to struggle with perfectionism over the years, I recently came across the following quiz.* Test yourself, indicating your own response with *Agree* or *Disagree:*

Agree   Disagree
_____   _____   1. I often put things off because I don't have time to do them perfectly.

*Dr. David Stoop, *Hope for the Perfectionist* (Nashville: Oliver Nelson Publications, 1987).

_____ _____ 2. I expect the best of myself at all times.

_____ _____ 3. I generally think I could have done it better.

_____ _____ 4. I get upset when things don't go as planned.

_____ _____ 5. Other people can't understand my desire to do things exactly right.

Agree   Disagree

_____ _____ 6. I am often disappointed in the quality of other people's work.

_____ _____ 7. I feel my standards should be the highest possible, allowing for a clarity of direction and a standard of performance.

_____ _____ 8. If anything I do is considered average, I'm unhappy.

_____ _____ 9. I think less of myself if I repeat a mistake.

I answered *Agree* to every statement, which places me in the category of hard-core perfectionist. I see now that while this particular compulsion helped me to succeed in certain areas (like making the majorette corps, achieving high marks at the Rhode Island School of Design and doing well in the working world), it led to deep frustration in the less quantifiable roles of wife and mother.

The perfectionist trait that really undid me was deciding so often not to do something at all unless I could do it "right." If I couldn't have a super birthday party for my small son or daughter, I wouldn't have one at all. If I couldn't get my closet organized perfectly, I wouldn't try even to keep it neat. After a while a sort of paralysis sets in that makes it difficult to achieve anything at all.

Since our marriage in 1985, Len has been helping me fight the "perfection demon." Shortly after we met, in fact, it reared its head—the afternoon I made the "Nancy Nice Nurse" visit to his hotel room. I was watching him chuckle through the items I had put into the first-aid kit when I realized I had left something out.

"The Pepto-Bismol! I left it sitting on the counter." My voice crackled with annoyance. How could I have goofed so badly?

The look on Len's face stopped me. He was studying me with a mixture of amusement and concern. "Sandy, all this was a great idea! I love it—just what the doctor ordered. Why get upset over one little detail?"

Why indeed?

It is the big question for all of us pursuing the fantasy of perfection. For some, even a 99% represents failure. Many of us will allow ourselves no satisfaction short of total success, total achievement.

As a new bride in 1985, I was eager to become involved in activities that interested Len. I knew his two great recreation loves were tennis and bridge. Bridge gave me gastrointestinal distress. I could never remember all the rules nor what cards had been played.

Tennis was different. I liked the clothes. The ambiance. Tennis was something I could learn to do—not just acceptably, not just well enough to keep Len company, but superbly.

Of course, perfectionism dictated first of all that I look the part. In April it was not hard to find some wonderful Easter clearance bargains on white shorts and tops to wear to my lessons.

My first session at the Gulfstream Tennis Club with tennis pro Fred Horenberger should have sounded a warning. I arrived fifteen minutes early, my stomach churning with little spasms as I pulled into the club parking lot. The busy courts were teeming with leaping white-clad figures.

As I entered the pro shop, I hoped I looked perfect because I didn't feel perfect. The heels of my new tennis shoes pinched against my new terry cloth tennis socks. It was too hot for panty hose, so I had applied erase makeup on the spider web of varicose veins on my thighs.

The lesson began. Fred, a tall, exuberant encourager, cheered me on in his most helpful tennis-coachy way. But I began to realize that my body was in lousy shape. After a short while I was puffing like an exhausted walrus. Before long my new outfit was a soggy mass of twisted fabrics, my leg makeup running in little rivulets onto my snow-white socks. Hardly the pristine vision that stepped onto the court minutes before!

As my errant tennis balls sailed into the adjoining courts, I was aware of stares of displeasure from fellow players. The inability to control the trajectory of these fuzzy little yellow spheres was especially maddening for a perfectionist.

The answer, obviously, was more lessons. After all, I intended to be ready for Wimbledon by the end of the month. (What would I wear?)

I practiced ferociously. I became obsessed with the game. I strategized shots in my dreams and designed tennis dresses in the margins of books. I bleached and starched and pressed my "whites" incessantly.

But I forgot one thing. I was putting enormous, unrealistic pressure on my fiftyish body.

And, of course, the inevitable happened. On the day Fred and I were going to work on my serve, I tossed the ball up over my head. Up went my right arm to smash the ball across the net. *Ping. Pop.* But it wasn't the ball making those sounds. It was my shoulder.

I groaned in pain and grasped the afflicted joint. My tennis career was over before it started.

Most people get tennis elbow. I got tennis shoulder. The white tennis frocks wound up in giveaway boxes and consignment shops.

Had I paced myself, been willing to settle for progress by degrees, the results might have been different. But the driven Sandy, the perfectionistic Sandy had to do it all at once. Compulsively. Perfectly. All or nothing.

Perfectionism, I have seen, was one of the factors leading to my alcoholism. Success had to be absolute. The smallest failure was unmanageable. And since some failure in the scheme of things is inevitable, I fled repeatedly into alcohol oblivion.

Bringing all this out with Len helped me begin to deal with it. Also this statement by addiction writer Anne Wilson Schaef: "The way to be perfect is to be perfectly you."

"That's it!" Len exclaimed when I showed him the Schaef quote. "You need to accept yourself just as you are. God created you with strengths and weaknesses. You're a good communicator. You have artistic flair. Develop them more. You're no good with numbers; you have trouble keeping your checkbook straight. So bridge is not for you. You do have athletic coordination, though. If you'd aimed at being an O.K. tennis player instead of a superstar, we could have had fun with it."

I grimaced, rubbing my aching shoulder. "So what's the answer for perfectionists like me?"

We sat down and worked out these five steps for perfectionists everywhere to follow. (I am working at them, imperfectly!)

1. Admit that perfectionism is a compulsive problem in your work and relationships, that you can never fit the dictionary definition: "Complete in all respects; without defect or omission; flawless."

2. Acknowledge that while some good can come out of perfectionism, if it helps you achieve a degree of excellence, all perfectionism has a root of selfishness and self-centeredness.

3. Realize that on your own, with your own strength and willpower, you cannot free yourself from this problem. Relinquish

to God your desire to be perfect and ask Him to free you from the inner focus on self that lies behind it.

4. Accept the fact that some of the endeavors you undertake will not meet your high standards; pledge to complete them anyhow. Finish everything you start.

5. Most important, accept yourself. Only the Creator is perfect. We are born with certain gifts, skills, strengths. The challenge for each of us, then, is to find that God-given gift, develop it and use it for the glory of God.

If we could achieve perfection, we would assume a godlike attitude and defeat would surely follow, then self-dissatisfaction and eventually depression. For in our humanness we can be neither God nor completely perfect, though many try.

As a recovering woman I am learning slowly to accept myself and enjoy doing what I can do well. Not that I won't accept a challenge to learn something new, try something different, even stick my neck out. But I am beginning to understand that it is unnatural for us to live in constant stress and tension. Our bodies soon react negatively, our spirits sag, our minds close up. Why? Because we weren't created to live this way.

Self-acceptance is a victory in its own way. It has an inherent element of relaxed power. There is a rhythm to acceptance that is good for body, mind and spirit. Pressure, tension, stress tend to ebb away from the person who knows who she is, why she is here on earth and what God's plan is for her life.

5

I Won't Be Home for Dinner

Recovery Principle # 5
SMELL THE FLOWERS

---

*I*F MY HANGUP WAS PERFECTIONISM, LEN'S WAS OVERABSORPTION IN work—the problem his family recognized when they sent him off to learn to smell the flowers.

This kind of relaxation has been hard for Len.

"You need to be a kid again," I told him one day early in our marriage, "learn how to play. That's another way to smell the flowers."

Len looked surprised. "I can be a fun person."

"But it doesn't come naturally. The fun person in you wants to come out, but you keep pushing him back. At times you're enjoying life, then I lose you. You're gone somewhere."

A week or so later Len and I were finishing the dinner I had prepared for the two of us in our own wing of Evergreen Farm. Four

373

lighted candles provided a cozy setting. But all through the meal Len had complained of a mosquito swarm of projects plaguing him. Nothing new about that. Len's list of things to do always filled an entire page of a legal-sized yellow pad.

Now he turned to me suddenly, a light in his blue eyes. "Sandy, I'm discovering things about my work habits."

"You mean your workaholism."

"Yes, I suppose you could call it that. To be honest, I've never really accepted that description of myself. Gave lipservice to it only. I love to work, always thought it was healthy for me."

"So what has changed?"

"The discovery that I've used work to avoid disagreeable situations. It began back in my first marriage when I felt so frustrated about Eve's drinking. Nothing I did or said made any difference. So I plunged myself into my work. It was a way to feel better about myself."

"Your thoughts about it may have changed, but your work patterns haven't," I reminded him.

"Not true. There's a big difference since our marriage. I love doing things with you—everything but shopping. I much prefer being with you than with my papers."

I acknowledged the compliment. "But Len, you really haven't learned to say no to people who want you to speak, or write an article, or be on a board or committee. As a recovering addict, I can still see in you the roots of your addiction."

"Come on, Sandy, work is not in the same addictive league as alcohol."

"I disagree." I pointed out to him how subtle workaholism is, that in some ways overworking is harder to kick than other addictions because it draws applause from the rest of us. Work addicts often have thicker denial systems than other people because overwork is rewarded at every level of society, especially in corporate America.

Work addiction destroys relationships and warps personalities. Amid praise and cheers health problems appear, marriages break, friendships dissolve. No one, least of all the compulsive worker, understands what has gone wrong. As their worlds crumble, work addicts respond by rolling up their sleeves and working all the harder.

In certain ways Len and I have discovered together that the perfectionist and the workaholic are similar:

Perfectionist	*Workaholic*
1) Finds self-esteem in being "complete" in all respects.	1) Finds self-esteem in gaining applause for work done well.
2) Obsession to be perfect is a cover-up for deep insecurity.	2) Obsession for work is a way of escaping problems at home or in the past.
3) Roots of the problem lie in a childhood dysfunctional family.	3) Roots of the problem lie in a childhood dysfunctional family.

At first Len believed his workaholism began as an escape from the pain and frustration of his first marriage, and he refused to accept the fact that he came from a dysfunctional family. "My parents loved each other throughout their marriage of 56 years. There were problems, but what marriage doesn't have problems?"

"But Len, you've told me that your mother was a compulsive eater, more than 75 pounds overweight, and that this led to a lot of emotional family upsets."

"True. But food problems are not in the same league as alcohol, Sandy."

"There you go again. Food disorders can be deadly to one's health, devastating to one's self-worth."

"Mother didn't seem to suffer any lack of confidence. In fact, she was an overachiever. She was president of every woman's club she belonged to, a delegate to church conventions, a top speaker. In 1956 she was honored as New York State Mother of the Year."

"What caused the emotional instability, then?"

Len thought for a few moments. "She was a strange mixture of strong leadership and immaturity . . . very sensitive to criticism. I admired her and loved her, but I resented the way she dominated our household through her emotional outbursts. That's how she got her way."

"What did your father do when your mother got upset?"

"He went outside and smoked a cigar."

"What did you do?"

"I took off—to the playground, to my room, wherever."

"So you had already established a pattern of escape from unpleasant confrontations."

Len nodded slowly. "If the definition of a dysfunctional home is a home disrupted by the emotional upsets of one family member, then I guess ours was dysfunctional."

"Mine certainly was," I said. "And in just this area of workaholism. It's why I'm so aware of the damage it can do."

I can still remember greeting my grandfather late on Friday afternoons when he returned from his week-long shift on the Boston and Maine Railroad. When I saw him appear over the crest of the hill, I would bound out the screen door and run to him. He would drop his metal lunch bucket and scoop me up into his arms with a bear hug.

"How's my honey bird?" he would always say. His engineer's clothes smelled of creosote and tar as I buried my head into his shoulder. Grandpa saw his family only on weekends.

As I look back on all the males in my family, a common trait is evident: They worked hard. And when they weren't working, they talked about all they still had left to do—an endless litany of "shoulds" and "have to's" and calls during the day saying, "I won't be home for dinner."

The women, too, were occupied constantly. In a household devoid of modern conveniences, it was literally true that "a woman's work was never done."

I remember my grandmother ironing with a heavy old cast-iron contraption with removable bases that she kept heating on the back of the kitchen woodstove. When one cooled off, she would snap on a red-hot alternate. Ironing was a major project: sprinkling the rumpled, line-dried cotton clothing with hefty shakes from a water-filled Coke bottle, rolling each garment into little jelly rolls, wrapping them in large terry towels so they wouldn't dry out.

I would watch her for hours, chatting from my child's "junior seat" next to the kitchen table. I felt so important when she let me fill the Coke bottle and sprinkle the clothes!

... A WOMAN'S WORK IS NEVER DONE."

Gram would stand for hours at the creaking wooden ironing board, looking fragile, her snow-white hair captured beneath a pristine white hair net. Her cotton housedress and apron were always starched, the stays of her corset forming ridges at her waist, her sturdy black work shoes tied with double knots.

On summer days I worried about her, she looked so hot and exhausted; but never a word of self-pity interrupted her ritual. When tiny rivulets of perspiration trickled down her temples, she would dab at them daintily with an ever-present white batiste hankie.

Stoic and uncomplaining, she became for me a model of virtuous womanhood.

Both my parents were raised in small New England communities, Dad in Vermont and Mother in Maine. The work ethic was the way of life in rural New England. My parents had experienced the Depression and were wary. "Work hard. Don't be caught napping. Save for a rainy day."

I never saw my father sit idle. When he wasn't at work selling appliances or automobiles, he was home mowing the lawn, papering, painting, tinkering with broken motors. His life was a litany of movement. Doing. Hurrying.

My mother, too, was constantly busy around the house. Dusting. Polishing. Cleaning. Washing. Ironing. I don't recall her taking time for leisure, to enjoy herself or to have fun. I used to wonder if she knew how!

Looking back at my family in the light of Len's work-oriented philosophy, I saw a sad procession of unhappy, unfulfilled people who felt they had to "earn their salt," perform to be accepted, forsake pleasure and leisure, toil at repetitive tasks to avoid having to deal with feelings.

The result: a dysfunctional family. Any home where feelings are not expressed—just as any home where feelings are used to bully and manipulate—produces emotional cripples.

Like so many others in my family, I was geared to be a workaholic, but as a doctor's wife with three small children I could hardly become a working mother. My husband would have forbidden it. So I became a compulsive volunteer.

Helping community causes is most worthwhile. I wish I could say I did it for the right reason—because of an unselfish, caring heart. Sadly, I see now it was an ego thing. Being on committees made me feel important, valued.

The children had good care at home, I rationalized. Though my heart was pricked with guilt at the bewildered little faces of my children as I whirled in and out of the house, my motor was running out of control. "You've got to produce to be somebody," I told myself. And my new "career" became volunteerism.

At one time I was decorations chairman of the Billings Symphony Ball, spending hundreds of hours making little black-and-white flowers, gluing jillions of sequins and feathers and doo-dads. I was newsletter editor of the Billings Junior League, community service chairman of the Auxiliary to the Montana Medical Society.

Any one of these jobs would have been more than enough. I took them on all at once. If I had not been institutionalized, I'm sure I would be dead today.

As Len and I had done for my perfectionism, we drew up a series of steps for him to follow out of work addiction and into a more balanced life:

Slow down.
Learn to say no.
Rest for an hour each day.
No work on Sunday.
Learn how to play.
Find more time for family.
Take long walks.
Eat fewer fats and sweets.
More discussion of feelings and emotions.
Attend a twelve-step support group.

6

How Can I Wash Her Feet If She's Wearing Pantyhose?

Recovery Principle # 6
OBEY THE INNER VOICE

MARRIAGE TO LEN PLUNGED ME INTO A SERIES OF ENCOUNTERS that tested my new relationship to the Lord and everything I had learned during five years of sobriety. While Len and I won the acceptance (and eventually the love) of our new family members, a few friends and associates of Len's and Catherine's were less than enthusiastic about my arrival in their midst.

One such friend was a board member, along with Len, of the Breakthrough prayer ministry. As Len's wife I had been voted into board membership soon after our marriage. My first "official" board meeting was in our own home over a three-day period with me as hostess. I was in a panic, in perfectionistic overdrive.

Living room chairs were set up in a circle for nine people. Nervously I fretted over the red-and-green-plaid Christmas decorations still in proliferation. Didn't everyone have their holiday decor intact in February?

It was always hard for me to admit that Christmas was finally, truly over; I decided to leave the ornaments where they were—including the little brown teddy bears I had attached to the crystal chandelier (a prized possession of Len's mother) that now hangs over the dining room table.

Len had regaled me with stories of his mother's Christmas parties in the 1930s when she would go out on Christmas Eve and buy up as many trees as she could find at bargain prices, transforming their Newton, Massachusetts, home into a winter wonderland. I understood this lady and felt somehow that she would approve of my compulsive style.

We had hired extra help to prepare meals for the board meeting, and the kitchen was abuzz with whirring and sizzling sounds. Everything was under control—except the butterflies in my stomach.

I had met the board members at the previous meeting six months before when Len and I were newlyweds. I remembered how nervous I had been when I entered the room and felt their friendly but close scrutiny. One woman who especially concerned me was Virginia Lively, a nationally known speaker and retreat leader. A tall, stately woman with penetrating blue eyes and an almost palpable aura of wisdom and depth, Virginia had been one of Catherine's closest friends.

I had sensed how hard it was for her to see me in Catherine's place. She had loved Catherine very much. In the presence of her still-fresh grief I had felt like an intruder. How could I or anyone else ever measure up to Catherine?

And, of course, I had promptly forgotten every recovery skill I had ever learned. My face had flushed. My hands had turned to ice. Rivulets of perspiration had run down my back and I had been convinced my deodorant was failing me. Before the evening was over, however, I had been voted unanimously onto the board.

Now, six months later, I was to be hostess for this same group.

The first evening was set aside for personal sharing. Again I felt in awe of these people, all with writing, teaching and prayer ministries that have had worldwide impact. I found myself trying hard to accept the fact that I was married to Len and part of this influential group.

The next day, as business matters were taken up, I focused on my duties as hostess, trying to be as inconspicuous as possible during discussions. After all, what could I with my short experience as a Christian contribute to compare with the expertise of these giants of the faith?

Again, I was terribly conscious of Virginia's strong presence and what I felt was her silent disapproval of me.

That night when Len and I went to bed, I silently thanked the Lord for seeing me through the day. A final meeting tomorrow morning, then lunch and it would all be over!

Len's steady breathing next to me indicated he had long since fallen asleep. I was strangely annoyed that he could sleep anywhere, anytime—a skill he said he had learned as an editor working at all hours. Lying there sleepless, I felt like the fabled "Princess and the Pea." Our mattress had never seemed lumpy before; now every crease and indentation irritated.

"Sandra, go to sleep," I kept ordering myself, to no avail. The idea of praying finally occurred to me. "Here you are on a prayer ministry board and praying is the last thing you try," I scolded myself.

"Lord, is there something You are trying to show me? Some reason I'm unable to sleep?"

Silence. And then the tiniest of thoughts in the back of my mind: *I want you to wash Virginia's feet.*

Startled, I was now more awake than ever. Footwashing! I had never done that. Sure, I recalled that Jesus had washed His disciples' feet to demonstrate His humility. And He had asked His disciples to wash one another's feet as a sign of their willingness to be servants, to be reconciled to each other. But no one did that today, did they? At least, no one I knew.

I dismissed it immediately. Wash her feet in the middle of a board meeting? Ridiculous! That couldn't have been God.

And yet . . . the idea refused to go away. At it I hurled first one objection, then another. "There's too much business to accomplish. It would be terribly awkward for everyone involved. And she always wears hose! How can I wash her feet if she's got pantyhose on?"

I'm asking you to wash her feet.

I awakened the next morning to the sounds of rustling pages. Len was already propped up in bed thumbing through the pages of *My Utmost for His Highest,* the classic by Oswald Chambers with which we began our morning devotions.

"Len, I had the most peculiar thought last night just before I finally dropped off to sleep," I told him. "It seemed as though the Lord was telling me—of all things—to wash Virginia's feet this morning at the meeting. Pretty ridiculous, don't you think?"

"Not at all," Len replied thoughtfully. "Let's pray about it."

I sighed. Deep down I knew a footwashing couldn't be my own idea. Where could it have come from but God?

Meanwhile, Len had found the reading for that day, February 19, in the Chambers book. He scanned it, then handed it to me without a word.

Read John 13. We see there the incarnate God doing the most desperate piece of drudgery, washing fishermen's feet, and He says . . . "If I then, your Lord and Master, have washed your feet, ye also ought to wash one another's feet."

I could not believe the words leaping at me off the page! Of all the days in the year for Oswald Chambers to write about footwashing!

Then a pang of sheer terror gripped me. "Does this mean I really have to do this in the middle of the meeting?"

"There's your answer," said Len. Then he looked at me tenderly. "Sandy, the Lord spoke to you last night, and now this incredible confirmation. He's saying you can trust Him."

The first half of the morning meeting passed in a blur. My mind was not on the agenda or anything anyone was saying. Preoccupied with the task before me, my palms were sweating, breakfast sitting undigested in my stomach.

I stared at Virginia across the room. She looked dauntingly imposing, sitting in the large white easy chair, her crisp, handpainted blouse set off by matching white slacks. The white sweater around her shoulders was trimmed with the same flowers that vined down the front of her blouse. On her feet, white sandals. And, of course, pantyhose.

New objections sprang to mind. Her feet would be terribly uncomfortable if I were to wash them in this air-conditioned room. There is nothing worse than having to sit around in wet hose. She could catch a bad cold.

The 10:30 refreshment break came. Len shot me a "you're-going-to-do-it-aren't-you?" look and I smiled back weakly. He grinned affirmation and love. I knew he was undergirding me with prayer. The word now confronting me was *obedience*.

From the kitchen cupboard I hauled out my largest stainless steel mixing bowl, then filled a large glass pitcher with warm water. Grabbing a hand towel from a kitchen drawer, I headed back to the living room.

The board members were settling into their chairs again, agendas in hand, pens poised to consider the next item of business. My appearance at the edge of the circle bearing footwashing paraphernalia created a shock wave of silence.

Inhaling deeply, I stepped into the circle and positioned myself before Virginia. She looked up at me, startled.

"Virginia, I feel I'm supposed to wash your feet. Last night the Lord showed me that I've had some feelings toward you that I need to confess. The words I heard Him say were *Wash her feet*."

"If it was His voice," she said quietly, "then you must do it."

I sat down on the floor before Virginia. To me she looked like Queen Victoria in her white outfit, sitting in the white chair. I removed her white sandals gently and placed both of her stocking-clad feet into the steel mixing bowl.

Such a touch of class, I thought to myself. *Couldn't I have at least found our glass punchbowl?*

The warm water from the pitcher poured over her right foot, turning her hose a dark brown.

"I need to ask your forgiveness, Virginia," I said as I washed the foot, "for some negative thoughts about you, thoughts that come from my own insecurity."

I lifted her right foot from the bowl and dried it. Next, the left foot, the same procedure.

Then I reached up and embraced her, tears of relief and freedom stinging my eyes.

As we broke from the embrace, Virginia's blue eyes glowed with love.

Quickly pushing the bowl, pitcher and towel under the coffee table, I settled into my chair, uttering a great sigh of relief. It was over.

But it wasn't.

The mood in the room had changed totally. The board members sat silent, tears in many eyes. Suddenly one of the women walked across the room to one of the men. "For some time I've held a resentment toward you concerning—. I feel I can't leave this place today without washing your feet and asking your forgiveness."

She washed his feet and he washed hers.

The agenda went out the window. The Holy Spirit blew through that living room like a hurricane. As one after another knelt to wash someone's feet there were healings and forgiveness and new understandings. We laughed and cried and laughed some more.

And even that was not the end.

Pastor Jamie Buckingham went back to his church and had a "Forgiveness Sunday" as members of his congregation washed one another's feet. Jamie reported to us later that nothing had so bonded his congregation in love and reconciliation as this mass footwashing experience.

And to think how hard I had resisted the inner message, which had gone against every instinct of self-preservation and social nicety!

Later Len and I reviewed the whole experience, marveling at the creative ways God uses to reach us with His guidance for our lives. The sad thing is how often we refuse to hear what He is saying to us. Or we hear but do not obey.

Hearing God is basic, vital and yet so difficult for many of us. Perhaps we expect His voice to command our attention. I am discovering that His voice is usually a gentle thought in my mind, a Spirit-to-spirit communique.

I want you to wash Virginia's feet was a quiet message but a firm one. No way could I slough it off as of the enemy or as coming from my own desires.

How is it that Len and I do at times hear God's voice? We have talked a lot about this and concluded that the more we pray, the more we read God's Word, the more we develop our relationship with Him, the more we open ourselves to receive communications from Him. If we stay close, we hear. If we draw apart, His voice fades. For us, it's as simple as that.

Hearing is one thing, of course, obeying quite another.

I am deeply saddened and convicted by the many requests I have received in my spirit and have done nothing about. It is easy to claim poor hearing or confusion ("I don't understand You, Lord") or fatigue or illness or fear or stubbornness as reasons for not doing what the Spirit tells me to do.

God understands our weak, indecisive natures only too well. He knows we want some confirmation that we are hearing Him correctly. It would have been easy for me to have dismissed the inner voice asking me to wash Virginia's feet as too far out. But the confirmation in *My Utmost for His Highest* on that very date could not be explained away. I would either obey or lose a blessing for many people.

I wonder how many such blessings I have lost in the past by my disobedience?

Going further, I am discovering through this episode that God has a specific solution for every one of my relationship problems, if I but ask Him.

This was a new thought. How would it work with my ex-husband Werner, for example? So far none of my efforts had lessened the hostility he had for me even slightly.

The key here, I am learning, is that my efforts, coming out of my own humanness, have little power or impact in easing strained, broken or severely ruptured relationships. But God's ways will work.

Wash Virginia's feet. I would never have thought of that in a million years!

So I need to keep asking, then be ready to obey when God gives me His solution.

7

"I Never Was Pretty, But I Had Good Teeth"

A S I HAVE MOVED ALONG ON THE HEALING ROAD, I HAVE BEEN surprised by the number of long-forgotten childhood memories that have reappeared. At first I didn't consider them especially significant. Then, as truth emerged through each one, I began to see a pattern of teachings that God was applying quietly to my life.

Like the apple episode when I was a pupil at Miss Hill's kindergarten.

That February morning began as every other winter morning. Mother had selected my clothes for the day and was warming them over the furnace radiator on a wooden rack. Mother believed it was unhealthy to wear cold clothes.

First I had to struggle into the inevitable garter belt with those ghastly hot buckles. On with the awful brown cotton stockings that bunched around the ankles. Into the sensible brown oxfords tied with double knots. The layers accumulated until buttoned, wrapped and swathed I waddled into the frigid Vermont morning like a little woolly Martian bound for Miss Hill's house a quarter-mile away.

Tucked into the pocket of my corduroy pinafore this particular day was a juicy red apple. At naptime when I thought no one was noticing, out came the apple from its hiding place.

Crickle . . . crunch. That first bite echoed through the quiet room like a rifle shot. Miss Hill bounded toward my rest pad and quickly had my apple in her hand. Up went the window shades.

"Roll up your nap rugs, children," she said. "Sandra is going to share her apple with *all* of us, aren't you, Sandra?"

My eight peers shuffled into a lopsided circle as Miss Hill dissected the apple with the skill of a brain surgeon into nine exactly even sections.

"What would have happened if Jesus had chosen to eat the loaves and fishes *all by Himself* instead of sharing them with the hungry multitudes?" she asked. "When we give something we want to others, we become like Jesus."

This unforgettable episode, deep in my subconscious for years, emerged during my recovery process, reminding me again to give of myself. I wasn't basically a selfish person; in fact, my compulsive nature often made me outgoing and giving.

Yet an addiction has a way of eating away good qualities like generosity, faithfulness, honesty. Soon self-centeredness takes over, dominates, destroys one's character.

How fascinating that a bit of wisdom learned in kindergarten would resurface at an unlikely place, the Montana State Hospital, on that sultry night when I got out of bed and comforted the distraught Karen! I had put self-pity aside for a moment as I gave myself to another. And at the exact moment I reached out to Karen, the healing process inside me had begun!

The give-yourself-away principle comes through often in the Bible. "Whatever measure you deal out to others, it will be dealt to you in return" (Luke 6:38). "He who has lost his life for My sake shall find it" (Matthew 10:39).

The principle is implicit in many treatment programs. Andrea, a recovering alcoholic at the halfway house, confessed to numerous suicide attempts. During group therapy we discovered Andrea to be a most articulate communicator. After she finished the course, she was invited back often to share her experiences with other groups. What a lift for Andrea! Seeing herself as a helper and giving of herself increased her self-confidence greatly and hastened her recovery.

Dr. Karl Menninger, the famous Kansas psychiatrist, was asked once what he would do if he felt a nervous breakdown coming on. If the questioner anticipated the doctor's saying, "I would see a psychiatrist," he must have been surprised to hear Dr. Menninger reply, "If you feel a nervous breakdown coming on, lock up your house, go across the railroad tracks, find someone in need and do something for him."

I was struggling with self-pity on Mother's Day in 1986 when I came out of a florist shop. In my hands were two plastic corsage boxes, not just the one I had intended to get for my husband's mother. Each one held a small yellow cymbidium orchid with a yellow ribbon and a pearl stickpin.

"You never know who might enjoy the extra flower," I said in answer to Len's quizzical look as I got into the car.

As we drove to the Gaithersburg, Maryland, nursing home where his 93-year-old mother, Lucile LeSourd, lay comatose, my emotions were spinning wildly. I wanted to pin one of those corsages on myself. For I couldn't ever recall receiving a Mother's Day corsage—not from the father of our three children; nor had I ever trained our two sons to send cards or give flowers (though my daughter Lisa regularly sent me beautiful remembrances that warm my heart).

I knew that my three children loved me very much, that they were proud (and bewildered, perhaps) over my recovery. But little cat paws of self-pity were leaving powdery prints on my fragile feelings this special day. The two orchid corsages lay next to me on the navy leather car seat, their delicate petals quivering rhythmically as our car sped down the interstate toward Gaithersburg.

Hmm, I thought to myself. *I'll just pin one of these corsages on and pretend it's from my sons.*

Something checked my spirit. *There you go again. Instant gratification, kiddo. There may be someone at the nursing home who needs this corsage today. Wait. Save it for someone else.*

I resisted thoughts like that. I still wanted what I wanted when I wanted it. Had I learned *anything* in recovery? At times like this I wondered.

We arrived at the nursing facility and the elevator door opened onto the fourth floor. As always the smells and sounds, even in this well-kept, beautifully decorated place, jolted us to the reality of human impermanence, made us aware of our own mortality.

To the left of the nurses' station, several Alzheimer's patients sat in their wheelchairs. Some stared off into another time, others flailed gnarled arms at imagined foes.

Len's mother was just as we had left her a few weeks earlier, her shrunken body motionless beneath the maroon coverlet. Her pale face never moved when Len and I leaned down to kiss her. As Len talked to the still form about their early life together, however, two tears slid down her face. Though she could not move a muscle, she had heard him and responded! Feeling I should leave Len alone with his mother, I slipped away into the hall, picking up the extra corsage as I left.

At the nurses' station I asked if there was anyone on the floor who received no visits.

"Go see Mary in 4G," one of the nurses suggested. "She's a love. You wouldn't believe she's 96."

The door to 4G was wide open. The sun streamed in on a scene I found startling. Seated in a green upholstered chair was an enormous woman. On her head was perched a Boston Red Sox cap, beneath which long wisps of white cotton candy hair fell far past her shoulders. Her bed was covered with stuffed animals.

"Mary, my name is Sandy," I said self-consciously. "I've come to pay you a Mother's Day visit."

"That's grand!" she boomed in a basso-profundo voice that shook her body from the top of her cap to the soles of her fuzzy blue slippers. "Sit down, child. I'm delighted you stopped by to see an old reprobate like me."

I pulled a worn red plastic ottoman close to her chair. Mary's moon face and bulbous red nose gave her the appearance of a kindly Mrs. Santa.

"See that table over there?" she asked, pointing beyond the foot of her bed. "That's about all that's left of my earthly treasures."

"MOTHER'S DAY MARY"

Wanting to appear interested, I turned and scanned several old photos, a copy of the Serenity Prayer, a battered cocoa brown leather family Bible and a needlepoint picture of a nurse with Mary's name appliqued on it.

"My friends gave me that needlepoint after I retired from 55 years of nursing," she offered with a noble sweep of her powerful hand. "Nursing was my life. What did you say your name was?"

I murmured my name, but she never stopped talking.

"I wanted to nurse since I was a little girl. We lived on a dairy farm not far from Boston"—here her eyes filled with tears—"and I was always patching up the animals. Some nights I'd stay till dawn with a sick cow. My dad told me somehow they'd find a way to send me to nursing school. How they did I'll never know.

"My two sisters were real pretty. They got married right out of high school. I never was pretty. There weren't many boys interested in a big moose like me. But I had good teeth.

"I never married and had children of my own," she continued. "But I sure mothered lots of young 'uns as a nurse. I have children everywhere. Of all ages. You'd be surprised how many said to me, 'Mary, I wish you were my mother!' I told them God was just using me to be His voice and tears and hugs. Hurting people need to know God loves them, that our Father God has a mother's heart."

Her watery gaze moved toward the window. She seemed to be tiring and I sensed it was time to wind up my visit.

"Uh, Mary . . . I'd like to leave something with you before we say goodbye. It's a corsage for Mother's Day. Perhaps you'd like me to pin it on for you?"

Her moist blue eyes flooded with tears as she cradled the oblong plastic container in her large hands. The flower looked so fragile, so jewel-like.

"Oh, no," she said. "It's much too lovely to wear. Let me just hold it and look at it. I always wanted a corsage like this. But not being a mother, no one ever gave me one."

In the rays of the fading sun, the dainty orchid seemed lit from within.

"It's so beautiful it makes my heart hurt," she whispered. "How can I ever thank you?"

I hugged her and kissed her damp cheek.

I thought about Mary all the way home—her lifetime of service to others, her self-discipline. I could see her striding tall in her nurse's whites down thousands of miles of hospital corridors, touching her patients' lives with her warmth.

And now she was winding all this up in a 12 × 15-foot room in a nursing home. Yet she still had her strength and her dignity. I felt privileged to know her.

All the rest of that day my spirit felt lighter. Freer. The selfish addict had given instead of taking.

Weeks later the door to Room 4G was only ajar. I pushed it open gently and walked into a darkened room. The gold drapes were closed. Mary was breathing with obvious difficulty, the long, white hair a tangle on her pillow.

"Mary?" I called softly. "It's me, Sandy, your Mother's Day friend."

Her eyes flickered open for a moment, then closed. Mary was dying of uremic poisoning and only semi-conscious, the nurse explained.

As I reached down to give her a final goodbye kiss, my eyes fell upon the table filled with her treasures. A shaft of light pouring through the crack in the drapes rested on a shining object. An oblong plastic box. Inside a yellow ribbon clung to a withered tendril of a flower.

It was her orchid. On top of her worn brown Bible.

"I'm Ready to Face 'Old Fang' "

Recovery Principle # 8
BE VULNERABLE

"*N*O MAN IS AN ISLAND." I don't know how many times I have heard this line from John Donne quoted, but it surely does apply to people in recovery from an addiction.

During the past twelve years, support groups have nourished and sustained me. They represent a lifeline for all of us working at fundamental changes in our coping strategies.

Whenever I felt depression coming on, I went to a support group.

When I was under severe tension or pressure, I went to a support group.

When I had a humiliating experience, a wrenching defeat, a painful loss, I went to a support group.

Today if I have had an exhilarating success, feel especially elated or have been on an ego trip, I look for a support group. I have learned that for a recovering person, any kind of high can precede a tumble into the abyss.

Support groups provide emotional and spiritual sustenance to those feeling low. They have a leveling, sobering effect on anyone who thinks he or she has it pretty much all together. And those of us in recovery need often to be checked by fellow travelers.

Because my husband and I move about a great deal, it seems I am always looking in a local paper for the address of such a group.* Here is a typical recent experience.

On this particular Saturday morning my car pulled into the parking lot of a large shopping center. My stomach was queasy, the apprehension I always feel approaching a new group of people in a family support group. *I hate to be late,* I thought, noting it was five minutes before the hour. Climbing out of the car, I rechecked the address clutched in my hand. Most of the stores had *To Rent* signs posted in their windows. So many people hurting economically.

Inside Room 706 men and women were setting up brown metal folding chairs and placing books and pamphlets on a long table by the wall. Feeling self-conscious, I concentrated on the available literature. Somehow I always felt more secure when my hands were full, and soon my hands bulged with brochures and pamphlets. Did I still need to fill that invisible hole of shame and low self-worth inside?

Even after years of working my recovery program, I realized once again how fragile I am, how uncomfortable in new situations.

People were heading for the circle of folding chairs. I selected a seat opposite the woman who seemed to be directing things. (Often when you sit next to the leader, you have to speak first!)

As I sat down, the pamphlets and brochures I was clutching slipped to the floor in a cascade of paper. When I leaned over to retrieve them, the glasses balanced on top of my head fell to the floor,

*See pp. 533–539 for the various headings under which these are listed.

too. I managed a nervous giggle and settled back self-consciously into my chair.

Gladys, the meeting leader, scanned the room like a mother hen counting her chicks. "Let's get started and introduce ourselves," she urged. One by one we gave our first names.

Obviously Gladys was a veteran of support group meetings. I was taken by her Easter-egg-like appearance. Thin legs protruded from a round body clad in a purple and red Hawaiian shirt and shorts combination. Her fuzzy salt-and-pepper hair was pulled back over her ears with two sparkly red barrettes; scarlet sandals housed her magenta-painted toes. She ran the meeting like a Marine drill sergeant.

Two chairs over from Gladys was Wanda, a divorced mother of three. She spoke first, running fingers through her long, black hair. "Say a little prayer for me. I'm flying to New York for my daughter's wedding next weekend and *he* will be there."

Several people in the group nodded; *he* was obviously her ex-husband.

But Wanda talked mostly about her mother, a manipulator who had decided her daughter couldn't handle the pressure of this event. Mentally I could envision little girl Wanda under the thumb of a controlling mother who made every decision for her. Now, however, there was something triumphantly defiant in Wanda's pale green eyes.

"I said to her, 'Mother, I can handle it.' I've come a long way in my alcohol program and I have the tools to get through an unpleasant encounter with 'Old Fang' and not fall apart. I do not intend to miss my daughter's wedding just because her father is going to be there. Maybe last year I couldn't have made it, but I can now. I feel good about myself and who I am."

I studied Wanda as she carefully rearranged the front of her oversized purple satin shirt that covered a ribbed black tank top. She was bra-less. Pretty brave for someone in middle age, I thought. Then I noted quarter-shaped calluses beneath each kneecap. Were they from a charwoman's work or years on her knees in prayer? She punctuated her speech by stabbing her index finger into the air, causing her purple metal earrings to swing about her face like chandeliers in an earthquake. Wanda, I concluded, could take care of herself. Her mother's days of domination were over.

The subject of the meeting was "letting go," a subject wrenchingly difficult for most of us.

Now Gladys told her story, in a way that indicated to me she had recited it countless other times.

"My husband was wounded in World War II and this guy hasn't given me a moment's peace ever since. Nothing is ever good enough or fast enough or hot enough or cold enough. He's negative, negative, negative from the time the sun comes up, and he made my life a living hell till I started to come to 'these rooms' {a term you hear at many meetings}.

"I've come to realize I am not responsible for how he thinks or what he says. I have to take care of Numero Uno." Gladys was drumming her chest with her fingers. "You know where I am now? I've let go of him and his power to get to me and keep me crazy."

She signaled the end of her remarks by folding her large arms over her bulging midriff and recrossing her knobby knees.

Kitty spoke up next. "This must be husband and ex-husband day," she joked, glancing apologetically at the five men in the circle. "Please forgive me, fellas, but all the guys out there aren't as nice as you! It's like my ex-husband has checked out on all responsibilities where our three grown children are concerned. He never writes or calls or pays any attention to them. They try to shrug it off, but I can tell they feel rejected and abandoned.

"This program has taught me that I need to let go of any expectations where he is concerned. For years I tried to make up for his lack of concern, financially and emotionally, and it darn near killed me. I've got to face the fact that I can do nothing about what he does and doesn't do.

"Sarah—she's my sponsor—had a bit of wisdom for me last night when I called her. I was upset that he hadn't remembered our son's twentieth birthday yesterday. No card. No call. She told me to pray that someday he would have the kind of loving relationship that I have with the children. I'd never thought of praying that way for him. In fact, I've been so exasperated with him lately I haven't prayed for him at all.

"But last night after I hung up, I did what she suggested and I felt much better. I felt a release from some of my anger. That's my gem to pass on to you about letting go."

Roger, seated next to Gladys, was clearly unsettled by what Kitty had said, rubbing the toes of his new Reeboks together and jamming his hands into the pockets of his jeans. He had said little about himself, other than that it was his second meeting. Now the muscles of his cheeks bulged as he gritted his teeth, some painful secret gnawing at him. He looked as though he wanted and needed to cry, but was fighting it with everything he had.

A pretty, fiftyish lady seated to my right cleared her throat. "My name is Amy, and I've been listening to all of you talk about letting go. I can let go of some things in my life and I think I have. But there is something that keeps tripping me up. I think I need to let it out.

"My mother always told me that when I was born I so crippled her that for a long time she had to get around in a wheelchair. How's that for a guilt trip? I remember her starting every sentence, whatever the subject, with 'If it hadn't been for Amy. . . .' Can you imagine growing up with that kind of guilt? 'My gosh, I've crippled my mother!'

"I know now that an infant's not to blame, but I still have this old record playing on and on in my brain, *You crippled your mother. You bad girl. You bad girl!*"

Amy's soft brown eyes were beginning to fill with tears. She pulled at a thread on her peach sweatshirt. "I've always tried to be perfect. The perfect daughter, the overachiever in school, the perfect wife and mother. What a joke. My life feels like it's been one big fat lie. I guess I need to come to more meetings. My mother eventually got better. I'm the one who's crippled."

As in most support groups, the women were more vocal than the men. I hoped Roger would speak up, but he didn't, even when he was asked if he had anything to say. The other men had only brief comments. Most men who come to support groups, I have noticed, have their emotions in check—at least until they have attended a number of meetings.

At the end we all stood in a circle holding hands to say the Lord's Prayer. All ages, sizes, men and women, young and old, blended our voices in the most famous prayer of all time.

I love to hear recovery groups say this prayer. There is something about the brokenness in all of our voices, the weakness reaching out for strength.

As people were hugging and wishing each other well, I noticed Roger bolting out the door. At the end of the Lord's Prayer I had heard Gladys tell him, "Keep coming back. It works if you work it."

Roger's pain must be enormous, I thought. *But he's come to the right place. I hope he comes back.*

Len, typical of males, was reluctant to go to a support group. One day I confronted him about this.

"I'm going to an alcohol support meeting tonight, Len. Why don't you go with me? There's a support group for families held in the same building."

"Why should I?"

"Because it's for people like you. Eve's drinking affected you both."

"That was 30 years ago."

"Well, your current wife is a recovering alcoholic. You may not realize it, Len, but you're a codependent. A family support group will help you see this."

I could see irritation beginning to rise in him.

"Exactly how do you see me as a codependent?" he asked.

I hesitated a moment to think through my answer. "When Eve was in deep trouble, you covered for her, made excuses, helped her avoid facing reality. The goal was peace at any price. In time, without knowing it, you developed a pattern of peacemaking, avoiding confrontation. This is codependency."

He shook his head. "I always thought of a codependent as the wife of a drunk. After a while she depends on her husband's drinking to evoke sympathy for herself. She also becomes the boss in the home. If her husband stops drinking and takes over as head of the household, it's hard for her to accept their changed roles."

"That's one pattern. But codependency is more complex than that. Come to the meeting and find out."

Reluctantly he did.

After the meeting as we drove home together, he didn't say much, but admitted he was glad he had come. There were more women than men attending, he said. A woman had led. She had gone around the circle asking everyone to identify their situations and where they were with them.

"What did you share?" I asked.

"I told about my marriage to Eve."

Len gave no details and I didn't press him.

But after going to several more meetings, he opened up.

"During the meeting the other night I realized not only what a failure my divorce represented, but also that for years I've been trying to block the whole ten-year marriage to Eve from my mind, as though somehow it didn't happen."

He paused, frowning. "We men often do anesthetize our feelings to block out painful experiences. I saw that for the first time."

"Women do that, too," I reminded him.

"I realized something else," he continued. "Though I've been faithful with my alimony support payments and always encouraged the children to maintain a relationship with their mother, I need to do more to try to heal the wounds of Eve's and my broken marriage."

"Why don't you go and see her?"

Len winced. "She's in a nursing home in Iowa. Confined to a wheelchair. Everyone in our family, many friends, all kinds of alcohol treatment centers, tried to help her. Nothing worked. It's so tragic."

"When was the last time you saw her?"

"I've talked to her on the phone occasionally, but we haven't met face to face in almost thirty years." He paused. "They tell you to let well enough alone in these situations. I wonder."

Months passed. One night Len's daughter, Linda Lader, called. As she and Len talked, I gathered Linda planned to take her year-and-a-half-old daughter, Whitaker, to visit Eve. Then I heard my husband say, "I think I should go with you."

Len came back from the telephone looking surprised. "Why did I say that?" he asked.

"Because something in your spirit said *go.*"

"Still, it'll be a most difficult weekend."

But when Len returned from that Iowa weekend, his face glowed.

Despite the tragedy of Eve's alcoholism, she had greeted Len with gratitude for his support of her over the years. Len, Linda and Eve had ended the visit by praying together, holding hands and asking forgiveness of one another for all the hurts inflicted over the years.

"A beautiful healing experience!" Len summed it up. "Why did I wait 30 years to do this?"

Support groups are crucially important to people like me who are attempting to work through past problems. Inner strength comes from hearing others talk about their struggles, which are similar to mine. I can identify immediately with someone grappling with a relationship problem, for example, especially an ex-husband. New thinking comes. I am encouraged to try again in my own life to establish friendlier relations.

Also, the we're-all-in-this-together atmosphere in a support group lessens my loneliness. Feelings long buried because they were so painful bubble up and say, "You have to deal with me!" I don't want to, but I know I have to if I am ever to become whole.

I am always intrigued by the chain-reaction effect a group meeting can have. I returned from one impressed by how a husband was able to forgive his estranged alcoholic wife. He had made an effort to see her and the result was healing. This is why I urged Len spontaneously to do the same, which he did with positive results.

The greatest support group was formed 2,000 years ago. Jesus gathered together twelve hurting, flawed men who would hardly have been called leadership types. They fellowshiped together, had disagreements, shared their hurts and grew stronger together. Their Leader taught them, brought out their gifts. As they were helped, they were able to help others.

And what they learned in a group situation gave strength to eleven of them to go boldly into the world and make an impact that is still being felt today.

9

Broken Relationships

Recovery Principle # 9
BE RECONCILED

Y EARS OF ALCOHOL ABUSE CAN LEAVE A TRAIL OF BROKEN RELA-
tionships—disappointed employers and co-workers, severed
friendships, family ruptures.

Most devastating to me were two broken marriages. One failure is
bad enough. Two made me desolate. Depressed and without hope, I
tried to end my life. A merciful Lord plucked me out of the miry pit
and put me onto the road to recovery, with this word of instruction:
Make amends to those you have hurt.

Making amends is not something one should do impulsively,
however. And I have found there are five categories of such people.*

---

*Drs. Robert Hemfelt and Richard Fowler, *Serenity, A Companion for Twelve-
Step Recovery* (Nashville: Thomas Nelson Publishers).

1. Those to whom we may turn immediately, such as spouses or close family members.

2. Those to whom only partial disclosure can be made, because to do more would cause harm to others. We need always to consider the risks to another's security, privacy and confidentiality.

3. Those to whom amends should be deferred until a later date. Perhaps the hurts are so fresh that to reopen them would only trigger rage on their part. Maybe we also need to work through anger and resentments of our own.

4. Those whom we should never contact, because doing so would only open up old relationship doors that need to stay closed. This may be true for a sex addict, for example, who wants to make amends to former partners.

5. Those who, because of death or illness, cannot be contacted. Three techniques can be used when we want to make amends with persons no longer living. One is called the "empty chair technique" in which we imagine the person sitting before us and talk with him or her. A second method is writing letters to the deceased as a form of journaling. Finally, if opportunity presents, we can visit the gravesite to offer our amends through a spoken monologue.

Making amends to my children Brad, Brent and Lisa is something I have been working at for years.

My son Brad is strong and independent. Friends recall an incident at a Little League baseball game when he was nine. An overzealous coach yelled at him for making an error. Seconds later Brad strode off the field and began to remove his uniform methodically, piece by piece, including his baseball shoes. He placed all these items in a neat pile along the foul line and walked out of the ballpark and home in his underwear without a word to anyone, or even a glance at his coach.

Brad never mentioned the incident to me. He never played ball again.

With this same stoicism, he suffered through two family breakups, deciding he had to make it on his own. When I finally became sober, I tried to appease my conscience and undo the harm to my children by giving them material things. They liked that, but it solved nothing and violated the principle of "Don't do for your children what they can do for themselves."

The time came when I had to say a firm *no* to one of Brad's requests. Soon thereafter I received this letter from him:

Dear ?

I just want to tell you how I feel even though you have never asked me. As a child you never had to wonder where your mother was or if she loved you. All the while you were never being beaten and locked up in closets by babysitters like I was! I had to wonder every day of my life where you were and why you did this to me.

How can *you* expect to be a part of my life now? You weren't there for me then and I don't want you here now. Even if I did, all you would worry about was if I wanted your precious money, instead of your moral support and love.

I don't believe you know what love really is. You have everybody snowed that you had real problems. Well, let me tell you about real problems. Sometimes we have to scrape up pennies just to eat. I helped Brent when he first came to live with me because he couldn't help with the finances. I felt good about helping him. If you are wondering why I felt good helping, it's called that "love" that you know nothing about.

Stay out of my life. Don't write, call or come by. If you want to talk with Brent, make arrangements with him. I never want to hear from or see you again.

Brad

At first I was devastated by the letter. Then I realized it was healthy that Brad had been able to get in touch with the pain and years of rage locked up within him. He was pouring out his feelings to me, gut-level feelings, for the first time in his life. I needed to accept his letter as an opportunity for an honest relationship with my son. I had tap-danced around many issues with him, not wanting to make waves, doing both of us a great disservice.

It was important that Brad know I loved him despite his anger, that our relationship would not dissolve because he had blown up at me. He needed to know I was still there for him, but that I was simply not going to grant his every financial wish.

Our relationship has been much better after this exchange. He learned he could be real with me, vent negative feelings and know that I still loved him.

Brent and Lisa are also learning to express themselves honestly, often bluntly. We are all beginning to communicate on a new level, not speak in the riddles of addictive lingo, skirting issues, telling half-truths or, worse yet, boldface lies.

How best to help my two sons? The answer came through a special course their grandmother and I were able to finance— the Film and Video Productions Program

JUNE 90

BRAD AND BRENT GRADUATE FROM FULL SAIL CENTER FOR THE RECORDING ARTS - WINTER PARK, FL at Full Sail Center for the Recording Arts in Winter Park, Florida. The boys worked hard, spending long hours in all-night labs, filming documentaries, learning every facet of this field.

Lisa flew to Florida from her home in Montana to attend her brothers' graduation. As a special treat we rented men's formal attire: tails, tuxedo shirts, satin bowties and cummerbunds for Brad and Brent to wear with their jeans and tennis shoes. When the four of us celebrated at a pre-graduation dinner, the boys looked handsome in their finery, complete with rose boutonnieres and sunglasses.

Before the diplomas became valid, Brad and Brent were required to complete six weeks of on-the-job internship at a production facility. They were both assigned to station WKCF in Orlando, worked diligently at their assignments, loved the challenge of live programming.

At the termination of the internship, the station manager called Brad and Brent into her office. "I regret to tell you this, but I have only one job. And two brothers. . . ."

Brent came quickly to her rescue: "Give the job to my brother."

Tears stung my eyes when I heard this story from Brad. His younger brother had unselfishly laid down a prize of great worth. Brent would have loved the job. But he deferred to his older brother, wanting to see him blessed with the opportunity. A role reversal here. My sons were now teaching me.

Making amends with my second husband, Randall, was crucial to my recovery. He had exhausted every effort to find help for me and had underwritten the expense of psychiatry and hospitalization. Since there were no children from this marriage, this divorce— painful though it was—was not as destructive as the first one. And my move from Montana to Vermont eased any awkwardness when Randall remarried. An obvious step on my part was to write him a letter expressing my gratitude for his love, support and understanding.

Making amends with Werner, my first husband and the children's father, was much more difficult. Our relationship had been strained and distant since our divorce twenty years before. My attempts to be friendly were usually met with stony resistance.

As in many such situations, the children had become go-betweens, sadly playing roles of wounded messengers with reports from the enemy camp. This always distressed me. I agonized for my children, for the heartbreak and devastation to their lives as they became helpless pawns in our acrimonious marital chess game.

After my marriage to Len, we began a prayer campaign for his ex-wife, Eve, and Werner. Each morning we lifted them to the Lord, asking His healing and blessing on their lives that day. We also prayed that the Lord would open doors of opportunity for reconciliation. This happened, as I have mentioned, with Eve and Len.

One morning while I was shampooing my hair, that inner voice I was learning to obey pounded against my skull like the pulsating jets of water from the shower head.

Call Werner. Ask him to forgive you for giving up on your marriage. His unforgiveness of you is standing in My way of working in his life as I need to.

Was this the Lord? Here was a message that once again I did not want to hear. I did not want to call Werner. He clearly resented any calls made to his home even to talk to our children when they were there. He was so abrupt on the phone that I could hardly complete a sentence.

Len's blue eyes brightened when I reported the shower message. "When are you going to do it?" he asked.

I groaned. I should have known this would be his reaction.

"Soon," I promised.

Though *Do it now!* had become a watchword of my recovery, the procrastinator I thought I had buried resurfaced. *Werner won't be home,* I told myself. *He always goes out for lunch about now. Call him in the morning when he's fresh and rested. And you're fresh and rested.* That was only sensible; I would call later.

Later was a lot later. The longer I put off the call, the more I dreaded the encounter. He would hang up. He would find some way to humiliate me. Days went by.

I felt guilty during our prayer time. I had prayed for a chance to heal the breach with Werner and now I was disobeying the prompting of the Holy Spirit.

Len sensed my struggle. In his loving way, he hadn't bugged me to make the call. But I knew it was on his mind.

Two weeks passed—two long weeks of evasion. The morning finally came when I could put it off no longer.

I sat down on the edge of our bed and stared at the phone. I could hear Len's warm voice dictating letters in the adjacent office. His presence nearby was reassuring.

I dialed Werner's number and waited. The phone rang several times. *He's not home,* I thought with relief. Just as I was about to hang up, he answered.

"Werner, this is Sandra. I need to talk with you about something that I—"

"Yes, I'm quite aware it's you. I'm not sure I want to hear anything you have to say."

"Please don't hang up," I pleaded. "I know how you feel about me and what's happened between us, but I hope you'll let me say what's on my heart."

Silence. At least he hadn't hung up!

"I can't let another day go by, Werner, without asking you to forgive me for giving up on our marriage. And for all the pain and grief I've caused you."

This time the silence lasted for what seemed an eternity. Then, in a thoughtful voice, he responded.

"I can't promise anything, Sandra, but I will try. That's all I can say."

It was more than I had dared hope for. The wellsprings broke

413

open and I began to chatter on about Brad, Brent and Lisa and the plans they were making for their lives.

Then: "Thanks for listening, Werner, and for your openness to what I've needed to say for a long time."

The call was over. I felt jubilant.

Len poked his head around the door. "That wasn't as bad as you thought it would be, was it?"

True. I could have saved myself days of anxiety by being more obedient. My call to Werner had eased the tension between us, but I knew there was much more work to be done. How to relate to a former spouse who lives alone? Werner's two marriages after ours had also ended in divorce. He was understandably bitter about women.

Months passed. Len and I continued our prayers for Werner and Eve. Then Marge Switzer, my closest friend in Billings, and Bob McFarlane decided to be married. I made plans to fly to Montana for the wedding. One morning this prayer came blurting from my lips: "Lord, if I am to contact Werner during my trip to Billings next week, please pave the way and prepare his heart. Make an opportunity available. And close the doors if it's not Your will that I see him."

My trips to Billings were always bittersweet. So many wonderful memories from the twenty years I lived there. But conversely, so many episodes I would rather forget from the worst of my alcoholism.

Now at least I could return with ten years of sobriety behind me. I truly was a new creation; old things had passed away. Or had they?

I especially looked forward to a reunion with Lisa. She had returned to Montana recently to live with her father and attend school. Our relationship had deepened and strengthened, restored by the Lord over the years of my recovery.

The day after I arrived in Billings and the day before the wedding, I felt a nudge to call Werner. I was learning my lesson about heeding these Spirit promptings, so I obeyed. This time Werner's tone was actually friendly.

As we chatted on about Lisa, I felt led to say something I hadn't intended. "Do you know that Len and I pray for you every morning?"

The silence was intense. What he said next I was most unprepared for.

"Do you suppose you could drop by the house sometime while you're here?" He had never before issued such an invitation.

We agreed upon six o'clock that evening, before I attended Marge and Bob's wedding rehearsal.

I shivered in the chilly Montana wind as I rang the doorbell of his ranch-style home on a large corner lot in one of Billings' loveliest neighborhoods. Massive chocolate brown wooden doors stood forbidding before me.

The doors opened and there he stood, taller and thinner than I had remembered, with the ever-present pipe clenched between his teeth. The years had grayed his thick blond hair, but his hazel eyes were warm. It was the first time in many years we had been alone together.

"Lisa just got home from work," he announced. "She's resting down in her room." I sensed his relief that someone else was in the house, and I shared it.

As Werner guided me around his home, I noticed that it lacked the coziness a woman would have given it, but it was comfortable and attractive. A bachelor pad. The tour over, we wound up sitting in the living room in front of a giant TV screen. Werner was obviously proud of his video and sound system.

I settled into a green leather chair across from his tan plush recliner, surrounded by mementoes of our life together. On the end table stood the beautiful crystal lamp his mother had given us for a wedding present. How many times had I dusted it?

Over the stone fireplace hung a large, ornately framed painting of majestic Swiss mountains. Werner had bartered for it for days with a local art dealer. How proud he had been the evening he brought it home and hung it in our brick home on Rimrock Road! It was our first painting. And how often I had stared at those magnificent Alps, longing to walk into the painting and wander in that flower-strewn meadow.

I was flooded now by a feeling of sadness for Werner. He had never known happiness in any of his marriages. If only he would trust the Lord to be his matchmaker, as I had.

As he flipped through the TV channels with his remote control, I was struck with a sense of *deja vu*. Just like old times, watching the 6:30 news.

During a commercial break I got up and started to put on my coat. "I have to be at the wedding rehearsal by seven, Werner, but first would you mind if I took a picture of us? I have a camera with an automatic shutter."

"Sure, go ahead." Then he laughed. "We should record this moment for posterity."

The wedding day dawned cold and windy. Lisa was to arrive at the church early so we could sit together. I breathed a sigh of relief as I saw her little black Ford Escort pull into the parking lot. When she got out of the car, though, I moaned under my breath. She wore no coat, only a lightweight sweater, while the October wind whipped her long, auburn hair across her face. The mother in me was horrified to see my daughter shivering in the cold.

"Relax, Sandy," I ordered myself. "She is 28 years old."

How many times I had agonized when Lisa had gone off to high school in freezing temperatures with wet hair and a light sweater slung over her shoulders! Nothing much had changed.

"Sweetheart, where is your coat?"

"Mom, I couldn't find a coat to wear."

What could I say? My instinct was to reiterate all the sermons I had received from my mother and grandmother as I was growing up, but I fought it. Lisa had heard them all anyhow.

The wedding began with an organ interlude. Looking around at the congregation I felt a sense of being home. So many loved ones . . .

those who had prayed for me and encouraged me during the dark years. . . .

As the ceremony progressed I glanced at Lisa's lovely profile next to me. She was listening intently. I found myself praying again, "Lord, please gift Lisa with a special Christian man as You have me. Whoever he is, I lift him to You right now."

Lisa was often attracted to "wounded bird" kinds of males—terribly needy, from dysfunctional homes like her own. She was following the pattern of many women drawn to men they hope to "fix," to change into the loving, warm caregivers their parents never were. Nice guys bored her. She felt a need to live on the edge in uncertain, undependable, ultimately destructive relationships. How I longed for that pattern to end for her as it had for me!

After the wedding Lisa came back with me to the friends' home where I was staying. We had barely arrived when the phone rang. It was Werner calling for—me!

"I tracked you down to get your help on something," he began uncertainly. I couldn't imagine what was coming next. "Do you realize Lisa was out today without a coat on? In this freezing weather?"

"Yes, I was distressed about it, too."

"Sandra, when are you leaving town?"

"Tomorrow afternoon at 1:50."

"You and I need to buy our daughter a coat."

I couldn't believe what I was hearing. Werner was inviting me to shop with him for a coat for Lisa!

"I suppose you'll be going to church tomorrow," he continued. "Well, when you get out of church, give me a call and we'll hit the stores. I'll have clipped the sale ads from the Sunday paper. I'm sure we'll find something she'll like."

"I'm sure we will, too," I agreed, still in a mild state of shock.

When I reported the conversation to Lisa, her beautiful hazel eyes stared at me in disbelief. "Dad actually wants to take you and me shopping tomorrow?"

After an early church service, Lisa and I met Werner at his home at 11 A.M. He was ready to go, clippings in hand. Then, just as we were to walk out the door, he stopped abruptly.

"Wait a minute, Sandra. I have something I want to give you."

He disappeared into the living room and returned with a slip of paper, which he handed to me with a flourish. The paper was covered with his familiar handwriting. "It's the secret recipe for the Windmill's barbecue sauce."

Then I remembered. When pregnant with Lisa, I used to crave barbecued spareribs from the Windmill Club, a popular Billings restaurant. I was touched.

"Thank you, Werner. This is really special."

Werner headed out the door for his car, leaving Lisa and me to follow him in hers.

"Mom, you should know that Dad doesn't give that recipe to just anyone," Lisa said, her eyes glowing.

Our first stop was Anthony's Department Store. As Werner steered us to women's coats, he reminded me of many men when they go shopping. Like single-minded hunters, they go out to bag a coat, to "shoot a coat" and do it with as few wasted motions as possible.

He plucked an enormous, plum-colored, quilted garment from a rack. Dutifully Lisa put it on; it was three times her size. In her eyes I saw apprehension. Was Dad going to come up with something really weird?

Since there were no coats her size at Anthony's, it was on to the next stop. I looked at my watch. An hour and fifteen minutes before I had to be at the airport.

Lisa seemed a bit discouraged.

"Don't worry, honey," I chirped. "We'll find you a wonderful coat."

At Rimrock Mall we hit the coat department of every store. By now we were almost running. Lisa tried on coat after coat. Nothing was right.

Werner pressed on. Thirty minutes to go. By now we were at the far end of the mall, Lisa looking doleful.

Then it happened. In the last store on a back rack at fifty percent off hung a beautiful black wool coat with a shawl collar and wide belt. She slipped it over her black print dress. Perfection. Werner was jubilant.

"It's gorgeous, honey," I told her truthfully. "It's you!"

Lisa's eyes danced as she stroked one soft sleeve with her hand. A time for celebration. We asked the saleswoman to take a photo of us linked arm in arm.

"This seems to be a very special occasion," she observed.

"You'll never know how special!" I answered.

The three of us marched down the mall still arm in arm. I looked over at Lisa, her hair flying as we strolled along, a look of sheer joy on her face.

"I just want you both to know," she said, "that I thank you with all of my heart for this beautiful coat. I love it. And I love you."

Lisa would have many coats in her life, but I knew this one would always be special. A coat of love and nurture and togetherness— things she did not always have growing up.

It was a bittersweet moment for me in a completely new way as we strode down the cobblestone mall, laughing and smiling and enjoying the stares of the other shoppers. Let them stare! We were celebrating a reconciliation. Werner's eyes sparkled with new life. He had been a provider. An encourager.

As we said goodbye I planted a sisterly kiss on his rough cheek. Inside were a jumble of feelings: tenderness, compassion, sadness, yet exhilaration, too, at the wonderworking power of prayer.

As Lisa and I drove to the airport, I knew I needed to say something to her that had been on my heart for a long time. But how to say it? How radiantly happy she had been with her mom on one side, her dad on the other. I knew how she felt. It had always made *me* happy to see my divorced parents together.

I found myself patting the arm of her coat. "Lisa, I know how much you love Dad and me. I know how hard you tried as a little girl to fix our marriage, how you agonized and prayed and hoped and finally despaired when we split up.

"Some people shouldn't be married to one another. They just can't make it work." My words were sounding mechanical and tinny, even to me, my effort to excuse myself threadbare. *Why couldn't the marriage have worked?* she would be thinking. *Why did it have to end with so much heartbreak for so many?*

Perhaps I should simply tell her the truth: Her parents were selfish, sinful people who hadn't known God when they broke up.

I thought back to how I had felt as a little girl trying to hold my parents' loveless marriage together. How responsible I had felt for their unhappiness. How hard I had tried to make everything O.K. How desperate and frightened and lonely I had felt. How lost and abandoned.

My voice choked. "Lisa, can you forgive me for giving up on the marriage? For divorcing your father and subjecting you to so much pain?"

Lisa was the nurturing one now. "Of course, Mom. I understand, I really do. I forgive you. It's O.K. It really is."

At the airport gate we clung to each other in a final embrace, tears streaming down our cheeks. Lisa's new black coat had that special store smell as I buried my head in her shoulder.

That night, reporting the Billings visit to Len, I said, "The Lord works in strange ways, doesn't He?"

"Strange indeed," Len agreed. "Who would have thought that reconciliation could be accomplished through a shopping trip and a recipe for barbecue sauce?"

Well, not exactly. I thought back to the day-by-day determined, persistent prayers that Len and I, along with our children, had offered since 1985 for reconciliation in our families. We hadn't known how the Lord was going to do this; that was His business. Our part was to pray and believe. And, of course, to listen to His instructions. And obey them.

Progress had been made. I had a good relationship now with all of my children and with Len's as well. We had taken steps to begin reconciliation and healing work with our living ex-mates—reconciliation that will continue to be needed, I am sure, the rest of our lives.

The Shopping High

Recovery Principle # 10
IDENTIFY YOUR REAL NEEDS

---

*D*URING MY BATTLE SINCE 1980 WITH MULTIPLE ADDICTIONS, I have experienced some definite successes. Alcohol, for one. I know I cannot take even one drink or I am in trouble. As I write this, I haven't had a drink in twelve years.

Smoking, too. Through prayer my craving for tobacco miraculously lifted one day.

Compulsive viewing of television (especially daytime soap operas), excessive exercising, compulsive volunteerism—these, too, I have learned to control.

But not food and shopping.

These two addictions may not seem life-threatening, but because they are ever-present, they are the toughest for me and millions of others to deal with. Unlike the bad habits that can simply be eliminated, we have to eat and we have to purchase a variety of things. Food and shopping are with us always.

Not too long ago I rushed through a crowded mall toward the department store, intent on the shower curtain I needed to buy. With houseguests arriving in the morning, the pressure was on—meals and sleeping arrangements to plan for, all the niggling details a hostess has on her mind.

Once inside the cavernous store, my nose twitched at the whiffs of perfume arising from the cosmetics counter. Like a moth to a flame, I flitted to the Estee Lauder display and sprayed little jets of fragrance on both wrists. The old familiar exhilaration was surging through my veins: *Buy! Buy! Buy!*

As I reached for my purse, a rack of colorful scarves and handbags caught my eye. I walked over for a better look. But wait! There was the best yet—a fifty percent off sale in designer dresses. Fingering through them, I pulled out eight or nine garments for closer perusal.

Then an inner alarm went off in my head.

I didn't need perfume.

I didn't need a handbag.

I didn't need a dress.

I needed a shower curtain.

With a stab of pain I recalled how often this kind of high had led me to spend money I didn't have for things I could do without. Loading my arms with bundles and boxes relieved my sense of low self-worth, made me feel important, cared for. What I didn't realize until I had gone through treatment for my compulsive nature is that shopping can become as addictive as drinking or overeating or smoking or taking drugs.

I comforted myself for years with the fact that I wasn't as bad as some I knew. One friend of mine blew $5,000 at L. L. Bean, the Freeport, Maine, outdoor clothing company, in a one-hour telephone spree. Her husband's annual income was $25,000. Needless to say, her marriage was in grave danger due to her out-of-control spending. She confessed to me that she had felt bored and depressed, that shopping helped her avoid the real problems in her life.

Like my friend, I, too, was trying to purchase self-esteem. Years ago when I lived in Billings, Werner would moan over the credit card receipts I racked up. At one point he revoked my check-writing privileges, until he grew tired of having to handle all the household accounts himself.

In looking back over my shopping excesses, I feel a deep shame for my wanton waste of resources. Anything and everything could trigger a shopping binge. I shopped when I was depressed. I shopped when I was happy. I shopped drunk and I shopped to sober up. "Creative shopping," I used to call it. It was a cry for help, that hole in my soul calling out to be filled.

I see now how cross-addicted I was—from alcohol to food to pills to shopping, whatever would take the pain away.

In *The Compulsive Woman* I described in detail my first shopping orgy when I purchased 22 pairs of shoes and five handbags. I was single then, just starting my first job. I spent an entire month's salary on these items and had to borrow to meet living expenses. But when I was acquiring all those lovely shoes, nothing mattered but the high. The fix.

I shopped frequently when I was angry with Werner. I bought hundreds of dollars' worth of things I really didn't want, as a way to get even when I had been hurt. I felt entitled. I deserved these things, I rationalized—only to be plagued with guilt afterward. Frequently I hid my purchases in the trunk of the car or under the bed.

My drawers bulged with yards and yards of fabric for future sewing projects. Once at a fabric sale (five cents a yard), I came home with 800 yards—enough to have wrapped up my entire neighborhood and tied it with a bow!

That unused fabric proved a source of great creativity for my son Brent, then twelve. One day he decided to redecorate his basement room by hanging yards and yards of cloth from the ceiling like multi-colored hammocks. He draped the walls and windows with huge cascades of fabric reminiscent of a sultan's tent.

Then he appropriated every plant in the house and placed them around the basement artistically on fabric-covered boxes. I had to marvel at his talent. He had transformed his living area into what looked like a Middle East nightclub. We heard the pounding of his hammer at all hours. Brent was trying to bring color and change into the bleak existence my drinking had brought about for him and his brother and sister.

Eventually Brent returned the drooping plants to their original locations. "Guess that wasn't such a swift idea, was it, Mom? I forgot plants need light."

I wanted to hug him, to tell him children could be deprived of essentials for their growth, too, and that I was going to do better as a mother. But I didn't. I felt too guilty. (My response to the guilt, of course, was to go out and buy more fabric.)

Months ago I came across a book that has helped me, *Women Who Shop Too Much* by Carolyn Wesson. I began by taking the self-evaluation test that follows:

1. Has shopping become the most frequent way you cope with up-setting feelings?

2. Do you feel uneasy without your credit cards?

3. Do you use shopping as a way of making contact with other adults?

4. Are you and the people close to you—husbands, lovers, children, parents—arguing or having long discussions about your shopping?

5. Do you usually hide what you buy or lie about the cost?

6. Do you find that you are not using many of the things you buy?

7. Are you paying only the minimum due on your charge accounts because you are short of money, or because you want to have more money available for shopping?

8. Do you buy items that don't fit your lifestyle—for instance, evening gowns or fancy clothes—even though you rarely have an opportunity to wear them?

9. Are you worried about your shopping?

10. When you shop, do you get a rush or a high, but at the same time feel uneasy?

11. Do you spend six hours or more a week shopping?

12. Do you feel guilty, embarrassed or anxious after you shop?

13. Do you spend more than an hour a week fantasizing about what you're going to buy?

14. Are you preoccupied with thoughts and worries about money, but continue to spend anyway?

If you answered yes to three or more of the following questions—numbers 1, 4, 5, 6, 7, 10, 11, 12, 13 or 14—you are probably an addicted shopper. If that is the case, don't panic. By summoning up the courage to take the test and acknowledge your behavior, you have taken the first step away from addiction.

Yes answers to questions 2, 3 and 8 and any one of the others indicate you may be a shopaholic. That means you use shopping occasionally to fill psychological needs in your life.

Reviewing my own shopping profile—yes to almost every question—showed me that:

I still use shopping to fill psychological needs in my life. I am still too much in the fast lane, still prone to needing quick fixes. I shop to nurture myself.

When I splurge and shop, it often originates from my sense of deprivation as a young woman. I had few clothes in high school as my parents struggled to provide necessities. Morning after morning as I stared at the same few garments, I vowed that someday, when I had enough money, I would have lots of clothes. I fulfilled that vow and then some.

I shopped to look well-dressed and put together on the outside so that no one would know what a mess I was inside.

I labored under the false impression that if I had a closet full of matching cashmere sweater sets and plaid pleated Pendleton skirts—the status symbol of the '50s—I would be happy. I have learned that a closet full of beautiful clothes does not bring happiness, only an insatiable craving for more.

The good news is that since taking the test, whenever I find myself relapsing into the old, destructive behavior, I have been programming myself to go through a change of thinking. I call it the Jesus Factor. (Since my conversion in the Billings Methodist Church in 1980, Jesus has been the biggest factor in my healing.)

The Bible describes "taking every thought captive to the obedience of Christ" (2 Corinthians 10:5). The moment a tempting thought enters my mind, as happened when I went shopping for the shower curtain, I measure it against the teachings of Jesus and the life He lived here on earth. If the temptation counters what I know Jesus would want for me, I reject it.

How does it work? In connection with my shopping addiction, I am learning to invite Him right into the mall or dress shop along with me.

I can only describe it this way. On my shower curtain expedition, my mind seemed like an internal television screen of whirling images, urging me to scoop up armfuls of goods. One of these, two of those—it was like temporary insanity. Unable to shut it off myself, I breathed a quick "Help me, Jesus! Please take control of my thoughts."

The moment I spoke His name, it was as though He stepped from the right side of my mind's screen and walked slowly across it, drawing behind Him a sliding glass door. As the door closed, those tempting clamorous images grew hazy and were soon obscured altogether. A radiant Jesus then turned to me with outstretched arms.

"Let Me fill those empty places inside you that you are striving to fill with things," He told me. "Let My love and grace assure you that you are special to Me. You are infinitely valuable just as you are; nothing you can buy or possess can add to your worth. Rest in Me and be satisfied."

The Jesus Factor has been with me now since 1980, but only recently have I been able to apply it to shopping. Yet I have learned that every slip in any area of my life starts with a tempting thought. That is why I take every such thought instantly to Christ.

Another little victory with compulsive shopping came when my friend Maria Santa Maria and I went to lunch in nearby Middleburg, Virginia. Middleburg is a quaint town filled with historic inns and lovely shops. A great place to take visiting friends!

Before lunch Maria and I wandered into one of the specialty dress shops, The Finicky Filly. A pert young salesgirl announced that everything in the store was thirty percent off, some items more than that. I could feel the old familiar feeling of exhilaration, the start of a high bubbling up.

As Maria and I headed for the jewelry counter, I did take captive every tempting thought. Strands of colored beads and pearls hung tantalizingly from brass racks. My mind went blank. I couldn't remember anything in my closet that would work with any of the beads.

Silver jewelry is my passion. There was lots of it.

But: "I really don't need anything here," I heard myself saying as I fingered a heavy link bracelet lovingly. I could hardly believe those words were escaping from my lips!

My resolve with the dresses was not so firm. Len and I had an upcoming convention that called for a special dress. It seemed I had found it.

It was a beautiful white cotton ankle-length summer frock trimmed with Battenburg lace. I had always wanted a white Battenburg dress, admiring them in the glossy catalogs that flowed into my mailbox almost daily. It was one of my fantasies, sipping lemonade at a garden party in a white lace dress.

The dress fit as though it had been made for me. The deep lace collar framed my face becomingly, and the ruffled hemline was especially feminine. Maria and the salesgirl oohed and aahed. It was perfect. I had to have it.

But deep inside a voice said quietly, *You really don't need this dress. You have other lovely dresses that would work. Think about it for now. Don't be impulsive.*

I didn't like to hear that little voice at times like this. Sometimes I ignored it and plunged on with the purchase, only to regret it later. Still, I knew that the dress, despite the thirty percent discount, was expensive.

"Please hold the dress," I heard myself say to the salesgirl, "while I have lunch and think about it."

What I didn't tell her was that I planned to pray about the purchase, too. Was it something I really needed or was it something I merely wanted?

Maria and I talked about the dress at lunch. It was wonderful to enjoy "owning" it for a while. I pictured myself at the convention banquet, the focus of all attention in white lace. But the inner voice was persistent. I didn't *need* the dress. I had other things to wear.

After lunch I headed for the phone and dialed The Finicky Filly.

"Thank you for holding the dress," I said, "but I won't be purchasing it."

An indescribably warm feeling flooded over me as I wheeled my car out of the restaurant parking lot. I had to smile. The Jesus Factor had come through once more.

He is my comforter, my healer, my helper, my strengthener, my special Friend. A Friend whose love is so all-fulfilling it sets me free of the never-ending pursuit for substitute satisfaction.

My suggestions for the shopaholic:

1. *Do a clothing inventory.* Use a small three-ring notebook so you can add or subtract pages and carry it in your purse. Put clothing into categories: dresses, blouses, skirts, accessories, evening, etc. Attach small swatches of fabric for outfits that need accessories or shoes. This is helpful when shopping for specifics. Make a list of accessories needed. And shop only for those things.

   Sounds tough, but I did it after months of procrastinating. I found my clothing way out of balance, but for the first time I knew my wardrobe and was doing something to put it in order.

2. *Be selective in using catalogs,* seeking only items you need. Television star Candice Bergen admits she buys "tons of stuff for the house" from catalogs. "I have a sort of catalog disorder," she confessed in the October 1991 issue of *McCall's.* "My eyes glaze over. I get compulsive. At work they confiscate my catalogs so I'll learn my lines."

3. *Pay with cash.* It is amazing, the impact of counting out cold, hard money as opposed to paying by credit card or even writing a check. Sometimes I have taken only one check, which eliminates impulsive (and usually unwise) purchases. Also tough but effective: Take the scissors to your credit cards. Ouch!

11

When Bed Was My Hiding Place

Recovery Principle # 11
EXPECT THE BEST

---

*T*HE VOICE ON THE OTHER END OF THE PHONE SOUNDED UNMIS-
takably British.

"Sandra, this is Jane Bolt from British Central TV in Birmingham, England. We'd very much like to do a story on compulsive behavior for our Central Weekend program."

The format, she explained, was something like the Phil Donahue
Show. "Would you be available to fly over for our March 6 broadcast?
We will pay all your travel expenses. . . ."

The heady intoxication of a summons from overseas drove every
other consideration from my mind. Normally I discuss speaking requests with Len, then we pray about them. But this opportunity was
too enticing.

"Yes, of course!" I gushed into the phone. "I'd be delighted."

"Splendid. I'll ring you up in a few days with final details." *Click.*

My ears rang with static from the call . . . or was it the static of excitement?

To my relief, Len was taken aback only momentarily by my unconsidered response. As we (belatedly) prayed about it, he had this intriguing comment: "Go with the expectation that God will use you in a surprising way."

At four in the morning of the day I was to fly to London, I awakened with a throbbing head, raspy throat and fever. Disaster! How could I travel 4,000 miles feeling like this?

Seven A.M. My attempts to medicate my malady had brought no improvement.

"What can I do?" I wailed to Len. "I don't feel good enough to walk across this room, let alone fly for nine hours over the Atlantic Ocean and then go on national television!"

He suggested I call Jane Bolt to see if I could do it another time.

"Oh, no!" Jane gasped into the phone. "My dear, if you don't come we'll have forty-five minutes of dead air! Can't you bundle yourself up with your aspirin bottle and hop on over?"

"I'll give it my best shot," I croaked into the receiver.

A decade earlier I would have used this fever to collapse into bed—for days, weeks. The slightest ache or pain gave me an excuse to retreat from responsibility, to seek attention, to take the focus off my drinking. Soon I would be in bed, phone off the hook, pillow plumped under my head.

Hypochondriac? In some ways, yes. But the teaching I received at the treatment center, halfway house and in support groups convinced me that fleeing to bed is not a solution to emotional problems. Today I am much more in touch with my feelings, have much to live for and hate to go to bed.

It was Joy Dawson, Christian prayer leader and teacher extraordinaire, who challenged both Len and me that an illness need not keep us from doing the Lord's work. Joy has a dynamo inside her that gives her seemingly inexhaustible energy. She would brush that aside, saying, "The Holy Spirit will give that to you, too."

I am convinced that only hospitalization, or perhaps a raging fever, would keep Joy from a Christian commitment. She would get up from a sickbed, trusting God to give her what she needs. Once she awoke with severe laryngitis the day she was to give a major speech. Though her voice was but a croak, she dressed, arrived at the event and stood before her audience *expecting the best,* in faith. The first few words came out in a whisper; then, slowly, her voice returned to full strength.

Was this my opportunity to test Joy's premise?

We started out by seeking extra prayer support. Len phoned a number of prayer warriors while I dragged myself through the motions of packing—sniffling and hacking all the way. The fever refused to abate despite megadoses of aspirin. My eyes were swollen almost shut.

I sensed that Len was about to assume husbandly authority and call the whole venture off when at two P.M. there was a near-miraculous change. My physical symptoms all but disappeared as renewed energy poured through me.

"I feel better!" I marveled to Len. "The prayers are being answered."

I couldn't wait to find out how God would use this overseas adventure!

The flight over was a blur of faces, interminable offerings of food and an almost sleepless night. Going through the customs line at Heathrow took an eternity. The sun was up when I met the limousine driver in the arrivals area arranged for by the television station. Two hours later we arrived at my hotel in Birmingham.

I had barely thrown my garment bag onto the bed when the phone rang. Jane Bolt and Sue Gay, the Central Weekend hostesses, would be right over.

I opened the door to two bright, shining faces.

"You look wonderful!" they encouraged me. "No one would ever dream you were so ill a few hours ago!"

The live one-hour show went on the air at nine P.M. At seven I arrived at the station armed with three copies of my book and wondering who the Lord would nudge me to give them to. That was part of the adventure of any trip.

Book one went to the makeup girl. A frail wisp of a brunette named Bridgette with inch-long scarlet fingernails, she flicked at tears as she poured out her heart to me regarding her marriage problems.

Jane Bolt appeared in a flurry of gold chiffon and led me down a maze of halls into the brightly lit studio.

"Marshall, dahling," she crooned to an orange-haired pot roast of a man wrestling with a headset, "this is Sandra LeSourd, the compulsive woman."

Marshall shot out a hand studded with diamond rings and squeezed my clammy one. "I loved your story about buying all those shoes. We'll want to do a shot of you surrounded by a mound of shoes."

Had I flown 4,000 miles for this? The most bizarre TV experience of my life was underway.

All of us participating in the show were herded into a corner of the studio where the air conditioner blew out great blasts of frigid air to counter the blazing lights overhead.

My teeth started to chatter uncontrollably. *Please, Lord, help me get through this program.*

Marshall was bouncing all over the set, dodging cables, barking signals into his headset, waving his clipboard in the air with diamonds flashing. His main concern seemed to be an enormous glass bowl heaped with hard-boiled eggs. "Did you boil them long enough? Do we have eighteen? Where is the stopwatch?"

Gradually I became aware that the main attraction of the program was a certain man named Peter, holder of more Guinness World Records involving eating and drinking than any human being alive.

Tonight before our very eyes—and those of the millions tuned in—Peter was going to try to break his own previous egg-swallowing record.

For the compulsivity segment of the program, I discovered, some twenty people had been assembled. How could there possibly have been 45 minutes of dead air without me?

The lights dimmed. Show time!

The first segment featured two gentlemen from Parliament who engaged in a furious exchange over a killing in a neighboring village. At issue: What punishment for the attacker? Anger erupted. Men and women in the studio audience jumped to their feet shouting, demanding justice.

I was beckoned to a side set where a beaming Sue Gay awaited me. "You're going to love this show. We've rounded up some really fascinating guests for your segment."

Right above my head the air conditioner belched icy gusts at me. My skin was turning blue, my nose running furiously. I wadded lumps of tissue up each nostril, then tried to talk. "Huddo, my nabe is Sander-ah. . . ."

"Welcome to this evening's special feature on compulsive behavior," Sue purred into the camera. "Tonight our special guest is Sandra Simpson LeSourd, author of *The Compulsive Woman,* who has flown all the way from Florida to be with us tonight. And now for a look at sexual compulsions, here's a film clip from the popular movie *Fatal Attraction.*"

The grisliest scene of the movie rolled for our edification. Knives flashed. Blood gushed.

Next, a full-screen shot of a grizzled sailor resembling Jack the Ripper. A trembling young woman related how this sexaholic was terrifying her with phone calls and beating on her door in the middle of the night.

Backstage, Marshall was losing his mind. Where was the man with the stopwatch? Did they have enough eggs? He gave the signal and a velvet-draped table was wheeled to center stage.

Now from behind maroon curtains burst Peter, his pock-marked face glistening with perspiration, his bulbous stomach protruding over his belt buckle. Settling his enormous frame behind the table, he reminded me of a Japanese sumo wrestler preparing to demolish a hated enemy. For Peter the enemy was a massive bowl of tubercular-looking gray eggs wilting under the intense TV lights. At Peter's left a nervous stagehand stood poised to activate the stopwatch that would verify for the world a new egg-swallowing record.

A drum roll underscored the taut scene.

"Now!" Marshall shouted. *Click* went the stopwatch. Peter dove into the bowl of eggs. One down. Two. With each gulp an egg disappeared into the huge, quivering, tattooed body. Peter's face was turning purple. Bits of yellow yolk tumbled onto his *Guinness World Recordholder* T-shirt. The bowl was emptying fast. Marshall was breathless.

Victory! Peter had broken his own world record, eating eighteen eggs in nineteen seconds. Marshall's face burst into a jubilant grin.

When the host asked Peter why he continued to break his own records, he replied—stifling a mighty burp—"So that my children will have something to be proud of their father for."

There followed multiple short interviews: a workaholic, a woman who went compulsively from relationship to relationship, a psychiatrist with bushy hair and a yin-yang earring who specialized in addiction problems.

I was struck especially by a fragile girl named Debra who suffered from obsessive-compulsive disorder, dressing and undressing fifteen times in the same clothes before she could go out the door to work. Needless to say, she was usually late and had been dismissed from job after job. My heart ached for her.

Last to be interviewed was a striking brunette named Carol. Her outpourings of frustration and pain revealed an articulate and bright woman.

"I can't seem to win my battle with the biscuit barrel," she moaned. "Why can't I stop my incessant binging?"

Now it was my turn.

"Sandra, do you have any advice for these people?"

My nose was running into my mouth in twin rivers. *How chic,* I thought. Freezing in my black chiffon evening dress, I was sure the air conditioner had frozen my mind as well.

"Most of us come from dysfunctional homes," I began. "We get trapped in our compulsive behavior." I launched into my own story. But already time was running out.

"Remember this," I concluded. "You can be freed from your addiction if you seek help. Go to a support group. Work some kind of program. There are no hopeless cases."

439

Sue Gay squeezed my hand enthusiastically. "Marvelous, simply marvelous. One of the best programs we've ever done."

I sneezed.

She led me back through the corridors to a room where a spectacular buffet had been set up for the post-show celebration: carved ice sculptures spewing champagne, fabulous bowls of peeled shrimp, trays and trays of hors d'oeuvres.

In my hands were the remaining two books I had brought to England. To whom should they go?

The woman with relationship problems spotted me and rushed to my side. "Oh, is that your book? I really need to read it." I signed it for her and moved on.

Carol, who couldn't win the battle with the biscuit barrel, lit up as I approached her.

"I can't tell you how much it has helped me just being here tonight," she said, her warm, brown eyes crinkling good-naturedly. "Just having the courage to admit I can't stop eating."

"Good for you, Carol," I agreed. "The first step is recognizing that you have a problem."

A man at her side cleared his throat. "I'm David, Carol's husband, and I want to thank you for coming. I'm willing to do anything it takes to help my wife. Do you have any suggestions?"

Briefly I told them about my own food problems and tried to encourage her to seek help, not knowing what support groups were available in England. We exchanged addresses.

Then, just before we parted, she shook my hand vigorously. "I don't believe in God. But I believe there is some reason I've met you. May we keep in touch?" Her eyes were pleading.

"Write me after you've read the book, Carol," I suggested.

As I flew home, I wondered again why I had made the trip. There had been enough of a physical healing to enable me to appear on the show. Yet my time on it was brief, and there had been no opportunity to honor God. *Lord, was this whole thing just my vanity at work?*

440

By the time the plane landed in Miami, the flu symptoms had returned with a vengeance. It was a week before I was functional again.

Two weeks after that, a letter from Carol appeared in my mailbox. She had made an important discovery—that anger was the dynamic of her overeating. But what thrilled me most from this nonbeliever was her last sentence.

"I don't know what it is that makes you different, but I want what you have."

My response to her was a package containing *Beyond Our Selves* by Catherine Marshall and *The Angry Book* by Dr. Theodore Rubin.

I heard nothing for months. Then one afternoon in September, five months later, the phone rang. It was Carol, calling from England.

"Sandra, I had to ring you up and tell you in person the incredible events of my life since I last wrote you. I have joined a church in Reddich and tomorrow evening I'm going to be baptized. I have never been so happy in all my life!"

David's eager voice came on. "Thank you, thank you, Sandra, for all you've done for my wife. She's a different woman."

"Don't thank me, David. Jesus is the one who deserves all the credit."

I hung up in a state of shock. Carol had gone from agnostic to baptized Christian in little more than six months. Wow!

My friendship with Carol has blossomed via the mail. Fourteen months after my Central Weekend TV experience, Carol became a member of the counseling corps for Billy Graham's England crusade. Then came a report that Carol's son was freed from anger and soft drugs, had asked to be baptized and was considering Bible college.

"To see him able to laugh, to hear him pray out loud and praise God is beyond belief," Carol wrote.

She now does visitation work for her church, helps organize local Christian rallies and, along with her husband and son, is setting up a youth club. (Carol's son plans to attend Bible college.)

I guess the words that touched me most came in her most recent letter: "That night on the TV program here in England, you shone like an angel, Sandy. In fact, you were my saving angel, sent by God to let me know that someone cared, that *He* cared."

My mind flashed back to 1979 . . . Montana State Hospital . . . the night Karen became *my* saving angel. *Karen, look what you started!*

The way the Lord used me with Carol was reason enough on its own for me to get out of a sickbed and go to England. Whereas my sicknesses in the past were often a subconscious way to avoid responsibility, when bed had been my hiding place, this is no longer true. I find that life today is exciting. I want to be where the action is. I have discovered the impact of those three words: *Expect the best.*

Something really sparked inside me when I told myself that good was going to happen on this trip to England. Right away my attitude changed from negative to positive.

In fact, I think that is what started the healing process inside me. I was opposing a stronghold of illness in my own body. I had an expectation in my spirit that, yes, the fever and the flu bug could be overcome.

Medication is a factor here, of course. But antibiotics and cold remedies go just so far. After taking them, I would still spend days in bed.

But it was more than medication that sustained me over that 48-hour period.

I know, too, that change began to work inside of me soon after we asked people to pray. For when people pray they use Scripture promises of belief. One of my favorites: "All things are possible to him who believes" (Mark 9:23). Prayer changes situations and people.

Does believing in prayer make it come true? Does your expecting the best ensure that it will take place?

Not always, of course, for there is much in the spiritual realm we don't understand. But from now on, when situations arise like the

British television invitation, I intend to move ahead with the following steps:

1. Ask God if this is something I should do.

2. If it has His O.K., pray that heavenly forces will clear the way.

3. Then expect the best to happen!

12

Second Chance

Recovery Principle # 12
SEIZE THE MOMENT

A FTER LEN'S AND MY PRAYER TIME THIS MORNING I LOOKED AT myself in the mirror, really looked at myself, with disbelief at the person staring back at me.

Part of me can barely remember, or perhaps chooses not to remember, the Sandy of years ago—bloated from the excesses of alcohol and food, dissipated from the ravages of addiction and excess.

The clear-eyed, slender, gray-haired woman in the mirror is an example of the mercy and grace of God's reconstruction, resurrection power. He does indeed restore the years the locusts have eaten. Not that we don't pay a price for our selfish, sinful behavior. We do. But the God of new beginnings is forgiving. In remaking us, He adds something new and beautiful that was not there before.

He is also the God of the second chance. And the third. Or however many others it takes.

I thought of Lauren, that irrepressible, free spirit who was my friend at the halfway house back in 1981. Still in bondage to alcohol and unhealthy male relationships, Lauren fled the halfway house to marry a man she met in treatment. Since both were in the early recovery stage, neither was ready for marriage and a second chance at a healthy life.

Over the next few years Lauren and I continued a Christmas card friendship. Each year her card came from a different address, indicating that her life was chaotic. I was now married to Len, working with compulsive-addictive people.

One Thanksgiving Lauren's face kept appearing before me. How was she? Sober? Still married to Mark?

The lesson I have learned in recovery when a thought like this comes is, *Seize the moment.* I felt prompted to write Lauren a letter of friendship and encouragement. So I wrote her a short note expressing my concern for her—for her health and healing, for her life with Mark. I sent it off feeling oddly relieved. Her face stopped haunting me.

No Christmas card from her that year. *Probably she moved again,* I thought, *and didn't get my note.*

The following October I was in Minneapolis for a conference and decided to try to contact Lauren. I got her phone number from Mark's legal secretary after much assurance I was a good friend.

Lauren's voice was crisp and bright on the other side of the phone.

"Oh, Sands, how incredible you would call just now. I have been trying to get in touch with you to tell you what happened. You'll never believe it!

"In August my life was unraveling so badly I just wanted to end it all. My marriage was a mess. I was a mess. One Tuesday morning I decided I didn't want to live anymore. I would take my life that day.

"I headed out the door with a prescription for sleeping pills in my purse. I planned to stop at the drugstore first, then get a bottle of vodka. Then, bye-bye, everybody and everything.

"Monday had been such a horrible day, I hadn't even bothered to pick up the mail in the box by our front door. But just as I was leaving, I noticed a pale blue envelope through the slits in the mailbox. Most of my mail was bills, but the blue envelope intrigued me and made me open the box. It was a note from you—a beautiful note dated last November, *nine months ago!*

"I sat down on the stairs and read it. Sands, your words of love and encouragement spoke life to me. My heart began to beat like crazy. It was as though God was telling me through you how much He loved me. It was incredible.

"I canceled my trip to the drugstore. In fact, I went into the bathroom and tore up the sleeping pill prescription and flushed it down the toilet. When Mark came home from work I told him what happened. We had a good cry and made a commitment to try harder, that we really loved each other and wanted to work on our marriage.

"He's just out of another treatment center and I'm seeing a counselor. Perhaps I'll go back for more help, too. But I just want you to know that your note saved my life. Thanks, Sands. . . ."

Who can explain the delivery of a letter, written in November, arriving in the receiver's mailbox the following August—at just the right time to stop her from an appointment with death? Only the divine Mailman could have made that happen and given Lauren and Mark the basis for a new start in their marriage.

I shuddered to think what would have happened to Lauren if I had not seized that moment to write the letter God had placed on my heart! God is merciful indeed.

Nowhere has His mercy been more evident than with my children. My alcoholism, my driven behavior, my compulsion to escape the home responsibilities of raising my three children robbed me of years of precious time with them.

They were well cared for, I rationalized. We had live-in help much of the time, plus a roster of eager young babysitters anxious to make spending money. Deep in my heart I knew all was not well, that I was violating basic qualities God had placed in me as a woman—as wife, mother, nurturer, keeper of the hearth.

In my creative fantasies I visualized happy hours with my sons and daughter doing wonderfully artistic things. I was always going to build an Indian fort and a doll house, to take them on picnics, to teach them to be creative with paints and glue and crafts.

My feeble attempts always ended in frustration for us all. Alcohol destroys creativity and the patience needed to hang in there with clumsy, small fingers that do not respond easily to adult directions.

One afternoon I did teach all three to sew on buttons. I can still see Brad, Brent and Lisa standing before me—ages eight, nine and ten—their fingers swathed with Band-Aids, clutching ragged squares of material covered with colorful buttons. Some had been sewn on top of each other. Others hung by a thread or two. But the triumphant looks in their eyes stabbed my heart. They had succeeded at doing something with Mom. And for Mom.

Why haven't you been doing things like this all along? I asked myself.

One day after Werner and I had separated, I heard the sewing machine whirring in the next room. Lisa had taught herself to sew by observing me. For hours her young, slender body sat patiently at the old Singer, stitching little purses of fabric. Small squares with foldover tops. She always sewed a snap under the flap to secure it. She made dozens of them in every material imaginable. I would return home and find a fresh stack of her offerings on the foot of my bed or neatly piled on my pillow. Perhaps it was her therapy, a way of escaping the pain and fear in her ten-year-old heart of missing her father and coping with an often-absent mother.

I weep today as I look at a multicolored cotton quilted purse from those dark days. The words *I LOVE YOU* cut out from red felt are pinned to the flap just as they were fashioned almost twenty years ago. My fingers trace the message of love from my child while a deep sense of loss gnaws at my soul. The loss of what I missed. What we all missed. . . .

That is when the words of my faith kick in and I hear God saying, "I will restore the years the locusts have eaten" (see Joel 2:25).

When I married Len in 1985, I inherited six delightful grandchildren ages four months to sixteen years. Clearly a challenge, but more important for me, a second chance! The passage of five years has brought us two more grandchildren. With my own three children, the total of my immediate family reaches 21.

At the end of July our clan gathers at Evergreen Farm for a two-week family time. What a lively, exuberant, heartwarming time it is! The farmhouse almost explodes with activity. Children's voices and bodies seem to be everywhere. The women cluster in the kitchen organizing meals and housekeeping details. The men plan entertainment and special groundskeeping projects around the farm. And the two cats run for their lives!

On the wall of the kitchen is posted a large yellow cardboard sign with the heading *Camp Evergreen.* Each family member is expected to sign up for one duty a day. It is the only way to handle such a large group of people.

The women sign up for a certain meal and are responsible for shopping and preparing the food. Others are enlisted to set up and clean up afterward. A "kitchen cop" is assigned for each day whose unpopular job it is to see that the kitchen is not a disaster area, that everyone does his or her assigned task.

Mealtimes are marvelous times of fellowship and fun. One outstanding such time was the occasion of Len's seventieth birthday. We decided to have a surprise "Teddy Bear Picnic and Hoedown" to honor the occasion, complete with scores of bears perched in trees, in flowerbeds, hanging from the pale blue umbrella over the food table. They were everywhere.

The entire family marched around the yard to the strains of the "Teddy Bear Picnic," snaking around the patio, past the white brick smokehouse and down the lawn and back to the patio.

Len was presented with a pair of jeans and a straw hat, which he donned good-naturedly for the occasion.

Len's daughters-in-law gave him a T-shirt with a huge black and white Holstein cow on the front—Len likes to call cows poochie-poochies.

"This is a *cow*, Dad," Linda joked. "Not a poochie-poochie. Cows are *not* poochie-poochies."

The entertainment for the evening was a family square dance. We had enough mobile family members for two squares of eight. A square-dance caller and his wife explained patiently the various dance calls and moves. Country music blared over loudspeakers from the front porch. People in cars passing by must have been curious. "Do-si-do, off you go." Right there on the front lawn.

We were convulsed with laughter and excitement. The children loved it as we all became a tangle of arms and legs, sometimes hopping in the right direction, often in the wrong.

As I clapped my hands to the catchy Western tunes, time stopped for a moment. I saw that God was not only restoring me and my children, He was giving me more family. I felt a sense of sacred trust as the matriarch of this beautiful, energetic creative group. He was indeed restoring. Not only restoring, but increasing!

And I was learning to grab hold of these opportunities and make something special of them. The recovery process had relaxed me, slowed down my motor and, most important, given me something new—an inner discernment to know how and when to seize a special moment.

How had this come about?

As I prayed about this, the Lord took me back to my early years and showed me that I always had a flair for remembering friends in small ways, sending them cards with drawings and scribbles. Alcohol had dulled this gift.

But when I became serious about my recovery and stopped abusing my body, I was given a second chance. Creativity returned.

Missed opportunities are still part of my life, of course. Fatigue, an overly heavy schedule or a bout of discouragement will keep me from seizing a special moment. But I am learning to rise above these low points because I want the joy these happenings bring to my spirit.

I have a choice, of course. I can give in to my temporary fatigue or busyness or discouragement and miss a special moment. Or I can choose to reach out for it.

On one rainy August afternoon the children were a bit restless, especially the little girls—Hadley, age six, Mary Catherine, age five, and Whitaker, age three. Suddenly I remembered something I always wished I had done for my daughter, Lisa—a dress-up tea party with hats and flowers and all the trimmings.

I asked Linda and Susan, the girls' mothers, what they thought of the idea. They were wildly enthusiastic, as were the girls.

The next two hours became a time of preparation, a large part of the fun. The girls dressed in their best dresses. I helped out with my treasure trove of fabrics, old jewelry, silk flowers and hats. Each girl was decked out for "high tea" in the most outlandish outfits imaginable.

Hadley selected a

headpiece of pink velvet ribbon and hot pink roses and petunias. Mary Catherine wore a long, printed cotton dress with her long hair tied up with navy ribbons and flowers. She carried a fan. Whitaker was dressed in white, a huge white net bow and silver ribbons perched precariously atop her dark hair.

They all wanted several necklaces and rings. And makeup. Each girl wore lipstick, blush, mascara and nail polish—a big treat!

They looked adorable in their finery, preening and posing self-consciously for my camera, a photo opportunity if ever there was one.

I had set a small table on the porch with a lacy white cloth and napkins, fresh flowers in a little crystal vase. Small white demitasse cups with gold trim marked each place. A colorful Miss Piggy teapot added a whimsical touch to the table. Treats included a large plate of cookies and pastel mints.

The girls giggled and sipped and chatted merrily. Linda, Susan and I observed from a distance the little drama before us, cameras clicking: three lovely little girls happily being little girls. There was something innocent and enchanting and nostalgic about it all.

As I watched, a part of me long forgotten was touched at a deep level. It was as though I could see myself with new eyes, eyes of forgiveness. Though I had not done something like this for my own children, God was giving me another chance with other little ones whom I loved, whose lives I could impact.

After dinner, when some rain had stopped, most of the family gathered on the croquet field. I remembered that the tea party table had not been cleared off from the front porch and headed there.

The evening sounds and colors were soft and comforting. Locusts hummed their special song from lush trees bordering the house. Fireflies sparkled tiny yellow greetings on the front lawn. Soon the air would be alive with thousands of little blinking lights.

For a moment I sat in a porch rocker listening to the sounds of a summer night mingled with the excited voices of our competitive family on the croquet field. I stared at the tea party table next to me, the pristine cloth now covered with spills and crumbs and knotted up napkins . . . three small chairs askew . . . flowers wilting in the vase.

Today would always carry for me a special memory, a moment seized and captured on film for generations to come. And perhaps, too, for three little girls.

13

Incest Comes Out of the Closet

Recovery Principle # 13
FORGIVE THOSE WHO HAVE HURT YOU

W HEN IT HAPPENED TO ME AT THE AGE OF FIVE, I GAVE MYSELF
an order: "I will never tell anyone." A beloved uncle had sexually molested me and I didn't understand anything about it. *Perhaps it's my fault,* I thought. Afterward I kept washing my hands
over and over.

As the months and years passed, I tried to forget what Uncle
Ralph had done to me when my parents were outside working in the
garden. I buried it in my subconscious. Years later while I was attending a compulsivity clinic, the subject of incest came up. I asked
the director if this single instance of sexual abuse could be one of the
underlying causes of my compulsive behavior.

"Yes," he answered. "Your shame/guilt reaction in this case was a major factor. You felt you couldn't talk to anyone. You tried ritual handwashing to cleanse yourself. You blamed yourself and forced the pain inward. This violation of your personhood seriously damaged not only the trust you had in yourself, but your trust in others. When the boundaries of your world as you knew it were stolen, the door was opened for compulsive-addictive behavior."

During my healing time at the halfway house just outside Minneapolis, I was told that underneath my smiling countenance was deep-rooted anger. So I was assigned "anger work." This meant going back as far as I could remember, noting events and people that made me angry.

Uncle Ralph!

"Go back to that place and that episode," the counselor instructed me. "Tell your uncle how you felt about his abuse of you. You're not a helpless little girl now. Tell him whatever you need to." She gave me several pillows to use.

Closing my eyes for concentration, I went back in time to Uncle Ralph's living room. I could smell the Sir Walter Raleigh tobacco he rolled into homemade cigarettes . . . hear the sound of several clocks ticking from the hallway.

Then I saw Uncle Ralph sitting in his squeaky wooden rocker. Felt his hands on me, heard him wheezing, clicking his teeth. I started to sob and beat my thighs.

"Use the pillows," the counselor ordered.

"I loved and trusted you, Uncle Ralph, and you abused me. I was little and couldn't resist. You hurt me! You scared me! I hate you for that! I hate you! I hate you!"

I was shouting now, my voice high and shrill. The five-year-old Sandy was doubled over, pounding the pillows with both fists.

During those sessions I realized that in the past my anger had erupted all right, only in indirect, inappropriate ways. Example: overeating. You could never have convinced me when I was binging on chocolate that I was really acting out my inner rage. Not just at Uncle Ralph, but at all the times I had swallowed my feelings and said nothing. It made no difference that my dress size was headed for the twenties, that I was totally repulsed at myself and nauseated physically by food. The raging dragon inside demanded to be fed. Or placated with cigarettes. Or booze. Or a new outfit.

The healing therapy I went through regarding Uncle Ralph became part of *The Compulsive Woman*. Soon after its publication in 1987 I received an astonishing letter from Marilyn Van Derbur, Miss America 1958. While traveling with Marilyn when I was a public relations specialist for one of the Miss America Pageant sponsors, we became friends and have kept in touch ever since.

She poured out her heart to me about the incestuous abuse she had received from her father:

Your book brought up such agony for me. You will be able to understand what a difficult journey I have had. I know now why people want to kill themselves—not because they want to die, but because they can't endure the pain one more day.

One of the ways I survived was typing, typing, typing. Sometimes I would type so furiously my fingers would type what my mind couldn't think . . . what my lips couldn't say. I would read what I had written and then just lie on the floor and sob.

I would type and edit. Type and edit. I seemed compelled to try to make sense out of what happened to me on paper. I spent hours doing that.

Without my husband, Larry, I would never even have tried to make it. I always thought I was tough and strong and smart. I found I couldn't control my body or my mind.

I'm so grateful that you found Len and that he found you. I think of you often and smile each time I do. I'm grateful, too, that you have found peace and love. I have had Larry every inch of the way and I am experiencing a peace that is indescribable . . . finally.

Here are excerpts from the "typings" Marilyn included in her letter to me. These typings later became the basis for articles she wrote for major American publications in 1991, drawing national attention to the problem of incest and winning widespread support for the cause she has undertaken of helping incest victims:

> My father was powerful, handsome, intelligent and so success-
> ful that, upon his death in 1984, his obituary ran on the front
> page of our Denver paper. . . . The F. S. Van Derbur Boy Scout
> Building was named after him.
>
> My mother and my three older sisters were beautiful and
> outstanding in their different ways. How lucky I was to have
> been born into such a family of influence and affluence. I be-
> lieved that with every ounce of my being. I had to, because by
> the time I was seven I was so traumatized I had begun to live
> in a fantasy world that I had created in order to survive.
>
> My day child, the happiest girl in the world, had already

separated from my night child. The two knew nothing of one another. I took my head off my body to live during the day. My body, hopeless and helpless, remained in my bedroom to take the endless degradation and humiliation from my father at night. To use the proper psychiatric term, I dissociated.

The more my nighttime child became ugly, filthy and despicable, the more my daytime child needed to excel in every area of her life. And she/I did! Whether it was in academics (Phi Beta Kappa honors) or sports (U. of Colorado ski team, AAU swim meets) or leadership as a college sophomore (I became Miss America) or an adult career of speaking to thousands at business and sales meetings (once named "Outstanding Woman Speaker in America"), I was the best!

But for reasons I would not understand until years later, I always felt guilty about the charmed life I had. I would never have survived emotionally or physically if my life had not been blessed by a young man I met when I was fifteen years old— Larry Atler, senior class president in our high school. I fell quickly and completely in love with him. It took me a full year to win his love, but once I did, it was a strong and abiding love that would, in time, teach me how to love, honor and trust again.

A year after her father's death, Marilyn revealed to her mother the sexual abuse she had endured. At first she refused to believe her, until Marilyn's oldest sister, Gwen, also disclosed that she had been victimized by her father.

Then, in an act of unprecedented courage, Marilyn went public with her story, convinced that she was just one of millions of women (and men) damaged by incest. The result: Marilyn has a national ministry to these people. In the Denver area she, with the Kempe National Center, formed a support group called Survivors United Network. More than 2,000 people are now involved.

The major point Marilyn makes: *Incest victims do not get healed until they go back in time to the abuse, face up to what really happened and work through it with professional counseling.*

The wounds of incest go deep. During every workshop or talk I give in which I mention my own molestation, women line up afterward to confide (often for the first time) their experiences. I suggest they go to support groups, seek professional counseling. In addition, I pray with them for God to heal them at a deep level.

Some of my most memorable encounters have taken place at the Aqueduct Conference Center outside of Chapel Hill, North Carolina. I have been there three times with Len and David Hazard to lead writers' workshops, and also with Edith Marshall, a psychotherapist in Chatham, Massachusetts, and daughter-in-law of the late Catherine Marshall LeSourd. Edith's sparkle, warmth and expertise win friends for her wherever she goes. With her I have done three weekend workshops on the general theme of overcoming compulsive behavior and finding healing and wholeness and freedom.

As soon as you arrive at Aqueduct, something in the quiet peace starts the healing process. The main building resembles a classic ski chalet with its ceiling-to-floor plate glass windows. In the lobby a long, hand-carved mahogany buffet holds conference literature and always a large basket of shiny red apples—a lovely touch of ambiance for the hungry traveler or conferee with a terminal case of the munchies.

To the left is a small chapel/counseling room decorated tastefully with antiques and brass lamps and Oriental rugs. At one end is a velvet-covered kneeling bench for prayer and meditation; a small rose love seat and chair grace the other end.

The central meeting room at Aqueduct looks, again, like the living room of a beautiful ski lodge. At one end is a massive gray flagstone fireplace with a raised hearth. In the center of the room are two light gray sofas arranged in a "U."

Aqueduct's host, Tommy Tyson, is a big teddy bear of a man with a booming voice, an infectious smile and vast experience as a teacher and pastor. His son Tom not only has many of his father's hospitality and teaching skills, but is an accomplished musician, especially on the piano, and manages the center with flair and skill.

On this particular Thursday night through Sunday noon conference, Edith and I began with a "Getting to Know You" evening. To set the theme we wore our *It's Never Too Late to Have a Happy Childhood* T-shirts with white slacks.

We told the women we wanted to dig deeply into women's issues, that our objective was to help them find freedom from any bondages they had arrived with. Many women smiled optimistically; others were wistful. Some were frozen-faced, probably with years and years of deep hurt.

Once Edith and I began with our own hurtful experiences, the women felt freer to open up and bare their hearts to the group. We asked that the confidentiality principle practiced in twelve-step recovery groups be in effect for the weekend. There were obvious sighs of relief.

Julie, a frail wisp of a young woman from the Northeast with whom I bonded one night at dinner, was one of the first to report her incest experience. She revealed at that evening's meeting that her father had molested her for over eight years. She suspected the abuse had started before that, when she was an infant.

Her warm brown eyes filled with tears and her face contorted in anger as she said, "My mother knew what was going on with Dad and me. And she never said anything. She never did anything to protect me. I can't forgive her for that.

"She always played the helpless one, the one who needed to be taken care of. She expected me to meet her needs when I was dying inside. She never could see my pain." Julie sobbed into the wad of tissues in her hand.

"I don't know why I've said all of this. But I've been sitting on this pain for so long, I can't stand another minute."

Just before the evening meeting broke up, Edith looked at Julie. "I have the feeling that you very much need one of the older women here to pray with you and tuck you into bed. You need a mother tonight to care for you and be with you. Does that sound silly to you, Julie?"

Julie's face exploded in a smile. "I'd like that very much. And I'd like Sandy to be my mother."

"O.K., then, you two take off."

As Julie and I walked down the winding path to her lodge, I knew this was to be a new experience for both of us. In a way, an adventure. I sensed that her trust in me had grown during the evening.

Lord, I prayed silently, *please be with both of us. You be the counselor by giving me just the right words to say.*

We entered a spacious wooden building serving as a dormitory and headed up the thickly carpeted stairs to her room on the second floor. The halls were silent now since we had arrived before the others. The whole building had a quiet, almost holy atmosphere.

The woman who was to be Julie's roommate had canceled at the last minute, so Julie had a private room.

She settled herself into a straight chair next to the dresser. Her tiny body looked almost childlike as she folded her hands in her lap and crossed her feet neatly, like a prim and proper little girl at a dance recital. Her soft brown eyes searched mine expectantly.

"Julie, let's start by doing some role-playing. I'll be your mother. You speak to me as though you were speaking to her. And don't hold back. Let it fly! Nothing you say will shock me or make me judge you or will cause me to flee. I'm here for as long as this takes. I don't have anything to do until breakfast at eight tomorrow morning."

After I pulled up another chair and sat directly in front of Julie, she began self-consciously, her voice cracking with emotion.

"Mother, *where were you?* Where were you all the times Daddy came into my bedroom, or when I was in the bathtub, or wherever I was that he got to me? Why, why, why didn't you help me? Rescue me? You knew what was going on. I could tell by the funny way you looked at me . . . almost like I was competition for you for Daddy's love, like I was a grown woman or something sick like that. You had to know even if you pretended you didn't. I was so little and so frightened and you never once came into my room and comforted me.

"Sometimes I heard your satin bathrobe rustling down the hall. You were listening, weren't you? *Weren't you?* And I hate you for that. I hate you! Why didn't you help me? Why did you let me suffer all those years?"

Julie was screaming now. The veins on her neck were bulging in rage. She was spitting out the words in my face, totally absorbed in the emotion of the minute. She started to shake. Her eyes were closed. Her body pitched backward. Her head hit the wall with a thud.

What is happening? I thought to myself. *I hope I'm not in over my head.*

Julie regained her composure briefly, hung her head and started to sob and heave. Her jeans soon were marked with tears.

My mind was racing. *Lord, give me the words her mother might have said to her that would comfort her and make her feel safe and valuable as a child.*

"Julie," I began, "you are right. I did know. I wanted to help you, to reach out to you and comfort you, but I couldn't. Your father terrified me with his violent temper, his threats to kill us all. There were many nights when he returned from your room that I wanted to stab him or shoot him, but I couldn't go through with it. I was too scared.

"Often I'd be there outside your room just to make sure he wasn't killing you or suffocating you. I didn't know what he would do to you. I felt powerless to stop him. He was so much like your grandfather. I was scared of him, too. Grampa did to me what your father has done to you. I've been an incest victim, too. I've never been able to deal with the trauma of my own childhood. And when the same things were happening to you, it was like your grampa was doing it all over again to me. And I felt small and helpless and terrified.

"That doesn't excuse me, sweetheart, for just standing by while you were being victimized, but perhaps it will help you to understand better why I was so paralyzed. I couldn't protect you. I couldn't even protect myself. Do you understand?

"Oh, Julie, can you ever forgive me? I am so sorry for what's happened to you, that I wasn't there for you. This awful secret has just about driven me crazy. Please, please forgive me. I'm so sorry I've hurt you and let you down. Please?" I was crying now, too.

Julie's brown eyes were shut tight in anguish, her mouth contorted in bitterness.

"Oh, Mother, everything in me wants to say no, I won't forgive you, but I know I must. Though my heart can't say I forgive you, I know I must *will* to forgive you. Yes, I will to forgive you. I'll have to trust God that He will make it real. That I'll have the feelings of forgiveness. But honestly, right now I don't have them. I wish I did, but I can't just manufacture them. I want to forgive you. I really *want* to."

I held the small, sobbing body in my arms for a long time. Julie wept convulsively, wetting the shoulder of my sweater through to the skin.

At some deep level I was being healed, too. Forgiveness for my uncle who had molested me when I was five solidified at a deeper level. I felt freer and more cleansed through the pain of Julie's experience. My situation was much less traumatic than her years of abuse. I suddenly felt very thankful and relieved and grateful.

We broke from the embrace and Julie reached for a wad of tissues she had jammed into the back pocket of her jeans. She blew her nose enthusiastically again and again. A triumphant smile crossed her pale face.

"Whew! I'm glad that's over. I feel so much better. I really do. Thanks, Sandy, for being here. And by the way, how did you know my mother was an incest victim, too? She confessed it to me just recently."

I was taken aback by what she said. How *had* I known?

"The Holy Spirit told me," I replied.

Julie emerged from the bathroom in a long white flannel night-gown ready for bed. She eased herself between the covers and pulled the blankets up to her neck. Only her head was peeking out. She looked so young, so little. I fluffed her pillow, making a nest around her head. She closed her eyes. A serene smile crept across her lips— a little girl's smile. A secure little girl's smile.

I sat down on the bed and stroked her forehead.

"I love you, Julie," I said as her mother would have said. "I'm sorry I wasn't there to tuck you in all the years you needed me, but I'm here now. I want you to know how very much I love you. How precious and special you are to me. Rest now, little one, and know you are safe and secure and loved very deeply."

Next I led Julie in "Now I lay me down to sleep" and the Lord's Prayer. I sang a little lullaby to her. Her breathing became regular. Deep. I knew she had drifted off to sleep. Then I stole from the room quietly, closing the door behind me.

The memory of Julie's peaceful, beautiful face stayed with me as I walked the short distance through the damp, pungent night air to the main lodge and to my room. And I carried Julie in my heart long after the Aqueduct conference ended. Sharing such anguish and joy had bonded us as spiritual mother and daughter.

Some weeks later this letter came from Julie:

Dear Sandy,

Because you ministered so lovingly to me at the conference, I have been praying for you ever since. The result—I have been shown a picture of the woundedness still in your heart.

Then came another picture, that of the woman caught in adultery waiting to be stoned by the crowd. In prayer, I saw all those accusers of 2,000 years ago standing with rocks in their hands ready to throw them at her. Suddenly your face was the face of every person in that crowd. One of self-hatred, an-other of self-condemnation, another of guilt, pain, anger, judgment, despair.

Then each one of those Sandys came forward and put down her rock into a basket at the feet of Jesus, and quietly walked away.

And you, the one "caught in sin" and filled with such pain, stood alone before the Lord. He looked into your tear-filled eyes and said with unfathomable kindness and tenderness, "Neither do I condemn you."

Sandy, I don't think you "goofed" when you said in your closing talk that the Lord was going to give you back diamonds.

I see Jesus, Sandy, back in that scene with you, picking up that basket filled with all those stones. Jesus lifts it up toward the Father and, as He prays, a shaft of brilliant white light shines down from heaven directly upon the stones, and they are transformed into many sparkling diamonds.

The rock labeled *self-condemnation* is turned into diamonds of mercy and compassion.

The rock of *guilt* becomes purity of heart and self-control.

The rock of *pain* becomes a diamond of healing grace.

Anger is changed into peace.

Judgment becomes forgiveness.

The rock of *despair* becomes diamonds of joy, hope, patience and trust.

Then the Lord lowers the basket. He looks into your eyes with great love and, reaching into the basket, pulls out a beautiful, sparkling necklace made of all these diamonds. They are strung together on a cord of God's love that can never be broken. Jesus puts this necklace on you, and as He does so, a shaft of light, His healing and transforming light, travels from each diamond into your heart, wherein the graces of the Spirit represented by each diamond will always be.

You kneel before Him, thanking Him, and He blesses you.

Healing the wounds of incest take time. If you are an incest victim I suggest the following procedure:

1. If the experience is buried deeply in your subconscious, go back in time, asking God to reveal to you what He wants you to see. Then let the pain of it come forth. Draw it up from your depths and face it. Healing won't start until you do.

2. Find someone to help you. A qualified counselor sympathetic to your faith is my recommendation. Don't try to do it by yourself. You need someone with experience to work with you.

3. Forgive the person or persons involved. This may take time and you will probably need help to do it. But forgiving the abuser is the key to your freedom and recovery.

4. Focus on this truth: God is the Healer. He loves you and wants you restored to healthy, joyful living.

14

The Conspiracy of Silence

Recovery Principle # 14
TALK ABOUT IT

I HAVE OFTEN WISHED OUR FAMILY HAD BEEN ABLE TO COMMUNI-
cate at a deeper level. The weather was always a safe subject.
When asked, everyone was always "Fine, thank you." (Horrors that
one would admit to physical weakness!) Superficial, non-confronta-
tional subjects were O.K., but I got the message at an early age that
serious subjects or topics that touched on personal issues were *ver-
boten.* We were not to talk about them.

A dome of quiet would descend over our home should feelings get
out of hand or an unpleasant subject come up. I used to wonder why
we couldn't talk about certain things, but I learned to keep my
mouth shut. I didn't get into trouble that way.

Nowhere is the conspiracy of silence more obvious than in the area of sexuality. Why is sex so hard to talk about in a family? My mother didn't tell me the facts of life. Her mother didn't tell her. And to my deep regret, I didn't tell my daughter—or sons, for that matter. They learned about sex from their peers.

As children, my friend of many years, Betty Lou, and I used to make drawings of boys and girls, scribbling in what we *thought* men's sex organs looked like. In retrospect the results were pretty hysterical. We giggled and tittered nervously for fear someone would catch us in this forbidden speculation.

Back in the '40s, especially in a little Vermont town, no one talked openly about sex. Once I saw our neighbor, Mr. Grant, frantically hosing down two dogs on his lawn who were locked in *l'amour*. He was so embarrassed he kept his back to me, muttering about "damn dogs in heat." I thought he was referring to the steamy August afternoon.

At dinner that evening I reported the afternoon adventures of the dogs next door to my assembled grandparents and aunts and uncles. I couldn't understand the sudden silence around the table, why some dove for their water glasses and napkins while my grandmother, red-faced, headed for the pantry. Absentminded, too, for she returned moments later without whatever it was she had jumped up to get.

The bathroom on the first floor of our St. Johnsbury Center home was just off the kitchen. On the rim of the large claw-footed bathtub, just peeking out from behind the white tieback curtains, a mysterious cobalt-blue box appeared and disappeared regularly. The white letters on the side of the box spelled K O T E X. *What a funny name!* I thought to myself. And under the delicate, stilt-like logo were inscribed the words *Sanitary Napkins*.

Those must be very special napkins, I decided. But why were they in the bathroom and not in the kitchen cupboard?

One day I asked my mother, "What are Kotex, Mummy? What are we saving them for?"

She got flustered. "I'll—er, er, er—tell you about them when it's time."

All this delaying tactic did, of course, was to further pique my curiosity. Kotex took on a mystery as deep and dark as the box in which they were stored.

I was haunted by *When it's time.*

Time for what?

Why had mother blushed so?

And why wouldn't Gram explain, either? She had gotten that "I think I've just smelled ammonia" look on her face and changed the subject.

Nor was my Aunt Ethel much help.

Nor my Aunt Dorothy.

They both smiled knowingly and looked away at some fly speck on the ceiling. Aunt Dorothy actually snickered out loud.

Was there anything funny about these little white gauze-covered pads?

One day I took one out of the box. What a peculiar, narrow shape it had! What a cute little doll mattress this would make! I could see why they were called "sanitary." They were even whiter than Gram's sheets, and that was saying a lot. My grandmother had the whitest sheets on any clothesline in St. Johnsbury Center.

One Sunday evening, as parishioners of the Congregational church, it was our family's turn to host our young pastor, Mr. Cushman, and his lovely bride of six months.

Great care and thought had gone into preparing a succulent baked ham. The scalloped potatoes were browned to perfection. Green beans picked fresh from the garden. A glistening strawberry Jello salad bursting with fruit cocktail. Homemade Parker House rolls. And Gram's famous raspberry-filled sugar cookies.

As family and guests took their places in the dining room, I was helping Mother with last-minute table settings when I realized she was going to be one napkin short. And it was at the pastor's place.

"Wait a minute, Mummy," I cried triumphantly. "I'll get a napkin for you."

Racing to the bathroom, I prayed that the cobalt-blue box would be on the back of the bathtub. It was! My heart raced with excitement. Who more than the pastor deserved the best napkin in the house?

Bursting back into the dining room, I headed for the pastor, now seated at the table and taking his first sip of iced tea. He saw me coming, waving the Kotex in the air by its gauze tab.

"Here, Mummy!" I crowed, relishing the knowledge that I had rescued the moment. "Here's a sanitary napkin for Pastor Cushman."

The iced tea in the pastor's mouth exploded in a stream.

Looks of shock. And disbelief.

Uncle Sam buried his face in his napkin.

Aunt Dorothy choked down a laugh.

My mother rolled her eyes heavenward and grabbed the back of Aunt Ethel's chair.

And my grandmother made another impromptu dash for the pantry.

It was years before I understood why no one ever thanked me for my clever solution to the napkin problem.

In fact, that evening was always referred to as *"that"* night when Pastor and Mrs. Cushman came to dinner. . . .

As I look back on our life in Vermont forty years ago, I can see a lot of things wrong about the conspiracy of silence in our family. Children learned about sex in an unhealthy way, whereas frank mother-daughter or father-son conversations would have cleared up a lot of confusion.

The conspiracy of silence in a family like Julie's, the young woman at the Aqueduct conference, allowed abusive incest to continue for years, seriously damaging all the parties involved. Such silence protected the course of infidelity, promoted distrust, resentment, pain.

In fact, this scenario is played over and over in millions of homes year after year, generation after generation. The three laws springing out of this conspiracy: *Don't talk. Don't trust. Don't feel.*

Yet the other extreme, which we have today care of the sexual revolution, is equally destructive. The new openness and frankness, which could be healthy, has led to a loosening of almost all barriers. As a result, free sex today is an untamed monster, destroying homes and damaging lives just as drugs do. Most people today consider affairs and adultery acceptable. The *f* word is said over and over in films, plays and conversations.

One of the worst results? Sex has become so talked about, so examined on television and in the movies, that it has become commonplace. The mystery is gone. And it often ends up being, well, boring. Ask a dozen women how they feel about sex, as I did recently. Most actually said, "I can live without it."

Children today know a great deal about sex as soon as they enter school. Where do they learn? Not usually from parents but from peers. Or from pornographic magazines and films.

Suddenly I have a warm, nostalgic feeling about my own childhood and the confusion I encountered with adults about sex. Their embarrassment made sex and the changes a woman's body went through seem mysterious and romantic and important.

If the long-ago conspiracy of silence in homes was wrong, and equally so the unbridled sexual revolution of today, what is the answer?

I have found the answer through readings and teachings on sexuality for Christians, and through the following principles, which I have been grappling with for a dozen years or more:

1. *Openness.* Support groups have helped me here as we share our pain, our experiences, our strength and our hopes.

473

2. *Trust.* For me, this began with a commitment to God. When I could trust Him, I could begin to trust people. And myself.

3. *Talking about it.* Learning to discuss sex in a healthy way has not taken away the mystery of it, but given me an infinite respect for the power and sacredness God meant it to have. Talking about sex openly with my children has lifted the code of silence in our family and opened the way for new honesty and healing among us.

15

Birthday Party Therapy

Recovery Principle # 15
CELEBRATE

THE WORDING ON THE T-SHIRTS THAT EDITH MARSHALL AND I like to wear when we minister to women has proven magnificently true: *It's Never Too Late to Have a Happy Childhood.*

True—and vitally important. There is great healing power in childlike joy and abandon. Thinking back to my own childhood, I am only too aware of how unacceptable it was in many of our families of origin to be either childlike or joyful.

Discovering one's lost childhood usually starts with the peeling away of layers and layers of hurt, abuse and trauma. It doesn't happen instantly. It took me several years to locate my inner child deep within the recesses of my subconscious. Inviting this child in me, and also in others, to come out and play has been exciting and deeply fulfilling.

My first experience with what I call "birthday party therapy" occurred several years ago at Evergreen Farm. Ellen, a good friend, was turning fifty, a birthday many women fear and dread.

I had known Ellen through prayer conferences in the Washington, D.C., area. News of the suicide of her beautiful daughter, Amy, at age eighteen had come to our Breakthrough intercession ministry months before in the form of a prayer request for strength for the family to endure this tragic loss. Ellen, her husband (from whom she was separated) and her son were devastated.

Somewhere along the way I learned that Ellen had been reared in a series of orphanages. She had never even had a birthday party. So some of us at Evergreen set about to rectify that with a fiftieth birthday extravaganza—an irresistible challenge for us compulsive women!

First, a trip to the toy department of the local drugstore. Our car's back seat bulged with paper bags: a soft brown teddy bear, a jump rope, a set of jacks, paper dolls, coloring book and crayons, puzzles, pinwheels, pickup sticks, checkers, a bag of marbles, a bottle of liquid soap bubbles, a makeup set with mirror, perfume and lipstick.

We got party hats, nut cups, Mickey Mouse plates and napkins, yards and yards of crepe paper streamers. Balloons and more balloons.

On the day of the party we hung a huge sign on the front door: *Happy 50th, Ellen.* Everywhere there were dolls and teddy bears. The table was a riot of flowers and confetti and favors. Tied to Ellen's chair was a bouquet of helium-filled birthday balloons.

The walls were decorated with *Happy Birthday* banners. Candles winked cheerily from wall sconces and candelabra on the buffet and dining room table. Ellen's gifts were placed in an ornately decorated bushel basket and set on her chair. The scene was outrageously festive.

When Ellen arrived accompanied by her handsome son, Mark, a college senior, her face exploded in joy and wonder and tears of unbelief over what had been prepared for her, and that a dozen friends would come to celebrate the occasion.

It had been fun for me, too. The compulsive quality in me that had for years focused on parties dominated by alcohol had been converted into something constructive, such as family birthday parties, household decorations, picnics for family and friends.

Now it was almost as though the Lord was saying to me, "You will be the instrument I have chosen to restore a sense of worth to Ellen so that she might catch a glimpse of how much I love her and how special she is."

As she sat down gingerly at her seat of honor trying to digest everything around her, Ellen's lovely face seemed to lose 45 years. It was the child inside her who opened the many cards and presents.

Later, Mark and the rest of us carried gifts, games, streamers and balloons to Ellen's station wagon. Ellen was still wearing her metallic red birthday hat. Confetti dotted her hair. Before getting into the car she pulled me aside.

"Sandy, there are just no words to tell you what is in my heart right now. I feel recreated and appreciated and loved. Special. I'm so glad, too, that Mark got to see a side of his mother he never knew existed. For the first time he saw the joyful, happy little girl I didn't know was inside me either, instead of the morose, weeping mother I've been for so long. For I want you to know that I do feel like a little girl. A special little girl.

"You should know something else. Today would have been Amy's birthday, too. Her twentieth." Ellen's eyes filled with tears. "She was born on my thirtieth birthday. And now here's something I want you to have."

She opened the back door of the car and retrieved an object from a shopping bag she had brought from home. Then she presented me triumphantly with a beautiful gray and silver tapestry teddy bear with golden eyes.

"This belonged to Amy. Knowing how you love bears, I want you to have it. It was her favorite. She had quite a collection." Her voice trailed off.

I accepted the bear, deeply touched.

"Amy loved Catherine Marshall's books," Ellen continued. "One of her dreams was to visit Evergreen. She never made it here, but I can't believe today was a coincidence. How thrilled she would have been by all this!"

"Now her bear will be a resident here," I added. "So Amy will be part of Evergreen Farm, too."

I waved goodbye to Ellen and Mark as their station wagon headed up the driveway, thinking, *Lord, You are indeed the Comforter and Healer. The passing years are surely no barrier to You as You help us redis-cover our childhoods.*

While leading a four-day workshop at Aqueduct Conference Center on the subject "Healing the Inner Child," Edith and I decided to try the birthday party therapy on Saturday night. The forty women attending were from 16 to 75, black and white, wealthy and poor. By Saturday evening they had received much teaching on wounded families, lost childhoods, compulsive behavior and generational patterns. We ended with this powerful prayer for the wounded inner child:

Heavenly Father, I come to You as a little child. Wounded. Abandoned. Rejected by important figures early in my life. I am afraid to trust and, I'm ashamed to say, afraid to trust You totally, Lord.

My inner child cries out to You from her dark hiding place. Weeping for what never was. My inner child hides, afraid to be hurt again. I need Your love, Your solace to give me courage to walk into the light.

If I did not have a mother's love, please send the Holy Spirit to hold me close, to rock me, to tell me stories, to fill in the empty parts of me that needed the comfort and warmth only a mother can give.

If I was deprived of a father's love and did not feel that I was wanted, I ask You to hold me, Lord, and let me feel Your strong, protective arms around me.

Walk through my life, Lord, and comfort me when others were not kind.

Heal the wounds of encounters that left me frightened . . . the person who disappointed me . . . the one who was cruel to me . . . the one who was insensitive to my feelings . . . the brother or sister who was preferred . . . my spouse or former spouse . . . any other family member who hurt me . . . the authority figure . . . anyone who wounded me physically, emotionally, sexually, spiritually . . . anyone who caused me to retreat into myself and erect barriers to You or to other people.

If I have felt unwanted, grant me through Your healing love a new sense of worth as a person.

Lord God, by the power of Your Spirit, help me to make a friend—namely myself. Empower me to forgive myself for my past failures, my mistakes, my moments of weakness and selfishness, my refusal to forgive myself, my self-hatred and self-loathing.

Help me to see myself as Your precious little girl, the apple of Your eye. May the reality of Your unconditional love be burned deeply into my spirit that I might be set free. To laugh. To play. To skip through a mud puddle . . . knowing my heavenly Father watches with delight.

How great it is, Lord, to feel safe in Your arms, to be able to trust, to be nurtured! And forgiven.

Thank You for drying my tears. For Your promise to restore the years the locusts have devoured.

Many of the women were now sobbing. Others reached out to hold the more distraught. Healing and love were flowing in a mighty way around the room.

Edith was comforting a particularly upset young woman. I marveled at Edith, the nurturer. So gentle. So wise. So caring. So gifted.

As the women regained their composure, I gathered them together.

"Tonight is a very special occasion. Special because we're all going to celebrate our birthdays! Regardless of what date yours is, tonight is going to be a celebration that we are women, that we are chosen and loved by our heavenly Father, that we are Daddy's little girls."

Edith started the tape *Celebration*. As the bouncy beat of the music caught us up in its infectious enthusiasm, the women started to clap their hands. Some began to dance.

Stashed behind one of the couches were two enormous bags of decorations and goodies. Pat Johnson, the Aqueduct office manager, and I had gone shopping for these surprises the day before. Now Pat burst into the room with fifty multicolored, helium-filled balloons. All the women were now in motion, laughing, singing. Some draped themselves with crepe paper streamers, tying them around their heads, waists, wrists or ankles. Others began blowing bubbles or skipping rope. Several women pranced about in a conga line doing Rockette kicks to the music.

Each woman was given a large plastic ring—Minnie or Mickey Mouse, Daisy or Donald Duck. One young woman attached her ring to her nose, to squeals of delight. Another took the little yellow felt hat off the Paddington bear she was carrying and attached it to her long blonde hair with bobby pins. What a picture of sheer delight, this lovely woman with a tiny yellow hat perched on her head, blowing hard on a pink metallic pinwheel, returning to the joyous little girl she had left behind twenty years before.

The noise level by now was deafening with the laughing and shrieking and shouts of glee. Pat looked at me with excited eyes. "Aqueduct has *never* seen anything like this before!" A short while later she returned with a large tray of chocolate cupcakes, each decorated with a candle. She and Edith arranged them on the coffee table in the center of the room.

"O.K., everybody," Edith hollered. "Pick up your birthday cake and come blow out your candle."

All forty of us clustered around the low table to sing "Happy Birthday" to ourselves. Forty voices blended in harmony. There was something almost angelic about each face as it was reflected in the candle glow—forty little girls rejoicing that they were little girls. And—for that moment, anyway—glad that they had been born. Pain, depression and darkness had been banished from our celebration. Only joy and acceptance and love were admitted here.

Then Edith announced it was game time. Cheers! Teams were drawn up; the under-35s against the over-35s for a lively session of charades.

At 11:30 P.M. we called it a night. As the women wandered off to their rooms, chatting happily, Edith and I collapsed on one of the large gray sofas, our feet propped on the coffee table.

"Well, Sandy, I don't know about you, but I had the time of my life," she yawned, a large blue crepe paper bow still draped over her forehead covering one of her eyes.

"Edith, you look ridiculously adorable."

But Edith had actually fallen asleep with a beautiful little smile.

Sunday morning was awards time, to recognize outstanding performances of the night before. To pretty blonde Ann went the prize for the limbo contest, a dance done in the Caribbean in which you slide under a pole that is lowered steadily until there is hardly room for a human form to pass under it.

The Mouseketeer Party Organizer Award went to Lottie, a vivacious redhead from Atlanta. Next, the drawing for a special teddy bear. With great fanfare, Edith drew a name from the box. "And the winner is—Rosemary!"

Rosemary was our oldest conferee who had come with many needs and hurts. The first evening she had sat stonily in her chair as the others shared. Slowly she opened up as the weekend progressed. The evening before she had stood arm in arm with her daughter, her Minnie Mouse ring reflecting the glow of the candle on her cupcake, her lovely face a wreath of smiles. What a contrast to the woman who had arrived! Rosemary had found the little girl within.

Slowly she came forward to receive the little gray teddy. She pressed the small bear to her chest and said, with tears misting behind her glasses, "I've never won anything before in my life."

As I looked at the balloons gathered into an enormous bouquet on the fireplace mantel, I marveled once again at how God had used a birthday party—this time to transform a group of forty women for a few shining moments into that magical place of childhood where joy can take root in the soul, no matter what the date on the calendar.

My recovery continues through workshops on compulsive behavior as I learn through reaching out to others. The birthday celebration helped me discover my own inner child who got lost years ago in the trauma of a dysfunctional home. In the process I see some of the steps* compulsive/addictive people like me—and there are millions of us—need to take to get well:

1. *Recognizing* that back there at an early age the natural progression of your childhood was stopped because of a sudden grief, family rupture, physical illness or some other deeply painful event. Because of this, your emotional growth was stunted and your behavior became erratic. Alcoholism or drug abuse, another type of compulsive behavior or a combination thereof tended to follow.

2. *Making contact* with that lost inner child. This can be done in a number of ways. Celebrating the discovery of the lost child is one, as I have done through the birthday party therapy. John Bradshaw suggests "embracing your lost inner child" through meditation.* This procedure involves *relaxing* the body; *breathing* exercises; *going back* in time to age seven or before; *walking down* the street to your house; *watching* the small child (you) coming out the front door; *walking up* to this child and telling him or her that you are his or her future; *asking him or her* to go home with you, then taking his/her hand; *turning the corner* to meet your cherished friends and Higher Power (God) waiting to greet you and embrace you.

3. *Being liberated,* which happens when you recognize the need to go back to your childhood, meet the lost child and set her free.

*John Bradshaw, *Reclaiming the Inner Child* (Los Angeles: Jeremy P. Tarcher, Inc., 1990).

Reconnecting with the inner child then enables you to discover your true self.

The above steps are not, of course, a substitution for twelve-step programs and related support groups that over the years have proven their value to the recovery process.

16

"*Sandy, I Hated Your Book*"

Recovery Principle # 16
BE HONEST

---

*T*HOSE OF US IN BONDAGE TO AN ADDICTION CREATE A WEB OF lies to protect ourselves. In time we come to the point at which we believe that these lies are truth; we live in delusion in order to feel good about ourselves. Sometimes we revise and rewrite our personal histories to excuse the shameful things we have done.

To move ahead with recovery, we must face up to our dishonesty and set the record straight whenever possible, even if it means painful confession and confrontation.

In speaking to groups I feel it is essential to be open, vulnerable and as honest as I can. Sometimes the results almost blow me away.

Like the Compulsive Woman Workshop we held in May 1990 at a church in Silver Spring, Maryland. Tina Haroldson, a lovely young woman from the Midwest, is a gifted soloist and provided our special music. Tina's mother was in the audience. Both were close friends of Dottie Schmitt, the pastor's wife, who was a co-speaker.

I had shared my personal story in the morning. The workshop was due to end with my giving a final teaching session on Saturday afternoon. Tina opened this session with a song in her strong soprano; her high notes were so penetrating that I expected the stained glass windows in the sanctuary to pop out. Then Tina drew a deep breath and prepared, we assumed, to give us a final song.

Instead, she turned her gaze to me where I was sitting in the front row. "Sandy, I read your book last year. And I just want you to know I hated it. Hated it because you were so honest. And I felt so convicted."

Tina stooped down for a moment and pulled off the high-heeled black pumps she had been wearing all day, giving herself in the process an aura of vulnerability and realness. I was intrigued that she was allowing herself to do what most people do when their feet hurt. Rarely do entertainers allow themselves this privilege while in front of an audience!

"You didn't write very much about my situation, Sandy." Her voice faltered for a moment. "I have a condition called obsessive-compulsive behavior. My particular problem is that I can't stop pulling out my hair."

There was shocked silence throughout the church. Two hundred women leaned forward, unable to believe the startling confession they were hearing.

None of us, looking at Tina, saw any evidence of a hair-pulling problem. Her carefully coiffed short brown hair was glossy and well-groomed, a fringe of bangs dusting her forehead.

No one was prepared for what happened next.

Carefully Tina placed the microphone back into its stand. Her right hand reached up under her bangs and she proceeded to remove a wig, placing it gently onto the lucite pulpit in front of her. It looked like a small, soft brown puppy curled up asleep next to her Bible.

Gasps of shock and disbelief. Here stood a beautiful young woman beneath an enormous stained glass window, stocking-footed, revealing her deepest, darkest secret to two hundred strangers. Tina's scalp glistened between wispy rows of thin, brown hair. It looked as though she had deliberately and neatly plucked out rows of hair the way a farmer would harvest rows of corn.

Suddenly, from the back of the church, Tina's mother raced down the aisle and up the carpeted steps to the pulpit where her daughter stood. She was in her stocking feet, too.

The two locked in an embrace, their bodies swaying as they wept in each other's arms. We were all weeping.

Mother and daughter broke from the embrace, and Tina reached for the microphone. Her final vocal tribute: "In Heaven's Eyes There Are No Losers."

Though her bald scalp shone under the bright overhead spotlights, on her face was the most radiant expression of peace. Tina's act had freed something inside her. The secret she had covered for so many years was out in the open at last. The Lord had given her courage to reach down into the darkness of her addiction and lift it into the dazzling light of His love.

She sang like an angel. She looked like an angel. I wondered for a moment if she *was* an angel who had been sent to us to show us how painful honesty and humility could set us all free.

We were all on our feet. We cheered. We danced in the aisles. Tina's moment of courage had, in different ways, set us all free.

Afterward Tina picked up her wig, seemingly nonchalant, hugged those of us in the front row and took her seat. I stepped up to the lectern to give the message.

The Spirit of the Lord was almost suffocating in His sweet power in that moment as I looked out at the tear-stained faces.

All I could do was weep into the microphone. No words came out, only the sounds of my sobs. The most eloquent teaching had already been given.

Fourteen months later I received a letter from Tina, along with a report she had sent out to followers of her singing and speaking ministry. Here are excerpts:

Since the age of twelve I have been in bondage to a form of obsessive-compulsive disorder (OCD) called trichatillamania. A person with this disorder has the strange desire to pull out his or her hair. For me the disorder became so uncontrollable that I eventually pulled out all the hair on top of my head and thus had to wear a wig.

Worse than the inconvenience of wearing a hairpiece was the feeling that I was a failure as a Christian. I had prayed and trusted and hoped, but nothing changed. In May 1990 I was in bondage and out of hope.

That May I was invited to Immanuel Church in Silver Spring, Maryland, for a women's weekend retreat. I was preparing to sing two songs when I sensed the Lord speaking to me:

Tina, I want you to tell these ladies about your affliction and then I want you to take off your wig.

My heart began to race. "No, Lord, they will think I have no faith."

But the Lord repeated the requests.

"How could You ask me to do such a thing?" I implored. "Why would You require me to face such pain, embarrassment and rejection?"

I decided I just could not do it.

Then Sandy LeSourd spoke. She was so transparent and willing to be real in her talk that my heart was touched. When it was time for me to sing, I knew I had to trust the Lord and be obedient.

When I removed my wig, I felt vulnerable and yet safe, transparent yet accepted, frightened and yet strangely free.

In Jeremiah 24:6–7 God has this promise to anyone who struggles with insecurity: "I will build them up and not tear them down; I will plant them and not uproot them. I will give them a heart to know me, that I am the Lord. They will be my people, and I will be their God, for they will return to me with all their heart" (NIV).

The Lord built me up because I had trusted Him enough to be obedient. From the time I took off my wig before those women, I have experienced complete deliverance from trichatillamania. Fourteen months later I was back singing in Immanuel Church. The tears rolled down my face on that morning of July 21, 1991, as I looked out across the congregation. Every person that Sunday morning was standing and praising the Lord for His faithfulness.

During my testimony I described how in one church I visited, crutches, canes and walkers were nailed to the wall as "evidence of healing." Then I presented my wig to be nailed to one of the church walls so that when people saw it they would be reminded that "in Jesus' name the blind shall see, the lame will walk, the deaf shall hear [and in Jesus' name the bald shall 'flip their wigs']."

So I left my wig there that day. I no longer need it; my thick, brown hair now grows so quickly it needs cutting often. Almost every time I look in the mirror I am reminded that God is faithful in freeing us from bondage when we are open and honest and obedient.

As I rejoice over Tina's new freedom, I am constantly amazed at the ripple effect of honesty. Facing the truth about myself and speaking it to others has been an important factor in freeing me from my compulsions. That my openness and candor could affect others like Tina excites me, of course, but it also reminds me all over again that the real power is from God. The more open and honest I am, the more He can do His work through me.

17

Letting the Tiger Out

Recovery Principle # 17
LIKE YOURSELF

---

*F*OOD ISSUES, I AM DISCOVERING, ARE THE MOST PREVALENT, PER-
sistent addiction problems with women. With men, too, but to
a lesser degree. Women have a particularly emotional relationship
with food. To us food can be a source of immense pleasure or intense
pain. It can be comforter, accuser, faithful lover, enemy to be
avoided.

Women live in a society in which they are judged by their
exteriors. Losing weight can somehow assume ultimate importance,
a way of waiting for life to happen: "Once I lose weight. . . ." All
of life would be better, happier, more rewarding if only we were
thin.

If and when all of us foodaholics manage to become thin, we find to our dismay that the anticipated paradise is a glittering sham perpetrated enthusiastically and profitably by Madison Avenue. The media has blitzed us with images of skinny models in diaphanous dresses sipping white wine on windswept beaches while slender men with perfect teeth nibble on their ears—the glorification of the body beautiful. If we but have one, all is well.

Not too long ago I went on a doctor's controversial diet, losing 25% of my body weight—about 40 pounds. Whoever said, "You can't be too thin," was wrong. I carried the diet to a compulsive extreme, starving myself in the process. My anorexic mindset was taking over again.

There was a lot of ego in my dropping several dress sizes, but the gaunt wisp I became hardly had the energy to pick up a Kleenex. I had little flesh. My breasts shrank. My eyeballs gaped like burnt holes in a blanket. To my alarmed husband I aged a decade in eight months. But I had ribs for a change and hip bones and a teeny waist.

I was not suddenly transformed into the devastatingly alluring creature I thought I would be if only I could lose those stubborn twenty pounds or so. Nor was I happier or more fulfilled. My problems did not suddenly vanish when I became thin. The mystique of skinny is just that—a mystique.

I found that some women resented my being thin. Heavier was better, less threatening to others. I would be asked, "What size are you now? A two?" These women were starving themselves on lettuce leaves and cottage cheese or liquid diets. Somehow they thought I had arrived at dieter's nirvana, that golden circle of wonderfulness where all is well.

It is a lie perpetrated by the multibillion dollar diet industry.

I went off that diet and got onto a sensible, more nourishing eating program. Now I am back at the insurance company's chart of ideal weight for my height, although it is a struggle to stay there as I crave the sugary, yeasty foods I shouldn't have. ("I don't need a cookie. There's always celery!")

Part of this new program is to allow myself two special treats weekly. A piece of pie . . . a divine cheese croissant . . . a dish of frozen yogurt. Otherwise I would go off the deep end.

In my recovery from addictions, while dealing mostly with overweight, I have discovered that the way to maturity where food is concerned is being aware of behavior patterns and feelings that have kept me in bondage to my need to overeat (and undereat). Mostly I was stuffing down my feelings—guilt, fear, anger, boredom, frustration.

Eventually I learned to check on my feelings when my tummy started rumbling. Exactly what was I trying to feed? Was it some psychological hunger (I'm eating because I'm scared of this situation)? Or was I *really* hungry?

Once I was able to spot-check my feelings, I could grab hold of that Scripture handle that has been so helpful to me in checking compulsions in general: "Take every thought captive to the obedience of Christ."

Freedom has come as I become more aware of who I am and how I use food to cope with stress, anger, rejection, shame. I feel a new kind of euphoria knowing I can now make choices, life-giving choices, that I don't need to be chained to old patterns.

For me, a journey to the past was necessary to understand why food gave me so many problems. For me as a child, as for so many, food represented security and love. Food was a reward, too. Mom baked a lot. There was always some fresh-baked love offering waiting for me when I got home from school: warm peanut butter cookies, gingersnaps or my favorite, chocolate chip.

"You've worked hard today at school; you deserve a special treat" was the message. Good girls got rewards, so I always worked hard to be not just good but *p-e-r-f-e-c-t!*

Since I was an only child, my mother hovered over my food intake, often insisting I eat her portion as well as my own, especially meat—a precious commodity in our meager budget. I remember how Mother would cut out the best part of her pork chop for me, content to chew on the fat and bone. Her sacrifice made me uncomfortable. Sometimes my tummy balked at swallowing what I felt should have been my mother's nourishment, that somehow I was taking what she needed.

We parents use food as a punishment, too. I think back with horror how I forced my firstborn, Brad, to sit in his high chair for over an hour until he cleaned his plate of the seven remaining garden peas. Finally, in desperation, he ate one and mashed the other six in his hair.

Have you ever noticed how angry people eat? They stab their food as if they expect it to attack them back. My Uncle Ralph used to eat that way, impaling each bite as though it were his mortal enemy.

I have watched anorexics eat—or not eat. I was one myself at one point. Food is merely rearranged on the plate, very little of it finding its way to the mouth. Meat is cut into tiny pieces and slipped under lettuce leaves. A nibbled roll lies nearby looking as though a mouse has chewed on it. It seems to the anorexic as though she has eaten a full meal.

At the other extreme are those (more typical of my own food abuse) who almost become human garbage pails. When most dysfunctional, I could all but inhale a two-pound box of chocolates. Another binge for me was a fresh-baked loaf of bread slathered with butter and peanut butter. My midnight raids into chocolate ice cream were hour-long orgies.

Chocolate was my smooth, undemanding, sensual friend. It lulled me. It seduced me. It satiated me—temporarily. The next night I would crawl back for more, coming to hate myself for my weakness. Indeed, a love/hate ambivalence has always characterized my response to food. It was my nurturer, my mother, my betrayer, my subtle poisoner. No wonder my weight ballooned upward of 200 pounds!

My shopping cart was a telltale giveaway. Chips, cookies, six-packs of beer, cartons of Twinkies and candy bars. Peanut M & Ms were utterly irresistible.

Once while standing in line at the neighborhood market checkout, I heard two women discussing me, thinking I was out of earshot.

"Doesn't she ever look at herself in the mirror?" one of them was saying.

To which the other replied, "Sad, isn't it, for someone who's been in the Miss America pageant to let herself go to seed the way she has. She couldn't win a cattle contest now!"

Those words should have seared themselves with white-hot pain into my heart and brain. But I shrugged them off, refusing to believe I looked as awful as I really did. My view of myself was most myopic—just what I saw in my hand mirror when I put on my makeup.

As my life turned around and I began to deal with my compulsive behavior, the first two enemies I confronted were alcohol and tobacco. Eventually, with God's help, I stopped drinking and smoking. Food, however, was hard to class as an enemy. After all, everyone has to eat.

At an eating disorder support group meeting I attended once, someone put it this way: "The alcoholics have it easy. They simply learn to put the cork in the bottle and keep it there. We food junkies have a tiger in the cage. Three times a day we have to let it out, feed it, pet it, make friends with it and then put it back in its cage."

The moment of truth came when I was looking for a dress to wear for my fortieth birthday celebration. In a three-way fitting room mirror I saw myself in full-length 3-D and couldn't believe the mass of flesh I had become. My upper arms looked like Smithfield hams, while bulges and rolls of fat creased my midsection. Heartsick, I ambled up to the cash register to purchase the only dress I could find that would fit: a dreadful black-and-rust print voile number with long sleeves and an elastic waist. It made me look like an overstuffed chair. I consoled myself on the way home with a triple-dip pecan and pralines ice cream cone.

At treatment centers and then later at the halfway house, I managed to bring my weight down from the 200 area to about 160. By the time I married Len I had dropped to around 150. Yet still I had not dealt with my food issues. I was still eating compulsively, then dieting compulsively.

Now that I am on a strict physician-prescribed eating program, I realize how often food has become that special treat I felt I deserved. After all, my codependent, people-pleasing self needed a fix when she took on the cares of the world. What better gift than something delectable to eat! I could space out. Medicate. Forget for a moment what feelings and problems were plaguing me.

Now my special treat to myself when I feel tempted to pig out is to take a few minutes to work on a crafts project, phone a friend, write a letter. One of my favorite treats: propping up lots of pillows on my bed and reading a news magazine. That is loving myself without involving food.

A recent incident during a family gathering at the farm tested my new food discipline. I knew that on top of the refrigerator sat a blueberry pie. Not some plastic bake-it-yourself frozen variety, but the *real thing,* a confection baked at a local Virginia dispensary of epicurean delights, Hill High Orchards.

Hill High pies are the ultimate treat for our family. People request them on birthdays. Some of us have been known to drive miles out of our way for Hill High pies. You're talking gourmet here.

This particular evening I happened to be returning from an errand to nearby Leesburg, Virginia. I knew the family planned to have that blueberry pie for dessert. It would be warmed in the oven, slathered with heavenly French vanilla ice cream and accompanied by piping hot chocolate raspberry coffee—none of which my food plan allowed.

But I didn't have to sit there and watch, drooling. I could have a special treat of my own. With sudden inner decision-making intensity, I wheeled my car into the parking lot of a super-market.

Seizing a grocery cart, I marched determinedly to the vegetable counter. The produce manager was misting his offerings. The tiny droplets did make them look a bit more appetizing lying there glistening seductively . . . if a beet can look seductive!

But not just any veggie would do. It had to be special. If I couldn't have blueberry pie, I would have an artichoke.

My exploring fingers plunged into the artichoke bin. After careful testing, I laid a pale green trophy lovingly into my grocery cart. It was gorgeous and I congratulated myself.

Chinese vegetables were next. I spent several minutes selecting the most perfect snow peas I could find. No blemishes. No spots. No splits. Perfect snow peas.

My heart leaped as I saw fresh parsnips smiling at me from little plastic bags. Parsnips excite me. My mouth was already watering as I fantasized a steaming plate of sweet parsnips dotted with my permitted small portion of butter.

At the far end of the counter, a siren vegetable sang a tantalizing song. Imported yellow peppers from Holland . . . $4.99 a pound. Should I?

"Why not?" I argued back.

I found the most lusciously tempting golden pepper in the bin, lifted it to my lips and gave it an enthusiastic kiss. Anyone watching me would have thought I had really lost it! Fortunately the produce manager had finished his misting duties. I was alone.

My spirits were soaring as my car purred down the winding road to Evergreen Farm. It was a dazzling night. The trees and fields were ablaze with thousands of tiny blinking lights from early summer fireflies.

What a fairyland! I thought to myself. *How could I get so wrapped up in a pie with all this beauty around? Forget the stupid pie. I have a bag full of perfect snow peas.*

During our evening meal I savored my special veggies for the benefit of the pie-eaters, although I have to admit I did have a few secret yearnings to join them. But I am working on it, trying to re-program myself.

Like most Americans I have been bewildered by the variety of diets screaming at me from television ads and headline stories in magazines at supermarket checkouts. What to believe? After extensive research, plus some sad experience with diets that take weight off but offer no formula for keeping it off, I have come up with ten general suggestions:

1. Find a food plan that is comfortable for you over the long term, allowing you special treats every now and then.

2. Cut down on portions at each meal, saying no to seconds.

3. Limit consumption of sugar, salt, bread, baked goods, junk foods. Eat less red meat, more fish and chicken.

4. Drink six to eight glasses of water every day.

5. Exercise five days each week. Daily, if possible. Brisk walking works for me.

6. If you are severely overweight, see a physician for a medical checkup and ask him or her for a food plan.

7. Don't put your life on hold waiting to be thin.

8. Combine disciplined eating and exercise with a spiritual plan that emphasizes quiet times, prayer, Scripture reading.

9. If you are struggling with a food problem, it is crucial that you attend a support group.

10. Remember, God loves you as you are. As one person put it at a support group meeting, "I can accept myself as I am because God has shown me I'm no less of a person in His eyes, in spite of the big numbers I put on the scale."

18

Learning to Say I'm Sorry

Recovery Principle # 18
CONFESS YOUR WRONGDOING

HE LOOKED FRAIL AND GAUNT IN HIS FAVORITE CHAIR, A ROSE-beige recliner. His calloused hands and stained fingernails told the story of years of long labor—repairing, renovating, refurbishing. Dad was one of those men who could fix most everything.

In my youth he and I had spent many hot summer days papering and painting the houses we lived in. I am grateful to him for helping me acquire so many home repair skills.

"I've always been the son you never had, Dad," I would tease as I climbed a ladder bearing a long strip of pasted wallpaper or a brush loaded with paint. He would always make sure his foot was planted securely on the lowest step of the ladder so it wouldn't fall over.

501

My heart was warmed now by the memory of that long-ago protective gesture.

"You're doing a fine job!" he would say.

Those were golden words of high praise from my father. His exacting eye and penchant for detail seldom missed a thing. How I wanted to please him, to do my very best!

We hung miles of wallpaper and spread a pond of paint in those days together. They were precious times of work and fellowship, times I needed to remember after he divorced Mother and moved out of our lives into a new one of his own. How angry I had been then!

That was forty years ago. Now I was sitting opposite him in the living room of his home in Barre, Vermont. My stepmother, Nora, had gone "downstreet"—a New Englandism for the shopping district—and I welcomed this time to be alone with him.

As I sat looking into his lined face, I thought back to the movie-star-handsome father of my youth. He was still attractive now and virile despite his siege of illnesses. His smile was warm and loving. His new false teeth seemed fashioned for a much larger face, giving him the appearance of being all teeth. His weary blue eyes shone with love for his only child.

Secretly I had always wondered what it would have been like to have had brothers and sisters. How would my life have been different? Would these siblings now be supportive to my parents as they grow older and the attendant infirmities set in? I felt very alone. Yet I had a special helper.

My mind flashed over to the guest house where Len and I were staying during our visit here. He had been poring over a manuscript, his black-rimmed half-glasses perched on the end of his slender nose. Looking up as I left the room, he had shot me a reassuring look.

"Call me if you need me."

Those words came back to comfort me as I sat in the silence of my father's living room. Len was there for me, whatever lay ahead with my parents. He was the brother I never had; he was friend, counselor, teacher, lover, all in one.

The late afternoon sun filtered through the sheer white curtains, highlighting my father's wispy gray hair. His skin was pale, splotched with red patches from his fever. Dark age spots dotted his forehead and hands and peppered his scalp. I bit my bottom lip in an attempt to keep from crying. He suddenly looked so vulnerable and helpless.

Perhaps he sensed my discomfort. He broke the silence.

"I just want you to know how much it means to Nora and me to have you and Leonard here. It seems there is never time enough. . . ." He dropped his eyes to the toes of his quilted brown leather slippers.

I jumped in. "Daddy, I only wish we lived closer, that our separations didn't have to be so long." I felt tears rising again. The lump in my throat ached like a stubbed toe.

"I guess I need to ask you if you have any fears right now, Daddy. Is there anything you're worrying about that we could talk about?" I felt awkward asking these questions.

"No, honey, there isn't anything in particular that I can think of. With the house paid off and no other major debts, I'd have to say things are O.K. When I get to feeling better, I'm going to get to the lawn outside with my weed-whacker."

Dad was doing what he always did—avoiding talking about feelings. I eased back in my chair, resigned to his changing the subject, knowing that we could never explore together a troubling concern on my heart: that before I was born my father had been so unhappy in his marriage that he had not looked forward to being a father. I had long since forgiven him for this. But how to show it?

Suddenly he looked me straight in the eye. "Honey, I'm worried about you. That I'm not doing enough for you."

Was this the confession of a man who felt remorse over his divorce and my subsequent alcoholism? Or a father's present concern for a very busy daughter?

His blue eyes filled with tears. He managed an embarrassed cough to cover the depth of his emotions.

I moved quickly to his side, kneeling before him on the floor in

503

front of his chair. "Oh, Daddy, don't be worried about me. I'm happy and fulfilled!"

I took his strong, rough hands in my own. Before I knew it we were embracing. His strong, wiry arms around me held me close. The roughness of his gray cardigan chafed my cheek in the gusto of the embrace.

"Daddy, I'm so sorry for everything I've done that has hurt you. Please don't blame yourself for what happened to me. I made some very foolish decisions in my life. It's not your fault that I became an alcoholic."

I sobbed into his shoulder, my hand tracing the sharp outline of his protruding shoulder blade beneath the sweater. He was fragile, a far cry from the robust man I had embraced so often in the past.

"Dad," I continued, "this may seem silly, but I want you to repeat after me: I am not responsible for Sandra's alcoholism. I am *not* responsible for Sandra's alcoholism."

Haltingly and self-consciously, he repeated the sentence twice, then smiled wanly at me as though he didn't really believe what he had just said.

His voice cracked again and his face crumbled in some long-held grief. "I'm sorry, too, dear, for everything that has happened. I hope you will forgive me, too. I love you."

"Oh, Daddy, I love you, too," I repeated, flooded with a great sense of relief. We hugged and swayed in our embrace.

My legs smarted with little prickles from the uncomfortable position. It didn't matter. I felt a new sense of freedom, of forgiveness and reconciliation with my father. I had waited many years for this moment.

Only the night before, when I was speaking with my mother on the telephone, she had broken down and said almost the same words: "I'm so sorry for what happened. I wasn't there for you in high school."

How well I recognized the guilty anguish in her voice. Not having been there for my own children in high school, I knew only too well how parents agonize over their children's addictions and pain, convinced somehow they are responsible.

"Mom," I said tenderly, "you aren't to blame for what happened to me. You really aren't. Can you understand and believe that?"

Silence at the other end of the phone.

"Mother, please repeat after me: I am not responsible for Sandra's alcoholism."

She laughed nervously. "I don't know if I can say that."

I insisted, making her repeat the sentence twice after me.

A pause, then a nervous chuckle of relief. Mom was working her way toward freedom, too.

My parents' marriage ended when I was sixteen. Dad moved out the night before my senior year began at Spaulding High School.

It was a difficult year. Not just "What am I going to be when I grow up?" or "Am I making the right career decision?" but feeling the burden of meeting my mother's burgeoning emotional needs now that Dad was gone.

At first I decided to enroll in the dental hygiene course at the University of Vermont. Yet when I entered my family dentist's office for a routine exam, the heavy medicinal aroma assaulted my nostrils with reality: This was not at all what I wanted to do.

Since I was a child I had loved to draw and paint and create crafts projects. Somewhere deep down inside, I had nurtured a dream of attending art school. So after deciding not to be a dental hygienist, I applied to the Rhode Island School of Design and, to my astonishment, was accepted.

This caused a major flap between my divorced parents. Dad thought I should not abandon the University of Vermont course, which he felt would lead to something practical for me; Mother favored art school. I went to art school.

I was nineteen when Dad remarried in 1955. Mother did so in 1961. Both second marriages were happy and fulfilling. But, as with most divorces, bitterness and resentment remained.

Ironically, it was the downturn in my life years later that resulted in their reconciliation. As I sank into alcoholism and life-threatening depressions, my parents had to communicate about the darkening situation of their one child. Soon parents and stepparents started having meals and get-togethers.

My father and stepmother were especially attentive to Mom during my stepfather's hospitalizations, leg amputations and death in 1983. They became an important part of my mother's support system.

After my session alone with Dad, I knew I had unfinished business with him and my stepmother regarding a bitter root judgment I had made against them years ago. When Dad married Nora, I vowed to myself that I would never forgive them. Over the years I made many more inner vows concerning men: Men were not to be trusted. They would let you down when you needed them. They would wind up hurting you. These all-but-forgotten oaths rotted away at my soul.

One night we were all three seated in their living room about to watch a Saturday night comedy show, when I asked Dad if he would mind turning off the television. There was something I had to say.

Dad and Nora both looked a bit startled, but switched off the TV, settled deeper into their recliners and fixed concerned stares on my face. I shifted uncomfortably on the sofa and dug my shoes into the soft carpet.

"It may seem to you that I've completely recovered from my alcoholism, that I'm now normal. Well, I'm not sure what normal is today. They say that 96% of all homes are dysfunctional in some way or another."

I paused, struggling for the right words.

"For years I covered up my deepest feelings. It was always important for me to put up a good front. Often I didn't even know what my real feelings were.

"But I was devastated when you left us, Daddy. I was angry at you. Mother fell apart and I felt totally responsible for her. She was so fragile and I became—well, like her mother. I felt so trapped and confused. Even though I threw myself into school and after-school activities, part of me was always with her, wondering if she was all right, wondering how she would be when I got home from school.

"Usually I found her in the same place—sitting on the footstool by the telephone, the curtain drawn back with one hand, her anxious, sad face peering out the window waiting for a glimpse of me coming up the street.

"The curtain would whish back into place as soon as she saw me, and she would be at the door to welcome me, smiling with her lips, her eyes hollow and haunted. She was such a fragile little bird. I wanted to make up to her what she had lost.

"I knocked myself out trying to be there for her, but what does a sixteen-year-old know about being a parent? Or a spouse?

"I blamed you, Dad, even though I knew it wasn't all your fault. I knew from the time I was a little child that you and Mother weren't suited for each other. I tried so hard to make the difference. To keep your marriage from collapsing. I tried to be everything you both wanted me to be. And somewhere along the way I got lost in the process. I am still finding out who I am today.

"I blamed you, too, Nora, for what happened, maybe wrongly. And I hardened my heart toward you both. Even though I was cordial on the outside, part of me on the inside reared up and said, 'I'll never forgive you for what you've done to Mother and me.'

"But over the years this unforgiveness has been a weight on my heart. I've known I needed to deal with it. So I'm asking you to forgive me for my judgment of you. I am truly sorry. Can you forgive me?"

After a stunned pause, Dad spoke first. "Well, of course, honey, I forgive you. Gee whiz, I never knew you felt that way. . . ."

His calloused hands picked at the fabric on the arms of his chair.

Nora broke the silence. "I didn't know you felt that way either, Sandra. But I've always loved you and thought of you as a daughter. . . ."

Then Dad started talking about how the house needed painting.

Nora commented on the rainy weather. I realized how uncomfortable it was for us all to talk about our feelings.

"If we could," I continued nervously, "let's get back to the subject at hand. I just want you to know that I love you both, and I want to thank you for standing by me and loving me when I wasn't lovable. For supporting me with your prayers. I am truly sorry for everything I've put you through."

I was starting to cry now. "Could I give you both a hug?"

They both stood up and all three of us joined in a hug. After much nose-blowing and wiping of eyes, the television blinked on.

My mind was not on the program. I closed my eyes, stretched out on the couch and fell asleep—a peaceful, blessed sleep freed from a long, dark shadow of the past.

Steps eight and nine of the twelve-step program of Alcoholics Anonymous stress the importance of making amends to those people "we have harmed." This is always difficult, sometimes impossible, because of circumstances.

Making amends, of course, often includes saying, "I'm sorry." Here again, many of us falter. The words we know we should say stick in our mouths.

"Why is this?" I have often asked myself. "Is my pride blocking the words?"

Pride, yes. Fear of showing weakness, too. Sometimes guilt freezes the words inside us. I have struggled with all of this.

What has helped me overcome these blocks is my daily times with the Lord. During these times I not only pray but listen to what He has to say to me. So often have I felt His love, His forgiveness, that it was easy to say, "I'm sorry, Lord, for making such a mess of my life. I'm sorry, Lord, for failing to keep Your commandments. I'm sorry, Lord, for all those years I wasn't a good wife and mother, daughter, friend. . . ."

Saying "I'm sorry" to the Lord this way has made it much easier to say "I'm sorry" to the people I have hurt.

More recently I have been able to say the following twelve healing words that can completely restore a relationship:

I am sorry.
I was wrong.
Please forgive me.
I love you.

During that same visit to Vermont, my mother and I were invited to dinner at Dad and Nora's. After the meal we settled into the music room—Nora at her bench before the small spinet organ, Dad in an old oak rocker to my left and Mother on his other side.

The tones of the organ filled the air with light melody. "When I grow too old to dream, I'll have you to remember. . . ."

Out of the corner of my eye, I witnessed a beautiful little vignette of forgiveness and reconciliation: Dad's hand, so thin from recent illness, rested on one arm of the rocker. For just a moment, Mother's small, arthritic hand moved from her lap and touched my father's hand ever so lightly, patting it gently. Then her hand disappeared back into her lap.

Being allowed to view this tender moment in that little window of time did a healing work in me.

Because so many of us have family relationships that need healing, I now use the following prayer for forgiveness in my talks and seminars, adapted from one I heard Brennan Manning use at a Life in the Spirit seminar:

Lord Jesus, I ask You into my heart.

Please touch those life experiences of mine that need to be healed.

Since You know me so much better than I know myself, bring Your love to every corner of my heart. Wherever You discover inner wounds, touch me . . . console me . . . release me.

Walk back through my life right now to the very moment in which I was conceived. Cleanse my bloodlines, Lord. Bless and protect me as I was being formed in my mother's womb. Grant in me a deep desire to be born. Heal any traumas that could have harmed me during the birth process.

Thank You, Lord, for being there to receive me into Your arms at the very moment of my birth, to welcome me onto the earth, to assure me that You would never fail me or desert me.

Jesus, please surround my infancy with Your light and Your love. If my earthly family failed to meet my physical or emotional or spiritual needs, supply them now from Your infinite store. Give me renewed confidence and courage to face the trials of the world because I know my Father's love will support me even if I stumble and fall.

Lord, by the power of Your Spirit, empower me to forgive myself for my past failures, for any hurts I may have inflicted on others, for my mistakes, for my moments of weakness and self-ishness.

Lord, I give myself to You body, mind and spirit, and I thank You for making me whole. My gift to You this day is to radiate Your Spirit of forgiveness, Your Spirit of love, Your Spirit of joy as I reach out to serve others for You.

Wounded in the Womb

Recovery Principle # 19
YOU ARE LOVED! BELIEVE IT

PEOPLE WITH LOW SELF-WORTH WHO ARE STRUGGLING TO FREE themselves from addictions to drugs, food, tobacco, *et al.,* are pursuing a new avenue of help these days—therapy for *in utero* wounding. Counselors are discovering that clients who fail to respond to regular techniques often improve when the stress and trauma of the time in their mothers' womb is probed.

John and Paula Sandford, well-known Christian authors and counselors, find that many of their clients experience major breakthroughs in healing when they are "prayed through" the rejection and abandonment that happened *before* birth. Thomas Verny, M.D., in his book *The Secret Life of the Unborn Child* (published by Dell in 1982 and still in print), discovered that the mother's and father's behavior toward the unborn child has major impact on the child's mental health and sense of well-being.

The moment a smoking mother thinks about lighting up a cigarette, the child in her womb will wriggle in anticipation; the little one is already addicted to nicotine that has entered its body through the placenta. News reports are full of articles and pictures of crack babies born from mothers on drugs.

My friend Dawn suffered for years from feelings of shame and low self-worth. When we prayed about this one day, she revealed to me that her father never knew who his father was, and that when drunk her father would scream out that he was a bastard, an accident, a heap of manure that nobody wanted. No wonder Dawn had no sense of her own value!

Dawn had also been a victim of abuse while in the womb. She told me tearfully that her father used to beat her mother during the pregnancy, hitting her and kicking her in the stomach. "I don't want you or this damned kid," he would bellow as he pummeled them both.

As Dawn grew up and learned of her mother's trauma during the pregnancy, she felt guilty that she had been such a terrible burden. She tried to take care of her mother, a frail, sickly, bedridden woman who gave birth to four more children after Dawn.

As Dawn became the surrogate mother of the brood, she was also the victim of an incestuous relationship with her father. As the oldest functional female in the home, she was expected to cooperate when her father wanted sex. She soon learned that he wouldn't beat her mother or siblings if she cooperated.

"I knew I was the child of a bastard," she told me. "My father drummed this constantly into my head. But he didn't need to. I already felt I was a mistake and worthless."

Dawn went on to tell me that she had received counseling and therapy for traumatic memories of incest, domestic violence and guilt toward her mother. She felt there had been some healing.

I sensed the Lord saying Dawn needed specific prayer for a healing of those experiences she had suffered in the womb. When we went back to her *in utero* experience she began to sob; then she gagged and choked and retched and whined like a whipped, helpless puppy.

I held her and in my prayer told her, "Dawn, you are loved and cherished and precious in the sight of God. You are a blessing, not a burden."

Her body gave a little shudder and then relaxed. As I ended the prayer, she was limp in my arms; then her teary eyes opened and a radiant smile crinkled her thin face. Some long-held burden had been lifted. A key had been given Dawn to unlock a dark room her memory had never been able to enter.

"Don't let Satan rob you of what has just happened," I advised her. "He'll try to steal your joy, your healing, and whisper doubts and judgments to you. But don't listen. He's a liar. Thank God every day for your healing and believe you have been healed, because you have."

Then I gave her an assignment. "Today I want you to do something that is childlike. I want you to get in touch with the little girl Dawn who never was able to play. Life has been serious for you from the time of your birth. I want you to give yourself permission to play."

Dawn looked doubtful. "I'm not sure I know how to do what you're asking. My mother always told me that play was a foolish waste of time. That's going to be a tough message to erase, but I'll try."

My experience with Dawn brought back a flood of memories of my own pregnancies. All three came in a 36-month period. I was unprepared emotionally, physically and spiritually to be a mother even of one. Two lively toddlers were already taking every ounce of my resources when the obstetrician gave me his stunning announcement: "You're pregnant."

"I can't be pregnant again," I gasped.

I was already in a downward spiral of addiction, and my marriage was in deep trouble. I felt trapped. Frantic. It wasn't right to bring another life into this troubled situation! I went from the doctor's office to my car and sat helplessly in the driver's seat, then pounded my stomach in desperation. A pathetic attempt to abort?

In the weeks and months that followed I raged mentally at the unborn child. Somehow the message must have been conveyed from my thoughts to the embryo in my body. Starting in the sixth month, the small life inside me tried to abort every day at twelve noon. It apparently found the womb a hostile place. Soon I was bedridden. And Lisa was born sensing she was not wanted.

As I learned more and more about *in utero* wounding of the fetus, I wept bitter tears over that time in my life. How could I make amends to Lisa? To help her know she was valued and loved?

During Lisa's first visit to Evergreen Farm after I began asking myself these questions, I felt a consuming desire to pray with her. To rock her. To go back in time and speak to that unborn child, little Lisa in the womb.

On the face of it, impossible! She was 27 years old. Yet I had learned we can go back and pray through traumatic situations in the distant past. I had received deeply powerful healings myself in this area.

Would Lisa think it was crazy or weird? Was it appropriate even to try? Would it turn her off?

The night before her visit was to end, I felt the time was right. Lisa and I had just spent several days in Charleston, West Virginia, visiting relatives, allowing us many hours together in the car. I had welcomed this opportunity to have her undivided attention. We had time to dig in on some painful issues.

The last leg of the seven-hour drive back to Virginia had been especially poignant. I had talked with her about my alcoholism and how it had robbed me of my ability to be a nurturing mother. We had wept together as the miles rolled by. I felt a new bond with my beautiful adult daughter. We were friends, more peers than mother and daughter. But always little Lisa was just below the surface. So many fears and insecurities. So much pain buried under years and years of denial.

We had finished dinner and she was in her room packing. I joined her there. The room was a clutter of bags and suitcases and girl things. The nudge to *Do it now* could not be ignored. "Lisa," I said hesitantly, "I'd like to pray for you in a way that may seem rather unusual. I'd like to just hold you and rock you and pray for healing deep inside you when you were damaged in the womb."

I felt frightened and vulnerable, but knew I needed to press on. Lisa looked startled.

"Would that be all right with you?" I continued. "Could we do it now before you have to leave?"

"Sure, Mom, that would be O.K."

Her willingness, guarded as it was, encouraged me that God was carving out this special time for us.

We struggled somewhat awkwardly to get our bodies into a comfortable position. I sat on the side of the bed and she placed her head against my chest, her arms around my waist, her long legs extended along the bedspread. We shifted our weight self-consciously, laughing nervously.

"Pretty tough to rock without a rocking chair, isn't it?" I laughed.

"No, Mom, this is fine."

I could feel Lisa's slim body relaxing in my arms. I smoothed her long hair away from her forehead and gently kissed the top of her head, her hair fragrant and flower-fresh.

How beautiful this precious child is, I thought. *How could I ever have considered aborting her? How horrible that would have been.*

Our bodies rocked together slowly. Forward and back. Forward and back. Lisa tightened her grip around my waist and snuggled her head closer to my chest.

As we rocked I gazed out through the sheer white Priscilla bedroom curtains to the verdant panorama of Evergreen Farm in the twilight. The bushes and trees and hedges rose from the lawn like hundreds of green guardian angels.

How safe I felt in this setting, my child nestled on my breast. Healing was happening without a word being spoken.

Finally I broke the silence. "Lisa, I want to speak to little Lisa in the womb, to hold her and rock her and reassure her of some things.

"Little Lisa, I need to tell you that I am filled with such joy that you are in my womb. You are wanted very deeply. You are precious and lovely. Feel the comfort and warmth of my love as you grow. You are treasured. I love you so much.

"I speak life and blessing and health and freedom to your little spirit and I thank God that He has given you to me as His incredible gift of love and trust.

"I welcome you onto the earth as your mother. How blessed I am that you are my little girl! For you are 'fearfully and wonderfully made.' Welcome, little one! Welcome."

Then I asked Lisa's forgiveness for neglecting her needs as a little girl, for being insensitive and selfish, for abandoning her to the care of babysitters while I pursued my own selfish interests. For all the hours she was left alone, waiting for me to come home. My "I'll be home in just a little while" meant hours and hours.

By now I was sobbing and so was she.

"Oh, Lisa, please forgive me. I only wish I could roll back the clock and have another chance to be the mom I could have been if I hadn't been a drunk."

"It's O.K., Mom," she whispered. "It's O.K. I always knew you loved me. It's O.K." I offered her a tissue and dabbed at her nose and snuggled closer. Neither one of us wanted this moment to end. We rocked some more.

Then, as we broke from the embrace, an astonishing ending. Suddenly I was aware of brilliant light all about my daughter. If the sun had not gone down, it could have been sunbeams through the window. I felt suffused in the glow of this light—warmed, bathed. Then it faded.

We both blinked and smiled and broke into girlish laughter.

But that wasn't all. The room was filled with the fragrance of lily of the valley. And neither of us was wearing perfume.

The next afternoon when Len and I drove her to Dulles Airport for her trip back to Montana, Lisa had a glowing smile on her face. She was radiant as she walked down the corridor to her plane. She walked proud and tall, with a new set to her shoulders. She had been affirmed. She knew she was loved, that she was precious. A weight laid on her in the womb had been lifted.

The "you are loved" affirmation contains great healing power. Receiving it from God washes me clean every day. Hearing it from others is balm to my spirit; it nourishes me, frees me from resentments and irritation, feeds my soul.

When I say it to others, I can see their eyes light up, tense faces soften, bodies relax. These three words are a form of therapy—not only to those who receive it, but for me, too, as the source. I can never say the words without feeling a warmth inside; yes, even an exhilaration and spirit-to-spirit connection to my God above and to the person I care about.

The healing that Lisa and I experienced at Evergreen Farm was a milestone in our mother-daughter relationship, but only one step on a long journey. There is always farther to go in this healing process.

Another get-together took place in Vermont when Lisa and I visited there in May 1991 to be with my father, who had gone through major surgery at the age of eighty. We stayed with Mother in her small Montpelier home and took daily trips to Barre to visit Dad and Nora.

One morning I awoke to a symphony outside Lisa's and my window as a flock of birds trilled their joyous alarm-clock greetings. I inhaled deeply the moist air, fragrant with lilac and honeysuckle. Nearby Lisa's beautiful face seemed almost angelic in the morning light, her long, chestnut hair cascading over her pillow.

What a treasure she is, I thought to myself. *Thank You, Lord, for such a precious gift.*

Unconsciously I extended my right hand close to her, resting it a few inches from her slumbering face. Suddenly she reached over for my hand and grasped it firmly with hers—like a little child reaching out in sleep for its mother's touch.

Lisa's breathing never changed, her eyelids never flickered. Before my eyes, her sleeping face took on a cherubic expression as this 29-year-old was transformed into a very little girl holding her mother's hand. Her face held such contentment! Peace. Trust.

Deep within my spirit I sensed healing happening to me as well, as though the Lord was doing a cleansing and restoring work in my heart. He knew my anguish for all the times I had failed Brad, Brent and Lisa during their infancy and growing-up years. I had been too self-absorbed and ill to be a real caring mother to them. I had asked both God and them to forgive me, but self-forgiveness was elusive.

I found myself praying, *O Lord, reach deep within Lisa's memory. Use this moment as our hands are clasped to heal those innermost hurts she carries—all the times she reached for me and I wasn't there for her.*

Then I prayed for myself. *Lord, please forgive me for all the times I neglected Lisa and Brad and Brent. Use this moment to wash away the guilt and pain and condemnation I can't seem to let go of.*

The tears were running down my cheeks, splashing onto the cool, white sheets.

I'm so tired of feeling guilty. I know You don't want me to feel this way. My head knows that, but my heart doesn't seem to. Please make it a reality.

Lisa's grasp relaxed a bit, but still she hung on. Such a bonding! I felt God's love in every fiber of my being. The room radiated it. And the birds outside rejoiced with us.

Lisa let go of my hand and rolled over.

I believe we had both been touched and transformed in mysterious ways we will never understand.

I Blew Them All Kisses

Recovery Principle # 20
REACH OUT

S I WRITE THESE WORDS I AM SUDDENLY AWARE THAT THE RE-
covery process in my life has been going on now for almost
fourteen years. It began in August 1978 when I met Karen at the
Montana State Hospital and she spoke to me of a Person whose
name I didn't want to hear: Jesus. Yet I discovered over time that
there was *hope for the hopeless* through that name.

The recovery road still stretches ahead of me for an indeterminate
stretch. But the slowness of the process does not discourage me. On
the contrary, the process itself has been so enriching, the experiences
I have had so edifying, that in some strange and hard-to-understand
way I am far ahead of where I would be without all the heartache and
tragedy.

The farther I travel, the stronger is my faith. Though excruciatingly difficult at times, the journey has been exhilarating, with many stimulating people met along the way. So much pain at times. But pain, I have discovered, is a necessary part of the journey.

Most of all, the journey has been an adventure. It became an adventure the moment I let go of my life and surrendered it to God.

"I've made a mess of it," I confessed. "Will You be in charge from now on?"

Being out of control is difficult for me, and there are times I try to take over and run my life as I used to. Thank You, Lord, for not letting me get away with that! For with Him in charge I have made wonderful new friends, have had a loving and fulfilling marriage, discovered gifts I never knew I had (like putting words together on paper), traveled to places I never dreamed I would see.

And the adventure goes on. . . .

I am astonished at how rapidly my healing continues when I *reach out* to help others.

Soon after my marriage to Len a recurring thought began to nag at me. The idea persisted. But it wasn't until June 1991, about a month after my healing experience with Lisa at Mother's house in Vermont, that I mentioned it to him casually.

"What do you think about my going out to see Eve?"

He looked at me in surprise. Then his face creased in thought.

"Why not?" he said slowly. "Your visit might give her a real lift."

Though Len's first marriage had been painful, his visit to Eve in the nursing home in 1989 had been surprisingly upbeat. Len, Eve and their daughter, Linda, had prayed together for a healing of all the hurts of the past.

But now I began to have mixed feelings about traveling all the way to Iowa to see Len's first wife. She might resent me and my role with Len and the three children she bore. It could be painful for me, too. Not just the encounter itself, but here I was going into another institution and reliving all those old emotions of being shut in because of my illness.

Yet I was continuing to learn to obey that inner voice. It had directed me into other difficult situations that had ended up aiding my recovery.

Eve and I had at least one thing in common: We were both dealing with the need for self-forgiveness.

Furthermore, as a recovering alcoholic myself, perhaps I could relate to Eve in a way no one else could.

When I called Linda for her reaction, she not only liked the idea but suggested that she and her daughter Mary Catherine, age six, go, too, since Eve had never seen her granddaughter. A great idea from my beautiful step-daughter! We chose a weekend that month.

The three of us met at the Des Moines International Airport and drove together to the nursing home in Albia.

When we walked into Eve's room, the stunning beauty of the former *Vogue* model was hauntingly apparent in her ashen face. Her large, warm brown eyes jumped to life as she saw us. Mary Catherine offered her a handmade paper Easter basket, which she had carried all the way from the airport in Washington, D.C.

Eve accepted this gift of love in her arthritic hands and held it tenderly. In a deep contralto voice choked with emotion she said, "My granddaughter made this for me?"

I was saddened to see this once vivacious soul, now bent and twisted, imprisoned in a wheelchair. There was a fragile birdlike quality about her—a tiny Dresden doll almost too delicate to touch.

During our weekend visit Eve stretched herself beyond her frailties, her earthbound restraints. Her spirit was buoyant. She thanked us over and over for coming to visit her. Several times she said to me, "Sandy, I feel like I've known you all my life."

I took that as a wonderful compliment, glad she felt comfortable with me, that she liked me. It was important to me to have the love and approval of the mother of Len's children.

Saturday evening was a special occasion, when we had dinner at a popular restaurant. As I looked at the three faces around the table I thought, *What an incredible happening!* This was the evening of June 22, 1991—the sixth anniversary of my marriage to Len, who was on this day giving a speech at a Presbyterian conference in Branson, Missouri. I was celebrating our anniversary with his first wife, their daughter, Linda, and his granddaughter, Mary Catherine, named after his second wife.

God, how amazing You are! I thought as I buttered my dinner roll. *You are in the business of bringing broken families together in ways no one could ever imagine.*

Eve asked me to please cut up her chicken breast, and added, "I really like you, Sandy. You're just like an old shoe."

Sunday morning we wheeled Eve into the Methodist church. At one point during the Sunday service I glanced over at her to see how she was getting along. Her doll-like frame was silhouetted against a large stained glass window. In the center section, Christ was pictured with His hand outstretched, a small white lamb nestled peacefully against His chest. In her white suit Eve looked somewhat like that little white lamb—small and fragile and vulnerable. I sensed that Jesus had also reached out for Eve and drawn her to His bosom.

The enormity of her loss struck me: three children relinquished to other mothers, five grandchildren she hardly knew, a life of missed opportunities.

The stark reality: I could just as well be the one in that wheelchair!

The high point of the weekend was our prayer time. The four of us held hands, three of us praying aloud for each other, with Mary Catherine's participation powerfully sweet in its silence. Then Eve and I were alone while Linda and Mary Catherine prepared for the drive to the airport.

"Is there anything else we should pray for?" I asked.

Then the thought came: "Eve, I feel we both know God has forgiven us, but have we been able to forgive ourselves?"

The look of pain on her face stabbed me. With tears streaming down her face, Eve asked God to help her forgive herself. I prayed the same prayer.

Later, as Linda, Mary Catherine and I drove to the airport, I made a discovery. I had gone to Iowa thinking that in some way I might be of help to Eve. Perhaps I had. But what came through strongly was how she had ministered to me. As her spirit bonded with mine, and as we prayed together for self-forgiveness, something had broken inside me. The barrier preventing me from truly forgiving myself was continuing to dissolve.

My recovery continues. Today I see myself as the not-so-compulsive woman. Yet I am staggered some days by the depth of woundedness inside me; layers and layers keep emerging to be dealt with.

On an occasion just recently the principle of reaching out collided with my inner fear of institutional confinement. After I spoke to a women's group one night in a coastal city in Florida, a gray-haired woman in her mid-sixties approached me. Bright brown eyes snapped beneath bushy salt-and-pepper eyebrows.

"I'm a social worker," she said, introducing herself. "Is there any way you could come and speak to my girls?"

Betty's girls, it turned out, were inmates in a correctional facility. Something pricked my heart. I remembered only too well what it was like to be locked up in an institution. I remembered with gratitude the dedicated people from the outside who cared enough to come and teach or bring music.

I said yes.

"Would you be able to come tomorrow morning?" she pressed.

"I guess so," I replied, taken back at the immediacy of her request.

I had some difficulty finding the facility, a low sandstone building in a remote section of town. Inside the front door stood a beaming Betty. Her cheeriness warmed my weary self. It had been a short night with little rest after a long evening of speaking and talking to people.

Inside the somber building, the sameness of institutional sights and smells hit me—disinfectant and floor wax and stale cigarette smoke. A shudder of thankfulness surged through me. *Thank You, God, that I am free of these places!*

Beyond the reception area was a glassed-in booth where an officious woman guard spoke to us through a small hole in the glass.

"Sign in, please," she said briskly, sizing me up through half-closed eyes.

In spite of my visitor status, the attitude of this young guard triggered feelings in me of helplessness and guilt from the past.

She's just doing her job, I reminded myself.

Betty clipped on her staff badge. "I'll lock Mrs. LeSourd's purse up in my closet," she told the woman in the booth. "But Sandy, you'll have to leave your car keys here." I pushed my keys under a small opening at the bottom of the glass cage.

Betty strode ahead down the hall, introducing me to colleagues along the way—the staff nurse in a white pantsuit, another nurse in a tailored gray suit.

Betty showed me her office, which she shared with the program director, an enormous black man named Lester. He pumped my hand enthusiastically, a gold front tooth glistening from his smile like a beacon light.

"Thank you so much for coming," he said. "Would you mind if some of the boys came to hear you, too?"

This was hardly what I expected.

"If they don't mind, I don't," I replied weakly, trying not to show my mounting panic. What in the world did I have to say to young men in a detention ward?

The cafeteria was a large room filled with fifteen or more round white tables, plus colorful plastic chairs—blue, red and orange. A large plate glass window looked out onto a grassy courtyard. To the left was the kitchen where an industrial-strength dishwasher chugged loudly. *Will anyone be able to hear me over that noise?*

My eyes turned to the double doors as the inmates entered slowly.

Five young black women ranging from 16 to 25, I guessed. They eyed me suspiciously, then slumped into chairs around a corner table.

Then the invasion of young men. Some looked to be in their teens, others in their early twenties. Dressed in navy regulation uniforms, they looked as enthusiastic as convicts en route to a firing squad.

As they filled up five or six tables, I was aware of scores of eyes sizing me up. Self-consciously I smoothed the pleats of my white cotton skirt and adjusted my knotted silk belt. *Am I overdressed?*

A tough-looking teenager in a Mohawk haircut caught my eye. He shot me a surly glance, then closed his eyes and pretended to sleep. A curly-haired boy perhaps sixteen smiled weakly, his puppy dog gaze strangely affirming. He seemed to be the only one even vaguely interested in my presence. The rest of the group wiggled and squirmed in the hard plastic chairs; some rested their heads on the tables.

Suddenly I felt very tender toward them.

"Mrs. LeSourd has come to be with us today to speak with you about her experiences," Lester said. "She is a former Miss Vermont."

This was met with stony indifference.

I began by telling them how I had been locked up in an institution for many months. Mild interest.

Then I told of being sexually abused at age five, and gave statistics on the number of boys and girls molested before age eighteen. Knowing looks, downcast eyes. The pain and shame in the room were palpable.

I told them of people praying for me while I was so ill in the institutions and "I believe these prayers changed my life." Shrugs.

Betty, who had heard my talk the night before, chirped, "Sandy, tell them about Karen."

"Yes. Karen. I met her when I was in the Montana State Hospital. What a wreck I was!" I told them how I sat around chainsmoking cigarettes, locked up as a hopeless alcoholic and prescription drug addict, when this new patient arrived. She kept talking about

Jesus and I tried to avoid her but couldn't. She was beautiful in an almost ethereal way.

"One night," I went on, "Karen came into my room, sobbing her heart out. She kept asking me if Jesus loved her. I got out of bed and held her in my arms and told her, 'Yes, Jesus loves you.'"

I went on to describe how something happened to me as I did that. "For a moment I stopped thinking only about myself and was concerned about someone else. And with that I began to get well.

"Strange thing, though. Karen left the hospital as suddenly as she arrived. I never had a chance to talk with her again."

Some interest.

"Years later I wanted to send a book to Karen. So I wrote to the Montana State Hospital asking for Karen's address. Guess what the hospital wrote back?"

Of the whole group, only Mohawk was not listening. His eyes were still closed.

"They had no record of Karen's ever being in that institution."

My young audience waited silently, expectantly.

"Does anyone here know why they had no record of Karen?"

The heads were all shaking *no.*

"It's my conviction that Karen was an angel, that God loved me so much—as He loves every one of you—that He sent an angel to rescue me."

Surprised looks. Expressions like "Wow!" and "Way to go!" Lester was grinning ear-to-ear. Mohawk opened his eyes for the first time.

"I believe each of you has a guardian angel," I continued. "And I hope you believe that, too."

One or two heads nodded. Others looked as though it was news too good to be true, at least for them. Undoubtedly many felt God had abandoned them or double-crossed them by giving them uncaring parents or no parents at all.

An announcement crackled over the public address system, my cue to stop. The exodus from the cafeteria began. The girls lined up and marched out first. The youngest smiled shyly at me in thanks.

The boys touched my heart. As they lined up to leave, I got several smiles. One young teenager with a thatch of honey-colored hair looked at me with moist eyes, his lips quivering. I could feel his spirit leap out to me in pain and desperation, and I wanted to hug him and take him home with me.

I BLEW THEM ALL KISSES...

As I walked down the hall I stopped briefly outside the boys' ward. A huge pane of gray glass separated me from them. I looked more closely. There was Mohawk. He was grinning. One of the boys waved at me. I waved back. Several others shot me the "V for victory" sign. I did the same. Mohawk and the others were now on their feet hopping up and down and waving at me.

Then I waved my arms as if they were angel wings. I must have looked pretty stupid to anyone who had not just heard the Karen story! But the boys loved it. Again I flapped my wings. They waved wildly.

Then I blew them all kisses. They blew kisses back.

My heart was full to bursting as I walked out of the building to my car.

RECOVERY PRINCIPLES

1 *Seek Prayers of Others*

2 *Say No*

3 *Trust God's Love for You*

4 *Accept Yourself*

5 *Smell the Flowers*

6 *Obey the Inner Voice*

7 *Give Yourself Away*

8 *Be Vulnerable*

9 *Be Reconciled*

#10 *Identify Your Real Needs*

#11 *Expect the Best*

#12 *Seize the Moment*

#13 *Forgive Those Who Have Hurt You*

#14 *Talk About It*

#15 *Celebrate*

#16 *Be Honest*

#17 *Like Yourself*

#18 *Confess Your Wrongdoing*

#19 *You Are Loved! Believe It*

#20 *Reach Out*

When You Need Help . . .

Here are addresses and telephone numbers of some of the programs available

1. ALCOHOL ADDICTION

Alcoholics Anonymous
World Services, Inc.
475 Riverside Drive
New York, NY 10115
(212) 870-3400

Alcoholics For Christ, Inc.
1316 North Campbell Rd.
Royal Oak, MI 48076
1-800-441-7877

Alcoholics Victorious
National Headquarters
P.O. Box 10364
Portland, OR 97236
(503) 245-9629

ACA
Adult Children of Alcoholics
P.O. Box 3216
Torrance, CA 90510
(310) 534-1815

Al-Anon Family Group Hdq., Inc.
1600 Corporate Landing Parkway
Virginia Beach, VA 23454
(757) 563-1600

2. CODEPENDENCY

Co-Dependents Anonymous, Inc.
(602) 277-7991

3. CHILD ABUSE

Child Help USA
1345 El Centro Ave.
P.O. Box 630
Hollywood, CA 90028
(213) 465-4016

National Child Abuse Hotline
1-800-422-4453

4. CULTS

International Cult Education
   Program
P.O. Box 2265
Bonita Springs, FL 34133
(212) 533-5420

Spiritual Counterfeits Project
P.O. Box 4308
Berkeley, CA 94704
(510) 540-0300

5. DRUGS

Cocaine Anonymous
World Services
3740 Overland Ave., Suite C
Los Angeles, California 90034
(310) 559-5833
1-800-347-8998 (meeting referrals)

Narcotics Anonymous
P.O. Box 9999
Van Nuys, CA 91409
(818) 997-3822

Cocaine Hot Line
1-800-COCAINE

Pills Anonymous
P.O. Box 248
New York, NY 10028
(212) 874-0700

The National Clearinghouse for
   Alcohol and Drug Information
P.O. Box 2345
Rockville, MD 20852
(301) 468-2600

Nar-Anon (Family Group)
P.O. Box 2562
Palos Verdes, CA 90274
(310) 547-5800

National Drug Abuse Information
and Referral Line
1-800-662-4357

6. EATING DISORDERS

Overeaters Anonymous, Inc.
8075 West Third Street, Ste. 405
Los Angeles, CA 90048
(213) 936-6252

O-Anon
General Service Office
P.O. Box 4350
San Pedro, CA 90731
(310) 547-1570

National Assoc. for Anorexia and
Associated Disorders
Box 7
Highland Park, IL 60035
(847) 831-3438

7. EMOTIONAL DISORDERS

Emotions Anonymous
International Services
P.O. Box 4245
St. Paul, MN 55104
(612) 647-9712

Recovery, Inc.
The Association of Nervous and
Former Mental Patients
802 North Dearborn St.
Chicago, IL 60610
(312) 337-5661

8. COMPULSIVE GAMBLING

Gamblers Anonymous
P.O. Box 17173
Los Angeles, CA 90017
(213) 386-8789

Gam-Anon/Gamateen
International Service Office, Inc.
P.O. Box 570157
Whitestone, NY 11357
(718) 352-1671

The National Council on
Compulsive Gambling, Inc.
445 West 59th St.
New York, NY 10019
1-800-522-4700

9. HOMOSEXUAL ISSUES

Exodus International
(For homosexuals and their
  families; also for sexual
  addiction)
P.O. Box 2121
San Raphael, CA 94912

Spatula Ministries
(Parents of homosexuals and
  children with AIDS) Barbara
  Johnson, founder/director
2230 Lake Forest Circle
La Habra, CA 90631
(562) 691-7369

10. INCEST

Incest Survivors Anonymous
P.O. Box 17245
Long Beach, CA 90807
(562) 428-5599

Kempe Foundation
1205 Oneida Street
Denver, CO 80220
(303) 355-9400

National Domestic Violence
  Hotline: 1-800-799-7233

VOICES in Action, Inc.
(Victims Of Incest Can Emerge
  Survivors)
P.O. Box 148309
Chicago, IL 60614
(773) 327-1500

11. INTERVENTION

For an intervention specialist, write:
  Families in Crisis, Inc.
  5200 West 73rd Street
  Edina, MN 55439
  (612) 893-1883
  or contact local support groups or
  health professionals for further
  information in your area.

12. OBSESSIVE-COMPULSIVE DISORDER

The OCD Foundation
P.O. Box 70
Milford, CT 06460
(203) 772-0565

13. SEX ADDICTION

International Service Organization of SAA
P.O. Box 70949
Houston, TX 77270
(713) 869-4902

Sex and Love Addicts Anonymous
Augustine Fellowship
P.O. Box 650010
Newton, MA 02165
(617) 332-1845

Co-SA
Codependents of Sex Addicts
P.O. Box 14537
Minneapolis, MN 55414
(612) 537-6904

Sex and Love Addicts Anonymous
Glendale, CA 93062
(213) 259-6549

14. SEXUAL ABUSE

Eleutheros
1298 Minnesota Ave., Suite D
Winter Park, FL 32789
(407) 629-5770

Christian Recovery International
Dale Ryan, Executive Director
P.O. Box 11095
Whittier, CA 90603
(562) 947-5140

Jan Frank
P.O. Box 1491
Placentia, CA 92871

15. SHOPPING/SPENDING

Debtors Anonymous Hotline:
(212) 969-8111

Debtors Anonymous
General Service Board
P.O. Box 400
Grand Central Station
New York, NY 10163-0400

16. SMOKING

The American Cancer Society
19 W. 56th St.
New York, NY 10019
(212) 382-2169

Smokenders
1-800-828-HELP

Quit and Stay Quit
Terry A. Rustin, M.D.
9731 Greenwillow
Houston, TX 77096

17. SUICIDE

For information write:
American Association of
  Suicidology
4201 Connecticut Avenue NW
Ste. 310
Washington, DC 20008
202-237-2280

For information on the workshop:
  "Suicide—The Preventable
  Tragedy" contact:
John Hipple, Ph.D.
North Texas State University
P.O. Box 310968
Denton, TX 76203
(817) 565-2741

18. OTHER
Post-Abortion Recovery

WEBA
(Women Exploited By Abortion)
Kathy Walker, Director
3553-B N. Perris Blvd., Suite 4
Perris, CA 92370
(714) 657-0334

Families Anonymous, Inc.
P.O. Box 3475
Culver City, CA 90231
(310) 313-5800
1-800-736-9805
For those with a concern about the
  use of mind-altering substances
  or related behavioral problems in
  a relative or friend

Ministry to Singles

The Tear Catchers
Harold Ivan Smith
P.O. Box 24688
Kansas City, MO 64131
(816) 444-5301

19. TREATMENT CENTERS

For information about the location of more than 1,600 centers offering various programs and services for recovery write:

Rapha—Christ-centered in-hospital counseling care units, treating psychiatric, substance abuse and other addiction problems for the Christian community. Has numerous locations nationwide.

Rapha
Box 580355
Houston, TX 77258
Nationwide number 1-800-227-2657

Ephesians 5:18 Life Ministries
1620 Elton Road, Ste. 204
Silver Spring, MD 20903
(301) 439-7191

Health Communications
and Journal Directory
Customer Services
3201 S.W. 15th St.
Deerfield Beach, FL 33442
1-800-851-9100

New Life Clinic—Comprehensive mental health care services, substance abuse, eating disorders and other addiction treatment. Numerous locations nationwide.

New Life Clinic
820 West Spring Creek Parkway,
Ste. 400
Plano, TX 75023
1-800-639-5433

20. OTHER HELPS:

Hazelden Publishing and Education
RW 15 P. O. Box 176
Center City, MN 55012
1-800-328-9000

Johnson Institute
7205 Ohms Lane, Ste. 200
Minneapolis, MN 55439-2159
(612) 831-1630

Recovery Publications, Inc.
P. O. Box 44
Curtis, WA 98538
(360) 245-3386

If you want more comprehensive information (self-assessment tests, suggested readings, etc.) on the compulsive-addiction problem, I refer you to my first book, *The Compulsive Woman* (Chosen Books, P.O. Box 6287, Grand Rapids, MI 49516-6287).